THE GREAT HISTORIES

A series under the general editorship of

Hugh R. Trevor-Roper,

REGIUS PROFESSOR OF MODERN HISTORY, OXFORD UNIVERSITY

THE AGE OF LOUIS XIV and Other Selected Writings

The first ten titles in

THE GREAT HISTORIES *series are:*

HERODOTUS, *edited by W. G. Forrest, Fellow of Wadham College, Oxford University.*

THUCYDIDES, *edited by P. A. Brunt, Fellow of Oriel College, Oxford University.*

POLYBIUS, *edited by E. Badian, Lecturer of Ancient History, Durham University.*

JOSEPHUS, *edited by M. I. Finley, Fellow of Jesus College, Cambridge University.*

TACITUS, *edited by Hugh Lloyd-Jones, Regius Professor of Greek, Oxford University.*

MACHIAVELLI, *edited by Myron P. Gilmore, Professor of History, Harvard University.*

GUICCIARDINI, *edited by J. R. Hale, Fellow of Jesus College, Oxford University.*

VOLTAIRE, *edited by J. H. Brumfitt, Senior Lecturer in French, St. Andrews University.*

GIBBON, *edited by H. R. Trevor-Roper, Regius Professor of Modern History, Oxford University.*

HENRY ADAMS, *edited by E. N. Saveth, Professor of History, The New School.*

VOLTAIRE

THE AGE OF LOUIS XIV
and Other Selected Writings

Newly Translated and Abridged
with an Introduction by

J. H. BRUMFITT

Senior Lecturer in French Language and Literature
St. Andrews University

TWAYNE PUBLISHERS, INC.
31 Union Square, N. Y. 3

Contents

Introduction

"The first historian of modern Europe": such is the title which H. N. Brailsford bestows on Voltaire, and many other writers have described him in similar terms. At first sight the claim may seem a surprising one. Voltaire was a prolific and many-sided genius: dramatist, poet, novelist, philosopher, scientist and social reformer. Could he really have managed to devote himself to all these interests and at the same time be the greatest historian of his age?

In one sense this question must be answered in the negative; there is no single work of Voltaire's which possesses the monumental qualities of, say, Gibbon's *Decline and Fall of the Roman Empire.* But what Voltaire lacks in concentration and depth, he makes up for by the remarkable range and variety of his historical works. He writes about every period of history from the remotest antiquity to his own times, and makes some contribution to the solution of nearly all the historical problems of his day. The selections from his work contained in this volume will give some idea of the scope of his activities. This Introduction will try to fill in the background by examining his career as a whole and giving some assessment of his contribution to the philosophy of history and to historical method. But first, in order to be able to appreciate his originality, it is worth while taking a brief look at the state of historical studies before his time.

In Voltaire's early years, the autocratic rule of Louis XIV was still at its height. This was not a stimulating period for historical thought in France, for the historian's speculative freedom was sharply limited by censorship in both the political and religious fields. It was an age which often produced a rather sycophantic, courtly type of historical writing which emphasized the pomp and pageantry of royalty, devoted a great deal of space to accounts of battles, and recorded the minor details of diplomatic negotiations. The most famous history of France written at this time, that by the Jesuit Father Daniel, is a typical example. But Daniel at least tried to be accurate, whereas many other writers made no very clear distinction between history and the historical novel and aimed at literary excellence rather than truth. Men like Sandras and Vertot come into this category, as does Saint-Réal, whose style Voltaire greatly admired. They strove to portray human nature, but felt free to manipulate the details of history in a way which is somewhat reminiscent of their contemporaries the great classical dramatists.

When they dealt with the more distant periods of history, the historians of the late seventeenth century tended to be even more uncritical. They were all too prone to accept the legends and miracles of the Middle Ages and had no rational criteria for distinguishing the probable from the improbable. They accepted the often fanciful accounts of the historians of antiquity in a spirit of unquestioning veneration. Above all, they considered the Old Testament to be an inspired historical document, accurate in every detail. Their accounts of the remote past were thus based entirely on the Bible, and not only had they to explain the repopulation of the world by the children of Noah, but they had to fit the whole of human history into less than six thousand years, since by adding up the ages of the patriarchs of the Old Testament, one could prove that the world had been created in approximately 4,000 B.C.

However, there is another side to this picture. If the historians were not using their tools to the best advantage, they were nevertheless being provided with more tools than ever before. A large number of scholars, who were learned if they were not always wise, were engaged in sifting and classifying historical evidence, particularly that relating to antiquity and the Middle Ages. The famous Benedictine schools of historians, whose outstanding figure was Mabillon, were examining medieval miracles and rejecting at any rate the more improbable ones. Auxiliary disciplines such as paleography and numismatics were being brought into existence. Chronologists were busy trying to reconcile the Old Testament chronology with the more recent discoveries about the early history of other nations, and if their attempts were increasingly unsuccessful, this was bound to lead them, sooner or later, to question the whole basis of their calculations.

In fact the traditional and orthodox view of history, which seemed so firmly established in Louis XIV's time, was being subtly undermined from all sides. And in the early eighteenth century, the edifice began to show visible cracks. More and more scholars began to use the phrase "the Pyrrhonism of history" to indicate their skepticism about the possibility of ever establishing any historical certainty, even with regard to relatively recent events. Typical of this tendency was Pierre Bayle, whose vast *Historical and Critical Dictionary* was one long alphabetical list of other people's errors and his own doubts. Elsewhere, Bayle went so far as to suggest that all that could be salvaged from the ruins of history were a few major facts. One could be sure, he said, referring to one of the military engagements of the sixteenth-century civil wars, that there had been a battle of Jarnac; one could be reasonably certain who had won it; but as to the details of the events and the motives of the participants, these were lost beyond hope of recovery.

However, not all the new ideas of this period were negative ones. If the details of intrigues and battles, and the motives of politicians and génerals remained shrouded in doubt, could not the historian turn his attention to something else? Social history, the history of institutions and forms of government, the history of the arts and sciences: here were fields in which it was still possible to arrive at a large measure of truth. Moreover, they seemed intrinsically more worth studying in the war-weary France of the years immediately following Louis XIV's death in 1715, when men had had their fill of patriotism and battles and were looking forward to a period of political and scientific progress. The phrase which summed up these aspirations, and which appears in the writings on the theory of history by men like Fontenelle and Fénelon, was *l'histoire de l'esprit humain*—the history of the human spirit. It was to become Voltaire's slogan.

The death of Louis XIV was followed by a revival of interest in political questions and a renewal of all forms of speculative thought. It saw the beginnings of the rise of the *philosophes*, the liberal, scientifically minded reformist propagandists who were to dominate the intellectual life of the later years of the century and who, for the most part, were to regard Voltaire as their master. In midcentury, in works like Rousseau's *Social Contract,* this new political interest was to take a largely theoretical form. But in the first part of the century, the questions which were asked were mainly historical ones. What had gone wrong with France, that she had suffered the misfortunes of despotism and war? What was the natural form of government which corresponded to the spirit and needs of the nation? Men like Fénelon and Boulainvilliers tried to answer these questions by discovering what the original form of French government had been, for they were traditionalist enough in their outlook to believe that whatever was was right. It seemed to them a matter of grave political importance to know whether the Franks had arrived in Gaul as conquerors or at the request of the Roman governors, and to know what their form of government was. In this way one could show that France was destined by nature to be either a monarchy or an elective aristocracy. Such an approach certainly had its pitfalls, but it stimulated interest in social and constitutional history. It had an important influence on Montesquieu, who was to be the outstanding theoretical sociologist of the next generation as Voltaire was to be its outstanding historian.

Such was the climate of opinion in which Voltaire grew up; his own historical works are full of references to these controversies and are, in part, an answer to some of the problems they raised.

Voltaire was born in Paris in 1694, the son of a fairly successful middle-class lawyer. His mother had been of noble birth, and it was through contacts on this side of the family that he was introduced, at a relatively early age, to some of the more skeptical and free-thinking elements of the Parisian aristocracy. He was also fortunate enough to be at school with a number of men who were destined to reach high office in the state, and he later cultivated these friendships assiduously. His wit, together with his skill as an occasional poet, allowed him to climb rapidly in society, and his fame was soon established by his success as a dramatist. *Œdipus,* the play which made his name, was first performed in 1718. After that, he continued to write for the theatre, but also turned to epic poetry. With his *Henriad,* a long poem on the civil wars of the sixteenth century which he wrote during the Twenties, he hoped to become the French Vergil.

Yet he was far from devoting himself uniquely to purely imaginative literature, even at this stage in his career. For one thing, he could not restrain his satirical pen, which landed him more than once either in the Bastille or in provincial exile. For another, he was already showing signs of hostility to orthodox religion, though he took care not to publish his criticisms too openly. But he was also a keen observer of the social and political questions of his day, as can be seen from the letters he wrote during an early stay in Holland. He had, too, a keen interest in history, and delighted in listening to the anecdotes of men like Caumartin, who had witnessed the closing years of Louis XIV's reign, or the theories of Bolingbroke, the former minister of Queen Anne, who was then living in exile in France and with whom he became closely acquainted in the Twenties. And if *The Henriad,* on which he was then working, had all the allegorical trappings of an epic poem, it had also a solid basis of historical fact. His interest in its historical accuracy can be seen from the many footnotes he added to the published editions.

But in 1725 an event occurred which was to transform Voltaire's life. Following a quarrel with a young nobleman, the Chevalier de Rohan-Chabot, he was set upon and beaten by the Chevalier's servants. When he expressed a desire for revenge, he was imprisoned in the Bastille, and only freed on the understanding that he would go into exile. He chose to go to England, and the two years he spent there were to have profound influence on him. English philosophy and science, in the persons of Locke and Newton, English religious tolerance and constitutional monarchy, all made a deep impression which was to last throughout his life.

The English exile was also to mark the beginning of his career as a historian. Indeed, his first historical work proper was actually written in England and in English. This was a brief *Essay upon the Civil Wars in France,* which was published in 1727 and was intended partly as a piece of publicity for *The Henriad,* which was to be published in England in 1728. It was little more than a summary of events, but it indicated the way in which Voltaire's interests were developing.

Moreover, circumstances were soon to hasten this development. During his stay in England he met another exile, Baron Fabrice, one of the men who had taken part in the strange events which had befallen Charles XII of Sweden during his captivity in Turkey. Here, as he no doubt realized, was a perfect subject for a historical narrative which would add to his fame. The glorious military career of the Swedish king had ended in his death only ten years before, and his name was probably still a household word in Europe. Voltaire persuaded Fabrice to supply him with an account of the events he had witnessed. He began, too, the task of collecting memoirs from others who had had direct contact with Charles: Villelongue, Poniatowsky, King Stanislas of Poland, the Chevalier Folard, the engineer Mégret and many more.

The History of Charles XII, which Voltaire published in 1731 soon after his return to France, is first and foremost an exciting adventure story; indeed there are occasions when, faced with two alternative accounts of an incident, he chooses the less likely but more romantic one. Yet the work had a more serious purpose too. It reveals the political and social interests of the author in its descriptions of the customs and institutions of Sweden, Poland, Russia and Turkey and in its presentation of the complicated diplomatic intrigues of Europe at that time. It also has a propagandist purpose, for although Voltaire is describing the career of a great conqueror, and although he is obviously fascinated by Charles's unique personality, yet his abhorrence of war and naked power politics, and his preference for the constructive greatness of Peter of Russia to the destructive brilliance of his rival, Charles, are themes which constantly reoccur. Voltaire the *philosophe* is already clearly visible in this work, even though it may be considered primarily as a superb piece of journalism rather than as a major historical study.

But the major historical study was not to be long delayed. By 1732, and possibly earlier, Voltaire had embarked on a far more ambitious historical work: *The Age of Louis XIV*.

He once described this book as his life's work; not without some justification, for it was twenty years before the first edition was published, and he later revised and added to it on a number of occasions. Here again, as in the case of *The History of Charles XII*, he spent a great deal of time writing to and interviewing many of the important surviving eyewitnesses of the events he was describing. His literary fame and his wide contacts with the nobility placed him in a unique position to do this. In the Forties, he enjoyed a brief period of success at the French court and was made Royal Historiographer; this gave him access to state papers and to unpublished memoirs, possibly including those of the greatest of all the memorialists of Louis XIV's court, the Duke of Saint-Simon. He himself claimed to have read some two hundred volumes of published memoirs on the period, and investigations of his sources testify to the remarkable thoroughness of the greater part of his work.

But important as this thoroughness is, it is not the outstanding quality of *The Age of Louis XIV*. *The History of Charles XII* had been thorough, but it had been traditional in form; Voltaire himself admitted that he had modeled his work on Quintus Curtius' history of Alexander the Great. But from the beginning, *The Age of Louis XIV* was intended to be a new type of history. It was not to be a mere life of the King himself, nor even an account of the political, diplomatic and military events of the reign. These were to play their part, but all the emphasis was to be placed on the social and cultural history of the period. For to Voltaire, this age seemed to have achieved something like perfection in the arts, to have made tremendous strides toward material and scientific progress, and to have set a new standard of civilized living for society as a whole. "A sluice gate on the canal joining the Atlantic and the Mediterranean," he wrote about this time, "a Poussin picture, a fine tragedy, or a real invention are worth a thousand times more than all the annals of the court and all accounts of military campaigns."

To emphasize the importance he attributed to these features of his work, he rejected the traditional, chronological way of presenting his material, and instead divided his history into three parts. First came the bulk of the narrative of political, military and diplomatic events; then came chapters of anecdotes designed to throw light on the character of the King himself and court and social life in general; lastly came the chapters to which he attached the greatest importance and which were to analyze the social, administrative and financial policies of the government, describe the religious disputes which had troubled society and, finally, reveal the great achievements of the age in literature, the arts, science and philosophy.

The publication of the *Philosophical Letters* in 1734, with their praise of English philosophy and institutions, resulted in a further period of semiexile for Voltaire. Much of it was spent in Cirey, the country seat in Champagne of his mistress, Mme du Châtelet. Here he busied himself with science and the theatre, but also spent considerable time working hard on *The Age of Louis XIV.* But as the work neared completion, he became increasingly aware of the difficulties which might attend its publication in France. Like everything else he ever wrote, *The Age of Louis XIV* was to no small extent a work of propaganda. One might imagine that propaganda in praise of Louis XIV, the achievements of his age and the greatness of France should have been highly acceptable to Louis XV and his government. But this was not altogether the case. The praise of the artistic achievements of the age, and of Louis XIV's efforts to foster them, could be interpreted as criticism of Louis XV in so far as he had failed to follow a similar policy; the admiration for the King's administration, and for his choice of efficient bourgeois ministers to carry out his plans, could reflect on the indolence of Louis XV and his predominantly aristocratic officials and advisers; finally, any attempt to describe the religious quarrels of the seventeenth century from a tolerant and rationalistic viewpoint such as Voltaire's was almost bound to give offense. Nevertheless he resolved to see what could be done, and in 1739 he published the opening chapters of the work in a volume which also contained some of his other writings. The government reacted immediately and suppressed the book.

With publication impossible in France, Voltaire began to lose interest in *The Age of Louis XIV*. He might have risked publishing it abroad, but he had his reasons for not wishing to do so. It was in the Forties that he enjoyed a brief period of relative favor at the French court. He had visions of himself as a minister, and determined to do nothing which might possibly give offense. His hopes, however, proved misplaced: Louis XV never really liked him, and he himself was constitutionally incapable of keeping out of trouble for long. A court scandal put an end to his period of favor. In 1749 Mme du Châtelet died, and feeling that France had now little to offer him, Voltaire at last lent an attentive ear to the pleas of his admirer Frederick the Great of Prussia, who had long been urging him to join him at his court in Potsdam.

When he arrived in Berlin in 1750, he at once set to work to complete *The Age of Louis XIV*. Frederick had repeatedly asked him to do this, and now that he had lost all hope of favor at the French court and could publish the work abroad, all obstacles were removed; however, he was still cautious enough to publish the first edition, which appeared in Berlin in 1751, under someone else's name.

The work was no longer quite the same as it had been in 1739. Many of Voltaire's views had changed and, in particular, his hostility to the Church had sharpened. Whereas the work had originally been intended to end in a blaze of glory with the chapters on the arts, it now ended with those on ecclesiastical controversies, Calvinism and Jansenism. These were considerably expanded, and a new final chapter was added dealing with the disputes between various Catholic religious orders as to whether the religious ceremonies of the Chinese were idolatrous or not. So instead of ending on a triumphant note, the work, in its final form, ended on a somewhat ludicrous one. Voltaire has been criticized for this. But it must be admitted that despite their propagandist element, these final chapters on religious controversies, taken as a whole, are among the best of his historical writings.

Long before this, however, Voltaire's historical interests had become much wider. At Cirey, he and Mme du Châtelet had worked together on scientific and mathematical questions, in which she was deeply interested. But "the divine Emilie," as he called her, asserted that she found the study of history both dull and valueless. It was partly to convince her that it could be interesting and useful that he began a work of much greater scope than any he had attempted hitherto. Up till then, he had been primarily interested in modern history, and he had absorbed enough of the skeptical attitude of the historical Pyrrhonists to regard the study of the more distant past as a relative waste of time. Bolingbroke had probably strengthened him in this belief. But now, if he was going to defend the cause of history as a whole, he could not confine himself to the events of the last hundred years; he had to go further back into the past.

So, in the Forties, he began work on a new universal history, choosing as his starting point the coronation of Charlemagne as emperor in the year 800 A.D. This work was to be known by a variety of titles until it finally became the *Essay on the Customs and the Spirit of Nations*. It is the longest of all his historical writings.

In some ways, he was less well equipped for this new task than for the writing of modern history. His knowledge of the Middle Ages, and of the auxiliary disciplines of the medieval historian, was relatively slight, and he became, for the most part, dependent on second-hand sources. But the freshness of his approach more than compensated for his lack of erudition. To begin with, he was still deeply interested in cultural history, and though his narrowly classical artistic standards often prevented him from appreciating the art of past ages (he had nothing but scorn for Gothic architecture), yet he strove to discover signs of artistic progress and eagerly sought for evidence of scientific and technological inventions and developments. Again, he had not lost his contempt for the unimportant details of battles, genealogies and court pageantry, and he made every effort to organize his account around a number of main themes: the growth of civilization, the conflict of empire and papacy, the reasons for the emergence of feudal society, the folly of the Crusades and of religious civil wars. Above all, he revealed himself throughout the work as an eighteenth-century moralist, condemning the barbarity of the past, proclaiming the superiority of the modern world and affirming the reality, though not the necessity, of material and moral progress.

He had, moreover, another important purpose: he intended that his universal history should be truly universal. This meant breaking away from the existing tradition and in particular from Bossuet, the great church orator of Louis XIV's time, whose eloquently written *Universal History* was still the most frequently quoted work on the subject. Bossuet had described the course of history from the Creation to the time of Charlemagne, basing his study almost exclusively on the Bible and the standard classical authorities, and consequently confining his attentions to the Middle East and Europe. At this time, Voltaire was unwilling to challenge him on his own ground (he knew it would have been highly dangerous to publish a work criticizing the historical authority of the Old Testament) but he deliberately set out to show the inadequacy of Bossuet's "universe" by describing a very different one himself. Though his own work began at the time of Charlemagne, the opening chapter did not deal with the Emperor of the West, but with the history of China. This was followed by a chapter on India, and throughout the rest of his work Voltaire devoted a considerable amount of space to these two countries, to Islamic civilization, and even to smaller and more distant lands. It is true, of course, that the bulk of his work is still devoted to Western Europe, for like all his contemporaries, he knew relatively little about China and India, and his chapters dealing with them tend to be geographical and sociological surveys rather than historical narrative. Yet Voltaire's gesture, even if it was no more than that, effected a profound transformation in the perspectives of history.

Fragments of the work, including the opening chapter, were published in journals in the Forties. But it was only in 1753, after Voltaire had quarreled with Frederick the Great and had returned to try to find a home in France or Switzerland, that part of it appeared in book form. The edition, or so he tells us, was published without his consent, and certainly contained a number of forthright phrases which he would have preferred not to see in print. To correct any unfortunate impression which these might have made, he hastily completed the work, which first appeared in complete form in 1756. However, in later years he was to rewrite and expand it more than once.

These three works, *The History of Charles XII*, *The Age of Louis XIV* and the *Essay on Customs*, are the finest of Voltaire's historical writings; they were the ones he wanted to write. But the works which he was prompted or commissioned to write, though they are less significant, are by no means unimportant.

In the Forties, when he was Royal Historiographer of France, he had written an account of the War of the Austrian Succession, which, in its emphasis on military matters and its rather fulsome praise of some of the French generals, exhibits qualities he had frequently condemned in other historians. He later revised and expanded this work, publishing it in 1769 under the title *Summary of the Age of Louis XV*, and though it still shows traces of its original inspiration, it is, in its final form, a balanced and informative account of Voltaire's own times. Certainly it is more important than his next piece of commissioned work, the *Annals of the Empire*, which he wrote at the request of the Duchess of Saxe-Gotha and published in 1753. This was a hurriedly written account using much material which he had already collected for the *Essay on Customs*. But if, as a whole, it cannot compare with the larger work, it does contain one of his most lucid analyses of the feudal society he detested.

His next commission came somewhat closer to being a labor of love. As early as 1745, he had written to the French Ambassador in St. Petersburg suggesting that he would like to write a history of Peter the Great. In 1757, he was asked to undertake such a work and was promised any documents and memoirs he needed from the Russian archives. Since the time of *The History of Charles XII*, Peter had been among his heroes, and he set to work eagerly, hoping to give a full account of Russian society and of the Czar's civilizing mission. However, things did not turn out quite as he had hoped. He lacked first-hand knowledge of the country and its language and had relatively few sources other than his Russian correspondents, on whom he largely depended for information. They did not always send him what he wanted, and what they did send was often subject to long delays, for by this time Europe was at war once again. He also found it difficult to reconcile his admiration for Peter's social reforms with his dislike of his outbursts of barbaric cruelty. His rather halfhearted attempt to justify Peter's judicial murder of his son seems strangely out of place coming from the pen of the man who was soon to be engaged in the defense of Calas, La Barre and other victims of legalized injustice in his own country. When *The History of Russia Under Peter the Great* finally appeared (the last volume came out in 1763) it was subjected to much criticism. Voltaire's reaction, according to one anecdote, was to remark cynically that he had at least been well rewarded. "My friend," he said, "they gave me some beautiful furs, and I am very sensitive to cold."

The last of these partly commissioned works was *The History of the Parlement of Paris* of 1769. As a contribution to constitutional history it is of some importance, for it traces the development of this institution, emphasizing the way in which its functions had changed. Yet it is also, though not outspokenly so, a work of propaganda against the claims of the parlement to represent the nation. The government, which had frequently been in conflict with the parlement, certainly encouraged Voltaire to write the work and probably supplied information too. But he himself had no love for an institution which was dominated by the Jansenists and had recently condemned La Barre to a cruel death on highly questionable charges of sacrilege. He was one of the first to applaud the dissolution of the parlements throughout the kingdom when the government ordered this in 1771.

However, in the last twenty years of his life, his main interests were of a different nature. Soon after his return from Prussia he had found refuge first at Geneva and then at Ferney, the small French village near the Genevan frontier which was to be his last home. It was from Ferney that he fought his campaigns in defense of victims of injustice, such as Calas, the Protestant who had been broken on the wheel after being condemned on an undocumented and almost certainly false charge of killing his own son to prevent his conversion to Catholicism. It was from Ferney, too, that he launched his "philosopher's war" against *l'infâme:* against religious intolerance everywhere, against the Roman Catholic Church in particular and, sometimes, against Christianity in general. This campaign involved him in the production of a ceaseless stream of books and pamphlets, often hastily written, often repetitive, and often naïve, not to say dishonest, in their propaganda. But the dishonesty was in the details, not in the main purpose, and the naïveté was that of his age.

The religious views he was attacking claimed to have their foundation in historical events, and inevitably, in order to refute them, he had to make use of history himself. More particularly, he had to turn to ancient history, and to what we should now term prehistory, and to attempt to throw light on ages which he had previously dismissed as being too full of myth and uncertainty to be worthy of the historian's study. He had always been a propagandist, but in this last period his propaganda became more blatant than ever. Yet it is nevertheless true that his demolition of the traditional edifice of ancient history, and the ideas he offered for the construction of a new one, were of great importance.

Voltaire's attack is directed mainly at the Jews, whom he dismisses as an unimportant, barbarous and relatively modern nation, and at their history, as revealed in the Old Testament, which is full of inconsistencies, improbabilities and examples of immoral behavior. These themes are hammered home by endless repetition in innumerable works. From the point of view of Voltaire's conception of history, however, they are less important than two of the principles which underly them. The first of these is that miracles are impossible. Voltaire occasionally pays lip service to the idea of the miraculous, but always in terms of ironic exaggeration. Elsewhere he gives his reasons for believing, as a deist, that an omnipotent and omniscient God could not possibly tinker with his creation in this way; and where non-Christian miracles are concerned, he is outspoken in his denunciations. With Newton, he insists that nature is and always has been the same everywhere, and that anything contrary to the ordinary course of nature should be disbelieved.

The second principle follows, to some extent, from the first. As human nature is part of nature, it too must be unchanging. Whatever is totally contrary to the moral sense of the patterns of behavior of eighteenth-century man can never have formed a permanent part of the moral doctrines or the way of life of man in any age.

Armed with these two principles, the Voltaire of Ferney sets out on a campaign of what might almost be termed "debunking" historical legends of all ages, and particularly those associated with the Christian tradition. Works like *The Philosophy of History* (1765), *The Defense of My Uncle* (1767), *The Pyrrhonism of History* (1769), and the *Fragment on General History* (1773) are all full of examples. Voltaire is one of the great destroyers of accepted myths, and though one or two truths also get swept away in the process of destruction, the general effect is a salutary one.

But his work has a positive side too. One of the main purposes of *The Philosophy of History* is to demonstrate the absurdity of any chronology based on a literal interpretation of the early books of the Old Testament. The alternative view of the distant past, which he propounds in this work, is necessarily a somewhat hypothetical one, for archaeological methods of investigating prehistory did not exist in the eighteenth century, and he had to base his own account on probabilities established from his general knowledge of human nature. But if he cannot describe the early history of man except in very general terms, he does at least establish the fact that man must have had such an early history, and that it must be thought of at least in terms of tens of thousands of years, rather than the four thousand or so of accepted chronology. Once again, he opens up new vistas to the student of history.

In these last years, he also carried on with his study of distant civilizations, particularly those of China and India. His *Historical Fragments on India* (1773) and his *Chinese, Indian and Tartar Letters* (1776) contain some of the fruits of these researches. Once again, a propagandistic purpose was mingled with his interest in these countries for their own sake. If civilizations existed which were both independent of and older than those of the West, then the latter's claim to be the unique source of religious truth appeared increasingly unlikely. It became even more so when many Judaeo-Christian beliefs were found to have been held in India long before they appeared in Palestine. Despite its obviously fabulous elements, and despite unpleasant features like sutteeism,* Voltaire was tempted to present an idealized picture of Indian religion. The fact that he did this partly as the result of receiving a document which he took to be of great antiquity, but which was in fact written in the eighteenth century, invalidates some of his arguments, but not their general principle.

If nature was the same everywhere, then all religious

* The Hindu custom of cremating the widow alive on the funeral pile of her husband.

beliefs must have developed on roughly the same lines. An attempt to demonstrate this is one of the main themes of *The Philosophy of History,* and in his comparison of the ways in which cults have developed in different primitive societies and early civilizations, Voltaire is something of a pioneer in the field of social anthropology. It is true that his predominant interest in religion leads him to deal more cursorily with man's material progress than he had done in the *Essay on Customs* and that, in consequence, his account of early human history lacks some of the qualities of the roughly contemporary *Discourse on Inequality* of Jean-Jacques Rousseau. It is also true that he is not altogether consistent, for though on the whole he tries to show the similarity of religious cults everywhere, he also has a tendency, when faced with wide divergences in beliefs and customs, to go to the opposite extreme of asserting that these cannot be explained or reconciled and that they fall within the province of that mysterious, powerful and irrational historical force to which he gives the name "opinion." Yet despite these limitations, and despite the fact that these late works lack the balanced judgment, the careful planning and the literary style of his earlier ones, their contribution to the formation of the modern conception of history is no mean one.

Voltaire's assumptions about the uniformity of nature, human and inanimate, form an integral part of his philosophy of history; so too do the principles which led him to emphasize certain aspects of historical development. But what of his philosophy of history in the narrower sense: how did he envisage the nature of causation in history, and to what extent did he consider the course of history as a whole as having a plan, a pattern or a goal? With his own work, *The Philosophy of History,* he was the first to give currency to a phrase which, in the following century, was to be on everyone's lips. Did he have a philosophy of history in this modern sense of the term?

In one sense, the answer is in the negative. Moreover, this is not surprising, for one of the characteristics of his approach to all philosophical questions is an innate hostility to what he terms "the spirit of system." He is suspicious of all generalizations from the facts, especially when he thinks that they may in reality be generalizations imposed on the facts. This accounts for his criticisms of philosophers like Descartes and Leibnitz, as well as for his lukewarm attitude to Montesquieu, whose *Spirit of the Laws* contains a great deal of this type of generalization.

Furthermore, one of his main purposes, in his later works, is to refute a philosophy of history rather than to create one. Here the main target of his criticism is once again Bossuet, though Bossuet's views were only an outstandingly clear formulation of a theory which went back at least as far as Saint Augustine. For Bossuet, the course of history was directly controlled by divine providence, and divine providence was primarily concerned to reward the virtues and punish the crimes of, first, the Jewish people and, later, the Christian community. It is true that Bossuet's formulation of this theory was a relatively modern one, in so far as his Providence did not act by direct miraculous intervention, but through the minds and hearts of men. But Voltaire was unwilling to accept the theory even in this modified form; nor was he willing to modify it even further himself, and produce a deistic version of it. He too believed in God, but in a God who had created man, given him an instinctive sense of right and wrong, and then left him to his own devices. "The finger of God," which controlled Bossuet's world, is absent from Voltaire's theories of historical causation.

It was perhaps a natural reaction to go to the other extreme and adopt what has been called the "Cleopatra's nose" view of history. Pascal had remarked that if the Egyptian queen's nose had been a little shorter, the whole course of history would have been changed. Voltaire, particularly in his later works, often does the same thing and almost seems to delight in pointing out the irrationality and unpredictability of historical events. There is a strong streak of pessimism in his nature, and he seems to take a certain savage pleasure not only in insisting that history is one long succession of crimes, misfortunes and stupidities, but also in showing that fate is the master of man rather than the other way round. Even in *The Age of Louis XIV* he likes to point out how chance events have overthrown deep-laid plans, as he does when he attributes the fall of Marlborough and the Whigs to the accidental spilling of a few drops of water.

Much of Voltaire's explicit "philosophy of history" is of this negative variety. What is rather surprising is that it should be found side by side with another view which seems to contradict it. Despite the cynicism which is usually attributed to him, and which he very often shows, he seems, in real life, to have had a certain addiction to hero-worship. The Duke of Richelieu, Frederick the Great and Catherine the Great of Russia were all, at some time or other, the object of his uncritical adulation. And the same spirit is often visible in his historical writings. When he finds a hero to admire, he tends to attribute everything to his actions. There is little doubt, for example, that he greatly overemphasizes the personal achievements of Louis XIV and the direct influence of the King on the men of genius of his age. The same is true of his praise of Peter the Great; even in the *Essay on Customs,* the heroes are still there, though they have by this time become less prominent. Of course, this attitude to history was nothing new and was indeed fairly characteristic of many classical historians as well as of the works of courtly flattery which abounded in Voltaire's own time. Yet the extent to which he adopted it may seem surprising when one considers that, throughout his life, he was in constant conflict with authority. It certainly surprised some of his "philosopher" contemporaries, such as Grimm, who regarded the praise of Louis XIV as something in the nature of a betrayal of their common liberal ideals.

These are the views which Voltaire most frequently expresses when he is discussing historical causation. But he expresses them, perhaps, because they are both easily formulated and easily memorable, rather than because they correspond to what is most fundamental in the spirit of his historical writing. For his work contains a more positive philosophy of history than this, one that is implicit rather than explicit but which is nonetheless all-pervading.

Essentially his attitude to history is an affirmation of values: reason, tolerance, social harmony, equality before the law, scientific progress, classical canons of culture and taste. These values may be said to result from the fusion of the seventeenth-century ideal of the *honnête homme,* which has a predominantly moral and literary content, with the eighteenth-century ideal of the *philosophe,* with its greater emphasis on scientific method and on social reform. To some extent, these values may be termed extrahistorical, for Voltaire believes that certain basic concepts of the human conscience are God-given and exist in all ages. But on the whole they belong to the sphere of history, for he is convinced that they have come to fruition through historical processes and have reached their highest point of development in his own age. It is in this development that he is primarily interested, and his best historical writings are devoted to showing how it has taken place.

However, he does not regard it as inevitable; he does not share the complacent belief of contemporaries like Condorcet, whose *Sketch for a Historical Picture of the Progress of the Human Mind* tries to demonstrate that things *must* improve. But his very denunciation of the errors and barbarities of the past is an affirmation that things *have* improved. It is also an exhortation to improve them still further, and a warning that, if the struggle to do so is not maintained, it is always possible to slip back into barbarism. Throughout his historical works, but particularly in the *Essay on Customs,* Voltaire acts as both judge and advocate and invites his reader to do the same. The past must be judged by the standards of modern civilization; but these standards must be constantly preached and defended, for only thus can they be made secure.

Man judges and makes history; but he is also made by history. And Voltaire is well aware of this in practical terms, even though he never discusses the problem as an abstract one. The emphasis he places on the role of insignificant causes or the achievements of great men, and his insistence on the need to struggle to preserve the values which men have created through history, do not exclude a simultaneous belief in more impersonal but more predictable forms of causation. On the contrary, he is to no small extent a forerunner of nineteenth-century economic determinism. On the one hand, he searches for the economic motives of events which otherwise strike him as irrational. He regards the Crusades as an outbreak of collective folly. But he also explains them as a series of highly profitable trading and looting expeditions. On the other hand (and this is a more important aspect of his thought), he constantly insists that economic prosperity is the key to all progress and that it develops independently of the tyrants who wish to destroy it and even, to some extent, of the great men who seek to foster it. The ants, as he says in the *Essay*, can carry on building their homes while the eagles and vultures fight overhead. The importance he attaches to economic matters is emphasized by the frequency with which he gives details of trade, of industrial production or of fluctuations in the value of money.

This philosophy of history has its limitations. In particular, Voltaire lacks a sense of evolution and relativity. He tends to give an absolute and timeless validity to the standards of his own age and to assume that they were incapsulated in human nature from the very beginning. His refusal to believe that moral standards can change with time is exemplified by his repeated attacks on Herodotus' account of ritual prostitution in Babylon, for he could not conceive that the sexual ethics of the ancient Chaldeans might have differed from those of eighteenth-century Parisian hostesses. His preoccupation with the values and standards of his own times is also largely responsible for his failure to understand or explain events or movements which seem to have no connection with his own day or with which he is out of sympathy. Thus, at the beginning of *The Age of Louis XIV,* he can dismiss practically the whole of French Renaissance art as worthless, and present the *Fronde* as a meaningless comic-opera civil war. And his views on, say, the value of medieval architecture are even less perceptive.

But contrast this with the closing chapters of *The Age of Louis XIV*, in which Voltaire describes the immediate origins of his own society. Here, in this more limited field, his presentation of the evolution and development of France in the economic, cultural and religious fields is masterly. And indeed, it is in the practical activity of writing history that he excels, and not in abstract theorizing about it. Here he is the odd man out, for he lived in an age addicted to theorizing. In a discussion of the philosophy of history, the names of Vico, Montesquieu, Condorcet or Herder are more likely to occur than is that of Voltaire. It is true their theories are more carefully elaborated than his; yet none of them could write history of the same caliber.

But if Voltaire was, above all, a practicing historian, how can this practice be described? What had he to contribute to methods of research and composition? And what can be said about his style and his understanding of human nature?

His contribution to historical method, in what might be called the academic sense of the term, does not amount to very much. He has no more than a smattering of the ancillary disciplines of the historian and, except when he is writing contemporary history, he tends to rely on second-hand sources. He insists that the historian should always quote his sources, but in fact he very rarely does so. He is capable of borrowing lengthy passages from other authors without acknowledgment, he frequently misquotes, and he quite often jumps to rash conclusions which he can then proceed to defend with great stubbornness and not a little dishonesty. One of the best illustrations of these tendencies is the long controversy in which he engaged to try to prove that Cardinal Richelieu had not written the *Testament* attributed to him. In this dispute, he cuts a rather poor figure compared with his scholarly opponent, Foncemange.

But such weaknesses are perhaps inevitable in a man who wrote on such a wide variety of historical subjects and had, at the same time, so many other intellectual and practical interests. And his achievements are more important. We have already described how he revolutionized the form of historical writing. But his critical method had a similar impact, not so much through its profundity (for it was often superficial) as through its omnipresent activity. The spirit of historical Pyrrhonism of the early years of the eighteenth century had been a predominantly negative one. Voltaire transformed it into something positive and active. "In everything I wrote," he says in a preface to the *Essay on Customs*, "I always put in the margin: *vide, quaere, dubita.*" Look it up, find out about it and, where necessary, doubt: these are the constant principles of his method. The scholars of the Benedictine type were all too willing to believe what their documents said; many of the *philosophes* were all too prone to engage in abstract speculation divorced from historical fact. Voltaire strikes a balance between them, constantly trying to document himself as thoroughly as possible, but never accepting without question what his authorities say. In the field of contemporary history, where he is really at home, he excels in the thoroughness of his documentation. But in other fields, he contributes almost as much by his omnipresent skepticism and his almost instinctive distrust of accepted ideas and beliefs.

There are two further qualities which one looks for in the really great historian: an exceptional understanding of human nature and an excellent literary style. The first of these is perhaps lacking in Voltaire. He was never a really great dramatist because he was unable to create great characters. His great works of imaginative prose are short stories like *Candide*, in which humor, rapid action and brilliant but concise description are all-important, but in which the characters tend to be marionettes. In his historical writings, he can present us with a clear picture of Charles XII or Louis XIV. But he does so very largely by relating anecdotes, not by direct description of character or by illuminating flashes of imaginative insight. And as, by instinct as well as by conviction, he believes men of all ages to be very much the same, he tends to assume that all men think and act from very much the same motives as he does himself.

But if his style lacks psychological insight, it has many

other excellent qualities. He himself frequently insisted that the literary value of a historical work was of vital importance, and more than once urged historians to write history with the same concern for form as if they were writing tragedy. Yet though he continued to make this point in his old age, he tended increasingly to neglect his own advice. The rapidly written works of his last years, such as *The Philosophy of History,* are almost conversational in tone, and contain many repetitions and even contradictions in places where he has changed his mind and introduced a new idea without bothering to remove the old one. To a lesser extent, the same is true of the *Essay on Customs,* where the style is a relatively matter-of-fact one. It is above all in *The History of Charles XII* and *The Age of Louis XIV* that he took pains to ensure that the literary excellence of his work should equal its historical merit. Admittedly, the former work has an exciting enough story; but the story gains in the telling, and the way in which Voltaire manages to include his more serious reflections on governments and customs without releasing the tension of the narrative is masterly. In *The Age of Louis XIV,* the problem was a more difficult one, because the picture he wished to present was far more complex. Critics have accused him of destroying the unity of his work by the way in which he divides up his material. Yet here again, particularly in the final chapters, dealing with government and religious matters, the balance between narrative and commentary is remarkably well maintained, neither being allowed to dominate the other. A glance at almost any modern French historical textbook will reveal the permanence of Voltaire's influence. The fact that both *The History of Charles XII* and *The Age of Louis XIV* continue to be widely read and frequently republished, although in a scholarly sense they are out of date, bears witness to their artistic power.

So we can understand why he has been acclaimed as the first modern historian. Not only did he make a great contribution to the sweeping away of the accepted legends and pious frauds of the past, but he enlarged the whole concept of history by making it more cosmopolitan and by opening up new vistas into distant prehistoric eras. More important, he created modern social history, showing the interaction and the unity of economic, cultural and religious factors and transforming, without destroying, the traditional form of historical narrative.

Above all he was a great reformer, preaching enlightenment, tolerance, peace, law and reason and human dignity. It is because of these qualities that a work like the *Essay on Customs* is still fascinating today although its facts are often wrong and its style lacks the brilliance of some of his other works. When Voltaire's remains were removed to the Pantheon in 1791, the last line of the inscription on his bier read: ". . . he prepared us for freedom." And this spirit of freedom breathes in his work even now.

The extracts which follow have been translated from the standard modern French edition of Voltaire's works —that by Louis Moland. This edition is based on the one published at Kehl shortly after Voltaire's death and presents his works, for the most part, in the final form he gave them. The passages I have chosen are intended to illustrate widely differing aspects of his historical writing, and at the same time to be, as far as possible, complete in themselves. They are as follows:

1. The second half (approximately) of *The History of Charles XII*. This is probably his most popular historical work and certainly one of his finest pieces of narrative writing. The second part is also the most interesting from the point of view of his historical method, for he makes use of a considerable number of eyewitness accounts.

2. Chapters I and XXIX to XXXVI of *The Age of Louis XIV*. In the first chapter Voltaire gives some account of his aims and an assessment of the importance of the age he is about to describe. The other chapters are those devoted to administrative, financial, artistic, scientific and religious affairs (though I have omitted the last three chapters, dealing with Jansenism, quietism, and the Chinese disputes). Together they illustrate all that is best in his

work as a social historian and as an analyst of the many factors which had gone to make the France of his own day.

3. From his longest work, the *Essay on Customs,* four passages, which reveal other aspects of his interests:

a. The first ten sections of the Introduction. This Introduction was originally an independent work published under the title *The Philosophy of History.* It appeared in 1765, and is thus later than the Essay as a whole. When Voltaire brought out a new edition of the *Essay* in 1769, he had this work reprinted as an introduction to it, and it has occupied this position in all subsequent editions. These opening sections examine certain general questions relating to the early history of mankind and thus illustrate Voltaire's contribution to the study of the remote past.

b. Chapter I of the *Essay* proper. This is the first of two chapters on China and gives some impression of the cosmopolitanism of his outlook.

c. Chapters LXXX to LXXXII. These offer a brief but balanced sample of his treatment of the Middle Ages. The first chapter is mainly narrative and deals with Joan of Arc and Jacques Coeur. The other two are predominantly descriptive and are devoted to the customs, usages and inventions of the thirteenth and fourteenth centuries and to their artistic achievements and religious beliefs and practices.

d. A very brief passage from the "Conclusion and Examination of This Historical Tableau," which he wrote for the 1763 edition of the *Essay.* It is an eloquent comment on the reformist spirit and belief in progress which inspired the *Essay* itself.

4. The article "History" from the *Philosophical Dictionary.* This was originally the article on the same subject which Voltaire contributed to the famous *Encyclopedia* of Diderot and d'Alembert. Later he revised the article and included it in his *Questions on the Encyclopedia,* a work similar in form to

the *Philosophical Dictionary*. Later editors fused these two works into one. The article "History" thus appears in its present form in most modern editions of his works, but it is, in fact, a compendium and includes quite a number of repetitions and not a few irrelevancies. Yet despite this it gives us the clearest picture of what Voltaire thought about a wide variety of subjects connected with the writing, interpretation and purpose of history, and constitutes his most important single pronouncement on the theory of the subject.

J. H. Brumfitt

SELECT BIBLIOGRAPHY

WORKS IN FRENCH

There are a number of complete editions of Voltaire's works, the most recent and the most thorough being that by Louis Moland: Voltaire, *Oeuvres Complètes.* (52 vols., Paris, 1877-85).

The best modern selection from his major historical works is a recent volume in the Pléiade series, edited by René Pomeau: Voltaire, *Oeuvres Historiques.* (Paris, 1958). It has a useful introduction and notes.

The edition of *Le Siècle de Louis XIV* by Emile Bourgeois (Paris, 1906) contains a very thorough introduction and many useful notes.

The eight volumes of G. Desnoiresterres's *Voltaire et la Société au XVIIIe Siècle* (Paris, 1869-76), although they are outdated in some ways, are still the most complete biographical study of Voltaire.

WORKS IN ENGLISH

Contemporary translations exist of all Voltaire's major works, the most important being *The Works of M. de Voltaire,* translated by T. Smollet and others (38 vols., 1771-75). However, copies of this translation are now rare.

There are modern translations in the Everyman's Library series of *The History of Charles XII* (by W. Todhunter, London, 1908) and of *The Age of Louis XIV* (by M. P. Pollack, London, 1926).

SELECT BIBLIOGRAPHY

AMONG MANY GENERAL AND BIOGRAPHICAL STUDIES OF VOLTAIRE, THE FOLLOWING MAY BE PARTICULARLY RECOMMENDED:

BRAILSFORD, H. N. *Voltaire*. London, 1935.
GAY, P. *Voltaire's Politics*. Princeton, 1959.
MORLEY, J. *Voltaire*. London, 1872.
TORREY, N. L. *The Spirit of Voltaire*. New York, 1938.

ON VOLTAIRE AS HISTORIAN, THE FOLLOWING MAY BE CONSULTED:

BLACK, J. B. *The Art of History*. London, 1926.
BRUMFITT, J. H. *Voltaire, Historian*. London, 1958.
GOOCH, G. P. *Catherine the Great and Other Studies*. London, 1954.

THE FOLLOWING WORKS CONTAIN MUCH USEFUL BACKGROUND MATERIAL:

BECKER, C. L. *The Heavenly City of the Eighteenth-Century Philosophers*. New Haven, 1932.
CASSIRER, E. *The Philosophy of the Enlightenment*. Princeton, 1951.
THOMPSON, J. W. *A History of Historical Writing*. New York, 1942.

SUMMARY OF THE LIFE OF VOLTAIRE

1694. Born in Paris, the son of a notary, Maître Arouet.

1704. Enters the Jesuit college of Louis-le-Grand, where he meets a number of fellow pupils who are to hold high office and be among his friends and protectors in later years.

1712. Becomes a law student, but is already devoting himself to society life and to literature.

1713. His Jansenist father, worried by his "dissipation," sends him to Holland as a member of the suite of the French ambassador. He is recalled as a result of his love affair with the Protestant Olympe Dunoyer.

1716. He is exiled from Paris, under suspicion of having written a satire against the regent, the Duke of Orleans.

1717. Another satire leads to imprisonment in the Bastille for nearly a year. In prison, he begins *The League,* the first version of his epic poem *The Henriad.*

1718. The success of his play *Oedipus* first brings him literary fame.

1723. Publication of *The League.*

1725. He is publicly beaten by the servants of the Chevalier de Rohan-Chabot, with whom he had quarreled. When he seeks revenge, he is imprisoned again in the Bastille.

1726. He is released on condition that he go into exile. He leaves for England, where he spends some two years. There he lives near London and meets many important people, including Peterborough, Bolingbroke (whom he had already known in France), Walpole, Pope, Gay, and the theologian and philosopher Samuel Clarke. *The Henriad* is published there in 1728.

1731. Soon after his return to France he publishes *The History of Charles XII*.

1734. His account of England, the *Philosophical Letters*, is published and is condemned by the parlement. To escape arrest, he flees to Lorraine and then to Cirey, the home of Mme du Châtelet, where he spends the greater part of the next ten years. During this period he produces further plays, writes a number of philosophical and scientific works, continues his *Age of Louis XIV* and begins the *Essay on Customs*.

1744. He begins to enjoy a period of relative favor at court. He is made Royal Historiographer the following year and elected to the Academy in 1746. He continues his poetic and dramatic work and also writes his *History of the War of 1741*. But his indiscretions lose him the King's favor.

1749. The death of Mme du Châtelet adds to his misfortunes. Convinced that France holds no future for him, he accepts the invitation of Frederick the Great and, in 1750, goes to Potsdam.

1751. Publication of *The Age of Louis XIV*.

1753. After quarrels with Frederick, he decides to return to France. He is arrested in Frankfurt by the envoy of the King of Prussia, who demands the return of his master's manuscripts. After this incident, knowing that Paris is closed to him, he searches for a home in France or Switzerland. He publishes the *Annals of the Empire*, and a

Summary of Universal History, a version of part of his later *Essay on Customs,* is published without his consent.

1755. He at last finds a home in Geneva.

1756. Publication of the first complete edition of the *Essay on Customs* and of his poem on the Lisbon earthquake.

1759. Publication of *Candide.* He buys the Château of Ferney, just outside Geneva but in French territory. It becomes his home for the rest of his life.

1762. He begins his long campaign to rehabilitate the memory of Calas. In the years which follow, he undertakes similar campaigns on behalf of victims of injustice and also publishes a large number of his deistic books and pamphlets.

1763. He completes his *History of Russia Under Peter the Great.*

1764. The first edition of his *Philosophical Dictionary.*

1765. Publication of *The Philosophy of History* under the pseudonym of the Abbé Bazin.

1769. Publication of the *Summary of the Age of Louis XV* and *The History of the Parlement of Paris.*

1778. Voltaire returns to Paris. Overwhelmed by his triumphal reception there, he falls ill and dies on May 30.

The History of Charles XII, King of Sweden

SYNOPSIS OF BOOKS I-III

[This extract begins at the turning point of Charles XII's career, the battle of Poltava in 1709, which put an end to a long series of victories. In the earlier part of the work, Voltaire has described the youth and education of Charles and the political situation in Europe when he came to the throne. He has given an account of his early victories over the Danes and of his great triumph at Narva, where a Swedish army of eight thousand men defeated ten times that number of Russians. He has described his subsequent campaigns in Poland against Augustus, Elector of Saxony and King of Poland, which culminated in the latter's defeat. By the treaty of Altranstädt, Augustus was forced to abdicate the Polish crown in favor of Stanislas Leszczynski, who, on Charles's orders, had already been elected to the throne.

Peter the Great of Russia had always been the Swedish King's most powerful and most dangerous enemy. Charles now resolved to invade Russia itself, and having secured the help of the Ukrainian leader Mazeppa, he marched into that country. Voltaire describes the Swedish advance, the difficulties it met with, the defection of the Ukrainians and the gradual weakening of the Swedish army during the terrible winter of 1709. However, with the coming of spring, Charles, ignoring these weaknesses, decided to continue to advance toward Moscow. The Swedes were held up by the Russian army before Poltava and Charles himself was incapacitated by a wound in the heel. He nevertheless resolved to attack the Russian positions.

The extract opens in the middle of Book IV, with Voltaire's account of the ensuing battle.]

BOOK IV

. . . It was on July 8, 1709, that the decisive battle of Poltava was fought between the two most remarkable monarchs then living. Charles XII had won fame through nine years of victories; Peter Alekseevich, through nine years of pains taken to train his troops to equal those of Sweden; the one was glorious for having given away dominions; the other, for having civilized his own; Charles loved danger and fought only for glory; Alekseevich did not run away from danger but only made war to further his own interests; the Swedish King was generous through his innate greatness of soul; the Muscovite never gave anything away without a purpose; the former was exceptionally sober and continent, naturally magnanimous, and only committed one barbarous action; the latter had never shaken off the roughness of his education and the harshness of his country and was as terrible to his subjects as he was admired by foreigners, as well as being too addicted to excesses, which even shortened his days. Charles had the title "Invincible," which he could lose at any moment; other nations had already given Peter Alekseevich the name "*Great*," which he could not forfeit by a defeat because he did not owe it to victories.

To have a clear idea of this battle and the place where it was fought, one must imagine Poltava on the north, the camp of the King of Sweden on the south, stretching a little toward the east, his baggage train about a mile behind him and the River Poltava, to the north of the town, running from east to west.

The Czar had crossed the river about a league to the west of Poltava, and was beginning to form his camp.

At daybreak, the Swedes issued forth from their trenches with no artillery other than four iron cannons;

the rest remained in the camp with about three thousand men; four thousand stayed with the baggage; so that the Swedish army attacked the enemy with about twenty-one thousand men, of whom about sixteen thousand were Swedes.

Generals Rehnsköld, Roos, Löwenhaupt, Schlippenbach, Hoord, Sparre, Hamilton, the Prince of Württemberg, a relation of the King's, and several others, most of whom had seen the battle of Narva, all reminded the junior officers of that day when eight thousand Swedes had destroyed an army of eighty thousand Muscovites in a fortified camp. The officers told the story to the soldiers, and they all encouraged one another as they advanced.

The King led the advance, carried on a litter at the head of his infantry. On his orders, part of the cavalry moved forward to attack that of the enemy, and the battle began with this engagement at half past four in the morning. The enemy cavalry lay to the east, on the right of the Muscovite camp; Prince Menzikov and Count Golovin had deployed it at intervals between redoubts armed with cannons. General Schlippenbach, at the head of the Swedes, charged this cavalry. All those who have served with the Swedish army know that it was almost impossible to resist the fury of their first attack. The Muscovite squadrons were broken and routed. The Czar himself arrived to rally them; his hat was pierced by a musket ball; Menzikov had three horses killed under him: the Swedes shouted, "Victory!"

Charles had no doubt that the battle was won; in the middle of the night, he had sent General Creutz with five thousand horsemen or dragoons to attack the enemy in the flank while he was attacking from the front; but as his ill fortune would have it, Creutz lost his way and did not appear. The Czar, who had thought himself lost, had time to rally his cavalry. In his turn, he charged that of the King, which, being without the support of Creutz's detachment, was likewise broken; Schlippenbach himself was made prisoner in this engagement. At the same time, seventy-two cannons were firing from the camp on the Swedish cavalry, and the Russian infantry, advancing from their lines, was moving to attack that of Charles.

Then the Czar detached Prince Menzikov, ordering him to place himself between Poltava and the Swedes. Menzikov executed this order ably and promptly; not only did he cut the communications between the Swedish army and the troops remaining in the camp before Poltava, but, having encountered a reserve body of three thousand men, he surrounded it and cut it to pieces. If Menzikov did this on his own initiative, Russia owed him her salvation; if the Czar ordered it, he was a worthy adversary of Charles XII. Meanwhile the Muscovite infantry had left its lines and was advancing in battle formation across the plain. On the other side, the Swedish cavalry was rallying a quarter of a league from the enemy army and the King, helped by Field Marshal Rehnsköld, was preparing for a general engagement.

He ranged the remaining troops in two lines with the infantry in the center and the cavalry on the flanks. The Czar disposed his army in the same way; he had the advantage of numbers and that of seventy-two cannons, while the Swedes had only four with which to oppose him and were beginning to run out of powder.

The Emperor of Muscovy was in the center of his army, having then only the title of major general, and he seemed to be obeying the orders of General Sheremetov. But he rode through the ranks as an emperor should, mounted on a Turkish horse which the Sultan had given him, exhorting the captains and the soldiers and promising them all rewards.

At nine in the morning the battle was renewed. One of the first salvos from the Russian guns killed the two horses which drew Charles's litter; he had two others harnessed, but a second salvo blew the litter to pieces, throwing the King out of it. Of the twenty-four drabants who were taking turns carrying him, twenty-one were killed. The Swedes, filled with consternation, began to lose their cohesion, and as the enemy guns continued to mow them down the first line fell back on the second and the second fled. In this last action, a single line of ten thousand Russian infantry was all that was needed to rout the Swedish army, so much had things changed.

All Swedish writers say that they would have won the

battle if mistakes had not been made; but all the officers say that it was a great mistake to fight at all and an even greater one to have advanced deep into this desert country, despite the advice of the wisest generals, against a warlike enemy three times stronger than Charles XII both in numbers of men and in resources which the Swedes lacked. The memory of Narva was the principal cause of Charles's misfortune at Poltava.

Already the Prince of Württemberg, General Rehnsköld and a number of leading officers were prisoners, the camp before Poltava was stormed, and everything was in a confusion which it was impossible to rectify. Count Piper, together with a number of officers of the Chancellery, had left this camp, not knowing what to do or what had happened to the King. They were scouring the plain until a major called Bere offered to take them to the baggage. But the clouds of dust and smoke which covered the countryside, and the mental turmoil natural amid this desolation, led them straight to the counterscarp of the town itself, where they were all captured by the garrison.

The King would not flee and yet was unable to defend himself. At this moment he had with him Count Poniatowski, a colonel of the Swedish guards of King Stanislas, a man of outstanding merit whose attachment to Charles's person had induced him to follow him into the Ukraine without any post in the army. He was one of those men who, in all the events and dangers of life in which others can do no more than show their courage, could always make up his mind promptly, wisely and successfully. He signaled to two drabants, who took the King under the arms and placed him on his horse despite the extreme pain of his wound.

Poniatowski, though he had no command in the army, now became a general by necessity and rallied five hundred horsemen around the King's person. Some were drabants, others officers and some simple troopers. This troop, once it was gathered together and inspired to action by the King's misfortune, cut its way through more than ten Muscovite regiments and took Charles for a whole league through the midst of his enemies, as far as the baggage of the Swedish army.

The King, closely pursued in his flight, had his horse killed under him; Colonel Gierta, who was wounded and spent with loss of blood, gave him his own. So this conqueror who had been unable to mount a horse during the battle was twice placed on one during his flight.

This amazing retreat was a great achievement in such a disaster; but it was necessary to fly even farther. Among the baggage they found Count Piper's coach, for the King had never used one himself since he left Stockholm. They put him into this vehicle and hurriedly took the road toward the Borysthenes. The King, who from the moment of being placed on horseback till his arrival at the baggage train had not said a single word, now asked what had happened to Count Piper. "He is captured, together with the Chancellery," was the reply. "And General Rehnsköld and the Prince of Württemberg?" he added. "They are prisoners too," said Poniatowski. "Prisoners of the Russians," said Charles, shrugging his shoulders. "Let us rather go to the Turks." There was no trace of dejection on his face and anyone who had seen him then, without knowing the situation he was in, would never have suspected that he was defeated and wounded.

While he was escaping, the Russians seized his artillery in the camp before Poltava, and also captured his baggage and his military chest, in which they found six millions in specie, the spoils of Poland and Saxony. Nearly nine thousand men, Swedes and Cossacks, were killed in the battle and about six thousand were captured. There still remained about sixteen thousand men, Swedes, Poles and Cossacks, who were fleeing toward the Borysthenes under the command of General Löwenhaupt. He marched along one road with his fugitive troops, and the King took another with a small number of horsemen. The carriage he was traveling in broke down on the way, and he was placed on horseback again. To complete his misfortune he lost his way in a wood during the night. There his courage could no longer overcome his exhaustion, and his tiredness made the pain of his wounds unbearable. His horse had fallen under him through weariness, and the King slept for some hours under a tree in constant danger of being surprised by the victors, who were searching for him everywhere.

At last, on the night of July 9th-10th, he found himself on the banks of the Borysthenes. Löwenhaupt had just arrived with the shattered remnants of his army. It was with an equal mixture of joy and sorrow that the Swedes saw their King, whom they had thought to be dead. The enemy were approaching. The Swedes had neither a bridge to cross the river nor time to make one, nor powder to defend themselves, nor provisions to maintain an army which had eaten nothing for two days. But the remains of this army were Swedes and the defeated King was Charles XII. Almost all the officers thought they would be ordered to halt there and make a last stand against the Russians, and that they would either conquer or die on the banks of the Borysthenes. Charles would undoubtedly have taken this decision if he had not been exhausted with weakness. His wound was suppurating and he had a fever, and it has been noticed that even the boldest men tend, during a fever of suppuration, to lose the instinct of valor, which, like all other virtues, demands a clear head. Charles was no longer himself; I have been assured of this, and it seems entirely probable. They carried him along like a sick man who is hardly aware of himself. Fortunately they still had a broken-down little carriage which by chance they had brought along with them. This was put on a little boat and the King and General Mazeppa were placed in another. Mazeppa had managed to save several coffers full of money, but as the current was too rapid and a strong wind began to blow, the Cossack threw more than three quarters of his treasure into the river to lighten the boat. Müllern, the King's chancellor, and Count Poniatowski, a man more than ever necessary to the King for his resourcefulness in misfortune, crossed in other boats with a number of officers. Three hundred troopers and a large number of Poles and Cossacks, trusting the strength of their horses, risked trying to swim the river. Their troop, keeping close together, resisted the current and broke the waves; but all those who left the main body and crossed lower down were carried away and drowned. Not one of the foot soldiers who tried to cross reached the other bank.

While the remains of the army were in this extremity, Prince Menzikov was approaching with ten thousand horsemen, each having a foot soldier behind him. The corpses of the Swedes who had died by the way of wounds, fatigue and hunger showed Prince Menzikov all too clearly the route which the fugitive army had taken. The Prince sent a herald to the Swedish general to offer him a capitulation. Löwenhaupt immediately sent four generals to receive the commands of the conqueror. Before this day, sixteen thousand soldiers of King Charles would have attacked the whole army of the Russian empire and would have perished to the last man rather than surrender; but after the loss of a battle and a flight of two days, deprived of the presence of their King, who was himself forced to flee, with every soldier's strength exhausted and courage no longer sustained by any hope, love of life overcame bravery. Colonel Troutfetre alone, seeing the Muscovites approach, began to advance with a single Swedish battalion to attack them, hoping by this means to induce the remaining troops to follow his example. But Löwenhaupt was obliged to stop this useless gesture. The capitulation was completed and the whole army were made prisoners of war. Some soldiers, in despair at the thought of falling into the hands of the Muscovites, threw themselves into the Borysthenes. Two officers of the regiment commanded by the brave Troutfetre killed each other, and the rest were made prisoners. They all filed past Prince Menzikov, laying their arms at his feet as thirty thousand Muscovites had done nine years earlier before the King of Sweden at Narva. But whereas the King had sent back all the Muscovite prisoners, as he had no fear of them, the Czar kept all those who were captured at Poltava.

These wretched people were later dispersed throughout the Czar's dominions, particularly in Siberia, a vast province of Great Tartary which extends eastward to the frontier of the Chinese empire. In this barbarous land where people did not even know how to make bread, the

Swedes became ingenious through necessity and practiced all the arts and crafts of which they had the slightest knowledge. All the distinctions which fortune makes between men were then banished. The officer who could not follow any trade was obliged to cut and carry wood for the soldier who was now turned tailor, draper, carpenter, mason or goldsmith and who earned enough to live on. Some of the officers became painters and others architects; some of them taught languages and mathematics. They even established some public schools, which in time became so useful and famous that the citizens of Moscow sent their children there.

Count Piper, the King of Sweden's prime minister, was for a long time imprisoned in Petersburg. The Czar was convinced, as was the rest of Europe, that this minister had sold his master to the Duke of Marlborough and led the Swedish army to invade Russia when they might have pacified Europe. As a result, he made his confinement all the more severe. The minister died some years later in Moscow, having received little help from his family, who lived in opulence in Stockholm, and vainly lamented by his sovereign, who would never condescend to offer a ransom for his minister for fear lest the Czar would refuse; for there was no agreement on exchange of prisoners between Charles and the Czar.

The Emperor of Muscovy, elated with a joy that he made no attempt to hide, received on the field of battle the prisoners who were brought to him in crowds. At every moment he kept asking, "Where is my brother Charles?"

He did the Swedish generals the honor of inviting them to dine with him. Among other questions which he put to them, he asked General Rehnsköld the number of his master's troops before the battle. Rehnsköld replied that the King always kept the muster roll himself and would never show it to anyone; but that for his own part he thought the total figure would be about thirty thousand, of which eighteen thousand were Swedes and the rest Cossacks. The Czar seemed surprised and asked how they dared penetrate into such a distant country and besiege Poltava with so few men. "We were not always consulted," replied the Swedish general, "but like faithful servants we obeyed our master's orders without ever presuming to contradict them." On receiving this answer, the Czar turned to some of his courtiers who had been suspected of engaging in a conspiracy against him. "Ah!" he said. "See how a king really should be served." Then, taking up a glass, he added, "To the health of my masters in the art of war." Rehnsköld asked him who were the people he honored with such a fine title. "You, gentlemen, the Swedish generals," replied the Czar. "Then your majesty is very ungrateful to treat your masters with so much severity," answered the general. After the meal, the Czar returned their swords to all the generals and behaved to them like a prince who wanted to give his subjects an object lesson in generosity and in politeness as he understood it. But this same prince who treated the Swedish generals with so much humanity had all the Cossacks who fell into his hands broken on the wheel.

So the Swedish army which had left Saxony in such triumph no longer existed. Half of them had died of hunger and the other half were either killed or enslaved. Charles XII had lost in one day the fruits of nine years' labor and of almost a hundred battles. He was now fleeing in a wretched old carriage, accompanied by Major General Hoord, who was gravely wounded. The rest of his troops followed, some on foot, some on horseback, and others in wagons, across a desert where neither huts, tents, men, beasts nor roads were to be seen. Everything was lacking, even water itself. It was now the beginning of July; the country lay in the forty-seventh degree of latitude; the dry desert sand made the heat of the sun even more insupportable; the horses fell by the wayside and the men were almost dying of thirst. A stream of muddy water which they found toward evening was all they met with; bottles were filled with this water, which saved the lives of the King of Sweden's little band. After five days' march, he reached the banks of the River Hypanis, now called the Bug by the barbarians who have disfigured even the names of those countries which once flourished as Greek colonies. This river joins the Borysthenes some miles lower down and flows with it into the Black Sea.

Across the Bug, on the south side, is the little town of Oczakov, which marks the frontier of the Turkish empire. The inhabitants, seeing a body of soldiers approaching, whose dress and language were completely unknown to them, refused to ferry them across to Oczakov without an order from Mehemet Pasha, governor of the town. The King sent a courier to this governor, requesting the right of passage; but the Turk, not knowing what to do in a country where one false step often costs a man's life, did not dare take anything upon himself without first obtaining permission from the seraskier of the province, who lived at Bendery, in Bessarabia. While they were waiting for this permission, the Russians, who had made the King's army prisoners, had crossed the Borysthenes and were approaching to take him too. At last the pasha of Oczakov sent word to the King that he would provide him with one small boat to transport himself and two or three attendants. In this extremity, the Swedes took by force what they could not obtain by agreement; a number of them crossed to the other bank in a small skiff, seized some boats, and returned to their own side with them. This proved to be their salvation, for the owners of the Turkish boats, fearing they would lose an opportunity of making a lot of money, at once came in crowds to offer their services. At that very moment, the favorable reply of the seraskier of Bendery also arrived. But the Muscovites arrived on the scene, and the King had the mortification of seeing five hundred of his men seized by the enemy and of hearing the insulting challenges they shouted at him. The pasha of Oczakov, through an interpreter, asked his pardon for the delays which had resulted in the capture of these five hundred men and begged him not to complain about the matter to the Sultan. Charles promised not to do so, but at the same time gave him a severe reprimand, just as if he had been speaking to one of his own subjects.

The commander of Bendery, who was also the seraskier (a title corresponding to that of general) and pasha of the province (its governor or administrator) hastily sent an aga to pay homage to the King and to offer him a magnificent tent, together with provisions, baggage, wagons, equipment, officers and all the attendants necessary to conduct him in splendor to Bendery; for it is a Turkish custom not only to pay the expenses of ambassadors as far as their place of residence but to provide abundantly for any princes who take refuge among them during the time of their stay.

BOOK V

[*The state of the Ottoman Porte. Charles resides near Bendery. His occupations. His intrigues at the Porte. His plans. Augustus regains his throne. The King of Denmark invades Sweden. All the rest of Charles's dominions are attacked. The Czar enters Moscow in triumph. The affair of the Pruth. The history of the Czarina, a peasant girl who became empress.*]

Ahmed III was at that time Emperor of the Turks. In 1703 he had replaced his brother Mustafa on the throne as a result of a revolution rather similar to the one which had transferred the crown of England from James II to his son-in-law William. Mustafa had been dominated by his mufti, who was hated by all the Turks, and had thus provoked the whole empire to rise against him. His army, which he had counted on to punish the malcontents, joined them instead. He was captured and formally deposed and his brother was taken from the seraglio and made Sultan, almost without a drop of blood being shed. Ahmed shut up the deposed Sultan in the seraglio of Constantinople, where he lived for several years, to the great astonishment of Turkey, which was accustomed to seeing the dethronement of one of her princes followed quickly by his death.

The new Sultan's only reward to the ministers, generals, Janizary officers and all others who had taken part in the revolution which had given him the crown was to put them all to death, one after another, for fear they should one day attempt a second revolution. By sacrificing so many brave men, he weakened the forces of the empire; but he strengthened his own throne, at least for some years. He then turned to the task of amassing wealth; he was the first Ottoman Emperor who dared to devalue the currency a little and to establish new taxes. But he was obliged to drop both these enterprises for fear of an insurrection, for the rapacity and tyranny of the sultans are usually felt only by the officers of the empire who, whatever their rank, are his domestic slaves; the rest of the population live in profound tranquillity, with no fear for their lives, liberty or fortunes.

Such was the Turkish Emperor to whom the King of Sweden fled for refuge. He wrote to him as soon as he arrived in his dominions; his letter was dated July 13, 1709. Several different copies of it were circulated, all of which are considered unfaithful today; but of all those I have seen, there is not a single one which does not exhibit the natural haughtiness of its author and is not more suitable to his courage than to his situation. The Sultan replied only toward the end of September. The pride of the Ottoman Porte made Charles realize the difference, in the Sultan's eyes, between a Turkish emperor and the King of a part of Scandinavia, a defeated and fugitive Christian. Otherwise, all these letters, which kings very rarely write themselves, are only vain formalities which serve to reveal neither the character of princes nor the state of their affairs.

In Turkey, Charles XII was really nothing more than a prisoner who was honorably treated. And yet he formed the plan of using the armies of the Ottoman empire against his enemies. He flattered himself that he could reconquer Poland and subdue Russia. He had an envoy at Constantinople, but the man who served him best in his vast projects was Count Poniatowski, who went to Constantinople without a commission and soon made himself necessary to the King, agreeable to the Porte, and finally dangerous to the grand viziers themselves.

One of the people who aided him most skillfully in his plans was a doctor called Fonesca, a Portuguese Jew established in Constantinople. He was a wise and versatile man, a competent organizer, and perhaps the only philosopher of his nation; his profession gave him entry to the Ottoman Porte and often gained him the confidence of viziers. I knew him well in Paris and he has confirmed all the details I am going to recount. Count Poniatowski has told me, both verbally and by letter, that he had been skillful enough to convey letters to the Sultana Valide, the mother of the reigning emperor, who had formerly been ill treated by her son but who was now beginning to regain some influence in the seraglio. A Jewess who was often admitted to her presence kept telling her of the exploits of the King of Sweden, and she was delighted by these stories. Moved by the secret inclination which most women feel toward extraordinary men, even when they have not seen them, the Sultana openly took the part of the King in the seraglio. She always spoke of him as her lion. "When are you going to help my lion to devour the Czar?" she would say to the Sultan, her son. She even ignored the austere laws of the seraglio to the extent of writing, in her own hand, to Count Poniatowski, who still possesses these letters at the time at which I am writing.

Meanwhile, the King was honorably conducted to Bendery, through the desert which used to be called the wilderness of Getae. The Turks took care that he should lack nothing on the way which might make his journey more agreeable. Many Poles, Swedes and Cossacks, who one by one had escaped from the Muscovites, came by different routes to increase his suite as he traveled. He had eighteen hundred men with him when he arrived at Bendery; and all these people were fed and housed, together with their horses, at the Sultan's expense.

The King chose to camp near Bendery rather than live in the town. The seraskier and pasha, Jussuf, had a magnificent tent erected for him and others were provided for all the nobles of his retinue. Some time later, the King had a house built for himself in the same place and his officers followed his example. The soldiers built barracks so that gradually the camp became a little town. The King's wound was not yet healed and he had to have a diseased bone removed from his foot; but as soon as he could mount a horse again, he returned to his usual hard life, getting up before sunrise, tiring out three horses a day, exercising his soldiers. His only amusement was an occasional game of chess, and if little things reveal men's characters, it is worth mentioning that he was constantly moving the king when playing this game; he used it more than any other piece and consequently lost every time.

At Bendery, he was abundantly supplied with everything he needed; a rare situation for a conquered and fugitive king. Apart from the more than sufficient provisions and the five hundred crowns a day which the Ottoman generously provided him with, he was also receiving money from France, and was borrowing from the merchants of Constantinople. Part of this money was employed in forwarding his intrigues in the seraglio, in buying the favors of the viziers or procuring their downfall. The rest was liberally distributed among his officers and among the Janizaries who composed his guards at Bendery. Grothusen, his favorite and treasurer, was the man who dispensed these liberalities; unlike most people who hold this office, he enjoyed giving as much as did his master. One day, he brought him an account of sixty thousand crowns in two lines: "Ten thousand crowns given to the Swedes and the janissaries on the generous orders of his majesty, and the rest eaten up by myself." "That's how I like my friends to render their accounts," said the King. "Müllern makes me read whole pages for the sum of ten thousand francs. I prefer Grothusen's laconic style." One of his old officers, who was suspected of being rather miserly, complained to the King that he gave Grothusen everything. "I only give money to those who know how to use it," replied Charles. This generosity frequently reduced him to a situation where he had nothing to give. A greater degree of economy in his acts of generosity would have served his honor as well and his interests better; but Charles's main vice was to carry his virtues to excess.

Many strangers came to Constantinople to see him. The Turks and Tartars of the neighboring districts arrived in crowds. Everyone respected and admired him. His stubborn refusal to drink wine and his regularity in taking part in public prayers twice a day caused them to say, "He is a real Moslem." They were eager to march with him to the conquest of Muscovy.

During this period of inactivity in Bendery, which turned out to be longer than he had anticipated, he gradually acquired a taste for reading. Baron Fabrice, a nobleman in the service of the Duke of Holstein and an attractive character with the gaiety and easy wit which princes like, was responsible for encouraging this taste for literature. He had been sent to the King at Bendery to look after the interests of the young Duke of Holstein, and he succeeded in doing so by making himself agreeable. He had read all the good French authors, and he got the King to read the tragedies of Corneille and Racine and the works of Boileau. The King had no liking for the latter's satires, which in fact are not his best work, but he admired his other writings. When the passage from the eighth satire was read to him, in which Boileau calls Alexander a fool and a madman, he tore out the page.

Of all the French tragedies, the one he liked best was *Mithridate,* because the situation of this king, defeated but breathing vengeance, was very like his own. He pointed out to Fabrice the passages which struck him most; but he refused to read any of them aloud and never risked speaking a word of French. Even when later at Bendery he met M. Désaleurs, the French ambassador at the Porte and a man of great distinction, who only knew his own language, he spoke to him in Latin; and when M. Désaleurs protested that he did not understand four words of that language, the King, rather than speak French, summoned an interpreter.

This was how Charles XII spent his time at Bendery while waiting and hoping for a Turkish army to come to his assistance. His envoy presented memoirs in his name to the grand vizier, and Poniatowski used the influence which he had achieved to support them. He managed to insinuate himself everywhere; he was always dressed in the Turkish fashion and had access wherever he wanted. The Sultan presented him with a purse of a thousand ducats and the grand vizier told him, "I shall take your

King by one hand and a sword in the other and I shall lead him to Moscow at the head of two hundred thousand men." This grand vizier was called Chourlouli Ali Pasha; he was the son of a peasant from the village of Courlou. Such an extraction is not considered a disgrace among the Turks, who have no ranks of nobility either attached to offices of state or deriving from the possession of titles. Services alone are the criterion by which men are judged, and this is the custom in almost every country in the East; it would be a natural and very desirable custom if only dignities were the reward for merit; but usually the viziers are merely the creatures of a black eunuch or a favorite slave.

The prime minister soon changed his mind. The King could only negotiate, but the Czar could hand out money, and this he proceeded to do. The money he used was the very same that had belonged to Charles XII, and the military chest which he had captured at Poltava furnished the Czar with new weapons against the defeated King. There was no longer any question of making war on the Russians. The Czar's influence became all-powerful at the Porte and his envoy was accorded honors which Muscovite ambassadors had never before enjoyed in Constantinople: he was allowed to have a seraglio—that is, a palace—in the Frankish[1] quarter, and to communicate with other foreign ambassadors. The Czar even felt powerful enough to demand the handing-over of General Mazeppa just as Charles XII had had the unfortunate Patkul delivered into his hands.[2] Chourlouli Ali Pasha could refuse nothing to a prince who backed his demands with millions. So this same grand vizier who had previously solemnly promised to lead the King of Sweden to Moscow with two hundred thousand men now had the temerity to suggest that he should agree to sacrifice

[1] The Turkish designation for European.

[2] Patkul was a Livonian, a subject of Charles XII, who became a plenipotentiary of the Czar. When Charles was victorious against Augustus of Saxony, he insisted that the latter should hand over Patkul, who was then in his power. He was convicted of treason and broken on the wheel. Voltaire condemns this execution as both unjust and illegal, and regards it as the one real atrocity of Charles's career.

General Mazeppa. Charles was outraged by this demand. It is hard to say how far the grand vizier might have pushed the matter if Mazeppa, who was then seventy, had not died at this juncture. The King's grief and indignation increased when he heard that Tolstoi, the Czar's ambassador at the Porte, was publicly served by Swedes who had been made slaves at Poltava, and that these brave soldiers were sold daily in the market at Constantinople. The Muscovite ambassador even said openly that the Turkish troops at Bendery were there to keep a guard on the King rather than to do him honor.

Charles, abandoned by the grand vizier and defeated by the money which the Czar had poured into Turkey, found himself deceived, despised by the Porte, and almost a prisoner among the Tartars. Those who were with him began to despair. He alone remained firm and never appeared in the least dejected. He believed that the Sultan was ignorant of the intrigues of his grand vizier Chourlouli Ali; he resolved to inform him about them and Poniatowski was charged with this dangerous commission. Every Friday the Sultan goes to the mosque surrounded by his solaks, a sort of guard who wear turbans with such tall plumage that they hide the Sultan from the people's views. When someone has a petition to present to him, he tries to mingle with the guards and hold the petition aloft. Sometimes the Sultan condescends to take it himself; but more often he orders an aga to see to it, and later, when he leaves the mosque, has the petitions presented to him. There is no danger of people daring to importune him with useless memoirs or trivial petitions, for they write less in Constantinople in a whole year than they do in Paris in a single day. People are even less willing to risk presenting petitions against the ministers, for normally the Sultan hands on such petitions to the ministers without reading them. This was the only means at Poniatowski's disposal for ensuring that the King of Sweden's complaints reached the Sultan. He drew up a damning indictment of the grand vizier. M. de Feriol, who was then French ambassador, and who has told me this fact, had the petition translated into Turkish. A Greek was hired to present it. This Greek mingled among the Sultan's guards and raised his paper so high and made so much noise that the Sultan noticed him and took the document himself.

This method of presenting the Sultan with petitions against his viziers was used several times; a Swede called Leloing handed in another one a few days later. Charles XII, in the Turkish empire, was reduced to using the same expedients as an oppressed subject.

Some days after this, the Sultan sent the King of Sweden, as the only answer to his complaints, twenty-five Arab horses, one of which had carried his highness himself and was covered with a saddle and housing studded with precious stones and had pure gold stirrups. This present was accompanied by an obliging letter, but one couched in very general terms, which led the King to suspect that the minister had done nothing without the consent of the Sultan. Chourlouli, who was a master of dissimulation, also sent the King five very rare horses. Charles said proudly to the man who brought them, "Go back to your master and tell him that I do not receive presents from my enemies."

Poniatowski, having already ventured to present a petition against the grand vizier, now formed the bold project of having him deposed. He knew that the Sultan's mother disliked this vizier and that the kislar aga, chief of the black eunuchs, and the aga of the Janizaries, hated him; he encouraged all three of them to speak out against him. It was a remarkable thing to see a Christian, a Pole and an unaccredited agent of a Swedish King who had taken refuge among the Turks, intriguing almost openly at the Porte against a viceroy of the Ottoman empire, who, moreover, was both useful and agreeable to his master. Poniatowski would never have succeeded and the very idea of the project would have cost him his life if a power stronger than all those working in his interest had not delivered a final blow to the fortune of the grand vizier Chourlouli.

The Sultan had a young favorite, who later governed the Ottoman empire and was killed in Hungary in 1716 at the battle of Peterwardein, in which the Turks defeated Prince Eugene of Savoy. His name was Coumourgi Ali Pasha. His birth differed little from that of Chourlouli: he was the son of a coal heaver, as the name Coumourgi implies, for *coumour* means "coal" in Turkish. The Emperor Ahmed II, uncle of Ahmed III, had met Coumourgi when he was still a child in a little wood near Adrianople and had been struck by his extraordinary beauty. He took him to the seraglio, where he was befriended by Mustafa, the eldest son and successor of Mahmud. Ahmed III made him his favorite. At the time he only held the post of selictar aga, or swordbearer to the crown. His extreme youth did not allow him to aspire to the position of grand vizier; but he had the ambition to attain it. The Swedish faction never succeeded in winning over this favorite. He was never a friend of Charles, nor of any Christian prince nor of their ambassadors; but on this occasion he served Charles XII without intending to do so; he joined with the Sultana Valide and the senior officers of the Porte to bring about the disgrace of Chourlouli, whom they all hated. This old minister, who had served his master long and faithfully, was the victim of a child's whim and a foreigner's intrigues. He was deprived of his dignities and his wealth; his wife, who was the daughter of the last Sultan, Mustafa, was taken from him, and he was exiled to Caffa, formerly known as Theodosia, in Crimean Tartary. The *bul,* or imperial seal, was given to Numan Couprougli, grandson of the great Couprougli who captured Candia. This new vizier was what ill-informed Christians can hardly believe it possible for a Turk to be: a man of inflexible virtue and a scrupulous observer of the law, who was prepared to oppose the cause of justice to the wishes of the Sultan. He would have nothing to do with war against Russia, which he considered both unjust and useless; but this same attachment to his law which prevented him from attacking the Czar in violation of existing treaties also made him respect the duty of hospitality toward the King of Sweden. He said to his master, "The law forbids you to attack the Czar, who has done you no harm; but it orders you to help the King of Sweden, who is an unfortunate prince in your dominions." He sent the King eight hundred purses—a purse is worth a hundred crowns—and advised him to return peaceably to his own dominions either by land through Germany or by sea in French ships which were then in the port of Constantinople and which M. de Feriol, French ambassador at the Porte, offered to Charles XII to take him to Marseilles. Count Poniatowski negotiated more than ever with this minister and acquired a superiority in these negotiations which outweighed all the gold of the Muscovites now that an incorruptible minister was in power. The Russian faction thought that the best thing it could do was to poison such a dangerous negotiator. One of his servants was bribed to put poison in his coffee, but the crime was discovered before it could be carried out and the poison was found in the servant's hands in a little phial which was taken to the Sultan. The poisoner was tried in a full divan and condemned to the galleys; for Turkish justice never inflicts the death penalty for crimes which have not been carried out.

Charles XII, who was still convinced that sooner or later he would succeed in getting the Turkish empire to declare war on Russia, would accept none of the proposals designed to ensure his peaceful return to his own dominions; he continued to try to convince the Turks that the Czar, whom he had so long despised, now constituted a serious threat to them; his envoys were constantly insinuating that Peter Alekseevich wanted to gain control of shipping on the Black Sea and that after having subjugated the Cossacks, he would turn next to Crimean Tartary. Sometimes these representations aroused the Porte; at other times the Russian ministers destroyed all their effect.

While Charles XII was thus making his destiny dependent on the will of the viziers, while he was receiving benefits and affronts from a foreign power, while he was presenting petitions to the Sultan and living off his generosity in a desert, all his enemies, reawakened at last, were attacking his dominions.

The battle of Poltava was the signal for a revolution in Poland. King Augustus returned there, protesting against his abdication and against the peace of Altranstädt, and publicly accusing Charles XII, whom he no longer feared, of brigandage and barbarity. He imprisoned Fingsten and Imhof, his plenipotentiaries who had signed his abdication, just as if they had exceeded their orders and betrayed their master. His Saxon troops, who had been the pretext for his dethronement, brought him back to Warsaw accompanied by the majority of the Polish palatines who, having formerly sworn fidelity to him, had later taken the same oath to Stanislas and were now returning to take a new one to Augustus. Siniawski[3] himself rejoined Augustus' party, and gave up any idea of becoming king, and contented himself with remaining grand general of the crown. Flemming, Augustus' prime minister, who had been obliged to leave Saxony for a time for fear of being handed over with Patkul, now contributed all his skill to the task of winning over to his master's side a large part of the Polish nobility.

The Pope relieved the people from the oath of allegiance they had taken to Stanislas. This action of the Holy Father, taken at the right moment and supported by Augustus' forces, had considerable effect; it strengthened the influence of the court of Rome in Poland, where no one at that time wanted to question the chimerical right of the popes to interfere in the temporal affairs of kings. Everyone was ready to submit anew to the authority of Augustus and to receive without repugnance an absolution which was of no use, but which the papal nuncio did not fail to represent as essential.

The power of Charles XII and the greatness of Sweden were now at their lowest ebb. More than ten crowned heads had long been fearfully and enviously watching Swedish power extending beyond its natural limits, on the other side of the Baltic, from the Dvina to the Elbe. The defeat and absence of Charles revived the interests and jealousies of all these monarchs, which had long been kept in check by treaties and by the fact that they dared not break these treaties.

The Czar, who was more powerful than all the rest of them put together, took advantage of his victory, captured

[3] Siniawski had been a third claimant for the Polish crown.

Viborg and the whole of Karelia, overran Finland with his troops, laid siege to Riga, and sent an army corps into Poland to help restore Augustus to the throne. The Emperor was now what Charles XII had earlier been: the arbiter of Poland and northern Europe; but he only consulted his own interests, whereas Charles had never listened to anything but his ideas of vengeance and glory. The Swedish King had helped his friends and crushed his enemies without demanding the least advantage from his victories; the Czar behaved more like a monarch and less like a hero, and would only help the King of Poland on condition that Livonia was ceded to him, and that this province, for which Augustus had started the war, should remain Russian forever.

The King of Denmark, forgetting the treaty of Travendal as Augustus had forgotten that of Altranstädt, immediately thought of gaining possession of the duchies of Holstein and Bremen, and he renewed his claims to them. The King of Prussia had ancient rights over Swedish Pomerania which he wanted to revive. The Duke of Mecklenburg was annoyed to see the Swedes still in possession of Wismar, the finest city in the duchy; this prince was to marry a niece of the Muscovite Emperor, and the Czar was only looking for a pretext to establish himself in Germany, following the Swedish example. George, Elector of Hanover, was also looking for a chance to enrich himself with the spoils of Charles's empire. The Bishop of Münster would also have liked to assert some of his rights if he had had the power to do so.

Twelve or thirteen thousand Swedes were defending Pomerania and the other countries which Charles possessed in Germany; it was there that war was likely to begin. The threatening storm alarmed the Emperor and his allies. It is a law of the empire that anyone who attacks one of its provinces is reputed to be an enemy of the whole Germanic body.

But there was another and still greater difficulty. All these princes, with the exception of the Czar, were at that time united against Louis XIV, whose power had for some time been as formidable to the empire as was that of Charles XII.

At the beginning of the century, Germany had found herself hard pressed by the French in the south and the Swedes in the north. The French had crossed the Danube and the Swedes the Oder, and if their then victorious forces had been able to unite, the empire would have been utterly defeated. A fate similar to that which had overcome Sweden had also humiliated France;[4] but Sweden still had resources, and Louis XIV was still fighting vigorously if unsuccessfully. If Pomerania and the duchy of Bremen became a theatre of war, it was to be feared that the empire would suffer, and that being weakened on this side it would have less strength to resist Louis XIV. To prevent this danger, the Emperor, the princes of Germany, Queen Anne of England and the States-General of the United Provinces concluded a treaty toward the end of 1709, which was one of the most curious agreements ever to be signed.

It was stipulated by these powers that the war against the Swedes should not be fought in Pomerania or in any of the provinces of Germany but that the enemies of Charles XII could attack him elsewhere. The King of Poland and the Czar themselves acceded to this treaty and they inserted in it an article which was as extraordinary as the treaty itself: this was that the twelve thousand Swedes who were in Pomerania should not be allowed to leave to go and defend their other provinces.

To ensure that this treaty was carried out, it was proposed that an army be assembled to preserve this imaginary neutrality; it was to be stationed on the banks of the Oder. An army raised to prevent a war would have been a singular novelty and the very people who were to subsidize it had for the most part a strong interest in prosecuting this war which they were claiming to prevent. The treaty stipulated that the army was to be composed of troops provided by the Emperor, the King of Prussia, the Elector of Hanover, the Landgrave of Hesse and the Bishop of Münster.

The result was what one might have expected from

[4] The French had been defeated by Marlborough and Prince Eugene at Blenheim in 1704 and had since suffered further disasters.

such a project: it was never put into effect. The princes who were to provide contingents for this army in fact provided nothing; less than two regiments were actually formed; there was a great deal of talk about neutrality, but nobody observed it and the princes of the north who had designs on the King of Sweden's territories were left perfectly free to fight over the spoils.

While this was happening, the Czar, having left his troops quartered in Lithuania and ordered the siege of Riga, returned to Moscow to show his people a sight as new as anything he had so far done in his kingdom, a triumph more or less like those of the ancient Romans. He made his entry into Moscow on January 1, 1710, under seven triumphal arches erected in the streets and decorated with everything these latitudes could produce and everything that commerce, made flourishing by his care, could provide. A regiment of guards led the march, followed by the pieces of artillery captured from the Swedes at Lesnoi and Poltava; each one was drawn by eight horses covered with scarlet housings which hung down to the ground. Then came the standards, the drums and the colors won in these two battles, carried by the officers and soldiers who had captured them. All these spoils of war were followed by the finest of the Czar's troops. After they had filed past, there came a specially made chariot bearing Charles XII's litter, which had been found on the battlefield of Poltava, shattered by two cannon shots. Behind this litter came all the prisoners, marching two by two; among them were Count Piper, Prime Minister of Sweden, the famous Marshal Rehnsköld, the Count of Löwenhaupt, Generals Schlippenbach, Stackelberg and Hamilton, and all the officers and soldiers who were later dispersed throughout Great Russia. The Czar appeared immediately after them, mounted on the same horse which he had ridden at the battle of Poltava. A few paces behind him came the generals who had had a share in the successes of that day; next followed another regiment of guards, and the whole procession was closed by wagons loaded with Swedish ammunition.

This triumphal entry was accompanied by the ringing of all the bells in Moscow, by the sound of drums, kettledrums and trumpets and of an infinite number of musical instruments as well as by the salvos of two hundred cannons and the shouts of five hundred thousand men crying, "Long live the Emperor our father!" every time the Czar paused in his triumphal progress.

This imposing exhibition increased the veneration which his people felt for him and perhaps did more to make him appear great in their eyes than all the useful things he had done for them. But the blockade of Riga went on. The Czar's generals occupied the rest of Livonia and part of Finland. At the same time, the King of Denmark sailed with his entire fleet to invade Sweden; he landed seventeen thousand men there and left them under the command of the Count of Reventlau.

Sweden was at this time governed by a regency composed of senators who had been appointed by the King before he left Stockholm. The body of the Senate, who thought the government rightfully belonged to them, were jealous of the regency. The state suffered from these divisions, but when, after the battle of Poltava, the first news to arrive in Stockholm was to the effect that the King was at Bendery at the mercy of the Tartars and the Turks, and that the Danes had invaded Skäne and captured Hälsingborg, the jealousies ceased and no one thought of anything but how to save Sweden. The country was becoming depleted of regular troops, for although Charles had always made his great expeditions at the head of small armies, yet the innumerable battles he had fought during nine years and the constant need to recruit troops, maintain garrisons and reinforce the armies which were needed in Finland, Ingria, Livonia, Pomerania, Bremen and Verden, had cost Sweden more than two hundred thousand soldiers during the course of the war. Barely eight thousand trained troops remained in the country, and these, together with the new militia, were all the resources Sweden possessed.

But the nation was warlike by nature and every people unconsciously adopts the attitude of its king. From one end of the country to the other, the only topic of conversation was the prodigious deeds of Charles XII and his generals and the old regiments which had fought under them at Narva, on the Dvina, at Clissau, at Polotsk and at Hollosin. The most insignificant Swedes were thus fired with a spirit of emulation and glory. To this were added affection for the King, pity, and an irreconcilable hatred of the Danes. In other countries the peasantry are slaves, or treated as such; those of Sweden formed a body within the state and considered themselves citizens and therefore capable of more exalted sentiments. As a result, these militiamen soon became the best troops in northern Europe.

On the orders of the regency, General Stenbock placed himself at the head of eight thousand trained troops and approximately twelve thousand of the new militia and advanced against the Danes, who were ravaging all the coast of Hälsingborg and who were already beginning to plunder far inland.

There was neither time nor the means to equip the militia with uniforms: the majority of these farm laborers arrived dressed in their flaxen smocks, with pistols at their belts tied on with cords. Stenbock, at the head of this strange army, came upon the Danes three leagues from Hälsingborg on March 10, 1710. He wanted to allow his troops a few days' rest, to dig entrenchments and to give the new soldiers time to get used to facing the enemy; but the peasants unanimously demanded battle the very day on which they arrived.

Officers who were present have told me how they saw these peasants almost all foaming with rage, so great is the national hatred of the Swedes for the Danes. Stenbock took advantage of these feelings, which, on the battlefield, are worth as much as military discipline. He attacked the Danes with a result which can scarcely have more than one or two parallels in the whole of military history: an untrained militia in its first battle equaled the bravery of an experienced body of soldiers. Two regiments of these hastily armed peasants cut to pieces the regiment of guards of the King of Denmark, leaving only ten survivors.

The Danes were completely routed and withdrew under the protection of the cannon of Hälsingborg. The crossing from Sweden to Zeeland is so short that the

King of Denmark learned the very same day of the defeat of his army in Sweden; he sent his fleet to embark the remnants of his troops. The Danes left Sweden in haste five days after the battle; but being unable to reembark their horses, and not wanting to leave them to the enemy, they killed them all near Hälsingborg and set fire to their stores. They burned their corn and their baggage and left four thousand wounded in Hälsingborg, of whom the majority died of infection from the dead horses and from the lack of provisions, which their own compatriots deprived them of, for fear they might fall into Swedish hands.

At the same time, the peasants of Dalecarlia, having heard, in the depths of the forests, that their King was a prisoner among the Turks, sent deputies to the regency at Stockholm offering to go at their own expense, to the number of twenty thousand men, to free their master from the clutches of his enemies. This proposal, which showed a great deal of courage and affection, but was not really very useful, was listened to with pleasure although it was rejected. The regency did not fail to tell the King all about it when they sent him an account of the battle of Hälsingborg.

Charles received this consoling news at his camp near Bendery in July, 1710. Soon after this, another event confirmed him in his hopes.

The grand vizier Couprougli, who was opposed to his designs, was deposed after two months in office. The little court of Charles XII and those who still supported him in Poland proclaimed that Charles was able to make and unmake viziers and that, from the depths of his retreat at Bendery, he governed the Turkish empire; but in fact he had no part whatever in the disgrace of the favorite. The rigid probity of the vizier was, so it is said, the sole cause of his fall; his predecessor did not pay the Janizaries out of the imperial treasury, but with money which he had procured by his extortions. Couprougli paid them with treasury money. Ahmed reproached him with preferring the interests of subjects to those of the Emperor. "Your predecessor, Chourlouli," he told him, "was quite capable of finding other ways of paying my troops."

The grand vizier replied, "If he knew how to enrich Your Highness by extortions, I am proud to say that this is an art of which I am entirely ignorant."

The profound secrecy that prevails in the seraglio rarely allows such statements to reach the public; but this one became known when Couprougli's disgrace was announced. The vizier did not pay for his boldness with his head because true virtue can sometimes make itself respected even when it displeases. He was allowed to withdraw to the island of Euboea. I learned these details through letters from a relative of mine, M. Bru, who was a principal interpreter at the Ottoman Porte, and I have repeated them here in order to give some idea of the spirit of that government.

The Sultan then recalled Baltagi Mehemet, the pasha of Syria, from Aleppo. He had already been grand vizier before Chourlouli. The baltagis of the seraglio, who get their name from *balta,* which means "ax," are the slaves who cut wood for the use of the princes of the blood and the sultanas. This vizier had been a baltagi in his youth and had always kept this name, as is the custom with the Turks, who are not ashamed to take the name of their first profession, or that of their father, or the name of their birthplace.

In the days when Baltagi Mehemet was a servant in the seraglio, he had had the good fortune to render a few small services to Prince Ahmed, who was then a state prisoner under the rule of his brother Mustafa. The princes of the Ottoman blood are allowed to keep for their pleasure a few women who are past the age of child-bearing (and this age arrives very early in Turkey) but still attractive enough to please. Ahmed, when he became Sultan, gave one of these slaves, whom he greatly loved, in marriage to Baltagi Mehemet. This woman, by her intrigues, made her husband grand vizier; another intrigue displaced him, and yet a third made him grand vizier again.

When Baltagi Mehemet received the *bul* of the empire, he found the King of Sweden's party dominant in the seraglio. The Sultana Valide, Ali Coumougri, the Sultan's favorite, the kislar aga, chief of the black eunuchs, and the aga of the Janizaries, all wanted war against the Czar; the Sultan was convinced on this step; the first order he gave to the grand vizier was to go and fight the Muscovites with two hundred thousand men. Baltagi Mehemet had never made war; but he was not a fool, as the Swedes who were displeased with him made him out to be. When he received a saber studded with precious stones from the Sultan, he said to him, "Your highness knows that I was brought up to use an ax to cut wood and not a sword to command your armies. I shall try to serve you well; but if I do not succeed, remember that I have begged you not to hold it against me." The Sultan assured him of his friendship, and the vizier prepared to obey his orders.

The first step taken by the Ottoman Porte was to imprison the Russian ambassador in the Castle of the Seven Towers. It is a Turkish custom to begin by arresting the ministers of countries on which they are declaring war. Though in other matters they observe the laws of hospitality strictly, in this they violate the most sacred rights of nations. They commit this injustice under the pretext of equity, for they imagine, or at any rate try to make others believe, that the only wars they engage in are just ones because they are consecrated by the approbation of their mufti. On this principle, they consider themselves to have taken up arms to punish the violators of treaties which they have often broken themselves, and imagine that they are punishing the ambassadors of enemy kings as accomplices in the treachery of their masters.

To this reason may be added the ridiculous contempt which they affect toward Christian princes and their ambassadors, whom they usually regard as mere trade consuls.

The Khan of the Crimean Tartars received the order to hold himself in readiness with forty thousand Tartars. This prince governs Nagaï, Budzhak, part of Circassia and the whole of the Crimea, a province known to antiquity as Tauric Chersonesus. The Greeks had carried their arms and commerce there and founded powerful cities, and later the Genoese penetrated as far as this when they were the masters of European trade. The ruins of Greek towns and a number of Genoese monuments can still be seen in this country, surviving amid the desolation and the barbarity.

The Khan is called Emperor by his subjects; but despite this impressive title, he is a slave of the Porte. The Ottoman blood which flows in the veins of the khans and the fact that they claim a right to the Turkish throne if the race of the sultans should ever die out makes them respectable as a family, but dangerous as individuals to the Sultan. It is for this reason that he dare not destroy the race of Tartar khans, but at the same time hardly ever allows any of them to occupy the throne for very long. Their conduct is closely inspected by the neighboring pashas, their dominions are surrounded by Janizaries, their inclinations are thwarted by the grand viziers, and their intentions are always suspect. If the Tartars complain about the Khan, the Porte uses this pretext to depose him; if he is too popular, this is an even greater crime, for which he is soon punished; so they are almost all driven from sovereignty into exile and end their days at Rhodes, which is usually both their prison and their tomb.

Their subjects, the Tartars, are the biggest brigands on earth and at the same time, though this seems inconceivable, the most hospitable of people. They will go fifty leagues from home to attack a caravan and destroy villages; but if a stranger, whoever he may be, enters their country, not only is he received, lodged and looked after everywhere, but wherever he goes the inhabitants dispute with each other for the honor of having him as their guest, and the master of the house, his wife and his daughters are all eager to serve him. This inviolable respect for the laws of hospitality has been handed down to them by their ancestors the Scythians, and they have conserved it because few strangers travel among them and the low price of all sorts of provisions does not make this virtue too onerous for them.

When the Tartars go to war in alliance with the Ottoman army, they are fed by the Sultan. Their only pay is the booty they capture; as a result, they are better at pillaging than at regular fighting.

The Khan, won over by the presents and the intrigues of the King of Sweden, first obtained permission for the general rendezvous of the troops to be at Bendery itself, under the eyes of Charles XII, so as to emphasize the fact that the war was being fought on his behalf.

The new vizier, Baltagi Mehemet, who did not lie under the same obligations, had no wish to flatter a foreign prince to this extent. He changed the order, and it was at Adrianople that this vast army finally assembled. The rendezvous of the Turkish armies always takes place in the vast plains of Adrianople when the Turks are making war on the Christians. The troops which have come from Asia and Africa rest and refresh themselves there for a few weeks. But to forestall the Czar, the grand vizier allowed the army to rest for only three days and then marched off toward the Danube and Bessarabia.

The Turkish troops are no longer as formidable today as they used to be when they conquered so many countries in Asia, Africa and Europe; in those days the physical strength, bravery and numbers of the Turks triumphed over enemies who were less robust than they and less well disciplined. But today, now that the Christians understand the art of war better, they almost always beat the Turks in a pitched battle, even when they are inferior in numbers. If the Ottoman empire has recently made a number of conquests, these have only been at the expense of the republic of Venice, which is generally considered to be more wise than warlike, is defended by foreign mercenaries, and receives little help from other Christian kings, who are always divided among themselves.

The Janizaries and spahis always attack in a disorderly manner and are incapable of obeying commands and of recovering their ranks. Their cavalry, which ought to be excellent, given the quality and speed of their horses, could not withstand the onslaught of German cavalry. Their infantry did not yet know how to make proper use of fixed bayonets. Moreover, the Turks have not had a great general since the time of Couprougli, the conqueror of the island of Candia. A slave nourished in the idleness and silence of the seraglio led a hastily raised, inexperienced and undisciplined army against the Russian troops, who were hardened by twelve years of war and proud of having defeated the Swedes.

On the face of things, the Czar should have defeated Baltagi Mehemet. But he made the same mistake with the Turks that the King of Sweden had made with him; he underestimated his enemy. When he heard that the Turks were arming, he left Moscow, and having ordered that the siege of Riga should be turned into a blockade, he assembled an army of eighty thousand men on the Polish frontier. With this army, he marched through Moldavia and Walachia, formerly the land of the Dacians but now inhabited by Greek Christians who are vassals of the Turks.

Moldavia was governed at that time by Prince Cantemir, who was of Greek origin and united the talents of the ancient Greeks with both literary and military knowledge. He was said to be a descendant of the famous Timur, known by the name of Tamerlane. This extraction seemed more impressive than a Greek one. His ancestry was proved by the name of the conqueror; Timur, it was said, is like Temir; the title of Khan, which Timur held before he conquered Asia, is found in the name Cantemir; therefore Prince Cantemir is descended from Tamerlane. The majority of genealogies have no more foundation than this.

Whatever family Cantemir may have sprung from, he owed his entire fortune to the Ottoman Porte. Scarcely had he received the investiture of his principality than he betrayed his benefactor, the Turkish Emperor, in favor of the Czar, from whom he hoped to obtain even more. He fondly imagined that the conqueror of Charles XII would easily triumph over a vizier who had little reputation, who had never made war, and who had chosen for his kehaya, or lieutenant, the Superintendent of Customs of Turkey. He reckoned that all his subjects would rally to his standard, for the Greek patriarchs had encouraged him to revolt. So the Czar made a secret treaty with this prince, and having received him into his army, continued his advance until, in June, 1711, he arrived on the north bank of the River Hierasus, now known as the Prut, near Iași, the capital of Moldavia.

As soon as the grand vizier heard that Peter Alekseevich was advancing in this direction, he immediately left his camp, and following the course of the Danube, crossed the river on a pontoon bridge near a town called Saccia at the very place where Darius had once built the bridge which bore his name. The Turkish army moved so swiftly that it soon came in sight of the Muscovites, the two armies being separated by the River Prut.

The Czar, sure of the Prince of Moldavia, never dreamed that the Moldavian people would fail him; but princes and their subjects have often very different interests. In this case, the subjects liked the Turkish government, which is only dangerous to the great, and which treats subject peoples leniently; they feared the Christians, and above all the Muscovites, who had always acted in an inhuman fashion toward them. They all took their provisions to the Ottoman army; traders who had promised to furnish supplies to the Muscovites carried out with the grand vizier the bargains they had made with the Czar. The Walachians, who were neighbors of the Moldavians, showed the same preference for the Turks, such was the extent to which Muscovite barbarity had aroused their hostility.

The Czar, finding himself deceived in the hopes which he had perhaps been rash in entertaining, now suddenly found that his army was without forage and provisions. The soldiers deserted in large numbers, and soon the army was reduced to less than thirty thousand starving men. The Czar experienced the same misfortunes on the banks of the Prut as a result of having trusted Cantemir as Charles XII had suffered at Poltava for having relied on Mazeppa. Meanwhile, the Turks crossed the river, surrounding the Russians and forming an entrenched camp before them. It is surprising that the Czar did not dispute the river crossing or at least that he did not attempt to repair his error by attacking the Turks immediately after they had crossed instead of giving them time to destroy his army through hunger and fatigue. It would seem, indeed, that the Emperor did everything he could in this campaign to hasten his own ruin. He found himself without provisions, with the River Prut behind him, a hundred and fifty thousand Turks in front of him, and forty thousand Tartars continually harassing his flanks. In this extremity he said publicly, "Here am I, at least as badly off as my brother Charles was at Poltava."

Count Poniatowski, the indefatigable agent of the King of Sweden, was in the grand vizier's army together with a number of Poles and Swedes who all thought the Czar's defeat inevitable.

As soon as Poniatowski saw that the two armies were bound to come to an engagement, he informed the King of Sweden, who immediately left Bendery with forty officers, savoring in advance the pleasure of fighting the Muscovite Emperor. After many losses and ruinous marches, the Czar found himself pushed back toward the Prut, where his only defenses were some *chevaux-de-frise* and a few wagons. A few detachments of Janizaries and spahis attacked these badly defended positions, but their assault was disorderly, and the Muscovites defended themselves with all the vigor that the presence of their king and their own despair lent them.

The Turks were repulsed twice. The following day, Count Poniatowski advised the grand vizier to starve out the Muscovite army, which, as it was short of everything, would be obliged to surrender unconditionally, together with its Emperor, within a day.

The Czar has since admitted more than once that in the whole course of his life he never felt anything as cruel as the dilemma which faced him that night; he turned over in his mind all the things he had done for so many years for the glory and happiness of his country; all these great works, which had constantly been interrupted by wars, would perhaps perish with him without ever having been completed. The choice was between dying of hunger or attacking nearly a hundred and eighty thousand men with weary troops whose numbers were only half what they had been—an almost entirely dismounted cavalry, and an infantry exhausted by hunger and fatigue.

Early in the night, he sent for General Sheremetov

and ordered him, without hesitation and without asking advice, to have everything ready for a bayonet assault on the Turkish positions at daybreak.

He also gave an express order that all the baggage should be burned and that each officer should keep only a single wagon so that, in case of defeat, the enemy would at least not get the booty they expected.

Having made all the preparations for the battle with the General, Peter retired to his tent, burdened with grief and racked with convulsions, a disorder which often attacked him and always recurred with redoubled violence when he was distressed. He forbade anyone to enter his tent during the night under any pretext whatsoever, as he did not wish people to come and reproach him for the desperate but necessary decision he had arrived at; still less did he want anyone to observe the sad state in which he felt himself to be.

Meanwhile, the greater part of the baggage was being burned as he had ordered. The whole army regretfully followed this example; several people buried their most precious possessions. The generals were already giving orders for the march and trying to inspire the army with a confidence they did not feel themselves. The soldiers, worn out with fatigue and hunger, marched without spirit and without hope. The women, of whom there were far too many with the army, were uttering cries which depressed the men all the more. Everyone expected death or slavery the next morning. This is no exaggeration, for it agrees to the letter with the accounts given by officers who served in this army.

However, the Muscovite camp contained a woman who was perhaps as extraordinary as the Czar himself. At this time she was known only by the name of Catherine. Her mother was a wretched peasant from the village of Ringen in Estonia, a province where all the people are serfs and which was at that time under Swedish domination. She had never known her father and had been baptized under the name of Martha. The curate of the parish brought her up out of charity until she was fourteen; then she became a servant at Malbork in the house of a Lutheran minister called Gluck.

In 1702, at the age of eighteen, she married a Swedish dragoon. The day after her wedding a section of Swedish troops was beaten by the Russians and the dragoon, who had taken part in the action, never returned. His wife could not discover whether he had been made prisoner and subsequently was never able to find out anything about his fate.

Some days after this she was made prisoner herself by General Bauer and became a servant of his and later of Marshal Sheremetov; he in turn gave her to Menzikov, a man who knew the most extreme vicissitudes of fortune, for he rose from being a pastry-maker's boy to the rank of general and prince, and was later deprived of everything once again and exiled to Siberia, where he died in poverty and despair.

It was at one of Menzikov's suppers that the Emperor first saw her and fell in love with her. He married her secretly in 1707, not because he was seduced by women's wiles, but because he found in her a strength of mind capable of helping him in his enterprises and even of continuing them after his death. He had already long ago repudiated his first wife, Ottokefa, the daughter of a boyar, for he accused her of being opposed to the changes he was making in his dominions, and this, in his eyes, was the greatest crime of all. He wanted his family to consist entirely of people who thought as he did. In this foreign slave he thought he had found the qualities of a sovereign, although she had none of the virtues of her sex. For her sake he brushed aside prejudices which would have stopped an ordinary man; he had her crowned empress. The same spirit which made her the wife of Peter Alekseevich later gave her the crown after her husband's death. Europe was amazed to see this woman, who could neither read nor write, compensate for her lack of education and her weaknesses by her courage and resolution, and occupy a legislator's throne with glory.

When she married the Czar, she renounced the Lutheran religion into which she had been born, and embraced that of the Russians; she was rebaptized according to the orthodox rite, and in place of the name Martha she took that of Catherine, the one by which she was known ever after. It was she who, in the camp by the Prut, held a council with the general officers and Vice Chancellor Schafirov, while the Czar was in his tent.

They decided that it was essential to sue for peace and to persuade the Czar to take this step. The Vice Chancellor wrote a letter to the grand vizier in his master's name, and the Czarina took this letter to the Czar's tent despite the fact that he had forbidden anyone to enter. By her prayers, her arguments and her tears, she finally got him to sign, and she immediately collected together all her jewelry, all her valuables and all her money. She even borrowed money from the generals, and having got together a considerable present, she sent it to Osman Aga, the grand vizier's lieutenant, together with a letter signed by the Muscovite Emperor. Baltagi Mehemet, maintaining at first all the pride of a vizier and a conqueror, replied, "Let the Czar send me his prime minister and I will see what can be done." Vice Chancellor Schafirov arrived at once, loaded with a number of presents which he himself publicly offered to the grand vizier. They were sufficiently large to show that they needed him, but not large enough to bribe him.

At first the vizier demanded that the Czar should surrender unconditionally. The Vice Chancellor replied that his master was going to attack him in a quarter of an hour and that the Muscovites would perish to the last man rather than submit to such infamous conditions. Osman added his remonstrances to Schafirov's words.

Baltagi Mehemet was no warrior: he had seen that the Janizaries had been repulsed the previous day. Osman easily persuaded him not to risk such certain advantages on the fate of a battle. He therefore agreed to a six-hour armistice, during which the conditions of peace would be settled.

During the parley, there took place a trifling incident which may serve to indicate that the Turks are far more scrupulous in keeping their word than we imagine. Two Italian noblemen, relations of M. Brillo, a lieutenant colonel of a regiment of grenadiers in the Czar's service, had gone off in search of forage and had been captured by the Tartars, who took them to their camp and offered to sell them to an officer of the Janizaries. The Turk was indignant that they should have dared violate the truce in this way, and he arrested them and himself brought them before the grand vizier, together with the two prisoners.

The vizier sent the two noblemen back to the Czar's camp and ordered that the Tartars who had been chiefly concerned in carrying them off should be beheaded.

Meanwhile, the Tartar Khan opposed the conclusion of a treaty which would deprive him of his hopes of plunder. Poniatowski supported the Khan with the most pressing arguments. But Osman won the day over the impatience of the Tartar and the insinuations of Poniatowski.

The vizier thought he was doing enough for the Sultan, his master, by concluding an advantageous peace. He demanded that the Muscovites should restore Azov and burn the galleys stationed in this port. He insisted too that they should demolish the important citadels built on the Palus Maeotis[5] and hand over all their cannons and munitions to the Sultan. The Czar was to withdraw his troops from Poland and to cease disturbing the small number of Cossacks who were under Polish protection and those who depended on Turkey. Lastly, he had to pay the Tartars a subsidy of forty thousand sequins a year, an odious tribute which had been imposed long ago, but from which the Czar had freed his country.

At last the treaty was on the point of being signed, without so much as making mention of the King of Sweden. All that Poniatowski could obtain from the vizier was the insertion of an article by which the Czar bound himself not to hinder the King in his return. And what is very remarkable, it was stipulated in this article that the Czar and Charles should make peace if they thought proper and if they could agree on the terms.

On these conditions, the Czar was permitted to retire with his army, cannon, artillery, colors and baggage. The Turks furnished him with provisions and there was plenty of everything in the camp two hours after the signing of

---

[5] The Sea of Azov.

the treaty, which was put into preparation on July 21, 1711, and completed on August 1st.

While the Czar, who had escaped from his predicament, was withdrawing with drums beating and banners flying, the King of Sweden arrived on the scene eager to fight and to see his enemy in his power. He had ridden more than fifty leagues from Bendery to near Iași. He arrived at the moment when the Russians were beginning their peaceful retreat; to reach the Turkish camp one could cross the Prut on a bridge three leagues from there, but Charles, who did nothing as other men did, swam the river at the risk of his life and passed through the Russian camp, where he might well have been captured. He reached the Turkish army and dismounted at the tent of Count Poniatowski, who has told me these facts both verbally and in writing. The Count advanced sadly toward him and told him how he had just lost an opportunity which might never arise again.

The King, furiously angry, went straight to the grand vizier's tent and heatedly reproached him for concluding the treaty. "I have the right," said the grand vizier calmly, "to make war and peace." "But," replied the King, "did you not have the whole Muscovite army in your power?" "Our law commands us," answered the vizier gravely, "to give peace to our enemies when they implore our mercy." "But," retorted the King angrily, "does it command you to make a bad treaty when you can impose whatever conditions you like? Were you not in a position to bring the Czar back to Constantinople a prisoner?"

The exasperated Turk replied coldly, "Yes, but who would govern his empire in his absence? It would be a bad thing if all kings were to be away from their own countries." Charles's only reply was an indignant smile; he threw himself on a sofa, and looking at the vizier with anger and contempt in his eyes, stretched out his leg toward him and deliberately caught his spur in the Turk's robe so that he tore it. He then got up at once, remounted, and returned to Bendery with despair in his heart.

Poniatowski still remained for some time with the grand vizier to try more persuasive methods of getting him to extract more favorable conditions from the Czar. But the hour of prayer had arrived, and the Turk, without answering a single word, went to wash and to pray to God.

BOOK VI

[*Intrigues at the Porte. The Khan of Tartary and the Pasha of Bendery try to force Charles to leave. He defends himself with forty servants against an army. He is captured and treated as a prisoner.*]

The fortune of the King of Sweden, now so different from what it had been, persecuted him in the most trifling things. On his return he found his little camp at Bendery and all his apartments flooded by the waters of the Dniester. He retired a distance of a few miles to near a village called Varnitza, and as if he had a secret foreboding of what was to happen, he had a large stone house built there, capable, if the need arose, of withstanding an assault for a few hours. He even furnished it magnificently, contrary to his usual custom, in order better to impress the Turks.

He also built two others, one for his chancellery and the other for his favorite, Grothusen, who kept a table at the King's expense. While he was building in this way near Bendery, as if he intended to spend the rest of his life in Turkey, Baltagi Mehemet, fearing his intrigues and complaints at the Porte more than ever, had sent the resident of the German Emperor to make a personal request in Vienna for free passage for the King of Sweden through the hereditary dominions of the house of Austria. Three weeks later this envoy returned with a promise from the imperial regency to pay Charles XII all the honors due to him and to guarantee his safe passage to Pomerania.

The application had been made to the regency in Vienna because at that time the Emperor Charles, successor of Joseph I, was in Spain, disputing the crown of that kingdom with Philip V. While the German envoy was carrying out this commission in Vienna, the grand vizier sent three pashas to the King of Sweden to inform him that he would have to leave Turkish territory.

The King, who already knew the orders with which they were charged, began by telling them that if they dared propose anything contrary to his honor or if they failed to show him proper respect, he would have them all three hanged on the spot. The pasha of Salonica, who was their spokesman, disguised the harshness of his commission in the most respectful terms. Charles ended the audience without even deigning to reply; his chancellor, Müllern, who remained with the three pashas, explained to them in a few words his master's refusal, which had already been made sufficiently clear by his silence.

The grand vizier was not to be put off; he ordered Ismael Pasha, the new seraskier of Bendery, to threaten the King with the Sultan's anger if he did not agree without delay. This seraskier had a mild and conciliatory nature which had won him the good will of Charles and the friendship of all the Swedes. The King conferred with him, but only in order to tell him that he would not leave until Ahmed had granted him two things: the punishment of his grand vizier, and a hundred thousand men with whom to return to Poland.

Baltagi Mehemet was well aware that Charles was remaining in Turkey in order to ruin him. He took care to place guards on all the roads from Bendery to Constantinople to intercept the King's letters. He did more than this; he cut down his *thaim*, that is, the allowance which the Porte makes to princes to whom it grants asylum. The King of Sweden had an immense *thaim*, consisting of five hundred crowns a day in silver and a profusion of all the things which contribute to maintaining a court in splendor and abundance.

As soon as the King learned that the vizier had dared to cut down his supplies, he turned to the steward of his household and said, "Up till now you have only had two tables; I order you to have four from tomorrow."

Charles XII's officers were accustomed to finding nothing impossible when their master ordered it; however, they had neither provisions nor money, and they were obliged to borrow at twenty, thirty or even forty per cent from the officers, servants and Janizaries who had become rich on the King's generosity. M. Fabrice, the Holstein envoy, Jeffreys, the English ambassador, together with their secretaries and friends, also gave what they could. The King, with his usual pride and lack of concern for the future, lived off these gifts, which would not have sufficed for long. It became necessary to elude the vigilance of the guards and to send secretly to Constantinople to borrow money from European merchants. But they all refused to lend money to a king who seemed to have put himself in a position where he would never be able to pay it back. A single English merchant called Cook finally risked lending about forty thousand crowns, content to lose them if the King of Sweden died. This money was brought to the King's little camp just when they were beginning to be short of everything and to give up all hope of relief.

Meanwhile, Poniatowski had written from the vizier's very camp an account of the Prut campaign in which he accused Baltagi Mehemet of cowardice and treachery. An old Janizary, who was indignant at the vizier's weakness and had also been bribed by Poniatowski, took charge of this account and, having obtained leave, presented it himself to the Sultan.

Poniatowski left the camp a few days later and went to the Ottoman Porte to organize further intrigues against the grand vizier, as was his custom.

Circumstances were favorable: the Czar, once he was at liberty, was in no hurry to fulfill his promises; the keys of Azov did not arrive; the grand vizier, who was responsible, rightly feared his master's indignation, and did not dare to appear in his presence.

The seraglio was then more than ever filled with intrigues and factions. These cabals, which are to be found in every court and which, in our own, usually end in the dismissal of a minister, or at the very worst in someone being exiled, always finish up, in Constantinople, with at least one execution. This one proved fatal to the former vizier Chourlouli and to Osman, the lieutenant of Baltagi Mehemet, who had been the principal author of the peace of the Prut and who since then had obtained an important post at the Porte. Among Osman's treasures were found the Czarina's ring and twenty thousand gold coins of Saxon and Russian origin; this proved that money alone had saved Peter from disaster and had ruined the fortunes of Charles XII. The vizier Baltagi Mehemet was banished to the island of Lemnos, where he died three years later. The Sultan did not confiscate his property either when he was exiled or on his death; he was not rich, and his poverty was a vindication of his memory.

The grand vizier was succeeded by Jussuf, or Joseph, whose fortune was as curious as those of his predecessors. He was born near the frontiers of Russia and was captured by the Turks, together with his family, at the age of six. He was then sold to a Janizary and for a long time was a valet in the seraglio. Finally he became the second person in an empire in which he had once been a slave. However, he was only the shadow of a minister; the young selictar, Ali Coumourgi, raised him to this dangerous post in the hope of one day filling it himself, and Jussuf, his creature, had nothing to do but set the imperial seal on whatever the favorite demanded. From the day of his appointment, the policies of the Ottoman court appeared completely changed; the plenipotentiaries of the Czar, who remained in Constantinople as ministers and hostages, were better treated than ever; the grand vizier ratified the peace of the Prut with them; but what was particularly mortifying to the King of Sweden was to learn that the secret links which were being formed between Constantinople and the Czar were the fruit of the mediations of the English and Dutch ambassadors.

Ever since Charles's arrival at Bendery, Constantinople had become what Rome has more often been: the center of the diplomatic negotiations of the Christian world. Count Désaleurs, the French ambassador at the Porte, supported the interests of Charles and Stanislas; the Emperor of Germany's minister opposed them; and the factions of Sweden and Muscovy clashed, as those of France and Spain have long done at the court of Rome.

England and Holland seemed to be neutral, but were not so in reality. The new trade which the Czar had opened at Petersburg attracted the attention of these two commercial nations.

The English and Dutch will always side with the prince who favors their trade the most; there were many advantages to be derived from a connection with the Czar; and therefore it is no wonder that the ministers of England and Holland secretly helped him at the Porte. One of the conditions of this new alliance was that Charles should be immediately obliged to quit the Turkish dominions, either because the Czar hoped to seize him on the road, or because he thought him less formidable in his own kingdom than in Turkey, where he was always on the point of arming the Ottoman troops against the Russian empire.

Charles was perpetually soliciting the Porte to send him back through Poland with a large army. The divan was resolved to send him back with a simple guard of seven or eight thousand men, not as a king whom they meant to assist, but as a guest whom they wanted to get rid of. For this purpose the Sultan Ahmed wrote him the following letter:

Most powerful among the kings who adore Jesus, redresser of wrongs and injuries and protector of justice in the ports and the republics of south and north, shining in majesty, friend of honor and glory and of our Sublime Porte, Charles, King of Sweden, whose enterprises may God crown with success.

As soon as the most illustrious Ahmed, formerly chiaoux pasha,[1] shall have the honor to deliver you this letter, adorned with our imperial seal, be persuaded and convinced of the truth of our intentions which are contained in it; namely that, although we had proposed to march our ever-victorious troops against the Czar, yet that prince, in order to avoid the just resentment occasioned by his delay in executing the treaty concluded on the banks of the

[1] First usher.

Prut and later ratified at our Sublime Porte, has now restored to our empire the castle and town of Azov and sought, through the mediation of the ambassadors of England and Holland, our old friends, to cultivate the ties of lasting peace with us. This we have granted him, and we have given his plenipotentiaries, who remain with us as hostages, our imperial ratification after having received his ratification from their hands.

We have given the most honorable and gallant Delvet Gherai, Khan of Budzhak, of the Crimea, of Nagai and Circassia, and our most wise counselors and generous seraskier of Bendery Ismael (may God perpetuate and increase their magnificence and prudence) our inviolable and salutary orders for your return through Poland, in accordance with your first plan, which you have presented to us again. You must therefore prepare to leave under the auspices of Providence and with an honorable escort, before the arrival of winter, to return to your dominions, taking care to pass in a friendly fashion through those of Poland.

Everything necessary for your journey will be provided by my Sublime Porte, money as well as men, horses and wagons. We exhort and recommend you above all to give the most positive and clear orders to all of the Swedes and others who are with you to commit no disorderly act and to do nothing which might tend, directly or indirectly, to violate this peace and friendship.

In this way you will conserve our esteem, of which we shall try to give you as important and as frequent tokens as opportunity allows us. The troops which we have chosen to accompany you will receive orders in conformity with our imperial intentions.

Given at our Sublime Porte of Constantinople, the 14th of the moon Rebyul Eurech 1124 [April 19, 1712].

This letter still did not make the King of Sweden lose hope; he wrote to the Sultan saying that he would be eternally grateful for the favors which His Highness had showered on him; but that he believed the Sultan was too just to send him back with a simple mobile escort through a country which was still inundated with the Czar's troops. And in fact, the Russian Emperor, despite the first article of the peace of the Prut, by which he had promised to withdraw all his troops from Poland, had actually sent fresh troops there. What seems surprising is that the Sultan knew nothing about this.

The Porte, for reasons of vanity, always allows ambassadors of Christian princes in Constantinople, but does not maintain a single agent in any Christian court. The result of this unfortunate policy is that foreigners can discover and sometimes even influence the Sultan's most secret resolutions, whereas the divan is always in complete ignorance of the things which go on openly in Christian countries.

The Sultan, shut in his seraglio with his wives and his eunuchs, only sees through the eyes of his grand vizier. This minister, as inaccessible as his master, occupied with the intrigues of the seraglio, and without any outside correspondence, is usually deceived. Alternatively, he himself deceives the Sultan, who then deposes him or has him strangled at the first mistake, replacing him by another, who is probably just as ignorant or perfidious, who behaves like his predecessors and who soon falls as they did.

This court is normally so inactive and filled with such a complacent feeling of security that if the Christian princes combined against it, their fleets would be in the Dardanelles and their armies at the gates of Adrianople before the Turks had even thought about defending themselves; but the different interests which will always divide Christendom will save the Turks from a fate which their lack of political skill and their ignorance of military and naval matters now seem to be preparing for them.

Ahmed was so badly informed about what was happening in Poland that he sent an aga to see if it was true that the Czar's armies were still there; two secretaries of the King of Sweden, who spoke Turkish, went with him to act as witnesses against him in case he made a false report.

The aga saw the truth with his own eyes and returned to report to the Sultan himself. Ahmed was indignant and was about to have his grand vizier strangled; but the favorite, who was protecting the vizier and who thought he might still have need of him, obtained his pardon and supported him for some time longer in the ministry.

The Russians were openly supported by the vizier and secretly supported by Ali Coumourgi, who had changed sides. But the Sultan was so angry, the infraction of the treaty was so manifest, and the Janizaries—who often cause ministers, favorites and sultans to tremble—were so openly in favor of war that nobody in the seraglio dared propose a more moderate course of action.

At once the Sultan shut up the Muscovite ambassadors in the Castle of the Seven Towers; they were by now just as used to going to prison as to attending an audience. War was declared again on the Czar, the horses' tails were displayed, and orders were given to all the pashas to assemble an army of two hundred thousand men. The Sultan himself left Constantinople and established his court at Adrianople so as to be nearer the theater of war.

Meanwhile, a solemn embassy, sent to the Sultan by Augustus and the republic of Poland, was on its way to Adrianople. The palatine of Masovia was at its head, with a retinue of more than three hundred people.

The whole of this embassy was arrested and imprisoned in one of the suburbs of the town. Never was the King of Sweden's party more hopeful than on this occasion; yet all these preparations were to prove useless once again, and all these hopes were to be disappointed.

If we can believe a public minister, a wise and far-sighted man who was then living in Constantinople, the young Coumourgi was already meditating plans very different from that of fighting a hazardous war with the Czar of Muscovy for a few stretches of desert. He was planning to drive the Venetians out of the Peloponnesus, now known as Morea, and to become master of Hungary.

To achieve these great ends, he was only waiting for the office of grand vizier, which he was still too young to hold. In this position, he needed the Czar as an ally rather than as an enemy; it was neither in his interest nor in accordance with his wishes to keep the King of Sweden any longer, still less to use Turkish arms on his behalf. Not only did he want to send Charles home, but he said openly that no Christian ministers should in future be tolerated in Constantinople, that all these ordinary ambassadors were nothing but honorable spies who corrupted or betrayed the viziers and had long been the cause of the intrigues in the seraglio, that the Franks who were established at Pera and in the Levantine ports were merely merchants who needed a consul and not an ambassador. The grand vizier, who owed his position and even his life to the favorite and who, moreover, was afraid of him, agreed with these aims all the more easily because he had sold himself to the Muscovites and hoped to avenge himself on the King of Sweden, who had tried to ruin him. The mufti, who was the creature of Ali Coumourgi, was also a slave to his wishes; he had advised war against the Czar when the favorite wanted it, and he found it unjust as soon as the young man had changed his mind. So no sooner was the army assembled than terms for a settlement were discussed. The vice chancellor Schafirov and the young Sheremetov, plenipotentiaries of the Czar and hostages at the Porte, promised, after many negotiations, that the Czar would withdraw his troops from Poland. The grand vizier knew perfectly well that the Czar would not carry out this agreement, but signed it nevertheless, and the Sultan, content with having given the appearance of laying down the law to the Russians, remained in Adrianople. And so, in less than six months, peace had been sworn with the Czar, war declared against him, and peace renewed once again.

The main article of all these treaties was that the King of Sweden should be forced to leave. But the Sultan was unwilling to compromise his honor and that of his empire by exposing the King to the danger of being captured on the way by his enemies. It was therefore stipulated that he would leave, but that the ambassadors of Poland and Muscovy would be responsible for the safety of his person. These ambassadors swore in the name of their masters that neither the Czar nor King Augustus would hinder him in his journey, and Charles, on his side, was to engage himself not to attempt to excite a rebellion in Poland. When the divan had settled Charles's destiny in this way, Ismael, the seraskier of Bendery, went to Varnitza, where the King was encamped, and informed him of the decisions of the Porte, leaving him in no doubt that he must delay no longer, but must leave.

Charles's only answer was to the effect that the Sultan had promised him an army, not an escort, and that kings should keep their word.

Meanwhile, General Flemming, the minister and favorite of King Augustus, was maintaining a secret correspondence with the Khan of Tartary and the seraskier of Bendery. La Mare, a French nobleman who was a colonel in the Saxon service, had made more than one journey between Bendery and Dresden, and all these journeys were suspect.

Precisely at this moment, the King of Sweden secured the arrest, on the Walachian frontier, of a courier sent by Flemming to the ruler of Tartary. The letters were brought to him and were deciphered. They showed that the Tartars and the court of Dresden were in constant touch with one another, but they were conceived in such ambiguous and general terms that it was difficult to make out whether King Augustus' aim was merely to detach the Turks from the interests of Sweden or whether he was trying to get the Khan to hand Charles over to the Saxons while he was taking him back through Poland.

It seemed difficult to imagine that a prince as generous as Augustus would, by seizing the person of the King of Sweden, hazard the life of his ambassadors and of the three hundred Polish noblemen who were detained in Adrianople as pledges of Charles's safety.

But on the other hand, it was known that Flemming, the all-powerful minister of Augustus, had few principles or scruples. The outrageous way in which the King of

Sweden had treated the Elector of Saxony, now King of Poland, seemed to excuse any act of revenge, and it might be thought that if the court of Dresden could buy Charles from the Khan of the Tartars, it could easily buy from the Ottoman court the liberty of the Polish hostages.

These arguments were discussed by the King, his chancellor, Müllern, and Grothusen, his favorite. They read and reread the letters, and as the wretched situation in which they found themselves made them all the more suspicious, they determined to believe the worst.

A few days later the King was confirmed in his suspicions by the sudden departure of Count Sapieha, who had taken refuge with him and who now left him in haste to return to Poland and throw himself into the arms of Augustus. In any other situation, Sapieha would have merely seemed to him to be a malcontent; but in his present delicate position, he did not hesitate to believe him a traitor. The fact that he was being continually pressed to leave turned these suspicions into certainty. The stubbornness of his character, combined with all these probabilities, made him convinced that he was to be betrayed and handed over to his enemies, although the existence of this plot has never been proved.

He may have been mistaken in his idea that Augustus had struck a bargain with the Tartars for his person; but he was still more mistaken in counting on help from the Ottoman court. However, he resolved to try to gain time.

He told the pasha of Bendery that he could not leave without first having the money to pay his debts; for although his *thaim* had been paid in full again for some time now, his liberalities had kept forcing him to borrow further sums. The pasha asked how much he wanted and the King replied, at random, "A thousand purses," which would be worth fifteen hundred thousand francs of our money. The pasha wrote to the Porte, and the Sultan, instead of the thousand purses he was asked for, sent twelve hundred, together with the following letter:

> The purpose of this imperial letter is to inform you that as a result of your recommendations and

representations, together with those of the most noble Delvet Gherai, Khan of our Sublime Porte, our imperial magnificence has granted a thousand purses to the King of Sweden. These will be sent under the care and conduct of the most illustrious Mehemet Pasha, formerly chiaoux pasha, to remain in your custody until the time of the departure of the King of Sweden, whose steps may God guide! They will then be given to him, together with a further two hundred purses, as an addition to our imperial liberality, which exceeds his requests.

As for the route through Poland, which he is resolved to take, you will take care, you and the Khan who are to accompany him, to ensure by wise and prudent measures that during the journey neither the troops under your command nor the King of Sweden's men cause any damage or commit any action which might be considered to infringe the peace which still exists between our Sublime Porte and the kingdom and republic of Poland: so that the King will pass as a friend under our protection.

If he does this (and you will expressly recommend him so to do), he will receive from the Poles all the honors and consideration due to his majesty, as we have been assured by the ambassadors of King Augustus and of the republic, who, on this condition, have even offered themselves, together with several other Polish nobles, as hostages, if required, for the safety of his passage.

When the time of departure, which you and the most noble Delvet Gherai will agree on, has arrived, you will place yourself at the head of your brave soldiers, among whom will be the Tartars headed by their Khan, and you will conduct the King of Sweden and his men.

May it thus please the only God, the Almighty, to direct your steps and theirs. The pasha of Aulos will remain at Bendery, with a corps of spahis and another of Janizaries, to protect it in your absence, and by following our imperial orders and intentions in all these points and articles you will deserve the continuance of our imperial favor as well as the praise and rewards due to all those who observe them.

Done at our imperial residence of Constantinople, the 2nd of the moon of Schewal, 1124 of the Hegira.

While they were waiting for this answer from the Sultan, the King wrote to the Porte to complain of the treason of which he suspected the Khan of the Tartars; but the roads were well guarded and the minister, moreover, was hostile; so the letters never reached the Sultan. The vizier even prevented M. Désaleurs from coming to Adrianople, where the Porte was, for fear that this minister, who was acting on Charles's behalf, might upset the plans which had been made for his departure.

Charles, angry at seeing himself being, as it were, driven from the Sultan's dominions, determined not to leave at all.

He could have asked to return through Germany, or to take a ship on the Black Sea and sail through the Mediterranean to Marseilles. But he preferred to ask for nothing and to await events.

When the twelve hundred purses had arrived, his treasurer, Grothusen, who had learned Turkish during his long stay in the country, went without an interpreter to see the pasha, with the intention of extracting the twelve hundred purses from him and then starting some new intrigue at the Porte, still vainly hoping that the Swedish party would be able to force the Ottoman empire into war with the Czar.

Grothusen told the pasha that the King could not get his equipment ready without money. "But," said the pasha, "we shall pay all the expenses of your departure; your master need spend nothing so long as he is under the protection of mine."

Grothusen replied that the difference between Turkish and Frankish equipment was so great that they would have to make use of the Swedish and Polish artificers at Varnitza.

He assured the pasha that his master was ready to leave, and that this money would both facilitate and hasten his departure. The pasha, who was too trusting, handed over the twelve hundred purses; a few days later he came to the King and, in a most respectful manner, requested him to give orders for the departure.

He was extremely surprised when the King told him that he was not yet ready to go and that he needed another thousand purses. Dumbfounded by this reply, the pasha was silent for some time. He went over to a window and was seen to shed tears. Then, turning to the King, he said, "I shall lose my head for having obliged your majesty; I have given you the twelve hundred purses despite my sovereign's express order." Having spoken these words, he turned away, full of sadness.

The King stopped him and said that he would make excuses for him to the Sultan. "Alas," said the Turk as he left, "my master does not know how to excuse faults; he only knows how to punish them."

Ismael Pasha went to convey this news to the Khan of the Tartars, who, having received the same order as the pasha prohibiting the handing over of the twelve hundred purses before the King's departure, and having himself agreed that the money should be delivered, was as apprehensive as the pasha of the Sultan's indignation. They both wrote to the Porte to justify themselves, protesting that they had only given the twelve hundred purses on a definite promise from the King's minister that he would leave without delay. They begged his highness not to attribute the King's refusal to leave to their disobedience.

Charles, still persisting in his idea that the Khan and the pasha intended to deliver him to his enemies, ordered M. Funk, his envoy to the Sultan, to complain of their conduct and to ask for a further thousand purses. His extreme generosity and his lack of concern for money made him fail to realize that he was acting contemptibly in making such a proposal. He only did it in order to be refused and to have a new pretext for not leaving; but things had come to a pretty pass when he needed to employ such subterfuges. Savary, his interpreter, an able and enterprising man, took the letter to Adrianople despite the strict guard which the grand vizier had placed on the routes.

Funk was obliged to present this dangerous request. The only reply he received was to be thrown into prison. The indignant Sultan called an extraordinary divan, which he addressed himself, as rarely happened. Here is a translation of his speech, made at the time:

> I have hardly known the King of Sweden other than by his defeat at Poltava and by the request he made to me to grant him asylum in my empire; I have, I believe, no need of him, and no occasion either to love or fear him; yet without consulting any other motives save those of Moslem hospitality and my own generosity, which sheds the dew of its favors on great and small, on foreigners as on my own subjects, I have received and assisted him, his ministers, officers and soldiers, and for three and a half years I have not ceased to load him with presents.
>
> I have granted him a considerable escort to conduct him back to his own kingdom. He asked for a thousand purses to defray a number of expenses, although I defray them all; instead of a thousand, I gave him twelve hundred. After having extracted these from the seraskier of Bendery, he now says he wants a thousand more and refuses to leave under the pretext that the escort is too small, whereas it is in fact only too large to pass through a friendly country.
>
> I ask you then if I am violating the laws of hospitality in sending this prince away and if foreign powers can have any reason to accuse me of violence and injustice if I should find myself obliged to compel him to leave.

The whole divan replied that the Sultan was acting justly.

The mufti declared that Moslems were not bound to show hospitality toward infidels, still less toward ungrateful ones. He gave his futwa, which is a sort of mandate which almost always accompanies the important orders of the Sultan; these futwas are revered as oracles, although those who issue them are slaves of the Sultan like everyone else.

The order and the futwa were taken to Bendery by the bouyouk imraour, grand master of horse, and a chiaoux pasha. The pasha of Bendery received the order while he was with the Tartar Khan; he at once went to Varnitza to ask the King whether he would leave as a friend or lay him under the necessity of executing the Sultan's orders.

Thus threatened, Charles could not restrain his anger. "Obey your master if you dare," he said, "and leave my presence." The indignant pasha returned at full gallop, contrary to normal Turkish usage. He met Fabrice and shouted to him as he passed, "The King will not listen to reason; you will see strange things presently." The very same day, he discontinued the supply of the King's provisions and removed his guard of Janizaries. He told the Poles and Cossacks who were in Varnitza that if they wanted any provisions, they must leave the King of Sweden's camp, go to Bendery and put themselves under the protection of the Porte. They all obeyed, and the King was left with only the officers of his household and three hundred soldiers to face twenty thousand Tartars and six thousand Turks.

There were now no provisions left in the camp for either men or horses. The King ordered that twenty of the fine Arab steeds which the Sultan had given him should be shot outside the camp. "I want neither their provisions nor their horses," he said. This provided a feast for the Tartars, who, as is well known, think horse meat delicious. But meanwhile, the Turks and Tartars surrounded the King's little camp on all sides.

Undismayed, Charles made his three hundred soldiers dig regular entrenchments; he even worked himself, and his chancellor, his treasurer, his secretaries, his valets and all his servants helped with the task. Some barricaded the windows, others fastened beams behind the doors to act as buttresses.

When the house was well barricaded, and the King had

inspected his so-called defenses, he sat down quietly to play chess with his favorite, Grothusen, just as if everything had been perfectly peaceful. Fortunately Fabrice, the Holstein envoy, was not living in Varnitza, but in a little village between Varnitza and Bendery, where the English envoy to the King of Sweden, Jeffreys, was also staying. These two ministers, seeing the storm about to burst, took it upon themselves to act as mediators between the Turks and the King. The Khan, and above all the pasha of Bendery, who had no wish to use violence toward the King, eagerly received the offers of these two ministers. They held two conferences at Bendery, at which the usher of the seraglio and the grand master of horse, who had brought the Sultan's order and the mufti's futwa, were also present.

M. Fabrice told them that the Swedish King had good reason to believe that they wanted to hand him over to his enemies in Poland. The Khan, the pasha and the others all swore on their heads and called God to witness that they detested such a horrible piece of treachery and that they would die rather than suffer even the least disrespect to be shown to the King in Poland; they said that the Russian and Polish ambassadors were in their hands and that their lives would answer for any affront offered to the King of Sweden. Finally they complained bitterly that the King should conceive such injurious suspicions about people who had received and treated him so well. Although oaths are often the language of treachery, Fabrice was persuaded by the Turks and thought he detected in their protestations an air of truth, which lying can only imitate imperfectly. He was well aware that there had been a secret correspondence between the Tartar Khan and King Augustus; but he was convinced that their negotiations had been concerned only with ensuring that Charles XII left Turkey. Whether he was right or not, he assured them he would tell Charles that he thought he was being unfairly mistrustful. "But do you intend to force him to leave?" he inquired. "Yes," said the pasha, "such are my master's orders." Then he begged them once again to consider carefully whether this order meant shedding the blood of a crowned head. "Yes," replied the Khan angrily, "if this crowned head disobeys the Sultan in his own empire."

Meanwhile, everything was ready for the assault and the death of Charles XII seemed inevitable. But the Sultan had not given definite orders for him to be killed in case of resistance, so the pasha persuaded the Khan to allow an express to be sent immediately to Adrianople, where the Sultan then was, to obtain final orders from his majesty.

Mr. Jeffreys and M. Fabrice, having obtained this short respite, hastened to warn the King. They came with all the eagerness of people who were bringing good news, but the King received them coldly. He called them self-appointed mediators, and persisted in maintaining that the Sultan's order and the mufti's futwa were forged. Had they not just sent a request for new orders to the Porte?

The English minister withdrew, determined to have nothing further to do with the affairs of such an inflexible prince. M. Fabrice, whom the King liked and who was more used to his moods than the English minister, remained with him and urged him not to risk so precious a life in such a useless venture.

For answer, the King showed him his fortifications and begged him to employ his good offices merely in procuring him some provisions. The Turks were easily persuaded to allow provisions to be taken to the King's camp until the return of the courier from Adrianople. The Khan himself had forbidden his Tartars, who were eager for pillage, to take any action against the Swedes until the arrival of fresh orders. So Charles XII was able to leave his camp at times with forty horses and ride through the midst of the Tartars, who respectfully left him a free passage. He even went straight up to their lines, which, instead of resisting, opened to allow him to pass.

Finally there arrived an order from the Sultan to put to the sword any Swedes who made the slightest resistance and not to spare the life of the King. The pasha had the generosity to show this order to M. Fabrice, so that he might make a last attempt to convince Charles.

Fabrice went immediately to inform him of this sad news. "Have you seen the order you talk of?" said Charles. "Yes," replied Fabrice. "Well, then, tell them from me that this is a second order they have forged and that I shall not leave." Fabrice threw himself at the King's feet and angrily reproached him with his stubbornness; but in vain. "Go back to your Turks," said the King with a smile. "If they attack me I shall know how to defend myself."

The King's chaplains likewise fell on their knees before him and begged him not to expose the wretched survivors of Poltava, and above all his own sacred person, to certain massacre. They assured him that such resistance was unjust and that he was violating the laws of hospitality by insisting on remaining forcibly among strangers who had helped him for so long and so generously. The King, who had not got angry with Fabrice, flew into a passion against his priests, telling them that he had brought them to pray for him and not to give him advice.

General Hoord and General Dahldorf, who had always been opposed to fighting a battle whose outcome could only be disastrous, showed him their bodies, covered by wounds received in his service. Assuring him that they were ready to die for him, they nevertheless begged that it might, at least, be on a more necessary occasion. "I know by your wounds and mine," said the King, "that we have fought valiantly together; you have done your duty up till now; you must do it again today." There was no alternative left but to obey, and they would all have been ashamed not to seek death with their sovereign. The King himself was ready for the assault and was secretly pleased at the thought of the honor he would win by withstanding the efforts of a whole army with three hundred Swedes. He assigned everyone to his post: Müllern, his chancellor, Ehrenpreuss, one of his secretaries, together with the clerks, were to defend the chancellery; Baron Fief, at the head of the officers of the household, was to occupy another position; the stable boys and cooks were also given battle stations, for with Charles everybody was a soldier. He rode between his entrenchments and his house, promising rewards to everyone, creating officers and assuring even the meanest servants that he would make them captains if they fought bravely.

They did not have long to wait before the Turkish army and the Tartars came to attack the little camp with ten pieces of cannon and two mortars. The horses' tails waved in the air, the clarions sounded, and the cries of "Allah, Allah" were heard on all sides. Baron Grothusen noticed that their shouts did not include insults to the King and that they merely called him *Demirbash*, "Head of Iron." Immediately he decided to leave the entrenchments alone and unarmed. He walked up to the ranks of the Janizaries, who had almost all received money from him. "What, my friends," he said, in so many words, "have you come to massacre three hundred defenseless Swedes? You, brave Janizaries, who pardoned fifty thousand Russians when they cried *amman* [mercy], have you forgotten the benefits you have received from us? And do you want to kill this great King of Sweden, whom you love so much and who has been so generous to you? My friends, he only asks for three days, and the Sultan's orders are not so strict as you have been led to believe."

These words produced an effect which Grothusen himself did not expect. The Janizaries swore by their beards that they would not attack the King and that they would give him the three days which he asked for. In vain the signal was given for the assault. Far from obeying, the Janizaries threatened to attack their leaders if the three days' grace were not given to the King of Sweden. They crowded around the pasha's tent, shouting that the Sultan's orders were forged. To this unexpected sedition the pasha could only oppose patience.

He pretended to be pleased with the generous resolution of the Janizaries, and ordered them to return to Bendery. The Khan of the Tartars, a violent man, was all for attacking at once with his own troops; but the pasha, who had no intention of allowing the Tartars to have all the honor of capturing the King while he was perhaps being punished for the disobedience of his Janizaries, persuaded the Khan to wait till the next day.

On his return to Bendery, the pasha gathered together the officers of the Janizaries and the veteran soldiers; he read and showed them the Sultan's definite order and the mufti's futwa. Sixty of the oldest, who had venerable white beards and had received a thousand presents from the King, proposed to go themselves to beg him to place himself in their hands and allow them to act as his guards.

The pasha gave his consent; he would have accepted any expedient rather than be reduced to having the King killed. And so these sixty old men went the next morning to Varnitza, armed only with long white sticks, for these are the sole weapons the Janizaries carry when they are not actually going to war. The Turks regard as barbarous the Christian custom of wearing swords in peacetime and entering their friends' houses and churches while bearing arms.

They addressed themselves to Baron Grothusen and Chancellor Müllern and told them that they had come with the intention of serving as faithful guards to the King and that, if he wished, they would take him to Adrianople, where he might himself speak to the Sultan. While they were making this proposal, the King was reading letters which had arrived from Constantinople and which Fabrice, who could no longer see him, had managed to smuggle through to him with the help of a Janizary. They were from Count Poniatowski, who could not come to help him either at Bendery or at Adrianople since he had been detained in Constantinople by order of the Porte ever since he had made the indiscreet demand for a thousand purses. He informed the King that the Sultan's orders to seize or kill him in case of resistance were only too authentic, that the Sultan was indeed deceived by his ministers, but the more he was deceived in this matter, the more he insisted on being obeyed. He advised Charles to submit to the times and yield to necessity and took the liberty of urging him to explore every possible form of negotiation with the ministers and not to remain inflexible when more subtle measures were needed, but rather to hope that wise policies and time would provide a remedy for an evil which violent measures would only render incurable.

But neither the proposals of the old Janizaries nor the letters of Poniatowski could make the King so much as consider the idea that he could compromise without dishonor. He would rather die at the hands of the Turks than be in some sense their prisoner. He sent the Janizaries away without seeing them, informing them that if they did not withdraw he would have their beards cut off, an affront which in the East is considered the most outrageous of all insults.

The old men, filled with the greatest indignation, went away crying, "Ah! Head of Iron! Since he wants to die, let him die." They returned to report to the pasha on their mission and to tell their comrades at Bendery of the strange way in which they had been received. Then they all swore to obey the pasha's orders without delay and were as impatient to begin the assault as they had been reluctant the previous day. At once the order was given. The Turks advanced to the Swedish entrenchments; the Tartars were already waiting for them there and the cannons began to fire.

The Janizaries on one side, and the Tartars on the other, forced their way at once into the little camp. There were hardly twenty Swedes who drew their swords, and the three hundred soldiers were surrounded and captured without resistance. The King was on horseback, between his house and his camp, together with Generals Hoord, Dahldorf and Sparre. When he saw that all the soldiers had allowed themselves to be captured in his presence, he said calmly to the three officers, "Let us go and defend the house." And he added, smiling, "We shall be fighting *pro aris et focis*."[2]

Immediately he galloped toward the house, where he had stationed about forty servants as sentinels, and which had been fortified as thoroughly as possible.

These generals, accustomed as they were to their master's stubborn bravery, could not help being amazed to see him resolve in cold blood, and with a joke on his

[2] "For home and country."

lips, to defend himself against ten cannons and a whole army; they followed him, together with a few guards and a few servants, about twenty people in all.

But when they arrived at the door they found it besieged by Janizaries; already some two hundred Turks or Tartars had entered by a window and had made themselves masters of all the apartments except for a large hall to which the King's servants had retreated. Fortunately this hall was near the door by which the King had intended to enter with his little band of twenty men; he jumped from his horse, sword and pistol in hand, and the others followed suit.

The Janizaries fell on him from all sides; they were encouraged by the promise which the pasha had made to them of eight golden ducats for anyone who so much as touched Charles's clothes, provided he was captured. But he wounded or killed all those who approached him. A Janizary whom he had wounded aimed his musket at him, and if the Turk's arm had not been jolted by the pressing throng, the King would have been dead. The ball touched his nose, carried away the end of his ear, and finished by breaking the arm of General Hoord, whose constant fate it was to be wounded at his master's side.

The King plunged his sword into the Janizary's stomach; at the same moment his servants, who had shut themselves in the large hall, opened the door; the King dashed in, followed by his little troop. They at once shut the door and barricaded it with everything that could be found. So Charles was shut up in this hall with the whole of his suite, which consisted of about sixty men—officers, guards, secretaries, valets and servants of all kinds.

The Janizaries and the Tartars were plundering the rest of the house and filled all the apartments. "Let's see if we can drive a few of these barbarians out," said the King, and placing himself at the head of his troop, he himself opened the door of the hall which led into his bedroom. He entered, and opened fire on the pillagers.

The Turks, loaded with booty and terrified by the sudden apparition of a King whom they were accustomed to respect, threw away their arms, jumped out of the window or took refuge in the cellars. The King, taking advantage of their disorder, and followed by his men, who were animated by their success, pursued the Turks from room to room, killing or wounding those who did not flee, and in a quarter of an hour he had cleared the whole house of the enemy.

In the midst of the battle the King saw two Janizaries hiding under his bed. One he killed with a sword thrust; the other begged for mercy, crying, "Amman." "I give you your life," said the King to the Turk, "on condition that you will go and give the pasha a faithful account of what you have seen." The Turk willingly promised what was asked of him, and he was allowed to jump out of the window like the others.

Now that they were masters of the house, the Swedes closed and barricaded the windows again. They were not short of arms, for a low room full of muskets and powder had escaped the tumultuous search of the Janizaries. They made good use of them, firing from the windows, almost at point-blank range, on the assembled crowd of Turks, of whom they killed two hundred in less than a quarter of an hour.

The cannons continued to fire on the house, but as the stone was very soft, the shot only made holes and did not destroy the building.

The Khan of the Tartars and the pasha, who wanted to take the King alive, were ashamed of losing so many men and of using a whole army against sixty people. They therefore decided to set fire to the house, to force the King to surrender. They had arrows twisted with lighted fuses fired at the doors and windows, and in a moment the house was in flames. The roof was fully alight and was about to fall in on the Swedes. The King calmly gave orders for the fire to be put out. Finding a barrel full of liquid, he picked it up himself and, helped by two Swedes, he threw it into the heart of the fire. The barrel was in fact full of brandy, but in the haste and excitement of the moment, this had not occurred to anyone. The fire raged with redoubled fury and the King's apartment was burned out. The large hall which the Swedes occupied was filled with thick smoke mingled with tongues of flame, which entered through the doors of the neighboring apartments. Half the roof had sunk into the house itself, and the other half fell outside, bursting into flames.

In this hopeless situation, a guard called Walberg dared to cry out that they must surrender. "What a strange man this is," said the King. "He imagines that it isn't a finer thing to be burned than to be a prisoner." Another guard, called Rosen, pointed out that the chancellery, which was only fifty yards away, had a stone roof and was therefore fireproof, and he suggested making a sortie, reaching this house and continuing resistance there. "There's a real Swede for you," cried the King, and embracing the guard, he created him a colonel on the spot. "Come, my friends," he said, "take as much powder and shot as you can, and let's fight our way to the chancellery, sword in hand."

The Turks, who were now surrounding the burning house, saw, with an admiration mingled with fear, that the Swedes were not leaving it. But their astonishment was even greater when they saw the doors opening and the King and his men making a desperate sortie. Charles and his principal officers were armed with swords and pistols; each of them fired two shots at once, the moment the door was opened; and in an instant, throwing away their pistols and drawing their swords, they drove back the Turks more than fifty yards. But a moment later this little band was surrounded. The King, who was booted as usual, tripped over his spurs and fell. A score of Janizaries immediately threw themselves upon him; he threw his sword in the air to spare himself the humiliation of having to surrender it. The Turks carried him to the pasha's quarters, some holding his legs and others his arms, in the same way as sick persons are carried to avoid their being hurt.

No sooner did the King find himself in their hands than the violence of his temperament and the fury which such a long and terrible fight must have induced in him gave place at once to calm gentleness. He did not utter an impatient word or cast an angry glance. He smiled at the Janizaries who bore him along, crying "Allah" in tones of mingled indignation and respect. His officers were captured at the same time and stripped of their possessions by the Turks and the Tartars. It was on February 12, 1713, that this strange event happened, which was to give rise to further curious consequences.

BOOK VII

[The Turks transfer Charles to Demirtash. King Stanislas is captured at the same time. M. de Villelongue's bold action. Revolution in the seraglio. Battle in Pomerania. Altona burned by the Swedes. Charles finally leaves to return to his own dominions. His strange manner of tråveling. His arrival at Stralsund. His misfortunes. The success of Peter the Great. His triumph in Petersburg.]

The pasha of Bendery was solemnly waiting for Charles in his tent, with Marco with him to act as interpreter. He received the King with profound respect and begged him to rest on a sofa. But the King ignored the Turk's civilities and remained standing in the tent.

"Blessed be the Almighty," said the pasha, "that your majesty is alive. I bitterly regret that your majesty left me no option but to carry out his highness' orders." The King, who was merely angry that his three hundred soldiers had let themselves be captured in their trenches, said to the pasha, "Ah! If they had only defended themselves properly, we should not have been overcome in ten days." "Alas," replied the Turk, "what a waste of courage." He had the King taken back to Bendery on a richly caparisoned horse. The Swedes had all been killed or captured; all his equipment, furniture, papers and even necessary clothes had been pillaged or burned. The roads were filled with almost naked Swedish officers, chained in pairs and following the Tartars or Janizaries on foot. The çhancellor and the generals suffered the same fate; they were the slaves of the soldiers to whose lot they had fallen.

Ismael Pasha, having taken Charles to his seraglio at Bendery, gave him his own apartment and had him treated as a king, though not without taking the precaution of stationing a guard of Janizaries at the door of his room. A bed was prepared for him; but he threw himself on a sofa without even taking his boots off and fell into a deep sleep. An officer who was standing near him covered his head with a cap, but the King threw it off when he woke from his first sleep, and the Turk was amazed to see a monarch who slept booted and bareheaded. Next morning, Ismael Pasha brought Fabrice to see the King. Fabrice found him with his clothes torn, his boots, his hands, and his whole person covered in blood and powder, his eyebrows burned, yet with a serene air despite his terrible appearance. He knelt before him without being able to speak a word; but he was reassured by the free and gentle way in which the King spoke to him and was soon back on familiar terms again. The two men talked laughingly of the battle of Bendery. "They claim," said Fabrice, "that your majesty killed twenty Janizaries with his own hand." "Good, good," said the King. "These things always get exaggerated by half." In the middle of this conversation the pasha presented the King with his favorite, Grothusen, and Colonel Ribbing, whose freedom he had had the generosity to purchase at his own expense. Fabrice undertook to ransom the other prisoners.

Jeffreys, the English envoy, helped to provide the money. A Frenchman who had come to Bendery out of curiosity and who has written an account of some of these events, also gave what he had. These foreigners, aided by the advice and even the money of the pasha, redeemed not only the officers but also their clothes from the hands of the Turks and Tartars.

Next day the captive King was put in a chariot covered in crimson and driven toward Adrianople; his treasurer, Grothusen, was with him, and Chancellor Müllern and a number of officers followed in another carriage. Several were on horseback, and when they looked at the King's chariot they could not restrain their tears. The pasha led the escort. Fabrice pointed out that it was shameful to leave the King without a sword and begged him to give him one. "God forbid," said the pasha. "He would cut our beards off with it." However, he gave it back to him a few hours later.

While they were taking away this captive and disarmed king who, a few years before, had given orders to so many states and had been the arbiter of the North and the terror of Europe, this same place witnessed another example of the fragility of human greatness.

King Stanislas had been arrested on Turkish soil and was being taken as a prisoner to Bendery, just as Charles was being removed from it.

Stanislas, being no longer supported by the hand which had made him King, and finding himself without money and consequently without a party in Poland, had retired to Pomerania, and as he could no longer keep his own kingdom, he had done his best to defend the dominions of his benefactor. He had even gone to Sweden to speed up the arrival of the reinforcements which were needed in Pomerania and Livonia; in short, he had done everything that might be expected of a friend of Charles XII. At this time, the first King of Prussia, a ruler of great prudence, was becoming justifiably worried by the proximity of the Muscovites, and evolved the plan of allying himself with Augustus and the republic of Poland to force the Russians to return home. He hoped to get Charles XII himself to take part in this plan. It was to have three main consequences: peace in northern Europe, the return of Charles to his own country, and the creation of a barrier against the Russian threat to Europe. The necessary precondition of this treaty, on which general peace depended, was the abdication of Stanislas. Not only did Stanislas accept, but he took upon himself the task of negotiating a peace which deprived him of his crown; necessity, considerations of public welfare, the glory of sacrifice and the interests of Charles, to whom he owed everything, determined him to take this step. He wrote to Bendery pointing out to the King of Sweden the nature of the situation, its evils and the remedy for them. He begged him not to oppose an abdication which circumstances had made necessary and which had the most honorable of motives. He urged him not to sacrifice the interests of Sweden to those of an unhappy friend who was willingly sacrificing himself for the public good. Charles XII received these letters at Varnitza. He said angrily to the courier, in the presence of several witnesses, "If my friend doesn't want to be King, I can easily make someone else King."

Stanislas was determined to make the sacrifice which Charles opposed. These times were destined to witness extraordinary sentiments and actions. Stanislas resolved to go in person to convince Charles and took greater risks to abdicate the throne than he had done to procure it. One day, at ten in the evening, he slipped away from the Swedish army which he was commanding in Pomerania and left, together with Baron Sparre, who later became ambassador in England and France, and another colonel. He took the name of a Frenchman called Haran, who was then a major in the Swedish service, and who later died as commandant of Danzig. He passed close to the enemy armies, being arrested several times and then released on the strength of his passport in the name of Haran. Finally, after many dangers, he arrived at the Turkish frontier.

When he reached Moldavia, he sent Baron Sparre back to his army and entered Iaşi, the capital of the province, imagining he was quite safe in a country where the King of Sweden had been so much respected; he was far from suspecting what was happening at the time.

He was asked who he was, and replied that he was a major in one of Charles XII's regiments. At once he was arrested and taken before the hospodar of Moldavia, who already knew from the gazettes that Stanislas had disappeared from his army and immediately began to suspect the truth. The King of Poland's face had been described to him and it was easy to recognize it from its open and pleasant expression and an exceptional air of kindness.

The hospodar questioned him insidiously and finally asked what post he held in the Swedish army. Stanislas and the hospodar were speaking in Latin. *"Major sum,"*[1] said Stanislas. *"Imo maximus es,"*[2] replied the Moldavian,

[1] "I am a major."
[2] "You must be the supreme commander."

and immediately offered him an armchair. He treated him like a king, but a king who was a prisoner, placing a strict guard around a Greek convent where he was obliged to remain until the arrival of orders from the Sultan. Orders came, to have him taken to Bendery, which Charles had just been forced to leave.

The news reached the pasha while he was accompanying the King of Sweden's chariot. The pasha told Fabrice, and the latter, going up to Charles's chariot, informed him that he was not the only royal prisoner in Turkish hands and that Stanislas was only a few miles away, in the custody of some soldiers. "Hurry to him, my dear Fabrice," said Charles, not in the least disconcerted. "Make it clear to him that he must never make peace with Augustus and assure him that our affairs will soon improve." Such was the inflexibility of Charles's opinions that although he was deserted by all his Polish supporters, attacked in his own dominions, captive in a Turkish litter and being taken, as a prisoner, he knew not where, yet he still believed in his good fortune and still hoped for the help of a hundred thousand men from the Ottoman Porte. Fabrice hastened to carry out his commission, accompanied by a Janizary, and with the pasha's permission. A few miles away he found the main body of the soldiers who were conducting Stanislas; he went into their midst and spoke to a horseman dressed in French clothes and poorly mounted. He asked him, in German, where the King of Poland was. "What," said the King, "don't you remember me any more?" Then Fabrice told him of the sad state of the King of Sweden and of the unshakable but useless firmness of his resolve.

When Stanislas was nearing Bendery, the pasha, who was returning after having accompanied Charles XII for a few miles, sent the Polish King an Arab horse with a magnificent harness.

He was received in Bendery with a salute of artillery, and except for the fact that he was not at first allowed to move about freely, he had no reason to complain of his treatment. Meanwhile Charles was being taken to Adrianople. The town was already filled with the news of his battle. The Turks both condemned and admired him;

but the divan was annoyed, and was threatening to confine him in one of the islands of the Archipelago.

The King of Poland, Stanislas, who has done me the honor of informing me of most of these details, has also assured me that a proposal was made in the divan to confine him too on a Greek island; but a few months later the Sultan became less hostile and allowed him to leave.

M. Désaleurs, who could have taken Charles's part and could have prevented this affront to Christian kings, was in Constantinople, as was M. Poniatowski, whose inventive and resourceful genius was still feared. The majority of the Swedes who remained in Adrianople were in prison; the Sultan's throne appeared everywhere inaccessible to the King of Sweden's complaints.

The Marquis de Fierville, who had been sent secretly to Charles at Bendery by the French government, was then in Adrianople. He risked coming to the King's aid at a time when he was abandoned by friends and oppressed by enemies. He had the good fortune to be helped in his plans by a French nobleman of an old Champagne family called Villelongue, a fearless man whose fortune was not equal to his courage and who, hypnotized by the King of Sweden's reputation, had come to Turkey to offer him his services.

With the help of this young man, M. de Fierville wrote a memorandum in the King of Sweden's name, in which this monarch demanded vengeance from the Sultan for the insult offered, in his person, to all crowned heads, and for the real or imagined treachery of the Khan and the pasha of Bendery.

The vizier and the other ministers were accused of having been corrupted by the Muscovites, of having deceived the Sultan, of having prevented the King's letters from reaching his highness, and of having, by these devices, extorted from the Sultan this order which was so contrary to Moslem hospitality and as a result of which they had violated the law of nations, in a manner most unworthy of a great emperor, by using twenty thousand men to attack a king who was defended only by his servants and who was relying on the Sultan's sacred word.

When this dispatch was composed, it had to be translated into Turkish and written in a particular hand on a special kind of paper, which must be used for anything which is presented to the Sultan.

They approached a number of French interpreters who were in the city; but the affairs of the King of Sweden were in such a desperate state and the vizier was so openly hostile to him that no interpreter would risk translating M. de Fierville's document. Finally they found another foreigner, whose handwriting was not known at the Porte and who, in exchange for a reward and the assurance of the strictest secrecy, translated the memorandum into Turkish and wrote it out on the appropriate paper. Baron Davidson, an officer of the Swedish army, forged the King's signature. Fierville, who had the royal signet, appended it to the document, which was then sealed with the arms of Sweden. Villelongue undertook to deliver the packet himself to the Sultan in the usual manner, when he was on his way to the mosque. This method had already been used to present the Sultan with notes against his ministers. But this very fact rendered the success of this enterprise more difficult, and the danger far greater.

The vizier, who had foreseen that the Swedes would demand justice from the Sultan and who had learned from the misfortunes of his predecessors, had expressly forbidden anyone to be allowed to approach the Sultan and had given special orders that anyone who appeared near the mosque with a petition should be arrested.

Villelongue knew of this order and was not unaware that he was risking his head. He changed from his Frank's dress into Greek clothes, and hiding the letter in his bosom, he set off early to place himself in the Sultan's path near the mosque. He pretended to be mad and danced his way through two rows of Janizaries, between which the Sultan was to pass, deliberately dropping a few coins from his pockets to distract the guards' attention.

When the Sultan approached, an attempt was made to remove Villelongue. He threw himself on his knees and struggled in the hands of the Janizaries; his hat fell off and his long hair at once showed him to be a Frank.

He received several blows and was roughly handled. The Sultan, who was now close by, heard the tumult and asked the reason for it. Villelongue shouted as loud as he could, "*Amman! Amman!*"—Mercy!—and drew the letter from his bosom. The Sultan ordered him to be allowed to approach. At once Villelongue ran up to him, kissed his stirrup and gave him the document, saying, "*Suet kral dan*"—The King of Sweden gives you it. The Sultan placed the letter in his bosom and continued on his way toward the mosque. Meanwhile Villelongue was seized and imprisoned in the outer buildings of the seraglio.

After leaving the mosque the Sultan read the letter and wanted to question the prisoner. What I am going to relate may perhaps sound incredible; but everything I say is vouched for by the letters of Villelongue himself, and when so brave an officer affirms something on his honor, he deserves some measure of belief. He has assured me that the Sultan took off his imperial dress and the special turban he wore and disguised himself as an officer of the Janizaries, and that this was something he often did. He took with him an old man from the island of Malta who acted as his interpreter. By virtue of this disguise, Villelongue enjoyed an honor which no Christian ambassador has ever obtained: he had a private conference with the Turkish Emperor for a quarter of an hour. He did not fail to explain to him the King of Sweden's grievances, to accuse the ministers and to demand vengeance, and he did this all the more freely because, though he was actually talking to the Sultan, he was only supposed to be talking to an equal. Despite the darkness of the prison, he had easily recognized the Sultan, and this made him speak out all the more boldly. The self-styled officer of the Janizaries spoke to him these very words: "Christian, be assured that my master the Sultan has the soul of an emperor, and that if your King of Sweden is right, he will obtain justice." Villelongue was soon set free and a few weeks later a sudden change was seen in the seraglio, which, according to the Swedes, was entirely due to this unique conference. The mufti was deposed, the Khan of the Tartars was exiled to

Rhodes, and the seraskier pasha of Bendery was confined in one of the islands of the Archipelago.

The Ottoman Porte is so subject to such storms that it is hard to say whether the Sultan really meant to appease the King of Sweden by these sacrifices. The manner in which Charles was treated does not suggest that the Porte was particularly interested in pleasing him.

The favorite, Ali Coumourgi, was suspected of having brought about all these changes to serve his own interests. It is said that he had the Khan of Tartary and the seraskier of Bendery exiled under the pretext that they had given the King the twelve hundred purses despite the Sultan's order. He placed on the Tartar throne the brother of the deposed Khan, a young man of his own age, who had little liking for his brother and whom Ali Coumourgi was counting on for support in the wars which he was planning. As for the grand vizier Jussuf, he was deposed only a few weeks later, and Soliman Pasha was given the post of grand vizier.

I am obliged to say that M. de Villelongue and a number of Swedes have assured me that the letter presented to the Sultan in the King's name was the sole cause of all these great changes at the Porte; but M. de Fierville, for his part, has assured me of the contrary. I have often found similar contradictions in the memoirs which have been entrusted to me. In a case like this, all the historian can do is give a straightforward account of the facts without attempting to penetrate the motives behind them, and limit himself to relating what he knows instead of speculating about what he does not.

Meanwhile, Charles XII had been taken to the little castle of Demirtash near Adrianople. A vast crowd of Turks had gone there to witness his arrival; he was carried from his chariot on a sofa, but in order not to be seen by the crowd, he covered his head with a pillow.

The Porte waited a few days before acceding to his request to live in Demotica, a small town six leagues from Adrianople near the famous river Hebrus, now called the Maritsa. Coumourgi said to the grand vizier Soliman: "Go and tell the King of Sweden that he can stay in Demotica for the rest of his life. I guarantee that before the year is up he will be asking to leave of his own accord; but above all don't give him any money."

So the King was transferred to the little town of Demotica, where the Porte assigned him a considerable *thaim* of provisions for himself and his suite. But he was only given twenty-five crowns a day in cash with which to buy pork and wine, two kinds of provisions which the Turks do not supply. The purse of a hundred crowns a day, which he had received at Bendery, was withdrawn.

Scarcely had he and his small court arrived at Demotica than the grand vizier Soliman was deposed; his place was given to Ibrahim Molla, who was proud, brave and excessively coarse. It is worth while recounting something of his history, so that the reader may have a more precise acquaintance with all the viceroys of the Ottoman empire on whom the fortunes of Charles depended for so long.

He had been a common sailor until the accession of Ahmed III. This Emperor often disguised himself as a private individual, as an imam or a dervish; he would slip into the cafés of Constantinople or into public places in the evenings in order to hear what was being said about him and to keep in personal touch with public feeling. One day he heard this Molla complaining that Turkish ships never returned with prizes and swearing that if he were a captain he would never enter the port of Constantinople without bringing back some infidel ship. The following day, the Sultan ordered that he should be given a vessel to command and sent out on a cruise. The new captain returned a few days later with a Maltese bark and a Genoese galley. At the end of two years he was made captain general of the navy, and finally grand vizier. As soon as he attained this post he thought he could do without the favorite, and in order to make himself indispensable, he planned to make war on the Muscovites; with this aim in mind, he had a tent put up near the place where the King of Sweden was living.

He invited the King to come and see him there, together with the new Khan of the Tartars and the French ambassador. But the King, whose pride had increased with his misfortunes, thought it an intolerable insult that a subject should dare send for him: he ordered his chancellor, Müllern, to go in his place; and for fear lest the Turks might not show him enough respect or might force him to compromise his dignity, the King, who was extreme in everything he did, took to his bed and resolved not to get up so long as he stayed in Demotica. He stayed in bed for ten months, pretending to be ill. Chancellor Müllern, Grothusen and Colonel Duben were the only ones who ate with him. They had none of the amenities which the Franks normally possess; these had all been pillaged at Bendery. So their meals were far from being characterized by pomp and delicacy. They served themselves, and for the whole of this period it was the chancellor, Müllern, who acted as cook.

While Charles XII was thus spending his life in bed, he learned of the sad fate of all the provinces of his kingdom outside Sweden itself.

General Stenbock, who had distinguished himself by driving the Danes from Skäne and by defeating their best troops with an army of peasants, still maintained for some time the reputation of Swedish arms. He defended Pomerania and Bremen and the remainder of the King's German possessions to the best of his ability. But he could not stop the combined Saxon and Danish armies from besieging Stade, a town of considerable strength and importance, situated near the Elbe in the duchy of Bremen. The town was bombarded and reduced to ashes, and the garrison was obliged to surrender unconditionally before Stenbock could advance to relieve it.

This general, who had about twelve thousand men, of whom half were cavalry, pursued the enemy, who were twice as numerous, and finally caught up with them in the duchy of Mecklenburg at a place called Gadebusch, near a little river of the same name. He came face to face with the Saxons and Danes on December 20, 1712. He was separated from them by a marsh. The enemy, camped behind the marsh, had a wood to their rear; they had the advantage of numbers and terrain and could only be attacked by crossing the marsh under the fire of their artillery.

Stenbock led his troops across, arrived in battle order on the other side, and began one of the most bloody and bitter battles which has ever taken place between these two rival nations. After three hours of sharp fighting, the Danish and Saxon lines were broken and they were obliged to retreat.

A son of King Augustus and the Countess of Königsmark, known by the name of Count Saxe, had his first experience of war in this battle. It was this same Count Saxe who later had the honor of being elected Duke of Kurland and who lacked only the necessary force to enjoy the most incontestable right a man can ever have to the sovereignty of a nation; by which I mean the unanimous vote of the people. This same man later acquired a more lasting glory by saving France at the battle of Fontenoy, by conquering Flanders and by deserving his reputation of being the greatest general of our times. He commanded a regiment at Gadebusch and had a horse killed under him. I have heard him say that the Swedes always kept their ranks and that even after the victory was won, and the first lines of these brave troops had their dead enemies at their feet, there was not a single Swedish soldier who so much as dared stoop down to despoil them until prayers had been said on the battlefield, so inflexibly did they adhere to the strict discipline to which their King had accustomed them.

After the victory, Stenbock, remembering how the Danes had reduced Stade to ashes, went to take revenge on Altona, which belonged to the King of Denmark. Altona lies downstream from Hamburg on the Elbe, and quite big ships can sail up the river to reach its port. The King of Denmark favored this town with many privileges, intending to make it a flourishing commercial center. Already the industry of the inhabitants, encouraged by the King's wise measures, was beginning to make their city rich and prosperous. Hamburg was becoming jealous of it and wished nothing more than to see it destroyed. As soon as Stenbock was in sight of Altona, he sent a messenger to tell the inhabitants that they must evacuate the town with everything they could carry with them; it was to be completely destroyed.

The magistrates came and threw themselves at his feet and offered a hundred thousand crowns ransom. Stenbock asked for two hundred thousand. The inhabitants begged that they might at least be given time to send to Hamburg, where they had correspondents, assuring Stenbock that they would bring the money the following day; the Swedish general replied that they must pay at once, otherwise Altona would be set on fire immediately.

His troops were already in the suburbs with torches in their hands; a weak wooden gate and a moat which had already been filled in were the only defenses the town possessed. The wretched inhabitants were obliged to leave their houses hurriedly in the middle of the night. It was January 9, 1713; the bitter cold was intensified by a strong north wind which helped to spread the fire more rapidly through the town and made the plight of the inhabitants who fled into the country even more unbearable. Men and women, bent under the heavy load of the goods they were trying to salvage, took refuge, weeping and wailing, on the ice-covered slopes of the nearby hills. Several young people were seen carrying paralyzed old men on their shoulders. Women fled with their newborn children and died of cold with them on the hill, watching the flames in the distance burning their homes. Not all the inhabitants had left the town when the Swedes set fire to it. Altona burned from midnight until ten the next morning. Almost all the houses were made of wood, and they were all destroyed. The next day it seemed as though there had never been a town there.

The old, the sick and the more delicate women, who had taken refuge in the icy countryside while their houses were burning, dragged themselves to the gates of Hamburg and begged the inhabitants to open them and save their lives. But they were refused entry because there had been a number of contagious diseases in Altona and the inhabitants of Hamburg did not like those of Altona enough to risk infecting their own city by admitting them. So the majority of these wretches died under the walls of Hamburg, calling on heaven to witness the barbarity of the Swedes and that of the inhabitants of Hamburg, which seemed no less inhuman.

The whole of Germany cried out against this act of violence; the ministers and generals of Poland and Denmark wrote to Count Stenbock to reproach him for this barbarous deed which, as it was both unnecessary and devoid of excuse, could not fail to provoke heaven and earth against him.

Stenbock replied "that he had only had recourse to these extreme measures in order to teach the enemies of the King his master to stop making war like barbarians and to respect the law of nations; that they had filled Pomerania with their cruelties, devastated this fair province and sold nearly a hundred thousand inhabitants to the Turks; that the torches which had reduced Altona to ashes were a reprisal for the red-hot bullets which had destroyed Stade."

Such was the fury with which the Swedes and their enemies fought each other. If Charles XII had then appeared in Pomerania, he would very probably have been able to recover his fortunes. His armies, although deprived of his presence, were still animated by his spirit; but the absence of the leader always jeopardizes the success of any enterprise and prevents full advantage being taken of victories. Stenbock lost in piecemeal engagements everything he had won by the remarkable victories which in other times would have proved decisive.

Victorious as he was, he could not prevent the Muscovites, Saxons and Danes from joining forces. Some of his quarters were captured; he lost many men in a series of skirmishes; two thousand of his troops were drowned crossing the Eider on their way to winter in Holstein. All these losses could not be replaced in a country where he was surrounded by powerful enemies on all sides.

He tried to defend Holstein against Denmark, but despite his ruses and his efforts the country was lost, the whole army destroyed and Stenbock himself taken prisoner.

Pomerania was now defenseless except for Stralsund, the island of Rügen and a number of neighboring places, and became the prey of the allies. It was occupied and handed over to the King of Prussia. The states of Bremen were filled with Danish garrisons. At the same time the Russians poured into Finland and defeated the Swedes, whose confidence was deserting them and who, being already inferior in numbers, were gradually losing their superiority in courage over their ever more experienced enemies.

To complete the misfortunes of Sweden, her King insisted on remaining in Demotica, still nourishing himself on hopes of Turkish help, on which he had no longer any reason to count.

Ibrahim Molla, the proud vizier, who was still insisting on war against Russia despite the opposition of the favorite, was strangled in a passage. The post of vizier had become so dangerous that nobody dared to occupy it; it remained vacant for six months. Finally the favorite, Ali Coumourgi, took the title of grand vizier. This put an end to the King of Sweden's hopes. He knew Ali Coumourgi, all the more because he had been helped by him when the interests of the favorite coincided with his own.

He had now been eleven months in Demotica, inactive and forgotten; this extreme idleness, following suddenly on the most violent activity, had finally given him the illness he had been pretending to have. The whole of Europe believed him dead. The council of regency which he had established in Stockholm when he left his capital no longer heard from him. The Senate as a body begged Princess Ulrike Eleonore, the King's sister, to take the regency into her own hands during her brother's long absence. She accepted, but when she saw that the Senate wanted to force her to make peace with the Czar and the King of Denmark, who were attacking Sweden on all sides, the Princess, who rightly judged that her brother would never ratify the peace, resigned the regency and sent a long account of the whole affair to the King in Turkey.

Charles received his sister's letters in Demotica. The despotic principles on which he had been nurtured made him forget that Sweden had once been a free country and that the Senate had formerly governed the kingdom in conjunction with the kings. He looked on this body as if they were a troop of servants who wanted to run the house in their master's absence; he wrote to them saying that if they claimed the right to govern, he would send them one of his boots, and that they would then have to take orders from that.

To put a stop to these so-called attempts to usurp his authority, to defend his own country at last, Charles informed the grand vizier that he wished to leave and return through Germany. He no longer hoped for any help from the Ottoman Porte, and prepared to rely on himself alone.

M. Désaleurs, the French ambassador, who was looking after the interests of Sweden, presented the request on his behalf. "Well," said the vizier to Count Désaleurs, "didn't I say that within a year the King of Sweden would be asking to leave? But let him make his mind up and fix the day, so that we don't have a repetition of the Bendery troubles."

Count Désaleurs softened the harshness of these words when he reported them to the King. But before leaving Turkey, Charles wished to display all the pomp of a great monarch although he was living in the poverty of a fugitive. He gave Grothusen the title of ambassador extraordinary and sent him to take formal leave in Constantinople, with a retinue of eighty people, all superbly dressed. The secret means which had to be used to collect enough money to pay for all this were even more humiliating than the ambassador's pomp was impressive.

M. Désaleurs lent the King forty thousand crowns; Grothusen had agents in Constantinople who borrowed in his name, at fifty per cent interest, a thousand crowns from a Jew, two hundred pistoles from an English merchant and a thousand francs from a Turk.

So they collected enough to play the brilliant comedy of the Swedish embassy in the presence of the divan. Grothusen received in Constantinople all the honors which the Porte confers on the extraordinary ambassadors of kings on the day of their audience. The purpose of all this fuss was to obtain money from the grand vizier; but the minister was inexorable.

Grothusen proposed to borrow a million from the Porte. The vizier replied coldly that his master could give when he wanted, but that it was beneath his dignity to lend. He said that the King would be abundantly provided with all he needed on his journey, in a manner worthy of the Sultan who was sending him home; and he added that the Porte might even make him a present of unminted gold, but that he should not count on it.

At last, on October 1, 1714, the King of Sweden set off to leave Turkey. A capigi pasha with six chiaoux came to collect him at the castle of Demirtash, where he had been staying for a few days. The pasha presented the King, on the Sultan's behalf, with a large crimson tent embroidered with gold, a saber with a jewel-studded hilt, and eight magnificent Arab horses with superb saddles and pure silver stirrups. It is worth recording that the Arab grooms who looked after these horses gave the King their genealogy; this is a long-established custom among these people, who seem to be more interested in the nobility of horses than in that of men, a view which is perhaps not unreasonable, for races of animals which are properly looked after and which remain unmixed never degenerate.

Sixty wagons, loaded with all sorts of provisions, and three hundred horses made up the convoy. The capigi pasha, knowing that a number of Turks had lent money to members of Charles's suite at a high rate of interest, told him that usury was contrary to Moslem law and begged him to liquidate all his debts and order the resident whom he was leaving in Constantinople to pay only the capital. "No," said the King, "if my servants have given bills for a hundred crowns, I will pay them even if they have received only ten."

He suggested to the creditors that they should go with him, promising that their expenses and debts would be paid. Several of them undertook the journey to Sweden and Grothusen took care to see that they got their money.

The Turks, in order to show more deference to their guest, made him travel in easy stages; but this slow and respectful progress irritated the King's natural impatience. He would get up at three in the morning as he always did. As soon as he was dressed, he would himself wake the capigi and the chiaoux, and order the march to begin in the middle of the night. The gravity of the Turks was disturbed by this new method of traveling; but the King took pleasure in their embarrassment, saying that he was getting a little of his own back for their behavior to him at Bendery.

As they were reaching the Turkish frontier, Stanislas left by another route and went to the German duchy of Zweibrücken, a province between The Palatinate and Alsace which had belonged to the King of Sweden ever since Charles X, the successor of Christine, had annexed this inheritance to the crown. Charles assigned Stanislas the revenues of this duchy, which were then worth about seventy thousand crowns. This was the end, for the time being, of all Stanislas' projects, wars and hopes. He would have liked to make, and could have made, an advantageous treaty with King Augustus; but Charles's indomitable stubbornness made him lose his lands and all his real property in Poland, to keep only the empty title of King.

He remained in this duchy until Charles's death. Then, because this province returned to a prince of the Palatine House, he retired to Wissembourg, in French Alsace. M. Sum, the envoy of King Augustus, complained of this to the Duke of Orleans, Regent of France. The Duke replied in the following memorable words: "Sir, tell the King your master that France has never refused asylum to monarchs in distress."

When the King of Sweden reached the German frontier, he learned that the Emperor had given orders for him to be received throughout his dominions with suitable splendor. The towns and villages through which the quartermasters had fixed his route were making preparations to receive him; all these people were impatiently awaiting the passage of this extraordinary man whose victories and misfortunes, whose smallest actions and whose very inactivity, had been the talk of Europe and Asia. But Charles had no wish to put up with all this pomp or to exhibit the prisoner of Bendery as a public spectacle; he had resolved never to return to Stockholm until his fortunes had improved.

When he reached Tergovitz, on the frontier of Transylvania, he took leave of his Turkish escort, assembled his suite in a barn and told them all not to worry about him but to return as quickly as possible to Stralsund in Pomerania, on the shores of the Baltic, about three hundred leagues from the place where they then were.

He took only Düring with him and gaily said farewell to the others, leaving them astonished, fearful and sad. He put on a black wig to disguise himself—for he still wore his hair long—dressed himself in a gold-edged hat, a thorn-gray coat and a blue cloak, took the name of a German officer and set off on horseback with his fellow traveler.

As far as possible, he avoided the territories of his open or secret enemies, and went via Hungary, Moravia, Austria, Bavaria, Württemberg, The Palatinate, Westphalia and Mecklenburg. So he almost toured the whole of Germany and went half as far again as he need have done. At the end of the first day, after having ridden without a break, the young Düring, who was not hardened to these excessive fatigues as the King was, fainted on dismounting. The King, who did not want to stop for a moment on the way, asked Düring, as soon as he had recovered, how much money he had. When Düring replied that he had about a thousand crowns in gold, the King said, "Give me half. I can see that you are not in a fit state to follow me; I shall go on alone." Düring begged him to rest for three hours at least, assuring him that by the end of this time he would be able to remount his horse and to follow his majesty; he urged him to think of all the risks he would run. But the King was inexorable and demanded the five hundred crowns and asked for horses. Then Düring, fearful of the King's resolution, thought of a harmless stratagem; he took the postmaster to one side and, pointing to the King, said, "This gentleman is my cousin; we are traveling together on the same business; he knows I am ill, but he won't even wait three hours for me; give him, I beg you, the worst horse in your stables and find me a chariot or post-chaise."

He gave two ducats to the postmaster, who did everything he was asked. The King was given a lame and restive horse: thus mounted, he left on his own at ten in the evening, while it was still dark, in the midst of snow, rain and wind. His traveling companion, after sleeping for a few hours, set off in a chariot drawn by strong horses. A few miles farther on, at daybreak, he caught up with the King, who could no longer get his horse to move, and was walking to the next stage.

He was obliged to get into Düring's chaise, where he slept on the straw. So they continued their journey, riding all day and sleeping in the chaise at night, without stopping anywhere.

After sixteen days' journey, during which they were more than once in danger of arrest, they finally arrived, on November 21, 1714, at the gates of the town of Stralsund, at one in the morning.

The King called out to the sentinel that he was a courier sent from Turkey by the King of Sweden and demanded to speak to General Dücker, governor of the town, immediately. The sentinel replied that it was late, that the governor had gone to bed, and that he must wait till daybreak.

The King retorted that he came on urgent business and declared that if they did not go and wake up the governor at once, they would all be punished the next morning. Finally a sergeant went to rouse the governor. Dücker imagined that it was perhaps one of the King of Sweden's generals. The gates were opened and the "courier" was taken to the governor's room.

Dücker, half asleep, asked him for news of the King of Sweden. The King took him by the arm and said, "What! Have my most faithful subjects forgotten me?" The governor, hardly able to believe his eyes, recognized the King; he jumped out of bed and embraced the King's knees, weeping tears of joy. Instantly the news spread throughout the town and everyone got up; the soldiers came and surrounded the governor's house. The inhabitants poured into the streets, asking one another, "Is it true that the King is here?" Lights were placed in all the windows; wine flowed in the streets to the light of a thousand torches and the sound of the cannons.

Meanwhile the King was taken to bed. He had not lain down for three days; his boots had to be cut off his legs, which had swollen with the extreme fatigue. He had neither linen nor clothes, and a wardrobe was hastily put together for him from everything suitable that could be found in the town. When he had slept for a few hours he got up, and at once went to review his troops and inspect the fortifications. The same day he issued orders to all his forces for an intensification of the war against his enemies. These details, which are so typical of the extraordinary character of Charles XII, were first communicated to me by M. Fabrice and have since been confirmed by Count Croissy, the French ambassador to the King.

Christian Europe was then in a very different state from that in which Charles had left it in 1709.

The war which had raged for so long in the south, and which had involved Germany, England, Holland, France, Spain, Portugal and Italy, had ended. This general peace had been the result of private quarrels in the English court. The Earl of Oxford, a capable minister, and Lord Bolingbroke, a most brilliant genius and the most eloquent man of his age, had overcome the famous Duke of Marlborough and had prevailed upon Queen Anne to make peace with Louis XIV. France, when she no longer had England for an enemy, was soon able to force the other powers to agree to terms.

Philip V, the grandson of Louis XIV, began to reign peaceably over what was left of the Spanish monarchy. The Emperor of Germany, having gained control of Naples and Flanders, had strengthened his position in his vast dominions. Louis XIV was now hoping only to end his long career in peace.

Anne, Queen of England, had died on August 10, 1714, hated by half of her subjects for having given peace to so many states. Her brother James Stuart, an unfortunate prince who had been excluded from the throne almost at birth, had not yet appeared in England to try to recover a succession which new laws would have given him if his party had prevailed. So George I, Elector of Hanover, was unanimously recognized as King of Great Britain. The throne belonged to this elector not by virtue of his blood, although he was descended from one of James's daughters, but by virtue of an act of Parliament.

George, who was called at an advanced age to govern a people whose language he did not understand and which was entirely foreign to him, still thought of himself as Elector of Hanover rather than as King of England. His only ambition was to extend his dominions in Germany. He crossed the sea almost every year to visit his subjects, who adored him. The pomp of royalty was a heavy burden for him. He lived with a small number of his old courtiers, with whom he was on familiar terms. He was not the most brilliant king in Europe, but he was one of the wisest, and he was the only one who occupied a throne and still enjoyed the pleasures of private life and friendship. Such were the principal monarchs and such was the situation in the south of Europe.

The changes which had taken place in the north were of a different nature. Its kings were at war, and were united against the King of Sweden.

Augustus had long since returned to the throne of Poland, with the help of the Czar and the consent of the Emperor of Germany, Anne of England and the States-General of Holland. For though they had all guaranteed the treaty of Altranstädt when Charles could impose his laws on Europe, they had withdrawn their guarantee when he was no longer to be feared.

But Augustus' reign was not undisturbed. The republic of Poland, when it had taken back its King, soon rediscovered its fear of arbitrary power; it had risen in arms to oblige the King to conform to the *pacta conventa,* and seemed to have recalled its master only in order to declare war on him. When these disturbances first broke out, the name of Stanislas was not heard; his party seemed completely destroyed. The King of Sweden was remembered only as a torrent which had changed the course of everything for a while in its passage.

Poltava and the absence of Charles XII, which had led to the fall of Stanislas, had also occasioned that of the Duke of Holstein, Charles's nephew, who had been despoiled of his dominions by the King of Denmark. The King of Sweden had loved Holstein's father tenderly and he was greatly touched and humiliated by the misfortunes of the son; moreover, as he had never done anything in life except for glory, the fall of sovereigns he had made or re-established moved him as much as did the loss of so many provinces.

There was a general scramble for the lands he had lost. Frederick William, the new King of Prussia, who seemed as warlike as his father had been pacific, began by gaining possession of Stettin and part of Pomerania, over which he had certain rights, and paying four hundred thousand crowns to the King of Denmark and the Czar for the privilege.

George, Elector of Hanover and now King of England, had occupied the duchy of Bremen and Verden, which the King of Denmark had ceded to him for sixty thousand pistoles. Thus the spoils of Charles XII were disposed of and the interests of the monarchs who had acquired Charles's territories in this way soon made them as dangerous enemies of the King as those who had actually conquered them.

As for the Czar, he was no doubt the one most to be feared. His former defeats, his victories, his very mistakes, his eagerness to learn and to show his subjects what he had learned—all this, together with his incessant labors, had made of him a great man in every respect. Already Riga had been captured; Livonia, Ingria, Karelia and half of Finland—all provinces conquered by Charles's ancestors—were now under the Muscovite yoke.

Peter Alekseevich, who twenty years earlier did not have a single ship on the Baltic, now saw himself master of this sea, with a fleet of thirty large ships of the line.

One of these had been built with his own hands; he was the best carpenter, the best admiral and the best pilot in the North. There was no difficult passage which he had not sounded himself, from the Gulf of Bothnia to the Ocean, for he had combined the work of a sailor with the experiments of a natural philosopher and the aims of an emperor, and had become an admiral by degrees and by dint of victories in the same way as he had reached the rank of general in the army.

While Prince Gallitzin, a general whom he had trained himself and who gave him the greatest help in his enterprises, was completing the conquest of Finland, capturing the town of Vaasa and defeating the Swedes, the Emperor put to sea and went to conquer the island of Aland, situated in the Baltic, a dozen leagues from Stockholm.

He left on this expedition at the beginning of July, 1714, while his rival, Charles XII, was keeping to his bed at Demotica. He embarked at Kronstadt, a port which he had built some years ago four miles from Petersburg. The new port, the fleet which it contained, the officers and the sailors—he had created them all himself, and wherever he looked he saw nothing for which he was not, in some sense, personally responsible.

The Russian fleet sighted Aland on July 15. The fleet was composed of thirty ships of the line, eighty galleys and a hundred half galleys. It carried twenty thousand soldiers. Admiral Apraxin was in command, and the Russian Emperor was serving as rear admiral. The Swedish fleet came to meet him on the 16th, commanded by Vice Admiral Ehrensköld. It had only a third of the Russian strength, but nevertheless fought for three hours. The Czar attacked Ehrensköld's ship and captured it after a stubborn engagement.

The same day he landed sixteen thousand men on Aland, and having captured a number of Swedish soldiers who had been been unable to embark on Ehrensköld's ships, he brought them back as prisoners on his own. He returned to Kronstadt with Ehrensköld's large ship, three smaller ones, a frigate and six galleys, all of which he had captured in the battle.

From Kronstadt he returned to the port of Petersburg, followed by his victorious fleet and the vessels captured from the enemy. He was greeted by a triple salute from a hundred and fifty guns. After this he made a triumphal entry which flattered him even more than that into Moscow, for he was receiving these honors in his favorite city, in a place where ten years ago there had not been a single hut and in which he now saw 34,500 houses. Above all, he was at the head not merely of a victorious navy, but of the first Russian fleet there had ever been on the Baltic, and in the midst of a nation to whom the very word "fleet" was unknown before his time.

His entry into Petersburg was accompanied by ceremonies very similar to those which had marked his triumph in Moscow. The Swedish vice admiral was the principal ornament of the new procession. Peter Alekseevich appeared as a rear admiral. A Russian boyar called Romandowski, who represented the Czar on solemn occasions, was seated on a throne with twelve senators beside him. The rear admiral gave him an account of his victories and was created vice admiral in consideration of his services. This was an odd ceremony, but a useful one in a country where military subordination was one of the novelties which the Czar had introduced.

The Muscovite Emperor, having conquered the Swedes on land and sea and helped to drive them out of Poland, now dominated that country in his turn. He had made himself mediator between the republic and Augustus, and the glory he obtained from this was perhaps as flattering as making a king would have been. The brilliance and fortune of Charles had passed to the Czar, and he put them to better use than his rival had done, for he employed all his successes to the advantage of his country. If he captured a town, its leading artisans were sent to employ their skill in Petersburg; the industries, arts and sciences of the conquered Swedish provinces were taken to Moscow; his dominions were enriched by his victories, and this made him the most excusable of all conquerors.

Sweden, on the other hand, deprived of almost all its overseas provinces, no longer had either trade, money or credit. Its veteran troops, who had been so formidable, had fallen in battle or died in poverty. More than a hundred thousand Swedes were slaves in the vast dominions of the Czar, and almost as many had been sold to the Turks and the Tartars. Men were clearly lacking, but hope revived when it was known that the King had arrived in Stralsund.

The feelings of respect and admiration for him were so deeply imprinted in the minds of his subjects that the young men of the countryside came in crowds to enlist, although the land had not sufficient hands left to cultivate it.

BOOK VIII

[*Charles marries the Princess his sister to the Prince of Hesse. He is besieged in Stralsund and escapes to Sweden. The plans of Baron Görtz, his prime minister. Projects for a reconciliation with the Czar and an attack on England. Charles besieges Fredrikshald in Norway. He is killed. His character. Görtz is beheaded.*]

In the midst of all these preparations, the King gave his remaining sister, Ulrike Eleonore, in marriage to Prince Frederick of Hesse-Kassel. The dowager Queen, grandmother of Charles XII and of the Princess, now aged eighty, did the honors of this celebration on April 4, 1715, in the palace of Stockholm, and died soon after.

This marriage was not honored by the King's presence; he remained in Stralsund, occupied in completing the fortifications of this important stronghold which was threatened by the Kings of Denmark and Prussia. However, he declared his brother-in-law generalissimo of his armies in Sweden. This Prince had served the Dutch in their wars against France; he was looked on as a capable general, and this quality had done more than a little to win him the hand of a sister of Charles XII.

Disasters now followed one another as rapidly as victories had done earlier. In June, 1715, the German troops of the King of England and those of Denmark besieged the fortified town of Wismar; at the same time, a combined Danish and Saxon army of thirty-six thousand men was marching to besiege Stralsund. The Kings of Denmark and Prussia sank five Swedish ships off Stralsund. The Czar was out on the Baltic with twenty large warships and a hundred and fifty transports carrying thirty thousand men. He was threatening to land in Sweden; first he sailed as far as the coast of Hälsingborg and then he appeared off Stockholm. The whole of Sweden stood to arms on the coasts, awaiting the moment of the invasion. At the same time, Russian armies were slowly driving the Swedes from their remaining possessions in Finland toward the Gulf of Bothnia; but the Czar did not carry his enterprises any further.

At the mouth of the Oder, a river which cuts Pomerania in two, and which enters the Baltic beyond Stettin, is the little island of Usedom, which occupies an important situation as it commands the Oder to right and left; whoever is master of it controls navigation on the river. The King of Prussia had dislodged the Swedes from this island and had seized it, together with Stettin, which he had sequestered—all, as he said, for the love of peace. The Swedes had recaptured Usedom in May, 1715. They had two forts there; one was the fort of Swine, on the branch of the Oder which bears this name; the other, which was more important, was Peenemünde, on the other branch of the river. To guard these two forts and the whole island, the King of Sweden had only two hundred and fifty Pomeranian soldiers, commanded by an old Swedish officer called Kuse-Slerp, whose name is worthy of being remembered.

On August 4, the King of Prussia sent fifteen hundred foot soldiers and eight hundred dragoons to occupy the island. They arrived and landed without opposition near the fort of Swine. The Swedish commander abandoned this fort as the less important one, and as he could not risk dividing the few troops he had, he withdrew with his small force into the castle of Peenemünde, resolved to defend it to the last.

So a regular siege had to be begun. Artillery was brought up from Stettin and the Prussian troops were reinforced by a thousand infantry and four hundred horsemen. On August 18, the siege was opened on two sides and the fortress was fiercely bombarded by cannon and mortars. During the siege a Swedish soldier, bearing a secret letter from Charles XII, managed to land on the island and slip into Peenemünde; he gave the letter to the commandant. It was couched in the following terms: "Do not fire until the enemy are on the edge of the moat; defend yourselves to the last drop of your blood; I wish you good luck. Charles."

Slerp, having read this note, resolved to obey and die as he was ordered, in the service of his master. On the 22nd, at daybreak, the enemy attacked. The besieged army, who only fired when they saw their assailants on the edge of the moat, killed a great number of them; but the moat was filled, the breach was a large one, and the number of the besiegers was overwhelming. They broke into the castle on two sides at once. The commandant then thought only of selling his life dearly and of obeying the King's letter. He abandoned the breaches by which the enemy had entered. His little troop, which was brave and faithful enough to follow him, was entrenched around a bastion in such a way that it could not be surrounded. The enemy attacked, amazed that he had not asked for quarter. Slerp fought on for a whole hour, and after having lost half his men was finally killed, as were also both his lieutenant and his major. Then the hundred soldiers who remained, together with a single officer, asked for their lives and were made prisoners of war. The King's letter was found in the commandant's pocket and taken to the King of Prussia.

While Charles was thus losing the island of Usedom and the neighboring islands, which were soon captured; while Wismar was on the point of surrender; while his navy no longer existed; and while Sweden itself was threatened, the King was in Stralsund, which was already besieged by thirty-six thousand men.

Stralsund, which has become famous throughout Europe as a result of this siege, is the strongest place in Pomerania. It is built between the Baltic and Lake Franken on the straits of Gella; it can be reached only by land across a narrow causeway defended by a citadel and by fortifications which were thought to be impregnable. It had a garrison of nearly nine thousand men and, in addition, the King of Sweden himself. The Kings of Denmark and Prussia undertook this siege with an army of thirty-six thousand men composed of Prussians, Danes and Saxons.

The honor of besieging Charles XII was such a powerful motive that all obstacles were overcome and the trenches were opened during the night of October 19-20, 1715. At the beginning of the siege, Charles said that he did not understand how a well-fortified and adequately garrisoned stronghold could ever be captured. It is true that in the course of his conquests he had captured several fortified towns, but never through a regular siege; the terror which his arms inspired had carried everything before it; moreover, he did not judge others according to the standards he applied to himself and had not a sufficiently high opinion of his enemies. The besiegers pressed on with their works with determination and enthusiasm and were aided by a very curious chance.

The Baltic, as is well known, has no tides. The fortifications which protected the town and which stretched from an impassable marsh on the west to the sea on the east seemed invulnerable. Nobody had noticed that when the west wind blew strongly it drove the waters of the Baltic eastward so that they were only three feet deep near the fortifications, which appeared to be surrounded by an impassable sea. A soldier who fell from the fortifications into the sea was amazed when he touched the bottom; he concluded that this discovery might make his fortune. He deserted and went to the headquarters of Count Wackerbarth, the Saxon general, where he gave his opinion that the sea could be forded and the Swedish fortifications penetrated without difficulty. The King of Prussia hastened to profit from this information.

The very next day, at midnight, while the west wind was still blowing, Lieutenant Colonel Köppen entered the water, followed by eighteen hundred men; at the same time, two thousand others were advancing along the causeway which led to the fortifications; the whole Prussian artillery opened fire and the Prussians and Danes created a diversion on another side.

The Swedes felt sure they could throw back these two thousand men whom they saw approaching along the causeway with such apparent rashness; but suddenly Köppen and his eighteen hundred men entered the fortifications from the sea. Surprised and surrounded, the Swedes could offer no resistance; the post was captured after a great slaughter. A number of Swedes fled toward the town; the besiegers followed them and they all entered the town mixed up together; two Saxon officers and four soldiers were already on the drawbridge; but there was time to raise it; they were captured, and for the moment the town was saved.

Twenty-four cannons were found in the fortifications and were turned against Stralsund. The siege was continued with all the stubbornness and confidence which naturally resulted from this first success. The town was bombarded almost incessantly.

Opposite Stralsund, in the Baltic, is the island of Rügen, which serves as a rampart for the town, and to which the garrison and citizens could have withdrawn if they had had boats to transport them. This island was extremely important for Charles. He could see that if the enemy captured it he would be besieged by land and sea and that in all probability he would then be reduced to being buried beneath the ruins of Stralsund or else to becoming a prisoner of the very enemies he had so long despised and on whom he had imposed such harsh laws. However, the wretched state of his affairs had not allowed him to place a sufficiently strong garrison on the island; there were no more than two thousand troops there.

For three months his enemies had been making all the necessary preparations for a landing on the island, which is very difficult to approach. Finally, when he had had enough boats built, the Prince of Anhalt, aided by favorable weather, disembarked on Rügen with twelve thousand men on November 15. The King, who was present everywhere, was on the island; he had joined his two thousand soldiers, who were entrenched near a little port some three leagues from the spot where the enemy had landed. He placed himself at their head and marched through the night in complete silence. The Prince of Anhalt, taking a precaution which seemed unnecessary, had already had trenches dug. The officers who commanded under him did not expect to be attacked the very same night and they thought Charles XII was in Stralsund; but the Prince of Anhalt, who knew what Charles was capable of, had had a deep ditch dug, surrounded by chevaux-de-frise, and was taking every precaution, just as if he were fighting an army superior in numbers.

At two in the morning, Charles reached the enemy without making the slightest noise. His soldiers said to one another: "Tear down the chevaux-de-frise." These words were heard by the sentinels; at once the alarm was given in the camp and the enemy sprang to arms. The King, having removed the chevaux-de-frise, saw a deep ditch in front of him. "Ah!" he said, "is it possible! I didn't expect it." But this surprise did not discourage him; he did not know how many troops had landed; and his enemies, for their part, did not know how small was the force they were facing. The darkness of the night seemed to favor Charles; he took his decision at once. He jumped into the ditch, accompanied by his bravest soldiers, and was immediately followed by the rest. The torn-up chevaux-de-frise, the piles of earth, the trunks and branches of trees which were found and the bodies of soldiers killed by random musket fire served as fascines. The King, the generals who were with him and the bravest officers and soldiers climbed on each other's shoulders as in an assault. The battle began in the enemy camp. At first the impetuosity of the Swedes threw the Danes and Prussians into disorder; but numbers were too unequal. The Swedes were repulsed after a quarter of an hour's battle and driven back across the ditch. The Prince of Anhalt then pursued them across the plain; he did not know, at that moment, that it was Charles XII who was fleeing before him. The unhappy King rallied his troops in open country and the battle began again, both sides fighting stubbornly. Grothusen, the King's favorite, and General Dahldorf were both killed beside him. In the heat of the battle, Charles stumbled over the latter's body while he was still breathing. Düring, who had been the only one to accompany him on his journey from Turkey to Stralsund, was killed before his eyes.

In the midst of the struggle, a Danish lieutenant, whose name I have been unable to discover, recognized Charles, and grasping his sword with one hand and his hair with the other, cried, "Surrender, Sire, or I shall kill you." Charles had a pistol at his belt: he fired with his left hand at the officer, who died the next morning. The royal title, which the Dane had pronounced, immediately attracted a host of enemies. The King was surrounded. He received a musket shot under his left breast. The wound, which he called a bruise, was two inches deep. The King was on foot and in danger of being killed or captured. Count Poniatowski was at this moment fighting near him. He had saved his life at Poltava, and had the good fortune to save it again in this battle of Rügen and to place him on a horse.

The Swedes withdrew to a part of the island called Altefähr, where there was a fort which they still held. From there the King returned to Stralsund, forced to abandon the brave troops who had helped him so well in this enterprise; they were made prisoners of war two days later.

Among these prisoners was the unfortunate French regiment composed of the remnants of the battle of Blenheim who had passed into the service of King Augustus and thence into that of Sweden. The majority of the soldiers were incorporated into the army of the Prince of Anhalt, who became their fourth master. The man who commanded this wandering regiment in Rügen was the same Count of Villelongue who had so generously risked his life in Adrianople to serve Charles XII. He was captured, together with his troops, and was later only poorly rewarded for all his services, labors and sufferings.

After all these prodigies of valor which only served to weaken his forces, the King, shut up in Stralsund and on the point of being defeated there, was in the same situation as he had been at Bendery. But nothing dismayed him; during the day he had ditches and entrenchments made behind the walls; at night he made sorties against the enemy. Meanwhile Stralsund was heavily bombarded; bombs rained on the houses and half the town was in ashes. The citizens, far from complaining, were full of admiration for their master, whose ceaseless activity, temperance and courage amazed them, and they had all become soldiers under his command. They accompanied him in his sorties and were as valuable to him as a second garrison.

One day, while the King was dictating letters to Sweden to a secretary, a bomb fell on the house, pierced the roof and exploded near the King's room. Half the floor collapsed; but the room in which the King was dictating was partly built into a thick wall and remained undamaged; by an astonishing piece of good luck, none of the flying fragments entered the room although the door was open. At the noise of the bomb and the crashes from within the house, which seemed to be collapsing, the secretary dropped his pen. "What's the matter?" said the King calmly. "Why aren't you writing?" The secretary could only reply, "Ah! Sire, the bomb!" "Well," said the King, "what has the bomb got to do with the letter I am dictating? Carry on."

Besieged in Stralsund with the King was a French ambassador, Colbert, Count of Croissy, a lieutenant general of the French army and brother of the Marquis of Torcy, a famous minister of state, as well as being a relation of the celebrated Colbert whose name should never be forgotten in France. To send a man to the trenches or to send him as an ambassador to Charles XII amounted to much the same thing. The King would talk to Croissy for hours on end in the most exposed places, while cannonballs and bombs were killing people all around them, without ever noticing the danger, and the ambassador, for his part, never even hinted that there might be more appropriate places to discuss business. This minister had done all he could before the siege to bring about an agreement between the Kings of Sweden and Prussia; but the latter asked too much, and Charles was prepared to cede nothing. So the only satisfaction that the Count gained from his embassy was that of enjoying close acquaintance with this unique man. He often slept by him under the same cloak, and by sharing his dangers and labors, he had acquired the right to speak to him freely. Charles encouraged this boldness in those he loved. He sometimes said to Croissy, "*Veni, maledicamus de rege*"—Come, let us say a few rude things about the King. The ambassador has told me this himself.

Croissy stayed in the town until November 13, and having finally obtained permission to leave, together with his baggage, he said farewell to the King of Sweden, leaving him amid the ruins of Stralsund with a garrison that had lost two thirds of its men, but still was ready to withstand an assault.

And in fact, two days later, such an assault was made on the hornwork. The enemy occupied it twice and were twice driven out. The King fought throughout the action in the midst of his grenadiers; but finally numbers prevailed, and the besiegers remained in occupation. Charles stayed two more days in the town, expecting a general assault at any moment. He stayed till midnight on the 19th, on a little half-moon fortification ruined by bombs and cannon shot. The following day his principal officers urged him not to stay any longer in a place which could not be defended; but it was now as dangerous to withdraw as to remain. The Baltic was covered with Russian and Danish ships. The only ship in the port of Stralsund was a little bark with sails and oars. The fact that all these dangers would make withdrawal glorious made Charles determined to try it. He embarked on the night of December 20, 1715, with only ten other people. They had to break the ice which covered the sea in the port; it needed two hours' hard work before the bark could sail freely. The enemy admirals had precise orders not to allow Charles to leave Stralsund, and to take him dead or alive. Fortunately the wind was against them and they could not get near him. The danger was even greater when they passed within sight of the island of Rügen near a place called La Babrette, where the Danes had stationed a battery of twelve cannons. These fired on the King. The sailors crowded on sail and rowed furiously to get out of range; a cannon shot killed two men at

Charles's side and another smashed the mast. By this perilous route the King at last reached two of his ships which were cruising in the Baltic. The next day Stralsund surrendered; the garrison were made prisoners of war. Charles landed at Ystad in Skäne and from there went on to Karlskrona, in a very different state from the one in which he had left it fifteen years before, on a ship with a hundred and twenty guns, to subjugate the North.

As he was so near his capital, people expected him to return there after such a long absence; but he was determined to do so only when he was victorious. Moreover, he could not bring himself to visit the people he loved while he was forced to oppress them in order to defend himself against his enemies. His sister was the only person he wanted to see; he arranged to meet her on the shores of Lake Vatter in East Götaland. He went there by the post route with a single servant and returned after spending a day with her.

From Karlskrona, where he spent the winter, he ordered new levies to be raised throughout the kingdom. He believed that his subjects were only born to follow him into battle, and he had accustomed them to believing it too. Young men of fifteen were enrolled, and in several villages there were only old men, women and children left; in many places women alone tilled the soil.

It was even more difficult to procure a fleet; to achieve this end, commissions were given to private fitters, who, in exchange for privileges which were both excessive and ruinous to the country, fitted out a few ships. To meet all these expenses, the people's standard of living had to be reduced. Every imaginable type of extortion was introduced under the name of tax or duty. Houses were searched and half the provisions were taken to increase the King's stocks; all the iron in the kingdom was bought up and paid for in notes, though it was later sold again for money. All those who wore clothes made partly of silk, or who had wigs or gilded swords, had to pay a special tax. The people, burdened by these exactions, would have revolted under any other king; but the most wretched Swedish peasant knew that his master was leading a life that was even harsher and more frugal than his own. So everyone submitted without grumbling to hardships which the King himself was the first to endure.

Public danger even caused private misfortunes to be forgotten. The Muscovites, Danes, Prussians, Saxons and even the English were expected to land in Sweden at any moment, and this fear was so well founded and so strong that those who had silver or other valuables buried them underground.

In fact, an English fleet had already arrived in the Baltic, although it was not known what orders it had received; and the King of Denmark had the Czar's word that the Muscovites would join the Danes in an attack on Sweden in the spring of 1716.

The whole of Europe had its eyes on Charles XII and was extremely surprised when, instead of defending his own country against the threat from so many monarchs, he entered Norway, in March, 1716, with twenty thousand men.

Since Hannibal's time, there had been no example of a general who, unable to defend his own country, had gone and made war in the heart of his enemies' dominions. The Prince of Hesse, Charles's brother-in-law, accompanied him on this expedition.

The only route from Sweden to Norway lies through dangerous passes; and when these have been negotiated, there are stretches of sea to be crossed between ranges of rocky mountains; bridges had to be built every day. A small number of Danes could have held up the whole Swedish army; but this sudden invasion had not been foreseen. Europe was even more astonished that the Czar remained inactive in the midst of these events, and did not attack Sweden, as had been agreed with his allies.

The reason for this inactivity was one of the greatest plans, but at the same time one of the most difficult to carry out, which the human mind has ever thought of.

Henry of Görtz, who was born in Franconia and was a baron of the empire, had rendered important services to the King of Sweden during his sojourn at Bendery and had since become his favorite and prime minister.

Never was a man more supple and audacious at the

same time, more resourceful in misfortune, more enterprising in his projects and more active in carrying them out; no plan was too daring for him and no method of achieving it was beyond his resources; gifts, promises, oaths, truth and lies—he used them all freely.

From Sweden he went to France, England and Holland to make personal contact with the forces he hoped to be able to bring into play. He would have been capable of throwing all Europe into confusion, and indeed such was his plan. Görtz in his cabinet was as dangerous as the King of Sweden at the head of his army, and it is not surprising that his influence over Charles was greater than that of any previous minister.

The King, who at the age of twenty had given orders to Count Piper, now received instructions from Baron Görtz, and he submitted to them all the more willingly because his misfortunes made it necessary for him to listen to advice, and the advice Görtz gave him was in keeping with his own courageous spirit. He observed that, of all the sovereigns who were united against Sweden, George, Elector of Hanover and King of England, was the one with whom Charles was most angry, because he was the only one Charles had not offended. He noticed too that George had entered the quarrel under the pretext of appeasing it, but really in order to keep Bremen and Verden, to which he seemed to have no other right than that of having bought them cheaply from the King of Denmark, to whom they did not belong.

He soon realized too that the Czar was secretly discontented with his allies, who had all stopped him from getting control of any part of the German empire, although expansion in this direction, dangerous as it was to the rest of Europe, had now become one of his main aims. Wismar, the only town on the German coast still held by the Swedes, had at last surrendered to the Prussians and Danes on February 14, 1716. These two allies refused to allow the Russian troops who were in Mecklenburg to take part in the siege. Such distrust, of which there had been other examples in the last two years, had aroused the Czar's hostility and had perhaps saved Sweden from ruin. There are many examples of allied states being conquered by a single power; there are very few of a great empire being conquered by several allies. If their united forces defeat it, their divisions soon allow it to revive.

As early as 1714, the Czar was in a position to invade Sweden. But either because he could not agree with the Kings of Poland, England, Denmark and Prussia, who were all jealous of him, not without reason, or because he did not think that his troops were yet sufficiently experienced to attack in their own homeland a people whose peasantry alone had conquered the elite of the Danish army, he kept putting off this enterprise.

Shortage of money had also made him delay. The Czar was one of the most powerful monarchs in the world, but also one of the least rich; at that time his revenues did not amount to more than twenty-four million francs. He had discovered mines of gold, silver, iron and copper; but it was not yet certain how profitable they would be, and work on them was extremely costly. He was establishing a vast trade, but in the beginning it brought him little more than expectations; his newly conquered provinces increased his power and glory without adding as yet to his revenue. Time was needed to heal the wounds of Livonia, a prosperous country, but one which had been ravaged by fifteen years of war, by the sword, by fire and by disease, and was now denuded of inhabitants and a burden on its conqueror. The fleets which he maintained and the new enterprises he was constantly undertaking exhausted his finances. He had been reduced to the unfortunate step of devaluing the currency, a remedy which never cures the ills of the state and which is particularly harmful to a country which imports more than it exports.

These were some of the foundations on which Görtz was building his plan for a diplomatic revolution. He risked advising the King of Sweden to buy peace with the Muscovite Emperor, whatever the price, suggesting to him that the Czar was angry with the Kings of Poland and England and insinuating that Peter Alekseevich and Charles XII, if they were united, could make the rest of Europe tremble.

There was no method of making peace with the Czar

without handing over some of the provinces to the east and north of the Baltic; but Görtz pointed out that by ceding these provinces, which the Czar already held anyway and which could not be recaptured, the King could have the glory of restoring Stanislas to the throne of Poland, re-establishing James II on that of England, and assuring the return of the Duke of Holstein to his dominions.

Charles, who was impressed by these vast schemes, though without relying on them too much, gave his prime minister a free hand. Görtz left Sweden with full powers which authorized him to do as he wished and allowed him to make any agreements he thought fit with the monarchs with whom he intended to negotiate. His first step was to sound the court of Moscow through a Scot called Erskine, the Czar's principal doctor, who was devoted to the Pretender's party, as were almost all the Scots who did not live off the favors of the court of London.

This doctor described the importance and greatness of the project to Prince Menzikov with all the vivacity of a man who was interested in its success. Prince Menzikov liked the proposal, and the Czar approved. Instead of attacking Sweden, as had been agreed with his allies, he wintered his troops in Mecklenburg and went there himself under the pretext of settling quarrels which were beginning to break out between the Duke of Mecklenburg and the nobility of the country; actually he was pursuing his favorite design of acquiring a principality in Germany and hoping to get the Duke of Mecklenburg to sell him his sovereignty.

The allies were annoyed by this action; they had no desire to have as a neighbor a man they feared so much and who, once he was established in Germany, might someday get himself elected Emperor and oppress the rest of the German princes. The more irritated they were, the nearer Görtz's project came to success. Yet to hide these secret intrigues all the more effectively, he was negotiating with the confederate princes at the same time. The Czar too kept them all occupied by arousing their hopes. Meanwhile Charles XII was in Norway with his brother-in-law the Prince of Hesse, at the head of twenty thousand men; the province was guarded by only eleven thousand Danes divided into several detachments, who were all put to the sword by the King and the Prince of Hesse.

Charles advanced as far as Christiania,[3] the capital of the kingdom; fortune seemed to favor him again in this part of the world, but he never took sufficient precautions to ensure supplies for his troops. A Danish army and fleet were approaching to defend Norway, and Charles, lacking provisions, retired to Sweden to await the outcome of his minister's vast projects.

To achieve his aims, Görtz needed both immense preparations and profound secrecy, and the two rarely go together. He even looked as far as the seas of Asia for help, which, however odious it might seem, would nonetheless have been useful for a landing in Scotland and which would at least have provided Sweden with money, men and ships.

For a long time the pirates of all nations, and particularly the English, had been working in association and had been infesting the seas of Europe and America. Mercilessly pursued on all sides, they had recently retired to the coasts of Madagascar, a large island to the east of Africa. They were desperate men, almost all famous for actions which would have been heroic if only they had been just. They were looking for a prince who would receive them under his protection, but the law of nations closed the ports of the world to them.

As soon as they knew that Charles XII had returned to Sweden, they hoped that this King, an enthusiast for war, obliged to make war, and lacking ships and soldiers, would come to a favorable understanding with them; they sent him a deputy, who arrived in Europe on a Dutch ship and proposed to Baron Görtz that they should be received in the port of Göteborg, where they offered to bring their sixty ships laden with riches.

The Baron got the King to agree to the proposal; the next year they even sent two Swedish noblemen, one

---

[3] Now Oslo.

called Cronström and the other Mendal, to complete the negotiations with the Madagascar pirates.

Later a more reputable and more important source of help was found in Cardinal Alberoni, the powerful and able minister who governed Spain long enough to ensure his own glory though for too short a time to make his country great again. He eagerly entered into the plan to make the son of James II King of England. Yet, as he had only just become a minister and wanted to set Spain on her feet before thinking about disturbing other countries, it seemed that it would be some years before he would be able to take part in this great enterprise. But in less than two years he changed the face of Spain, restored its reputation in Europe, engaged, or so it is said, the Turks to attack the German Emperor, and tried at the same time to deprive the Duke of Orleans of the regency of France and King George of the crown of Great Britain. All this shows how dangerous a single individual can be when he is absolute master of a powerful state, and has a mind full of great ideas and courage.

Görtz, having kindled the first sparks of the conflagration he was planning, in the courts of Muscovy and Spain, went secretly to France, and thence to Holland, where he met a number of the supporters of the Pretender.

He was particularly interested in finding out the strength, numbers and disposition of the potential rebels in England, the money they could provide and the troops they could raise. These malcontents were only asking for the help of ten thousand men, and claimed that with these troops a rebellion was sure to succeed.

The Count of Gyllenborg, Swedish ambassador in England, on the instructions of Baron Görtz, had a number of meetings in London with the Jacobite leaders. He encouraged them, and promised them everything they asked; the Pretender's party went so far as to provide considerable sums of money which Görtz was able to draw on in Holland. He negotiated the purchase of a number of ships, and bought six in Brittany, together with arms of all kinds.

Then he secretly sent a number of officers to France,

among whom was the Chevalier Folard, who, having fought for thirty years in the French army without adding much to his fortune, had recently come to offer his services to the King of Sweden, less from selfish motives than from a desire to serve under a king who had such an amazing reputation. Folard hoped, moreover, to interest this monarch in the new ideas he had about war; he had spent the whole of his life studying war scientifically and had recently published his conclusions in his *Commentaries on Polybius.* His views were appreciated by Charles XII, who had himself made war in a new way and who never allowed himself to be guided by custom. He intended that Folard should be one of the instruments he would use in his projected landing in Scotland. When he arrived in France, this nobleman carried out Görtz's secret orders. Many French officers and a large number of Irish joined this new type of conspiracy which was being carried on simultaneously in England, France and Russia and which had secret branches in every part of Europe.

These preparations were only a beginning for Görtz, though it was a great achievement to have even begun. The most difficult step, without which further progress was impossible, was to conclude peace between the Czar and Charles; many difficulties had still to be ironed out. Baron Osterman, the minister of state in Russia, had not at first allowed himself to be won over to Görtz's point of view. He was as circumspect as Charles's minister was enterprising. His policies were slow and measured and he liked to wait for things to ripen. Görtz, on the other hand, was impatient enough to expect to be able to reap as soon as he had sown. Osterman was afraid that the Emperor his master would be dazzled by the brilliance of this plan and would grant the Swedes a too advantageous peace, and he kept delaying this by a series of obstacles and procrastinations.

Fortunately for Görtz, the Czar himself came to Holland early in 1717. He intended to go on to France, as he had never visited this famous country which for the last hundred years has been criticized, envied and imitated by all its neighbors; he wanted to satisfy his insatiable desire to see and learn and at the same time further his political designs.

Görtz saw the Emperor twice at The Hague; he made more progress in these two conferences than he had done in six months of negotiations with plenipotentiaries. Everything seemed to be turning out satisfactorily; his great plans appeared to be hidden in impenetrable secrecy and he felt sure that Europe would hear of them only when they were put into effect. Yet at The Hague, he spoke only of peace, proclaiming loudly that he regarded the King of England as the peacemaker of the North and even feigning to press for the holding of a congress at Brunswick where the interests of Sweden and those of its enemies would be discussed amicably.

The first man to discover Görtz's intrigues was the Duke of Orleans, the French regent, who had spies throughout Europe. These spies, whose job it is to sell the secrets of their friends, and who live by being informers and often slanderers, had increased so much in France under his government that half the nation seemed to be spying on the other half. The Duke of Orleans, who was bound to the King of England by personal ties, informed him of the plot which was being formed against him.

At the same time, the Dutch, who were becoming suspicious of Görtz's behavior, communicated these suspicions to the English government. Görtz and Gyllenborg were busy furthering their plans when they were both arrested, one at Deventer in Gelderland and the other in London.

As Gyllenborg, the Swedish ambassador, had violated the law of nations by conspiring against the prince to whom he was accredited, the English government had no scruples about violating the same law in arresting him. But it was more surprising that the Dutch should have taken the unheard-of step of imprisoning Baron Görtz to please the King of England. They even ordered the Count of Welderen to interrogate him. This formality was only an additional outrage, and as it produced no results, it merely served to cover them in confusion. Görtz asked Welderen if he knew him. "Yes, sir," replied the Dutchman. "In that case," said Görtz, "you should know that I shall say no more than I want." The interrogation did not get much further. All the ambassadors, and particularly the Marquis of Monteleon, the Spanish minister in England, protested against the violation of the rights of Görtz and Gyllenborg. The Dutch had no excuse; they had not only violated a sacred right by arresting the prime minister of the King of Sweden, but they were acting directly against the precious principles of liberty which had attracted so many foreigners to their country and had been the foundation of their greatness.

As for the King of England, he had acted perfectly justly in arresting an enemy. To justify himself he published the letters of Görtz and Gyllenborg which were found among the latter's papers. The King of Sweden was then in the province of Skäne; the printed letters were taken to him at the same time as the news of the arrest of his two ministers. Smilingly he asked if his own had not been printed too. He immediately ordered the arrest of the English resident in Stockholm, together with all his family and his servants; he forbade the Dutch resident to appear at court and placed him under surveillance. But he neither recognized nor disowned Baron Görtz; he was too proud to deny an enterprise which he had approved, and too wise to admit to a plan which had been stifled almost at birth. He maintained a disdainful silence toward England and Holland.

The Czar adopted a different tactic. As he was not named but only obscurely hinted at in the letters of Gyllenborg and Görtz, he wrote to the King of England a long letter full of compliments on the discovery of the plot and of assurances of sincere friendship. King George received these protestations without believing them, but pretended to accept them at their face value. A conspiracy undertaken by private individuals is destroyed when it is discovered; but discovery only adds new strength to a conspiracy of kings. The Czar arrived in Paris in May, 1717. He was not solely occupied in looking at the beauties of art and nature, visiting academies, public libraries, private collections and royal palaces; he proposed to the Duke of Orleans, regent of France, a treaty which, if it had been accepted, would have set the seal on Russian greatness. His plan was to unite with the King of Sweden, who would cede large provinces to him, to completely deprive the Danes of control of the Baltic, to weaken the English by civil war, and to attract the whole of the trade of the North to Russia. He was even prepared to help Stanislas to challenge Augustus once again so that, when every corner of Europe was alight, he could go from place to place, stirring up or damping down the fires as best suited his purpose. With these aims in view, he proposed that the French regent should act as mediator between Russia and Sweden and should sign an offensive and defensive alliance with these two states and with Spain. This treaty, which seemed so natural and so useful to these nations and would have made them masters of Europe, was nevertheless not accepted by the Duke of Orleans. At that very time, he was entering into engagements of a totally different kind; he was allying himself with the Emperor of Germany and George, King of England. Reasons of state had so much altered the viewpoints of all the princes of Europe that the Czar was ready to declare himself against his ancient ally King Augustus and to side with his mortal enemy Charles, while France was going to help the English and the Germans by making war on the grandson of Louis XIV after having supported him for so long against these same enemies at a terrible cost in blood and treasure. All that the Czar could obtain, and then only indirectly, was that the regent would use his good offices to secure the liberation of Görtz and Gyllenborg. He returned to Russia at the end of June after having given France the rare spectacle of an Emperor who traveled to instruct himself; but too many Frenchmen noticed only his unpolished manners, which his bad education had failed to eradicate; and the legislator and creator of a new nation, the great man, entirely escaped them.

What he was looking for in the Duke of Orleans he soon found in Cardinal Alberoni, who had become all-powerful in Spain. Alberoni wanted nothing so much as the restoration of the Pretender, both as a minister of

Spain, which England had so ill-treated, and as the personal enemy of the Duke of Orleans, who was England's ally against Spain, and finally as the priest of a Church for the sake of which the Pretender's father had so unnecessarily lost his crown.

The Duke of Ormond, who was as loved in England as the Duke of Marlborough was admired, had left his country on the accession of George I and gone to Madrid. Now, vested with full powers by the King of Spain and the Pretender, he went to meet the Czar at Mitau in Kurland, together with another capable and enterprising Englishman called Irnegan. He asked the Czar to give his daughter Anna Petrovna in marriage to the son of James II, hoping that this union would strengthen the bonds between the Russian Emperor and this unfortunate prince. But instead of forwarding the progress of negotiations, this proposal almost led to their being put off. In Baron Görtz's plans, this princess had long been destined for the Duke of Holstein, who, in fact, did marry her later. As soon as he heard of the Duke of Ormond's proposal, he became jealous and did all he could to ensure that it would not succeed. He was freed from prison in August, as was Gyllenborg, although the King of Sweden had not deigned to offer the slightest excuse to the King of England or to show the least sign of displeasure at the way his minister had behaved.

At the same time, he freed the English resident at Stockholm and all his family, who had been treated much more severely than Gyllenborg had been in London.

Görtz, once he was at liberty, was an implacable enemy who now had the extra motive of personal vengeance to add to the powerful political ones which had inspired him hitherto. He traveled at once to see the Czar, who was more than ever convinced by his arguments. Firstly, he assured him that in less than three months he would, with the help of a single Russian plenipotentiary, remove all the obstacles holding up the conclusion of a peace treaty with Sweden. He picked up a map which the Czar had drawn himself, and tracing a line from Viborg through Lake Ladoga to the Arctic Sea, he promised that he could get his master to cede everything to the east of this line as well as Karelia, Ingria and Livonia. Then he put forward proposals for a marriage between the Russian Emperor's daughter and the Duke of Holstein, assuring the Czar that the Duke might be willing to cede his dominions in exchange for some equivalent. Thus he could become a member of the empire, and Görtz proceeded to paint a picture of the Czar or his descendants wearing the imperial crown of Germany. By this means he flattered the ambitions of the Russian ruler, and deprived the Pretender of the Czar's daughter while at the same time opening the road to England for him; he was achieving all his objectives at once.

The Czar designated the island of Aland for the conferences which his minister of state Osterman was to have with Baron Görtz. The Duke of Ormond was asked to return so as not to give too much offense to England, with which the Czar did not want to break until the invasion was imminent. Ormond's confidant Irnegan stayed behind alone in Petersburg and lodged in the town with so many precautions that he went out only at night and, disguised either as a peasant or as a Tartar, saw only the Czar's ministers.

As soon as the Duke of Ormond had left, the Czar informed the King of England of his friendly action in dismissing the most important follower of the Pretender; and Baron Görtz, full of hope, returned to Sweden.

He found his master at the head of thirty-five thousand regular troops; the coasts were lined with militia. The only thing the King lacked was money; credit was exhausted both at home and abroad. France, which had granted a number of subsidies during the last years of Louis XIV, no longer did so under the regency of the Duke of Orleans, whose policies were the direct opposite of his predecessor's. Spain promised money, but was not yet in a position to provide much. So Baron Görtz put into general effect a plan which he had already tried out before going to France and Holland: it was to give copper the same value as silver so that a copper piece which was intrinsically worth a halfpenny became worth forty pence when it had the royal stamp on it. In the same way, in besieged towns, governors have often paid the soldiers and citizens in money made of leather while waiting for the arrival of real coin. These fictitious kinds of money, which are invented through necessity, and to which good faith alone can give a lasting value, are like bills of exchange whose imaginary value may easily exceed the actual funds which exist in a state.

These expedients are very useful in a free country and have sometimes saved a republic; but they almost inevitably ruin a monarchy, for the people soon lose confidence and the minister is reduced to breaking his word. The fictitious money multiplies excessively and people hide their real money. So the whole machine breaks down and the resultant confusion is often accompanied by great distress. This is what happened in Sweden.

Baron Görtz had begun by introducing the new currency discreetly, but was soon forced to go beyond his original intentions by the pressure of events he could no longer control. All merchandise and all commodities had become excessively expensive and he was forced to increase the quantity of copper coins. The more there were, the less they were worth, and Sweden, flooded with this false coin, sent up a general cry against Görtz. The people, who still venerated Charles XII, could not bring themselves to hate him, and all their anger was directed at a minister who, as a foreigner and a finance minister, was doubly exposed to public detestation.

A tax which he attempted to impose on the clergy was the final straw which made him the object of the nation's hatred. The priests, who too often join their own cause to that of God, publicly called him an atheist because he was asking for their money. The new copper coinage was stamped with the images of a number of the gods of antiquity, and as a result these coins were called "the gods of Baron Görtz."

To this public hatred against him was joined the jealousy of the other ministers, which was all the more implacable for being, at that time, powerless. The King's sister and the Prince her husband feared him as a man attached by his birth to the Duke of Holstein and capable of one day placing the crown of Sweden on his head. The only person in the kingdom who had ever liked him was

Charles XII, but the general hatred of him only served to confirm the King's friendship, for Charles's feelings always thrived on contradiction. His confidence in the baron at this time was carried almost to the point of submissiveness; he left him absolute power in the internal government of the kingdom and relied on him unquestioningly in all matters concerning negotiations with the Czar; above all, he urged him to press on with the Aland island conference.

And in fact, as soon as Görtz had completed the financial arrangements which necessitated his presence in Stockholm, he left to complete with the Czar's minister the great work which he had begun.

Here are the preliminary conditions of this alliance which was to change the face of Europe and which were found among Görtz's papers after his death.

The Czar, keeping the whole of Livonia and part of Ingria and Karelia for himself, was to return everything else to the King of Sweden; he would ally himself with Charles XII with the aim of restoring Stanislas to the throne of Poland and promised to re-enter that country with eighty thousand Russians to dethrone the same King Augustus on whose behalf he had fought for ten years. He would provide the King of Sweden with the necessary ships to transport ten thousand Swedes to England and thirty thousand to Germany; the united forces of Peter and Charles were to attack the King of England in his dominions of Hanover and above all in Bremen and Verden; the same troops would have served to restore the Duke of Holstein and forced the King of Prussia to accept a treaty which deprived him of part of his spoils. From this time onward, Charles acted as though his victorious troops, reinforced by those of the Czar, had already executed everything that was being planned. He haughtily demanded that the German Emperor should carry out the treaty of Altranstädt. The court of Vienna scarcely deigned to reply to the proposal of a monarch from whom it thought it had nothing more to fear.

The King of Poland did not feel so secure; he saw the storm gathering on all sides. The Polish nobility was in league against him and ever since his restoration he had constantly been obliged either to fight his subjects or to treat with them. The Czar, a mediator who was to be feared, had a hundred galleys near Danzig and eighty thousand men on the Polish frontier. The whole of the North was filled with jealousies and alarms. Flemming, the most mistrustful of men, and the one whom neighboring powers distrusted most, was the first to suspect the plans of the Czar and the King of Sweden in favor of Stanislas. He wanted to have him kidnaped in the duchy of Zweibrücken as Jacob Sobieski had been seized in Silesia. One of those enterprising and restless Frenchmen who go to seek their fortune in foreign lands had recently introduced a small number of partisans, Frenchmen like himself, into the King of Poland's service. He communicated to Flemming a plan for taking thirty resolute French officers, kidnaping Stanislas in his palace, and bringing him back a prisoner to Dresden. The plan was approved. Such enterprises were fairly common in those days. Some of the people who are known in Italy as *braves* had carried out similar exploits in the province of Milan during the war between Germany and France. Even later, a number of Frenchmen who were refugees in Holland had got as far as Versailles with the intention of abducting the Dauphin and had actually seized the first equerry almost under the windows of Louis XIV's palace.

Accordingly, the adventurer disposed his men and his horses to surprise and carry off Stanislas. The enterprise was discovered the day before it was to be carried out. Some of the plotters escaped; others were captured. They could not expect to be treated as prisoners of war, but rather as bandits. Stanislas, instead of punishing them, contented himself with reproaching them in a kindly fashion and even gave them money to pay their expenses, showing, by this generosity, that his rival, Augustus, had good reason to fear him.

Meanwhile, in October, 1718, Charles set off for the second time to conquer Norway. He had made his preparations so thoroughly that he expected to occupy the kingdom in six months. He preferred to go and conquer a rocky country covered with snow and ice, in the bitter depths of winter, which kills animals even in Sweden where it is a little milder, rather than to try to recapture his fair German provinces from his enemies; the reason for this was that he hoped that his new alliance with the Czar would soon place him in a position to recover these provinces; more important, his glory was tempted by the idea of capturing a kingdom belonging to a victorious enemy.

At the mouth of the Tistedal River near the Skagerrak, and between the towns of Bahus and Anslo, lies Fredrikshald, an important fortress town which was considered to be the key to the kingdom. Charles besieged it in December. His soldiers, numbed by cold, could hardly break the ground, which was frozen under the ice; it was like digging trenches in rock, but the Swedes could not object when they had at their head a king who shared their labors. Never had Charles worked harder. His constitution, toughened by eighteen years of hard living, had become so strong that he could sleep in the open in Norway in the middle of winter, on straw or on a plank, and wrapped only in a cloak, without his health suffering. Many of his soldiers dropped dead at their posts; the others, almost frozen, did not dare complain when they saw that their King was suffering as they were. Some time before this expedition he had heard talk of a woman in Skäne called Johns Dotter who had lived on water alone for several months, and as he had spent his life trying to find out how to withstand the most arduous conditions possible for a human being, he wanted to try to see how long he could resist hunger and remain active. He spent five whole days without food or drink. On the morning of the sixth day he rode for two leagues and visited the Prince of Hesse, his brother-in-law. There he had a large meal, and suffered no ill effects either from the five-days fast itself or from following it with a banquet.

With this iron constitution and his bold and inflexible spirit, none of his neighbors could do other than fear him, whatever the state to which he was reduced.

On December 11, St. Andrew's Day, he went to visit the trenches at nine in the evening, and finding that the parallel trench was not so far advanced as he expected, he appeared very dissatisfied. M. Mégret, the French engineer in charge of the siege, assured him that the place would be taken in a week. "We shall see," said the King, and he continued his inspection of the engineer's works. He stopped at a spot where a branch made an angle with the parallel. He knelt on the inner ramp, and resting his elbows on the parapet, remained for some time watching the workmen, who were continuing to dig the trenches by the light of the stars.

The slightest details become important when it is a question of the death of a man like Charles XII; so I must warn the reader that the whole conversation which so many writers have described between the King and the engineer Mégret is completely false. Here are the true facts which I know about this event.

Almost half the King's body was exposed to a battery of cannon which were trained on the angle where he was kneeling. Near him there were only two Frenchmen: one was M. Siquier, his aide-de-camp, a thoughtful but active man who had entered his service in Turkey and was particularly attached to the Prince of Hesse; the other was the engineer. The cannon fired on them with grape-shot, to which the King, because of the position he was occupying, was the most exposed. A few paces behind him was Count Schwerin. Count Posse, captain of the guards, and an aide-de-camp called Kaulbars were receiving his orders. Siquier and Mégret saw the King instantly fall on the parapet with a deep sigh. They ran to him, but he was already dead. A ball weighing half a pound had struck him on the right temple and made a hole in which three fingers could be inserted. His head had fallen on the parapet, his left eye had been driven inward and his right eye was out of its socket. He must have died instantly but he had had the instinctive strength to place his hand on the hilt of his sword, and he remained in that posture. At this sight, Mégret, a curiously indifferent man, merely said, "That's the end of the play; let's go and eat." Siquier ran at once to tell Count Schwerin. Together they decided to hide the fact of Charles's death from his soldiers until the Prince of

Hesse had been told. The body was wrapped in a gray cloak; Siquier put his wig and hat on the King's head; and in this state he was carried, under the name of Captain Carlberg, through the midst of his troops, who little dreamed that it was their dead King who was passing through their ranks.

At once the Prince ordered that no one should leave the camp and placed a guard on all the roads to Sweden in order to have time to take the necessary measures to ensure that his wife should inherit the crown and to exclude the Duke of Holstein, who might lay claim to it.

So, at the age of thirty-six and a half, Charles XII, King of Sweden, met his death, after having experienced the heights of prosperity and the depths of adversity yet without having been softened by the one or even momentarily cast down by the other. Almost all his actions, even those of his private life, were far beyond the realms of probability. He was perhaps the only man, and certainly the only king, who showed no weakness throughout his life; he had all the heroic virtues and he carried them to such extremes that they became almost as dangerous as the opposite vices. His firmness, which became stubbornness, led to his disasters in the Ukraine and kept him five years in Turkey; his liberality, which degenerated into lavishness, ruined Sweden; his courage, which he carried to the point of rashness, caused his death; his justice sometimes became cruelty; and, in the last years of his reign, he enforced his authority by methods which came near to tyranny. His great qualities, any one of which would have sufficed to immortalize another prince, caused the downfall of his country. He never attacked anybody but he was not as prudent as he was implacable in his acts of revenge. He was the first king to have the ambition of being a conqueror without having the desire to enlarge his dominions; he wanted to win empires in order to give them away again. His passion for glory, war and vengeance prevented him from being a great statesman, a quality which every really successful conqueror must have. Before the battle and after the victory he showed nothing but modesty; when he was defeated, nothing but resolution. He was hard toward others as he was toward himself and he thought no more of the labors and lives of his subjects than he did of his own. He was a unique rather than a great man; one to be admired rather than one to be imitated. The story of his life should teach kings how much a peaceful and happy rule is superior to so much glory.

Charles XII was tall and noble in stature; he had a fine forehead, large blue eyes full of kindness, and a well-shaped nose, though the lower part of his face was less attractive and was often disfigured by his way of laughing through scarcely opened lips. He had hardly any beard or hair. He spoke little and often replied only with a short laugh which had become a habit with him. Complete silence was observed at his table. In the inflexibility of his character there was more than a trace of the timidity which is called false modesty. He would never have been able to shine in conversation because he had devoted himself entirely to work and war, and had never mixed in society. Before his years of inactivity in Turkey, he had read nothing other than Caesar's *Commentaries* and the *History of Alexander;* but he had written a number of reflections on war and on his campaigns from 1700 to 1709. He admitted this to the Chevalier Folard and told him that this manuscript had been lost at the battle of Poltava. Some people have suggested that he was a good mathematician; no doubt he had a penetrating mind but the proof of his mathematical knowledge which has been offered is far from convincing; he wanted to change the method of counting in tens, and he proposed in its place the number sixty-four because it contains both a cube and a square and one can go on dividing it by two until one is left with unity. This idea merely proves that he liked the extraordinary and the difficult in all things.

As for his religion, although the beliefs of a monarch should not be allowed to influence those of other men, and although the opinion of a king as uninformed as Charles was cannot be given much weight, yet I must try and satisfy people who are interested in every aspect of this prince, on this matter as on others. I know from the man who gave me the principal memoirs on which this history is based that he was a convinced Lutheran until 1707. Then, in Leipzig, he met the famous philosopher Leibnitz, who thought and spoke freely and who had already communicated this freedom of thought to other princes. I do not believe, as I have been told, that the views of this philosopher led Charles to adopt an attitude of indifference toward Lutheranism, for their conversations lasted only a quarter of an hour. But M. Fabrice, who spent seven years in close contact with him, has told me that owing to his stay in Turkey and his experience of various religions there, his indifference increased. Even La Motraye, in his *Travels,* confirms this idea. The Count of Croissy has the same opinion and has often told me that the only part of his original faith that the King retained was his belief in absolute predestination, a doctrine which favored his courage and justified his rashness. The Czar had similar beliefs about religion and destiny; but he spoke of them more often, for he used to converse freely with his favorites and had both the knowledge of philosophy and the gift of eloquence which Charles lacked.

I cannot refrain from mentioning here a calumny which is all too often renewed at the death of princes; credulous and malicious people always claim that they have been either poisoned or assassinated. A rumor spread in Germany that M. Siquier had himself killed the King of Sweden. This brave officer was for a long time in despair at this slander; one day he said to me, in these very words, "I could have killed the King of Sweden; but my respect for this hero is such that even if I had wanted to do so, I would not have dared."

I know that Siquier himself had given rise to this terrible accusation, which is still believed by some people in Sweden. He admitted to me himself that when he was delirious with fever in Stockholm, he had shouted out that he had killed the King of Sweden; that he had even opened the window and publicly asked pardon for this murder. When he was cured, and learned what he had said during his illness, he nearly died of grief. I did not want to reveal this anecdote while he was still alive. I saw him some time before his death and I can assure the reader that far from having killed Charles XII, he would have died a thousand deaths for him. If he had been guilty of such a crime, it could only have been in order to serve some power which would, no doubt, have rewarded him richly; yet he died in poverty in France and even had to live on the charity of friends. If these reasons are not sufficient, it should also be remembered that the ball which struck Charles XII could not have been fired from a pistol and that the only possible way in which Siquier could have carried out this detestable deed would have been with a pistol hidden under his cloak.

After the King's death the siege of Fredrikshald was raised. In a moment everything was changed: the Swedes, who by this time were more overpowered than flattered by the glory of their monarch, thought only of making peace and of putting an end to the absolute power of which Baron Görtz had made them feel all the excesses. In a free election, the states chose the Princess, Charles XII's sister, as their Queen and obliged her to renounce solemnly any hereditary right to the crown, so that she should only owe it to the wishes of the nation. She promised, in repeated oaths, that she would never try to re-establish arbitrary power. If ever she was jealous of the title of Queen, she later sacrificed this jealousy to conjugal love by ceding the crown to her husband and persuading the states to elect this prince, who mounted the throne on the same conditions as she had done.

Baron Görtz, who was arrested immediately after the death of Charles, was condemned by the Swedish Senate to have his head cut off in front of the town gallows of Stockholm. This was perhaps more an example of vengeance than of justice and was a cruel affront to the memory of a king whom Sweden still admires.

The Age of Louis XIV

CHAPTER I *Introduction*

This work is not intended to be just a life of Louis XIV; it has a more important purpose. Its aim is not merely to describe the actions of a single man, but to provide posterity with an account of the achievements of the human spirit in the most enlightened age there has ever been.

Every age has produced its heroes and its statesmen, every people has experienced revolutions, and all histories are pretty much the same for anyone who only wants to memorize facts. But for men who think and for those even rarer individuals who have good taste, there are only four ages in the history of the world which really count. These four happy ages are those in which the arts were perfected and which, serving as epochs of the greatness of the human spirit, are an example to posterity.

The first of these truly great ages is that of Philip and Alexander, or still more, that of Pericles, Demosthenes, Aristotle, Plato, Apelles, Phidias and Praxiteles. This greatness, moreover, was confined within the limits of Greece at a time when the rest of the known world was still barbarous.

The second age is that of Caesar and Augustus, made still more famous by the names of Lucretius, Cicero, Livy, Vergil, Horace, Ovid, Varro and Vitruvius.

The third age is that which followed the conquest of Constantinople by Mohammed II. It was at that time, as the reader may remember, that Italy witnessed the spectacle of a family of ordinary citizens achieving what should have been undertaken by the kings of Europe. The Medici summoned to Florence the scholars whom the Turks had driven out of Greece. This was the age of Italy's glory. The arts had already taken on a new lease of life there and the Italians honored them with the name of virtue just as the ancient Greeks had given them the name of wisdom.[1] Everything was advancing toward perfection.

The arts, which have always tended to migrate from Greece to Italy, found a favorable soil there and immediately blossomed forth. France, England, Germany and Spain, in their turn, longed to possess their fruits; but either they never reached these latitudes or they degenerated too quickly.

Francis I encouraged scholars, but they tended to be nothing more than scholars; he had architects, but there were no Michelangelos or Palladios among them; he tried in vain to establish schools of painting; the Italian painters he sent for made no French disciples. Our poetry consisted only of a few epigrams and some rather coarse tales. Rabelais was our only popular prose writer at the time of Henry II.[2]

To sum up, the Italians alone had everything, except music, which was still in its infancy, and experimental philosophy, which was unknown everywhere until Galileo finally introduced it to the world.

The fourth age is that which we propose to call the age of Louis XIV, and it is perhaps the one of the four which approaches most nearly to perfection. Enriched by the discoveries of the other three, it has, in certain fields, achieved more than all of them put together. It is true that not all the arts reached greater heights than under

---

[1] Voltaire uses the words "arts" and "beaux-arts" in the widest possible sense, to mean all the products of a fully developed intellect and imagination. In this sense, the word includes the qualities which the Italians designated by *virtú* and the Greeks by *sophia*.

[2] Partly as a result of his own classical prejudices, partly in order to emphasize the greatness of the age of Louis XIV, Voltaire tends to minimize the achievements of the Renaissance in sixteenth-century France, which produced poets of the stature of Ronsard and Du Bellay, and prose writers like Montaigne, to mention only a few.

the Medicis, the Augustuses and the Alexanders, but human reason in general made remarkable progress. Sound philosophy only became known at this time, and it is true to say that, beginning with the last years of Richelieu and ending with those following the death of Louis XIV, there has taken place, in our arts, in our minds, in our manners and in our government, a general revolution which should serve as an eternal monument to the true glory of our country. Moreover, the influence of this welcome change has not been confined to France; it has extended to England and excited there the spirit of emulation which this intelligent and bold nation stood in need of; it has carried good taste into Germany and introduced the sciences into Russia; it has even revived a languishing Italy. Europe is indebted for her culture and her social spirit to the court of Louis XIV.

It would be wrong to believe that these four ages were exempt from misfortunes and crimes. Peaceful citizens may cultivate the arts to perfection, but this does not stop princes from being ambitious, peoples from being seditious and priests and monks from being sometimes turbulent and dishonest. Human wickedness is the same in all ages, but I only know these four which have been distinguished by great talents.

Before the age which I call that of Louis XIV and which begins, approximately, with the establishment of the French Academy,[3] the Italians called all the peoples beyond the Alps barbarians, and one must admit that the French partially deserved this insult. Their forefathers combined the romantic chivalry of the Moors with a Gothic coarseness of manners. They possessed hardly any of the arts which delight the mind, and this proves that the useful arts were neglected, for when a people has provided itself with all that is necessary, it soon turns to what is beautiful and pleasant. It is not surprising that painting, sculpture, poetry, rhetoric and philosophy were almost unknown to the French, when one sees that although they had ports on the Atlantic and the Mediterranean they had no fleet, and that although they had an

[3] Founded by Richelieu in 1635.

excessive love of luxury they only possessed a few primitive manufacturing industries.

The Jews, the Genoese, the Venetians, the Portuguese, the Flemish, the Dutch, the English—each in turn carried on the commerce of France, while France herself remained ignorant of the very principles of commerce. Louis XIII, on his accession to the throne,[4] did not have a single ship; Paris had less than four hundred thousand inhabitants and no more than four fine buildings. The rest of the kingdom was like those country towns you can still see south of the Loire. The nobility were scattered throughout the country like garrisons in their moated castles, and oppressed those who cultivated the land. The highways were almost impassable; the towns were without police; the state without money; and the government almost always without credit among other nations.

It would be wrong to hide the fact that, ever since the decline of the family of Charlemagne, France had been more or less languishing in this same state of weakness, because she had hardly ever enjoyed a good government.

For a state to be powerful, either the people must have liberty founded on laws or the sovereign authority must be accepted without question. In France the people were slaves until about the time of Philip Augustus; the nobility were tyrants until Louis XI; and the kings, constantly occupied in maintaining their authority against their vassals, had neither the time to think of the happiness of their subjects nor the power to make them happy.

Louis XI did a great deal to increase the royal power, but nothing for the happiness or the glory of the nation. Francis I promoted commerce, navigation, literature and all the arts; but his reign was too unhappy for him to succeed in getting them to take root in France, and they all died when he did.[5] Henry the Great was on the point of rescuing France from the calamities and the barbarity

[4] In 1610.

[5] Louis XI (1461-83) was the first of the powerful centralizing kings of modern France. Francis I (1515-47) was a true Renaissance monarch, but his reign was marred by wars and by the

into which thirty years of civil discord had plunged it, when he was assassinated in his capital in the midst of a people whose happiness he was just beginning to achieve.[6] Cardinal Richelieu, occupied in reducing the power of the house of Austria, the Calvinists and the nobility, never enjoyed a period of peaceful power in which to reform the nation; but he did at least begin this worthy task.[7]

So for almost nine hundred years, the genius of the French was almost continuously inhibited by a Gothic government, plagued by divisions and civil wars, lacking fixed laws and customs, and changing, every two hundred years, its perpetually untutored tongue. Its nobility were undisciplined, knowing only war and idleness; its churchmen lived in disorder and ignorance; its peoples, bereft of industry, stagnated in poverty.

The French had no part in the great discoveries and the admirable inventions of other nations. Printing, gunpowder, mirrors, telescopes, proportional compasses, the air pump, the true system of the universe—all these were no property of theirs. They employed themselves in tournaments while the Portuguese and Spaniards were discovering and conquering new worlds to the east and to the west of the known world. The Emperor Charles V had already filled Europe with the treasures of Mexico even before some of Francis I's subjects had discovered the barren country of Canada. But the little the French did achieve at the beginning of the sixteenth century gave some idea of what they are capable of when they are properly led.

We propose to show what they were like under Louis XIV.

One must not expect to find here, any more than in the account of earlier centuries, endless details of wars or of towns captured and recaptured by arms or surrendered

religious discords which led, after his death, to the civil wars of the late sixteenth century.

6 Henry IV (1589-1610), who reunited the country after the civil wars, was always an object of Voltaire's admiration and was the hero of his epic poem *The Henriad*.

7 Richelieu was the all-powerful first minister of Louis XIII from 1624 to 1642.

and restored again by treaties. A thousand circumstances which might have interested contemporaries become of no consequence to posterity and therefore disappear, leaving only the great events which have decided the fate of empires. Not everything that has been done deserves to be written about. In this history we shall be concerned only with what merits the attention of all ages; with what depicts the genius and the customs of men; and with whatever can serve for instruction and recommend the love of virtue, of the arts and of our country.

We have already seen[8] what France and the other states of Europe were like before the birth of Louis XIV; here we shall describe the great political and military events of his reign. The internal government of the kingdom, a much more important object of interest to the public, will be treated separately. The private life of Louis XIV, and details about his court and his reign, will occupy considerable space. Other chapters will be reserved for the arts, the sciences and the progress of the human mind during this period. Lastly we shall speak of the Church, which for so long has been closely linked with the government; which has alternately disturbed and strengthened it; and which frequently gives itself over to politics and to human passions although it was instituted to teach morals.

CHAPTER XXIX

Internal Government/Justice/Commerce/ Police/Laws/Military Discipline/ Marine, Etc.

We owe it to public men who have benefited their age to look at the point from which they started in order better to appreciate the changes they have brought about in their country. Posterity owes them an eternal debt of gratitude for the examples they have given, even when

[8] Voltaire is referring here to his own *Essay on Customs*, which, in some editions, was printed together with *The Age of Louis XIV*.

their achievements have been surpassed, and this well-deserved glory is their only reward. It was certainly the love of this sort of glory that inspired Louis XIV when, as soon as he began to govern for himself, he set out to reform his kingdom, embellish his court and perfect the arts.

Not only did he impose upon himself the duty of working regularly with each one of his ministers, but any man of repute could obtain a private audience with him, and every citizen was free to present him with petitions and projects. The petitions were received, first of all, by a master of requests, who noted his comments in the margin and sent them on to the offices of the ministers. The projects were examined in Council when they deserved it and their authors were more than once admitted to discuss their proposals with the ministers in the King's presence. In this way, despite Louis's absolute power, the nation could still communicate with the monarch.

Louis XIV trained and accustomed himself to work, and this work was all the more difficult because it was new to him and because he could easily be distracted by the lures of pleasure. The first dispatches he sent to his ambassadors he wrote himself, and he later often minuted the most important letters in his own hand. None were written in his name without his having them read to him.

After the fall of Fouquet,[1] Colbert had scarcely re-established order in the finances when the King canceled all the arrears due on taxes from 1647 to 1656 and, above all, three millions of the taille.[2] Five hundred thousand crowns' worth of onerous duties were abolished. So the Abbé de Choisi seems to be either very misinformed or very unjust when he says that the receipts were not decreased. It is clear that they were decreased by these remissions, though they were later increased again as a result of better administration.

[1] Louis XIV's first finance minister, who was disgraced in 1661.

[2] This tax on land or income was paid only by the non-noble class and was one of the most unpopular forms of taxation under the Old Regime.

The efforts of the First President of Bellièvre, helped by the generosity of the Duchess of Aiguillon and several other citizens, had already established the general hospital in Paris. The King enlarged it and had others built in all the principal towns of the kingdom.

The highways, which up till then had been impassable, were no longer neglected and gradually became what they are today under Louis XV—the admiration of all foreigners. Whatever direction one goes from Paris, one can now travel for nearly two hundred miles, except for a few places, on well-surfaced roads lined with trees. The roads built by the ancient Romans were more lasting, but not as spacious or as beautiful.

Colbert directed his genius principally toward commerce, which was still largely undeveloped and whose basic principles were still unknown. The English, and still more the Dutch, carried almost all French trade in their ships. The Dutch in particular loaded their ships with our goods in our ports and distributed them throughout Europe. In 1662 the King began to exempt his subjects from a duty called the freight tax, which all foreign vessels had to pay, and he gave French merchants every facility for transporting their goods themselves more cheaply. It was then that our maritime trade began to develop. The council of commerce, which still exists today, was established, and the King presided over it every fortnight.

The ports of Dunkirk and Marseilles were declared free, and very soon this advantage attracted the trade of the Levant to Marseilles and that of the North to Dunkirk.

A West India company was formed in 1664 and the East India company was established in the same year. Before this, France had had to pay tribute for her luxuries to the industry of the Dutch. The partisans of the old economy, timid, ignorant and constricted, declaimed in vain against a commerce in which there was a continuous exchange of permanent cash for perishable commodities. They failed to realize that these Indian goods, which had become necessities, would have cost even more abroad. It is true that more money is sent to the East Indies than is brought back from them and that, as a result, Europe is impoverishing itself. But this money comes from Peru and Mexico; it is the price paid for the goods we send to Cádiz, and more of this money remains in France than is absorbed by the East Indies.

The King gave more than six millions of our present-day money to the company. The queens, the princes and the whole court provided two millions in the currency of that day. The superior courts gave twelve hundred thousand francs;[3] the financiers, two millions; the company of merchants, six hundred and fifty thousand francs. The whole nation followed the example of its ruler.

This company still exists; for although the Dutch captured Pondichéry in 1694 and trade with India languished from that time onward, it revived under the regency of the Duke of Orleans. Pondichéry then became the rival of Batavia, and this East India Company—founded with extreme difficulty by the great Colbert and revived in our own day by remarkable methods—was for several years one of the great resources of the kingdom. In 1669 the King also created a Northern company, and he placed funds in it as he did in the East India Company. This clearly showed that commerce is no disgrace, for the greatest families, following the monarch's example, interested themselves in these establishments.

The West India company was encouraged no less than the others; the King supplied a tenth of all its funds. He gave thirty francs a ton on exports and forty on imports. All those who had ships built in French ports received five francs for each ton their vessel could carry.

It is amazing to find that the Abbé de Choisi, in his not altogether reliable *Memoirs,* has criticized these new

---

[3] The prerevolutionary words for money can be somewhat confusing, as different terms were used for actual coinage and for money in account. Voltaire sometimes uses *livre* (the term for money in account), and sometimes *franc* (the coin). For simplicity's sake, we have used the word *franc* throughout.

A crown (*écu*) was worth three francs, and a *louis* 24 francs. Mr. Besterman, in his edition of *Voltaire's Correspondence,* suggests that the purchasing power of the franc in the eighteenth century was roughly equal to that of the present-day U.S. dollar.

establishments. Today we realize how much Colbert did for the welfare of the kingdom;[4] but this was not felt at the time; he was working for an ungrateful people. In Paris he was disliked for having suppressed the interest on certain Paris municipal stocks which people had been able to buy for a song ever since 1656, and for the discredit into which the exchequer bills had fallen after their misuse by the preceding minister, much more than he was admired for the general good he was doing. There were more selfish bourgeois than good citizens in the capital, and few people thought in terms of public welfare. We know the extent to which private interests absorb the attention and cramp the mind; this is true not only of the interests of a merchant, but of those of a company or a whole town. One merchant, called Hazon, consulted by the minister, said to him, "You found the carriage overturned on one side and you have overturned it on the other." This remark was still quoted with approval in my youth. Indeed the anecdote is still to be found in Moreri's *Dictionary*. It was not until the philosophic spirit, introduced very late into France, had reformed popular prejudices that full justice was finally done to the memory of this great man. He had the same exactness as the Duke of Sully,[5] but far wider views. The one only knew how to economize, but the other could create great establishments. After the peace of Vervins, Sully's only difficulty was to maintain a rigid and severe economy; whereas Colbert had to find immediate and immense resources for the war of 1667 and that of 1672. Henry IV aided Sully in his plans, but the magnificence of Louis XIV continually ran counter to Colbert's system.

Yet almost everything was either restored or created in his time. The reduction to five per cent of the interest on royal and private loans, which took place in 1665, gives tangible proof of an abundant circulation of money.

---

[4] In fact, Colbert's policies, particularly his rigid controls and his opposition to free-trade in grain, had many critics in the eighteenth century as well as in the seventeenth. Voltaire is one of his most outspoken admirers at this time, and much of this and the following chapter is a lengthy plea on his behalf.

[5] Henry IV's finance minister.

He strove to enrich France and to populate it. He encouraged marriages in country areas by exemptions from the taille for five years for those who set up a household at the age of twenty, and every father of a family of ten was exempted for life because he had given more to the state through the labor of his children than he would have done by paying the taille. This regulation should never have been withdrawn.

From 1663 until 1672, each year of his ministry was marked by the creation of some new industry. The fine cloths which were previously imported from England and Holland were now manufactured in Abbeville. The King advanced the manufacturer two thousand francs for each working loom, not to mention other considerable gratifications. In 1669 there were 44,200 woolen looms in the kingdom. The silk factories were improved and produced a trade of more than fifty millions in the currency of that time; and not only were the profits made far greater than the cost of the necessary silk thread, but the cultivation of mulberry trees allowed the manufacturers to dispense with foreign threads for the weaving of their materials.

In 1666 mirrors as fine as those of Venice, which had always supplied the whole of Europe, began to be made in France; they attained a size and beauty which has never been successfully imitated elsewhere. Turkish and Persian carpets were surpassed by those of the Savonnerie. The tapestries of Flanders were inferior to those of the Gobelins, a vast factory which employed over eight hundred workers, of whom three hundred lived there. The best painters directed the work, either from their own designs or from those of old Italian masters. Within these same precincts there were also produced fine examples of inlaid mosaic work, and the art of marquetry was brought to perfection.

In addition to this fine tapestry factory of Les Gobelins, another was set up at Beauvais. The first manufacturer employed six hundred workmen in the town, and the King made him a present of sixty thousand francs.

Sixteen hundred girls were employed in lacework; thirty key workers were brought from Venice and two hundred from Flanders, and they were given thirty-six thousand francs to encourage them.

The cloth factories of Sedan and the tapestry factories of Aubusson, which had degenerated and fallen into decay, were re-established. The manufacture of rich fabrics in which silk is mingled with gold and silver was revived in Lyons and Tours.

It is well known that the ministry bought from England the secret of that ingenious machine with which stockings are made ten times as quickly as with needles. Tin plate, steel, fine porcelain and Morocco leather, which had always been brought from abroad, were now made in France. But the Calvinists, who possessed the secret of making tin plate and steel, carried it with them into exile in 1686 and imparted it, together with many other advantages, to foreign nations.

Every year the King bought about eight hundred thousand francs' worth of the most tasteful products made in his kingdom, and gave them away as presents.

Paris in those days was very far from being what it is now. There was neither lighting, police protection nor cleanliness. Provision had to be made for the continual cleaning of the streets and for lighting them every night with five thousand lamps; the whole town had to be paved; two new gates had to be built and the old ones restored; a permanent guard, both mounted and on foot, was needed for the security of citizens. All this the King took upon himself, allotting the funds for these necessary expenses. In 1667 he appointed a magistrate whose sole duty was to supervise the police. Most of the large cities of Europe only imitated these examples many years later; none has equaled them. There is no city paved like Paris, and even Rome has no street lighting.

Everything was beginning to improve so noticeably that the second holder of the office of lieutenant of police in Paris acquired a reputation which placed him among the distinguished men of his age; and indeed he was a man of great ability. He was afterward in the Ministry and he would have made a fine general. The post of lieutenant of police was below his birth and merit, and yet it gained him a much greater reputation than did the uneasy and transient ministerial office which he obtained toward the end of his life.[6]

It is worth noting here that M. d'Argenson was not the only member of the old nobility to hold the office of magistrate. Far from it; France is almost the only country in which the old nobility has often worn magisterial robes. Almost all other states, from motives which are a remnant of Gothic barbarity, fail to realize that there is greatness in this profession.[7]

From 1661 onward, the King was continually occupied in building the Louvre, Saint-Germain and Versailles. Private individuals, following his example, built hundreds of superb, spacious buildings in Paris. Their number increased to such an extent that there sprang up around the Palais-Royal and Saint-Sulpice two new towns vastly superior to the old one. This same time saw the invention of that splendid convenience the coach ornamented with mirrors and suspended on springs; thus a citizen of Paris could travel about this great city in far greater luxury than that in which the ancient Romans rode in triumph to the Capitol. This custom, which began in Paris, soon spread to the rest of Europe and has become so common that it is no longer a luxury.

Louis XIV had a taste for architecture, gardens and sculpture, and his taste was characterized by a liking for grandeur and impressiveness. In 1664, Controller General Colbert assumed the office of director of buildings (which is really the Ministry of the Arts), and no sooner had he done so than he set about furthering his master's schemes. The first task was to complete the Louvre. François Mansart, one of the greatest architects France has ever had, was chosen to construct the vast buildings that were planned. He was unwilling to undertake this commission unless he had freedom to reconstruct any

---

[6] In this praise of d'Argenson, Voltaire is perhaps indulging in a little flattery of the father of two men who were, to some extent, his friends and protectors: the Marquis d'Argenson, who became foreign minister, and his brother, the Count.

[7] The nobility who had obtained their titles through administrative or legal office (nobility of the robe) were looked down on by the old, military nobility (nobility of the sword).

parts of the edifice which seemed to him defective when he had completed them, and this mistrust of himself, which might have involved too great an expenditure, led to his exclusion. The chevalier Bernini was then sent for from Rome, a man whose name was famous by virtue of the colonnade surrounding St. Peter's Square, the equestrian statue of Constantine and the Navonna fountain. Carriages were provided for his journey. He was brought to Paris like a man who came to honor France. Apart from five louis a day during the eight months he stayed, he also received a present of fifty thousand crowns, together with a pension of two thousand, and one of five hundred for his son. Louis XIV's generosity to Bernini was even greater than that of Francis I to Raphael. By way of acknowledgment, Bernini later made, in Rome, the equestrian statue of the King which is now to be seen at Versailles. But when he arrived in Paris with so much circumstance, he was amazed to see the plan of the façade of the Louvre which faces Saint-Germain-l'Auxerrois, and which soon after, when executed, became one of the most august monuments of architecture in the world. Claude Perrault had made this plan, and it was put into execution by Louis Levau and Dorbay. Perrault invented the machines by which were transported the stones, fifty-two feet long, that formed the pediment of this majestic edifice. Sometimes people go a long way to find what they already have at home. No palace in Rome has an entrance comparable to that of the Louvre, for which we are indebted to the Perrault whom Boileau dared to ridicule. Travelers admit that the famous Italian villas are inferior to the château of Maisons, which was built at such a small cost by François Mansart. Bernini was magnificently rewarded and did not deserve his rewards; he merely furnished plans which were never put into execution.

While building the Louvre, the completion of which is so greatly to be desired, while creating a town at Versailles near the Château which has cost so many millions, while building the Trianon and Marly and embellishing many other edifices, the King also built the Observatory, which was begun in 1666, at the same time as he founded the Academy of Sciences. But his most glorious monument, by its usefulness and its greatness as much as by the difficulties of its construction, was the canal which joins the two seas and which finds an outlet at the port of Sète, built especially for the purpose. All this work was begun in 1664 and continued without interruption until 1681. The foundation of the Invalides, with its chapel, the finest in Paris, and the establishment of Saint-Cyr, the last of many works built by the King—these by themselves would suffice to make his memory revered. Four thousand soldiers and a large number of officers find consolation in their old age and relief for their wounds and wants in the first of these great institutions; two hundred and fifty daughters of noblemen receive an education worthy of them in the other; together they are like so many voices praising Louis XIV. The establishment of Saint-Cyr will be surpassed by the one which Louis XV has just created for the education of five hundred noblemen; but so far from causing Saint-Cyr to be forgotten, it serves to remind one of it; the art of doing good has been brought to perfection.

At the same time, Louis XIV wanted to achieve something even greater and more generally useful, though more difficult; he wanted to reform the laws. For this task he employed the Chancellor Seguier, Lamoignon, Talon, Bignon, and above all, the councilor of state, Pussort. Sometimes he attended their meetings himself. The year 1667 was marked both by his first laws and by his first conquests. The civil ordinance appeared first and was followed by the code for the rivers and forests, and then by statutes concerning all the industries, by a criminal code, one for commerce and one for the marine. These followed one another in an almost annual succession. New laws were even established in favor of the Negroes of our colonies, a race of men who had hitherto not enjoyed the common rights of humanity.

One cannot expect a sovereign to possess a profound knowledge of jurisprudence, but the King was well informed about the principal laws; he was imbued with their spirit and knew how to enforce or mitigate them as the occasion demanded. He often judged his subjects' cases, not only in the Council of the Secretaries of State, but also in the so-called Council of Parties. There are two celebrated judgments of his in which he decided against his own interest.

In the first, in 1680, the issue was one between himself and some private citizens of Paris who had built on his land. He decided that they should keep the houses, together with the land which belonged to him and which he ceded to them.

The other case concerned a Persian called Roupli, whose goods had been seized by his revenue commissioners in 1687. His decision was that all should be returned to him, and the King added a present of three thousand crowns. Roupli returned to his country full of admiration and gratitude. When we later met Mehemet Rizabeg, the Persian ambassador to Paris, we found that he had known about this incident for a long time, for it had become famous.

The abolition of dueling was one of the greatest services he rendered to his country. These combats had sometimes been authorized by the kings and even by the parlements and the Church, and although they had been forbidden since the time of Henry IV, this baneful custom persisted and grew stronger than ever. The famous combat of the La Frettes, with four participants on each side, which took place in 1663, finally determined Louis XIV to condone such activities no longer. His severity proved beneficial, for it gradually reformed our nation; even foreign nations came to conform to our wise customs after having adopted our bad ones. There are a hundred times fewer duels in Europe today than in the time of Louis XIII.

He was the legislator of his armies as well as of his people as a whole. It is surprising that, before his time, there was no uniform dress among the troops. It was he who, in the first year of his administration, ordered that each regiment should be distinguished by the color of its dress or by different badges; this regulation was soon adopted by all other nations. It was he who instituted brigadiers and who put the household troops on their present footing. He turned Cardinal Mazarin's guards into a company of musketeers and fixed the number of men in the companies at five hundred; moreover, he gave them the uniform which they still wear today.

Under him there were no longer constables, and after the death of the Duke of Epernon, no more colonel generals of infantry; they had become too powerful, and he quite rightly wanted to be sole master. Marshal Grammont, who was only colonel of horse of the French Guards under the Duke of Epernon and who took his orders from this colonel general, now took them only from the King, and was the first to be given the title of Colonel of the Guards. The King himself installed his colonels at the head of their regiments, giving them with his own hand a gilt gorget with a pike, and afterward, when the use of pikes was abolished, a spontoon, or kind of half-pike. In the King's Regiment, which he created himself, he instituted grenadiers, on the scale of four to a company in the first place; then he formed a company of grenadiers in each regiment of infantry. He gave two to the French Guards. Nowadays there is one for each battalion throughout the whole infantry. He greatly enlarged the Corps of Dragoons, and gave them a colonel general. The establishment of studs for breeding horses, in 1667, must not be forgotten, for they had been completely abandoned beforehand and they were of great value in providing mounts for the cavalry, an important resource which has since been too much neglected.

It was he who instituted the use of the bayonet affixed to the end of the musket. Before his time, it was used occasionally, but only a few companies fought with this weapon. There was no uniform practice and no drill; everything was left to the general's discretion. Pikes were then thought of as the most redoubtable weapon. The first regiment to have bayonets and to be trained to use them was that of the Fusiliers, established in 1671.

The manner in which artillery is used today is due entirely to him. He founded artillery schools, first at Douai, then at Metz and Strasbourg; and the Regiment of Artillery was finally staffed with officers who were almost all capable of successfully conducting a siege. All the magazines in the kingdom were well stocked, and they were supplied annually with eight hundred thousand pounds of powder. He created a regiment of bombardiers and one of hussars; before this only his enemies had had hussars.

In 1688 he established thirty regiments of militia, which were provided and equipped by the communes. These militia trained for war but without abandoning the cultivation of their fields.

Companies of cadets were maintained in the majority of frontier towns; there they learned mathematics, drawing and all the drills, and carried out the duties of soldiers. This institution lasted for ten years, but the government finally tired of trying to discipline these difficult young people. The Corps of Engineers, on the other hand, which the King created and to which he gave its present regulations, is an institution which will last forever. During his reign the art of fortifying strongholds was brought to perfection by Marshal Vauban and his pupils, who surpassed Count Pagan. He built or repaired a hundred and fifty fortresses.

To maintain military discipline, the King created inspectors general and later directors, who reported on the state of the troops; from their reports it could be seen whether the war commissioners had carried out their duties.

He instituted the Order of Saint-Louis, an honorable distinction which was often more sought after than wealth. The Hôtel des Invalides put the seal on his efforts to merit loyal service.

It was owing to measures such as these that he had, by 1672, a hundred and eighty thousand regular troops, and that, increasing his forces as the number and strength of his enemies increased, he finished with four hundred and fifty thousand men under arms, including the troops of the navy.

Before his time such powerful armies were unknown. His enemies could scarcely muster comparable forces, and to do so they had to be united. He showed what France, on her own, was capable of, and he always had either great successes or great resources to fall back on.

He was the first to institute full-scale warlike maneuvers in peacetime. In 1698 he assembled seventy thousand men at Compiègne and made them carry out all the operations of a campaign. He did this for the instruction of his three grandsons, but the ostentatious luxury of the occasion turned this military school into an occasion for sumptuous festivities.

The care which he took to form powerful and well-disciplined land armies even before he went to war was also seen in his efforts to secure command of the seas. In the first place, the few vessels which Cardinal Mazarin had allowed to rot in the ports were repaired. New ones were brought from Holland and Sweden, and in the third year of his personal reign, he sent his naval forces to try out their strength at Gigeri, on the African coast. The Duke of Beaufort cleared the sea of pirates by 1665, and two years later France had sixty ships of war in her ports. This was only a beginning; but while new regulations and new efforts were being made, Louis was already beginning to feel his strength. He refused to allow his ships to strike their flag to that of England. The Council of King Charles II insisted in vain on this right, which their strength, their industry and the passage of time had given to the English. Louis XIV wrote to the Count of Estrades, his ambassador: "The King of England and his chancellor can see what my forces are, but they cannot see into my heart; I set everything at nought in comparison with my honor."

He said no more than he was resolved to maintain, and in fact, the usurpation of the English gave way before natural right and the firmness of Louis XIV. The two nations came to treat each other on equal terms at sea. But while he was establishing his equality with the English, Louis was asserting his superiority over Spain. He forced the Spanish admirals to strike their flag before his, in virtue of the precedence which had been solemnly conceded in 1662.

Meanwhile, work was in progress on every side toward the establishment of a navy capable of justifying these arrogant sentiments. The town and port of Rochefort were built at the mouth of the Charente. Sailors were enrolled and conscripted to serve both on merchant ships and in the Royal Navy. There were soon sixty thousand of them registered.

Naval construction councils were established in the ports so that ships should be built in the best possible way. Five naval arsenals were built at Brest, Rochefort, Toulon, Dunkirk and Le Havre. In 1672 there were sixty ships of the line and forty frigates. In 1681 there were a hundred and ninety-eight ships of war, including tenders, and there were thirty galleys in the port of Toulon, either armed or on the point of being so. Eleven thousand regular troops served on the ships and there were a further three thousand for the galleys. There were a hundred and sixty-six thousand men enrolled for all the various naval services. In subsequent years a thousand noblemen or men of good family were to be found in this service, acting as soldiers on the ships and learning the arts of navigation and maneuver on shore; these were the marine guards, and their role at sea was comparable to that of cadets in the land forces. They had been instituted in 1672, but in small numbers. This body was the school from which the best ships' officers came.

Up to this time there had never been marshals of France in the navy, a fact which indicated the extent to which this essential part of the armed forces of the country had been neglected. Jean d'Estrées was created the first marshal in 1681. It seems clear that one of Louis XIV's main preoccupations was to inspire, in every field, that spirit of emulation without which all enterprise languishes.

In all the naval battles which the French fleets fought, the advantage was with them until the battle of La Hogue in 1692, when the Count of Tourville, carrying out orders received from the court, attacked a fleet of ninety English and Dutch ships with forty-four of his own. Numbers won the day, and fourteen ships of the first class were lost; having run aground, they were burned in order to prevent their falling into the enemy's hands. Despite this defeat, the naval forces still held their own, but their strength declined during the War of Spanish Succession. Cardinal Fleury subsequently neglected them, during the leisure of a prosperous peace which ought to have offered a favorable opportunity for re-establishing them.

These naval forces served to protect trade. The colonies of Martinique, Santo Domingo and Canada, which had formerly languished, now flourished to a hitherto unexpected extent, for from 1655 to 1665 they had always been a burden to the state.

In 1664 the King established a colony in Cayenne, and soon after that another one in Madagascar. He did everything in his power to make amends for the mistakes and misfortunes from which France had so long suffered as a result of her neglecting the sea while her neighbors had created empires for themselves at the ends of the earth.

This short account is enough to illustrate the changes which Louis XIV brought about in the state; and that they were useful changes is shown by the fact that they still exist. His ministers vied with each other in furthering his plans. They were responsible for all the details and for the actual execution, but the over-all plan was his. Of one thing one can be certain: the magistrates would not have reformed the laws; order would not have been restored in the finances; discipline would not have been introduced into the armies and into the general policing of the kingdom; there would have been no fleets; the arts would not have been encouraged; and all this would not have been achieved in such an organized and determined fashion at one single time (though under different ministers) if there had not been at the head of affairs a master who conceived in general terms all these great aims, and had the will power to accomplish them.

He never separated his own glory from the well-being of France, and he never looked on his kingdom in the same light as á lord looks on the lands from which he extracts all he can in order to live a life of luxury. Every king who loves glory loves the public welfare; Colbert and Louvois were no longer there when, in 1698, he ordered each intendant[8] to produce a detailed description of his province for the instruction of the Duke of Burgundy. In this way it was possible to have an exact account of his kingdom and an accurate census of his peoples. This was a most useful achievement, although not every intendant had the capacity or the attention to detail of M. de Lamoignon de Bâville. If the King's intentions had been carried out as thoroughly in every other province as they were by this magistrate in his census of Languedoc, this collection of reports would have been one of the finest monuments of the age. Several others were well done; but a general plan was lacking, insofar as the intendants did not all receive the same instructions. What would have been most desirable was for each intendant to give, in columns, an account of the number of inhabitants of each district—nobles, citizens, farm workers, artisans and workmen—together with livestock of all kinds, lands of various degrees of fertility, the whole of the regular and secular clergy, their revenues, those of the towns and those of the communes.

In most of the reports returned, these aims are confused; some subjects are dealt with superficially and inaccurately, and it is often quite difficult to find the information one is looking for and which should be immediately available to a minister wanting to discover, at a glance, the forces, needs and resources of the community. The plan was an excellent one, and it would be most useful if someday it is executed in a uniform manner.

This, then, in general terms, is what Louis XIV did or tried to do to make his country more flourishing. It seems to me hardly possible to consider all this work and all these efforts without a feeling of gratitude and without being filled with the concern for the welfare of the people which inspired them. Consider what the country was like at the time of the *Fronde*[9] and what it is like

[8] The intendants were officers of the central government in the provinces.

[9] The revolt against the authority of Cardinal Mazarin during the minority of Louis XIV.

today. Louis XIV did more for his people than twenty of his predecessors put together; and even then he did not do everything he might have done. The war which ended with the Peace of Rijswijk[10] began the ruin of the flourishing commerce established by his minister Colbert, and the War of Spanish Succession completed it.

He spent immense sums on the aqueducts and works of Maintenon and on conveying water to Versailles, and both these projects were abandoned and thereby rendered useless. If he had spent this money, or a fifth part of what it cost to force nature at Versailles, on embellishing his capital, Paris today would be, throughout its whole extent, as beautiful as is the area around the Tuileries and the Pont-Royal, and would have become the most magnificent city in the universe.

It is a great achievement to have reformed the laws, but legal chicanery could not be abolished by legislation. The government tried to make justice uniform, and it has become so in criminal matters and in those of commerce and procedure; it could become so in the laws regulating the fortunes of individual citizens. It is most inconvenient that the same tribunal often has to give judgment on the basis of a hundred different customs. Certain land rights, which are either equivocal, onerous or harmful to society, still exist like remnants of a feudal government which no longer survives; they are the rubbish from a ruined Gothic building.

We are not claiming that the different orders in the state should all be subjected to the same laws. It will be realized that the customs of the nobility, the clergy, the magistracy and the peasantry must be different. But there is no doubt that it is desirable that each order should have its own law, which should be uniform throughout the kingdom, and that what is just or true in Champagne should not be considered false or unjust in Normandy. In every branch of administration, uniformity is a virtue; but the difficulties of achieving it have deterred people from the attempt.

Louis XIV could much more easily have done without

[10] Louis XIV's first major war against much of the rest of Europe, which ended in 1697.

the dangerous assistance of tax-farmers, to whom he was forced to have recourse because he almost always anticipated on his revenues, as will be seen in the chapter on finances.

If he had not believed that his will was sufficient to make a million men change their religion, France would not have lost so many citizens. Yet despite these upsets and losses, the country is still one of the most prosperous in the world, because all the good which Louis did remains and the evil which it was difficult to avoid doing in those stormy times has been repaired. In the final analysis it is posterity which judges kings and of whose judgment they must always be mindful; and when it comes to weigh up the virtues and weaknesses of Louis XIV, posterity will admit that, although he received too much praise during his lifetime, he deserves the praise of all future ages and was worthy of the statue which was erected to him at Montpellier, with a Latin inscription the sense of which is "To Louis the Great after his death." Don Ustariz, a statesman who has written on the finances and commerce of Spain, calls Louis XIV "an astounding man."

All these changes in government and in all the orders of society, which we have just examined, necessarily produced a vast change in our manners. The spirit of faction, intemperance and rebellion which had possessed the citizens of France ever since the time of Francis II[11] gave place to a desire to excel in serving the King. The lords of large estates no longer remained quartered at home; the governors of provinces no longer had important posts to bestow; and as a result, the sovereign's favors were the only ones people strove to deserve; in this way, the state acquired a sort of geometrical unity, with each line leading to the center.

These developments delivered the court from the factions and conspiracies which had troubled it for so many years. Under Louis XIV's administration there was only one plot, which took place in 1674 and was contrived by La Truaumont, a Norman nobleman sunk in

[11] 1559-60.

debt and debauchery and supported by a member of the Rohan family, a master of hounds of France, who had a great deal of courage and very little prudence. The haughtiness and harshness of the Marquis de Louvois had so enraged him that, on leaving an audience with him, he went straight to M. de Caumartin's house, still beside himself with passion. He flung himself down on a couch and said, "Either this———Louvois dies or I do." Caumartin took this threat to be merely a passing outburst of anger; but the next day, when this same young man asked him if he thought the people of Normandy were loyal to the government, he began to suspect some dangerous design. "The days of the *Fronde* are over," he said. "Believe me, you will ruin yourself and be regretted by nobody." The chevalier did not believe him, and rashly flung himself into La Truaumont's conspiracy. The only other man to join the plot was a certain Chevalier de Préaux, La Truaumont's nephew, who was led astray by his uncle, and who, in turn, won over his mistress, the Marquise de Villiers. They could not expect or even hope to gain considerable support in the country; they merely intended to sell and hand over Quillebeuf to the Dutch, thus giving the enemy a foothold in Normandy. This was a badly planned act of cowardly treachery rather than a conspiracy. The execution of all the guilty parties was the only result of this stupid and useless crime, which is hardly remembered today.

If there were a few seditious outbreaks in the provinces, they were nothing more than feeble popular risings and were easily suppressed. Even the Huguenots remained perfectly peaceful until the time when their churches were destroyed. In short, the King succeeded in turning a previously turbulent nation into a peaceful people which was dangerous only to its enemies after having, for over a hundred years, been dangerous to itself. Their manners became more civilized without any lessening of their courage.

The houses which all the nobility built or bought in Paris, and their wives, who lived there with fitting dignity, formed schools of politeness which gradually drew the young people from the tavern life which was still the fashion and which only encouraged reckless debauchery. Manners depend on such little things that the custom of riding on horseback in Paris created a disposition toward frequent quarreling, which came to an end only when this usage was abolished. Decorum, for which we were mainly indebted to the ladies who gathered society together in their houses, made people pleasanter, and reading, in the long run, made them wiser. Acts of treachery and great crimes of the sort which are not dishonorable in times of faction and strife became almost unknown. The villainies of the Brinvilliers and the Voisins[12] were only passing storms in an otherwise clear sky; and it would be as unreasonable to condemn a nation on the basis of the striking crimes of a few individuals as it would be to canonize it for the reform of the abbey of La Trappe.[13]

Every station in life had hitherto been recognizable by the faults which characterized it. The soldiers and the young people who intended to enter the military profession had been noted for their hotheadedness; the lawyers, for a repellent gravity to which their habit of always wearing their robes, even at court, contributed. The same was true of the universities and of the doctors. Merchants still wore their short robes when they assembled or when they visited the ministers, and the greatest among them were still uncouth. But the houses, the theatres and the public walks where people began to gather to enjoy a more civilized life gradually led all the citizens to adopt more or less the same outward appearance. Even the courtesy one now receives from shopkeepers makes one aware of the extent to which politeness has gained ground in all ranks of society. With the passage of time, the provinces too have felt the effects of these improvements.

Luxury has now become something associated only with good taste and convenience. The crowds of pages and liveried servants have disappeared, and there is more

---

[12] The Marquise de Brinvilliers and La Voisin were two notorious seventeenth-century women poisoners.

[13] This monastic order, famous for its extreme austerity, had been reformed by its abbot, Rancé, about 1664.

comfort in the interior of homes. Vain pomp and pageantry have been left to those nations who only know how to show off in public and are ignorant of the real art of living.

The extreme ease which has been introduced into social intercourse, affability, simplicity and the culture of the mind have turned Paris into a town which is probably far superior, as regards civilized living, to Rome and Athens in the days of their splendor.

The many kinds of help so promptly and willingly given for all the sciences and the arts, and for every taste and every need; the combination of so many solid advantages with so many agreeable things, to which may be added the openness peculiar to Parisians—all this leads a large number of foreigners to visit or reside in this homeland of sociability. If natives occasionally leave it, they are usually those who are called elsewhere by their talents and who continue to honor their motherland, or else they are the dregs of the nation, who try to profit from the consideration it inspires; sometimes, however, they are emigrants who still prefer their religion to their country and who go elsewhere to find poverty or wealth, following the example of their fathers, who were driven from France by the fatal injury done to the memory of the great Henry IV when his Edict of Nantes, which should have lasted forever, was repealed; or, finally, they may be officials discontented with their minister, or accused men who have escaped from the rigors of a law which is sometimes badly administered; this, after all, happens in every country in the world.

People have complained that the court no longer has the same proud dignity as in former times. And, indeed, there are no longer any petty tyrants as in the days of the *Fronde,* under Louis XIII and in previous ages. But vast numbers of the nobility enjoy true greatness again after having been so long forced to serve subjects who had grown too powerful. Today one finds noblemen and citizens who would formerly have considered themselves honored to be the servants of these lords becoming their equals and very often their superiors in military service;

and the more merit of every kind prevails over titles, the more flourishing the state becomes.

The age of Louis XIV has been compared to that of Augustus. It is not that they are comparable in power, or in the lives of individuals. Rome and Augustus were ten times as powerful in the world as Louis XIV and Paris, but one must remember that Athens was the equal of the Roman empire in all those things which did not derive their value from force and power. And one must consider too that, though there is nothing in the world today like ancient Rome, and no one like Augustus, yet Europe as a whole is vastly superior to the entire Roman empire. In Augustus' day there was only one nation; today there are several which are civilized, valiant and enlightened, and which possess arts unknown to the Greeks and Romans; and among all these nations, there is not one which has been more distinguished in every field, for nearly a century, than the nations which Louis XIV did so much to form.

CHAPTER XXX

Finance and Administration

If Colbert's administration is compared with all those that preceded it, then posterity will admire this man whose body a senseless populace wanted to tear to pieces after his death. Frenchmen certainly owe him their industry and their commerce, and consequently that wealth whose springs are sometimes diminished by war, only to flow abundantly again in time of peace. Yet in 1702 people were still ungrateful enough to blame Colbert for the languor which was beginning to be felt in all the sinews of the state. A certain Bois-Guillebert, a lieutenant general in the district of Rouen, printed at that time his *Description of France,* a work in two small volumes, in which he claimed that everything had degenerated since 1660. The exact opposite was actually the case. France had never been so flourishing as it was between the death of Cardinal Mazarin and the war of 1689; and even during this war, the body of the state, though showing signs of illness, remained basically sound because of the vigor which Colbert had infused into all its limbs. The author of the *Description* claimed that since 1660 the value of landed property in the kingdom had declined by fifteen hundred million. Nothing could be both falser or more improbable. And yet these captious arguments persuaded those who wanted to be persuaded that this ridiculous paradox was true. In the same way in England when things are at their most prosperous, one finds a hundred pamphlets published proving that the state is ruined.

It was easier in France than elsewhere to discredit the finance minister in the public mind. This ministry is always the most hated because taxes are always hated; besides, there was generally as much prejudice and ignorance to be found in financial administration as there was philosophy.

Greater knowledge came so late that even in 1718, in our times, we have heard the Parlement telling the Duke of Orleans that "the intrinsic value of the silver mark is twenty-five francs" as if it could have any real intrinsic value other than that of weight and standard. Moreover, the Duke of Orleans, enlightened though he was, was not sufficiently well-informed to be able to point out their error to the Parlement.

Colbert, when he took control of finance, showed both knowledge and genius. He began, as the Duke of Sully had done, by putting a stop to the abuses and peculations, which had been enormous. Methods of collection were simplified as far as possible, and by economies which were little short of miraculous, he increased the King's revenue while diminishing the taille. The memorable edict of 1664 shows that about a million of the money of that time was earmarked every year for the encouragement of manufactures and of maritime trade. He was so far from neglecting agriculture, which up till then had been abandoned to the rapacity of the tax-farmers, that when in 1667 some English merchants approached M. Colbert de Croissi, his brother, who was ambassador at London, offering to provide Irish cattle for France and salted meat for the colonies, the controller general replied that for the last four years they had been able to export these themselves.

To achieve such a successful administration, a special court of justice and a number of major reforms had been necessary. Colbert was obliged to withdraw over eight millions of Paris municipal stocks, which had been bought at a very low price and were reimbursed at the rate of purchase. These various changes demanded special edicts. Since the days of Francis I, the Parlement had had the right of examining and registering such edicts.[1] It was proposed simply to have them registered by the Court of Exchequer, but the ancient usage prevailed. So, in 1664, the King went in person to the Parlement to see that his edicts were recorded.

He still remembered the *Fronde,* the decree of proscription passed against a cardinal, his prime minister, and other decrees by which the parlement had seized the royal funds and pillaged the property and money of citizens attached to the Crown. All these excesses had begun with remonstrances against edicts concerning the revenues of the state, and in 1667 he ordered that Parlement should make no remonstrances except within eight days, and then only after having obediently registered the edicts. This edict was itself renewed in 1675. As a result, throughout the whole course of his administration, he never received a single remonstrance from any court of justice, except in the fateful year 1709, when the Parlement of Paris pointed out in vain the harm that the finance minister was doing to the state by varying the price of gold and silver.

Most citizens considered that if the Parlement had always limited itself to making well-informed submissions to the King about the difficulties and needs of the peo-

---

[1] There were thirteen parlements in France. That of Paris was the most important and had the right of registering and making representations about royal edicts. The parlements were legal tribunals, composed of lawyers who had usually bought their offices, and unlike the English Parliament, were neither legislative nor elected bodies. Nevertheless, they claimed to represent the nation, and except under a strong king like Louis XIV, wielded considerable power. Voltaire was hostile to the parlements particularly because, in his own day, they were responsible for judicial barbarities such as the execution of Jean Calas.

ple, the dangers of taxation and the even greater perils of the sale of these taxes to tax-farmers who deceived the King and oppressed the people, then this custom of making remonstrances would have been a venerated institution of the state, a curb on the greed of the financiers and a continual lesson to the ministers. But the strange abuses of what might have been so valuable a remedy had so irritated Louis XIV that he saw only the abuses and refused the remedy. The indignation which he always felt in his heart was carried so far that on August 13, 1669, he went in person to the Parlement to revoke the privileges of nobility which he had granted in his minority, in 1644, to all the higher courts.

However, in spite of this edict, which was registered in the King's presence, the custom has continued of allowing all those whose fathers have spent twenty years exercising a judicial function in a higher court or had died in office to enjoy the privileges of nobility.

While thus humbling a body of magistrates, the King strove to encourage the nobility who defend their country and the farm workers who feed it. Already, by his edict of 1666, he had granted a pension of two thousand francs, which would be worth about four thousand today, to any nobleman who had twelve children, and a thousand to any who had ten. Half this sum was granted, on similar conditions, to all citizens exempt from the taille, and among those normally subject to it, any father of ten children was freed from all taxation.

It is true that Colbert did not do all he could have done, and still less all he wanted to do. In those days, men were not sufficiently enlightened, and in a great kingdom there are always great abuses. The arbitrary taille, the multiplicity of taxes, the customs duties between one province and the next which make one part of France foreign and even hostile to another, the inequality in weights and measures from one town to the next—these and many other diseases of the body politic could not be cured.

The greatest fault of which Colbert is accused is that of not having dared to encourage the export of grain. For a long time none had gone abroad. Agriculture had been neglected during the stormy years of Richelieu's ministry, and it was even more neglected during the civil wars of the *Fronde*. A famine in 1661 made the ruin of the farming areas complete, though nature, aided by hard work, can always bring about a recovery from this type of ruin. In this unhappy year, the Parlement of Paris issued an edict which, though it seemed just in principle, was almost as disastrous in its consequences as all the edicts the Parlement had been made to issue during the civil war. Merchants were forbidden, under the gravest penalties, to form any trade association, and individuals were forbidden to hoard grain. This was a good thing during a passing period of shortage, but it became pernicious in the long run and had a depressive effect on all agriculture. To revoke such a decree, in a time of crisis and prejudice, would have been to invite popular revolts.

The minister had no alternative but to buy back at a high price, from foreigners, the very grain which the French had earlier sold them in the years of plenty. The people were fed, but the cost to the state was heavy. Fortunately the order which Colbert had already restored in financial matters made the losses slight.

Fear of renewed shortages closed our ports to the export of grain. Even worse, every intendant considered it his duty to oppose the transport of grain from his own province to neighboring ones. In good years they could sell their grains only by making a special request to the King's Council. These disastrous regulations seemed justified by past experience. The Council as a whole was afraid that free trade in grain would later force it to spend large sums by buying back, from other nations, a vital commodity which, owing to the selfishness and improvidence of the farmers, had been sold ridiculously cheaply.

As a result, the farmer, who was more timid than the Council, became afraid that he would ruin himself by producing a commodity from which he could not expect much profit, and lands were not cultivated as well as they should have been. The fact that all the other branches of the administration were in a flourishing state prevented Colbert from remedying the fault in this most important field.

This is the only blot on his ministry. It is an important one, but what excuses it and proves how difficult it is to destroy prejudices in the French administration, how difficult it is to do good, is the fact that this fault, which was realized by all thoughtful citizens, was not remedied by any minister for a hundred years until the memorable date 1774, when a more enlightened controller general rescued France from profound distress by freeing the grain trade, except for a few restrictions similar to those to be found in England.

In order to pay for the King's wars, buildings and pleasures, Colbert found in 1672 that he had to re-establish taxes which he had hoped to abolish forever: those on contracts, on annuities, on new offices and on increases in wages. In short, he had to take measures which strengthen the state for a while, but which burden it for centuries.

He had to take measures he never intended. For all the surviving instructions which he himself wrote show that he was convinced that the wealth of a country consists only in the number of its inhabitants, the cultivation of its lands, its industry and its commerce. They show too that a king who owns little personal property and is only the administrator of that of his subjects can only be truly rich through taxes which are easily collected and equitably distributed.

He was so afraid of abandoning the state to the tax-farmers that some time after the dissolution of the Court of Justice which he had had set up to deal with them, he persuaded the Council to issue an edict establishing the death penalty for anyone found advancing money on the new taxes. By this threatening edict, which was never printed, he hoped to inhibit the cupidity of the financiers. But soon after, he had to make use of them, even without revoking the edict; the King was impatient and prompt measures had to be found.

The farming of taxes had been introduced from Italy into France by Catherine de Médicis, and had so corrupted government by its pernicious facility that after the practice had been suppressed during the glorious years of Henry IV's reign, it reappeared throughout that of Louis XIII, and infected, above all, the last years of Louis XIV.

The real difference between Sully and Colbert is that the former enriched the state by wise economy, helped by a king who was as parsimonious as he was valiant, who was a soldier at the head of his armies and a father to his people. Colbert, on the other hand, sustained the state in spite of the luxury of an extravagant monarch who spared no expense to increase the splendor of his reign.

We know that after Colbert's death, when the King proposed to put Le Pelletier in charge of finances, Le Tellier said to him, "Sire, he is not fitted for this post." "Why?" asked the King. "He is not hardhearted enough," said Le Tellier. "But, really," said the King, "I don't want my people treated harshly." The new minister was, in fact, both goodhearted and just, but when in 1688 war broke out again and it became necessary to withstand the attacks of the League of Augsburg (that is, almost the whole of Europe), he found himself saddled with a burden which had been too heavy for Colbert. In these circumstances, the easy but unfortunate expedient of borrowing and creating new loans was his first recourse. Later he tried to diminish luxury; but such a step, in a manufacturing country, reduces industry and the circulation of goods, and it is therefore really appropriate only for countries which buy their luxuries abroad.

All solid-silver ornaments (which were common at that time in the houses of great lords and were regarded as a sign of wealth) were ordered to be taken to the Mint. The King set an example by depriving himself of all his silver tables, candelabras, solid-silver couches and similar furniture. These were masterpieces of chased work created by Ballin, a man unequaled in his own field, and based on designs by Le Brun. They had cost ten million francs, but their sale produced only three; the silver ornaments of private individuals produced three more; the whole operation proved of little value.

There was then committed one of those enormous mistakes which the government has corrected only in recent times; it was decided to alter the currency, to issue new coinage with a different content of precious metal, to give crowns a value disproportionate to that of quarters. The result was that, as quarters were now proportionally more valuable than crowns, they disappeared abroad, where they were reminted into crowns, which could then be returned to France at a profit. A country must be pretty sound in itself to remain strong after having experienced shocks like this. Ignorance was still common, and finance was then, like physics, a science of vain conjectures. The tax-farmers were charlatans who deceived the ministry, and they cost the state eighty millions. It takes twenty years' hard work to repair this sort of damage.

By 1691 or 1692, then, the finances of the state appeared to be seriously disorganized. Those who attributed this drying up of the springs of abundance to Louis XIV's lavish spending on buildings, arts and entertainments did not realize that, on the contrary, expenditure which encourages industry enriches a state. It is war which necessarily impoverishes the public purse, unless the spoils of the vanquished replenish it. I know of no nation which has enriched itself by its victories since the time of the ancient Romans. Italy in the 16th century was rich only through her trade. Holland would not have lasted long if she had contented herself with capturing the Spanish silver fleet and if the Indies had not nourished her strength. England has always impoverished herself by war, even while she was destroying the French fleets, and commerce alone has enriched her. The Algerians, who have hardly anything other than what they gain by piracy, are a very wretched people.

Among European nations, a few years of war cause as much distress to the victor as to the vanquished. War is like a chasm which swallows up all the streams of abundance. Ready money, which is the mainspring of all material good and evil and which is raised with such difficulty in the provinces, finds its way into the coffers of a hundred financiers and tax-farmers, who then lend the money and by doing so acquire the right to plunder the nation in the King's name. Private individuals come to regard the government as their enemy and hide their money; and as circulation declines, the country is impoverished.

No hasty remedy can take the place of fixed and stable arrangements established well beforehand and intended to cover unforeseen contingencies. The poll tax was instituted in 1695, to be suppressed at the Peace of Rijswijk and reinstituted later. The controller general, Pontchartrain, sold patents of nobility worth two thousand crowns in 1696; five hundred people bought them, but the expedient brought only temporary relief, whereas the shame lasted. All the nobility, old and new, were obliged to register their coats of arms and to pay for the permission to seal their letters with them. Unscrupulous tax-farmers got control of this affair and advanced the money. The government confined itself almost entirely to these small-scale measures in a country which could have furnished it with greater resources.

It was only in 1710 that it finally dared to impose the *dixième* (a tax of one tenth on all incomes). But this tax, imposed on top of so many other burdensome duties, seemed so harsh that the government did not have the courage to apply it rigorously. It only brought in twenty-five millions each year, at forty francs to the mark.

Colbert had made few changes in the value of the coinage. It is better to make none at all, for gold and silver as tokens of exchange should be invariable measures. He had only increased the nominal value of the silver mark from twenty-six francs, the figure when he assumed office, to twenty-seven and later twenty-eight; but after his time, in the last years of Louis XIV, the devaluation of the franc was continued until it stood at forty to the mark. This was a fatal expedient, for the King was relieved of his difficulties for a moment, only to be ruined in the long run because instead of a silver mark, he now received only about half. Anyone who owed twenty-six pounds in 1668 paid a mark, and anyone who owed forty pounds in 1710 still paid only a mark. The lowering of the rate which followed some time later was just as harmful to what little trade remained as the original increases had been.

The introduction of paper money would have been a great help, but such paper money should only be brought into circulation in times of prosperity, so that it may then maintain its value in harder times.

In 1706 the minister, Chamillart, began paying in special paper currency for specie handed in at the Mint, and for goods and services in connection with the billeting of troops, but as this paper money was not accepted by the Royal Exchequer, its value fell almost as soon as it appeared. The government was forced to continue borrowing on onerous terms and to use up four years of crown revenue in advance.

It also made continual use of what were called extraordinary expedients. Ridiculous offices were created, and these were always bought by people who wanted to escape from the taille, for this tax is regarded in France as being particularly degrading, and as all men are vain, they are always ready to fall for any scheme which offers them relief from this shameful burden. Moreover, the high salaries attached to these new offices in difficult times tempt people to buy them, for they do not stop to consider that these salaries will be abolished when things improve. So in 1707 the dignity of royal counselor of wine tasting and wine broking was invented, and it brought in a hundred and forty thousand francs. Royal registers were created, and subdelegates of provincial intendants. The government thought up the idea of appointing royal counselors to control the storing of wood, police counselors, official barbers and wigmakers, inspectors of fresh butter and tasters of salt butter. These extravagances make people laugh today; but they made them weep then.

Desmarets, a nephew of the great Colbert, who succeeded Chamillart as controller general in 1708, was unable to find a remedy for a disease which everything helped to aggravate.

Nature conspired with fortune to overwhelm the state. The severe winter of 1709 forced the King to cancel nine million francs of the taille at a time when he did not have enough to pay his soldiers. The shortage of provisions was so great that supplies for the army cost forty-five millions. Expenditure in 1709 totaled 221 millions, and the King's ordinary revenue produced only forty-nine. The state had to be ruined from within so that its enemies should not conquer it from without. There was such financial chaos, and so little was done to remedy it, that long after peace had returned at the beginning of 1715, the King was obliged to sell thirty-two millions in notes to get eight millions in specie. Finally he left at his death debts amounting to two billion six hundred million francs, at twenty-eight to the mark, the rate to which the currency had by then been reduced. This would be about four billion five hundred millions of our current money in 1760.

It is surprising and yet true that this immense debt would not have proved an unbearable burden, if trade had been flourishing, if paper money had been in circulation, and if this paper money had been guaranteed by reliable companies, as was the case in Switzerland, England, Venice and Holland; for when a powerful state owes money only to itself, confidence and the circulation of money are enough to ensure that the debt is paid. But at that time France was very far from possessing the resources to set such a vast and complicated machine in motion, and was overburdened by its weight.

During his reign, Louis XIV spent eighteen billions, the equivalent, in an average year, of three hundred and thirty millions of our present money, taking into account the various revaluations which have taken place in the meantime.

Under the administration of the great Colbert, the ordinary revenues of the crown never exceeded a hundred and seventeen millions at the rate of twenty-seven and later twenty-eight francs to the mark. Consequently all the rest had to be provided by extraordinary measures. Colbert, who was most strongly opposed to taking such fatal steps, was nevertheless obliged to have recourse to them in order to obtain money quickly. During the war of 1672, he borrowed eight hundred millions in terms of our present currency. Very few of the old royal domains remained crown property. Every parlement in the kingdom declared them inalienable, but they were nearly all sold nevertheless. Today the King's revenue consists in that of his subjects and results from the perpetual circulation of debts and payments. The King owes his people more money every year, in the form of interest on Paris municipal stocks, than any monarch ever received from the crown lands.

To gain some idea of the tremendous increase in taxes, debts, wealth and circulation, and at the same time in difficulties and troubles, which France and other countries have experienced, one has only to consider that at the death of Francis I the state owed about thirty thousand francs in these perpetual municipal stocks, whereas today it owes over forty-five millions.

Those who have tried to compare the revenues of Louis XIV with those of Louis XV have discovered that, taking only fixed and current revenue into account, Louis XIV was much richer in 1683, the date of Colbert's death, with a revenue of a hundred and seventeen millions, than his successor was in 1730 with nearly two hundred millions; and this is very true if we consider only these fixed and ordinary revenues, for a hundred and seventeen millions at twenty-eight to the mark are more than the two hundred millions at forty-nine to the mark, which was the royal revenue of 1730. The increased charges due to royal borrowing ought also to be taken into account. Yet it is also true that the revenues of the King, that is to say of the state, have increased since then, and that the understanding of finance has developed to such an extent that, in the ruinous war of 1741, credit was never for a moment in danger. Sinking funds were established on the English model; France had to adopt part of the financial system of the English as well as their philosophy, and if only a purely monarchical state could introduce the circulating notes which, at the very least, double England's wealth, France would reach her highest degree of perfection. In a monarchy, however, such perfection would be dangerously liable to abuse.

In 1683 there were about five million francs' worth

of minted silver coin in circulation in France; in 1730 the figure was about twelve hundred millions of our present currency. But the real value of the coinage under Cardinal Fleury's ministry was only about half what it had been in Colbert's time. It seems, then, that France was only about a sixth richer in circulating money than she had been at Colbert's death. But she is far richer than this when one takes into account the gold and silver which has been manufactured into articles for use or for show. In 1690 these were worth only four hundred millions of our present currency, whereas by 1730 their value was equal to that of all the coins in circulation. Nothing illustrates more clearly the extent to which commerce, which Colbert was the first to develop, has subsequently increased, especially since the restrictions imposed on it by war have been removed. Industry has improved too, despite the emigration of so many craftsmen dispersed by the revocation of the Edict of Nantes, and it is still expanding. The nation is capable of things as great as, and even greater than, those it achieved under Louis XIV, because genius and commerce always strengthen each other when they are encouraged.

Looking at the affluence of individuals, at the prodigious number of attractive houses built in Paris and in the provinces, at the vast number of carriages, and at all the commodities and refinements which go by the name of luxuries, one would think that France is twenty times as rich as formerly. All this, however, is the fruit of ingenious labor rather than of wealth. It hardly costs more to be comfortably housed today than it did to be badly housed under Henry IV. The fine mirrors made in our own factories, which now decorate our houses, cost far less than did the little ones which used to be imported from Venice. We have beautiful and ornamental materials which are both cheaper and better than those brought from abroad. In fact it is not gold and silver that procure the comforts of life for us; it is the creative activity of the nation. A people which had nothing but precious metals would be wretched; a people which, without these metals, made the fullest use of all its natural products would be truly rich. France is in this fortunate position and has, in addition, far more precious metals than she needs to put into circulation.

The spirit of industry which grew up in the towns also spread to the country. There will always be complaints about the lot of the ordinary farm worker. They are to be heard in every country in the world, and they usually come from rich and idle people who are moved by a desire to criticize the government much more than by any real concern for the people. It is true that in almost every country, those who spend their lives in agricultural labor would, if they ever had enough leisure to complain, protest against the exactions which deprive them of part of the fruits of their toil. They would express their detestation of having to pay taxes which they have not imposed on themselves and to bear the burdens of the state without enjoying the advantages of other citizens. It is not the task of the historian to inquire how the people can make a just contribution without being exploited, nor to discover the precise point, so difficult to ascertain, at which the execution of the law becomes abuse of the law and taxation becomes robbery. But history should show that it is impossible for a city to flourish unless the surrounding countryside is prosperous too; for clearly, it is this countryside that feeds it. On certain fixed days, in every town in France, one hears reproaches from those whose profession allows them to declaim against the consumption of all those different articles which are known as luxuries. Yet it is clear that these articles are provided only by the hard work of those who cultivate the land; and this work is always well paid.

More vines have been planted, and their cultivation has been improved; new wines have been made which were not known before, like those of Champagne, which have been given the color, flavor and strength of those of Burgundy, and which are now sold abroad at considerable profit. This increase in the production of wines has led to a similar increase in that of spirits. Horticulture, the cultivation of vegetables and fruits, has increased tremendously, and the trade in provisions with the American colonies has grown as a result. The complaints which have always been voiced about the poverty of the countryside have thus ceased to have any justification. Moreover, in these vague complaints, no distinction is made between peasant owners and farmers, on the one hand, and mere laborers, on the other. The latter live by the work of their hands; and this is the case in every country in the world, where the majority must toil to live. But there is no kingdom on earth where the farmer is more prosperous than in some of the provinces of France; England alone may dispute this advantage with her. The substitution of a proportional taille for the arbitrary one, which has taken place in several provinces, has contributed still further to the prosperity of those farmers who possess plows, vineyards and gardens. The laborer, the worker, must be reduced to necessity before he will work; such is the nature of man. The great majority of men must be poor; but this does not mean that they must be wretched.

The middle class has enriched itself by its industry. Ministers and courtiers have become less wealthy because, while money has been devalued by nearly half, salaries and pensions have remained the same and the price of commodities has more than doubled. This has happened in every country in Europe. Rights and fees have everywhere remained on the old footing. An elector of the empire receiving the investiture of his estates still pays what his predecessors paid in the days of Charles IV, in the fourteenth century, and the fee payable to the Emperor's secretary in this ceremony is only one crown.

What is even more strange is that, though everything has increased, including the nominal value of money in circulation, the quantity of manufactured articles of gold and silver, and the price of goods, yet the soldier's pay remains the same as it was two hundred years ago; a foot soldier receives five sous, as he did in the days of Henry IV. This vast number of ignorant men who sell their lives so cheaply do not realize that, as a result of devaluation and increased prices, they actually receive two thirds less than the soldiers of Henry IV. If they did realize it and demanded a two-thirds increase in pay, it would have to be granted. The result would be that every European power would maintain two thirds fewer troops; the armed forces would remain in equilibrium, and agriculture and industry would benefit.

It should also be noted that as commercial profits have increased and the salaries attached to important offices have decreased in real value, the great have become less wealthy and the middle classes more so. This has lessened the distance between different social classes. In the past, the man of small means had no alternative but to serve the great; but today industry has opened up to him a thousand possibilities which were unknown a hundred years ago. Finally, in whatever way the finances of the state may be administered, France now possesses in the labor of nearly twenty million inhabitants an inestimable treasure.

CHAPTER XXXI

The Sciences

This fortunate age, which was to witness a revolution in the human spirit, did not to begin with seem destined to such greatness. Take first the case of philosophy. In Louis XIII's time, there was nothing to indicate that it was on the point of emerging from the chaos in which it was plunged. The Inquisition in Italy, Spain and Portugal had linked philosophical errors with religious dogmas; the civil wars in France and the quarrels between Catholic and Calvinist constituted a climate of opinion which was no more likely to promote the cultivation of human reason than was the fanaticism of Cromwell's time in England. If a canon of Thorn[1] had revived the ancient planetary system of the Chaldeans, so long forgotten, this truth was condemned in Rome. When the congregation of the Holy Office, consisting of seven cardinals, had declared that the theory that the earth moved (a theory without which true astronomy was impossible) was not only heretical but also absurd, and when the great Galileo, at the age of seventy, had had to ask par-

[1] Copernicus, whose theory that the earth rotated around the sun was published in 1543.

don for being right, there seemed little chance of truth being received on earth.

Sir Francis Bacon had already pointed, from afar, to the road which could be taken;[2] Galileo had discovered the laws governing falling bodies; Torricelli was beginning to understand the pressure of the air which surrounds us; a number of experiments had been made at Magdeburg. Apart from these feeble attempts, all the schools remained wedded to absurdity, and the world plunged in ignorance. Then Descartes appeared;[3] he did the opposite of what he ought to have done; instead of studying nature, he tried to guess its secrets. He was the greatest geometer of his century; but geometry leaves the mind as it finds it. Descartes's mind was too prone to invent, and the greatest of mathematicians produced nothing but romances in the field of philosophy. A man who disdained experiments, who never quoted Galileo and who tried to build without bricks could only construct an imaginary edifice.

All that was fantastic in his work succeeded; and the few truths which were mixed in with these new fantasies were at first contested. But finally these truths gained acceptance, with the help of the method he had originated; for before him, men had no thread to guide them through the labyrinth, and he at least provided one, which others used after he himself had lost his way. It was no small achievement to have destroyed the fantastic theories of the Peripatetics[4] even if he created new ones of his own in doing so. For some time they fought each other; but finally one after the other they collapsed, and reason at last arose on their ruins. In Florence there

[2] In his *Philosophical Letters,* Voltaire speaks approvingly of Bacon's attempts to encourage experimental science. Bacon's influence was important in the eighteenth century, particularly on the Encyclopedists.

[3] Voltaire's assessment of Descartes contains more blame than praise. It must be remembered that, as a disciple of Newton and Locke, he was frequently in conflict with the Cartesians of his own day. As a result, though he tries to discuss Descartes impartially, he does not altogether succeed.

[4] The Aristotelian school of philosophy, which had a profound influence on the medieval schoolmen and still largely dominated philosophical thought up to Descartes's time.

was an academy called *del Cimento,* established about 1655 by Cardinal Leopold de' Medici, where experiments were conducted. In this motherland of the arts, people already felt that they could come to understand something of the great edifice of nature by examining it piece by piece. After the death of Galileo, and from the time of Torricelli, this academy rendered great services.

In England, under the stern administration of Cromwell, a few philosophers gathered together to search peaceably for truths while fanaticism was oppressing all truth. Charles II, recalled to the throne of his ancestors by the repentance and the inconstancy of his nation, gave letters patent to this budding academy; but this was all the government provided. The Royal Society (which would be better entitled the Free Society) of London worked for the honor of working. It is from this body that there have come in our own time the discoveries about light, about the principle of gravitation, about the aberration of the fixed stars, about transcendental geometry and a thousand other inventions which, from this point of view, might well lead us to call this age the Age of the English as well as that of Louis XIV.

In 1666 Colbert, jealous of this new glory, wanted France to share it; and at the request of a number of scientists he got Louis XIV to agree to the establishment of an Academy of Sciences. It was free from control until 1699, like that of England and like the French Academy. By offering them considerable pensions, Colbert attracted Domenico Cassini from Italy, Huygens from Holland and Roemer from Denmark. Roemer calculated the speed of light from the sun; Huygens discovered the ring and one of the satellites of Saturn, and Cassini discovered the four others. We owe to Huygens, if not the first invention of pendulum clocks, at any rate the true principles of the regularity of their movement, which he deduced by a superb piece of geometrical reasoning. Gradually knowledge was acquired of all branches of physics, while at the same time all arbitrary systems were rejected. The public was astonished to see a chemistry which was no longer concerned with seeking the philosopher's stone or the elixir of life, an astronomy which did not predict future world events and a medicine independent of the phases of the moon. Putrefaction was no longer thought to be the source of animals and plants. There were no more miracles, once nature was better understood. It was studied in all its manifestations.

There was an amazing increase in geographical knowledge. No sooner had Louis XIV finished building the Observatory than he invited Domenico Cassini and Picard to undertake the task of measuring a meridian. This work, begun in 1669, was continued toward the north in 1683 by La Hire, and finally in 1700 extended to the far boundary of Roussillon by Cassini. This great astronomical achievement is itself sufficient to immortalize the age.

In 1672 a party of physical scientists was sent to Cayenne to make useful observations. From this voyage came the first knowledge of the flattening of the earth's poles, later to be demonstrated by the great Newton; and it prepared the way for the more celebrated voyages which have since added luster to the reign of Louis XV.

In 1700 Tournefort was sent out to the Levant. His task was to collect plants to enrich the Royal Garden, which had hitherto been neglected, but which was then restored and has since become one of the curiosities of Europe. The Royal Library, which was already well stocked, was enriched by more than thirty thousand volumes under Louis XIV; and this example has been so thoroughly followed in our own day that it now contains more than a hundred and eighty thousand. Louis had the Law School reopened, after it had been closed for a hundred years. He established a chair of French law in every French university. There would seem to be no need for any others, for the wise laws of the Romans, incorporated with those of France, should form a single body of law for the nation.

It was during his reign that Journals were first published. As is well known, the *Journal des Savants*, which began in 1665, is the prototype of all such works. They abound in Europe today, though a number of abuses have crept into them, as often happens with the most useful things.

The Académie des Belles-Lettres was first formed in 1663 from a number of members of the French Academy for the purpose of handing down to posterity the deeds of Louis XIV by striking medals to commemorate them. It became useful to the public when it ceased to concern itself only with the King, and applied itself to researches into antiquity and to the judicious criticism of opinions and facts. It had roughly the same effect on history as the Academy of Sciences had on physics: it dissipated errors.

The scientific and critical spirit which was gradually spreading, destroyed almost imperceptibly a great deal of superstition. This new spirit of reason was responsible for the royal declaration of 1672 which forbade tribunals to accept simple accusations of sorcery. No government would have dared to make such a prohibition under Henry IV or Louis XIII. Since 1672 people have still been accused of sorcery, but normally judges have only condemned them as blasphemers who used poison into the bargain.

It used to be quite common to try sorcerers by tying them with cords and throwing them in the water; if they floated, they were convicted. Many provincial judges had ordered these trials by ordeal, and among the people they continued for a long time. Every shepherd was a sorcerer, and amulets and magic rings were worn by townspeople. People were convinced that hazel wands were effective in discovering springs, treasures and thieves, and this belief is still common in more than one province of Germany. There was hardly anyone who did not have his horoscope cast. The secrets of magic were a constant subject of conversation and illusions were to be found everywhere. Scholars and magistrates wrote on these matters in all seriousness and there was even a group of authors known as demonographs. There were rules for distinguishing real magicians and real demoniacs from false ones; in short, up to this time hardly anything had been adopted from antiquity except errors of all kinds.

Superstitious ideas were so deeply rooted among men that in 1680 they were still frightened by comets. The more enlightened hardly dared combat this popular fear. Jacques Bernoulli, one of the greatest mathematicians in Europe, gave a sort of reply to the partisans of superstitious prejudice when the comet appeared. He said that the head of the comet could not be a sign of divine wrath because this head was eternally unchanged; the tail, however, might be such a sign. Yet neither the head nor the tail are really unchanging. We had to wait for Bayle to destroy this popular prejudice by writing a famous book which the subsequent progress of human reason has made less controversial than it was at the time.[5]

One might not think that sovereigns had an obligation to philosophers. Yet it is true that this philosophical spirit, which has spread to almost all social classes except the common people, has made a great contribution toward establishing the rights of kings. Quarrels which in former times would have produced excommunications, interdicts and schisms have ceased to do so. It has been said that peoples would be happy when they had philosophers for kings; it is equally true to say that kings are happier when many of their subjects are philosophers.

It must be admitted that this spirit of reason which is beginning to dominate education in our large towns has not been able to prevent the furious outbursts of the fanatics of the Cévennes[6] or the crazy behavior of the Paris populace around the tomb at Saint-Médard;[7] nor has it succeeded in appeasing quarrels, as bitter as they were frivolous, between men who ought to have been wiser. But in previous times these disputes would have caused disturbances in the state; the miracles of Saint-Médard would have been believed by citizens of the highest standing, and the fanaticism which was confined to

[5] The comet had appeared at the end of 1680. Bayle's *Pensées diverses sur la comète,* a lengthy work which refuted the idea that the comet was a sign of divine wrath and dealt also with many other philosophical topics, was first published (in its full version) in 1683.

[6] See Chapter XXXVI.

[7] This was the tomb of the Jansenist leader Pâris, in the cemetery of the Church of Saint-Médard in Paris. Miraculous cures were said to be worked there and large crowds frequently gathered, exhibiting all the manifestations of religious hysteria. The cemetery had to be closed in 1732.

the mountains of the Cévennes would have spread to the towns.

Every branch of science and literature was developed during this period, and so many writers have helped to increase human knowledge that those who, at other times, would have been considered prodigies have been lost in the crowd. Because of their number their glory is slight, but the glory of the age is all the greater.

CHAPTER XXXII

The Arts

True philosophy did not make such great progress in France as it did in England and Florence, and if the Academy of Sciences rendered great services to the human spirit, it did not place France above other nations. All the really great inventions and discoveries came from elsewhere.

But in rhetoric, poetry, literature, in all forms of writing, both for instruction and for delight, the French were the legislators of Europe. Italy was devoid of good taste. Previously, true eloquence had been unknown everywhere, religion had been preached in a ridiculous manner, and cases pleaded equally absurdly at the bar.

Preachers would quote Vergil and Ovid; lawyers, St. Augustine and St. Jerome. No genius had yet appeared who was capable of giving the French language the right turns of phrase, propriety of style and dignity. A few of Malherbe's verses[1] made one realize that it was capable of grandeur and force; but this was all. Men of genius who wrote well in Latin, such as President De Thou or the Chancellor de L'Hôpital,[2] were no longer the same when they handled their own language, which they could not control. The only admirable feature of French was a

[1] Malherbe (1555-1628) was the most important precursor of the classical school of poetry in France.

[2] The historian De Thou wrote his major work in Latin in the early seventeenth century. The Chancellor de L'Hôpital, who held office in the middle of the sixteenth century, was a Latin poet as well as an important political figure.

certain naïveté, which constituted the only merit of Joinville, Amyot, Marot, Montaigne, Régnier and the *Satire Ménippée*. And this simplicity went hand in hand with a great deal of inaccuracy and coarseness.

Jean de Lingendes, Bishop of Mâcon, who is unknown today because his works were never printed, was the first orator to preach with real eloquence. His sermons and funeral orations, though still stained with the rust of his time, were a model for the orators who imitated and surpassed him. The funeral oration for Charles Emmanuel, Duke of Savoy, called The Great in his own country, which Lingendes delivered in 1630, was full of such flashes of eloquence that Fléchier, many years later, took the whole of the exordium, as well as the text and many other sizable passages, and inserted them in his own famous funeral oration for Viscount Turenne.

At the same time Balzac[3] was giving regularity and harmony to prose. It is true that his letters were bombastic in style; he wrote to the first Cardinal de Retz: "You have just taken up the scepter of kings and put on the livery of roses." He wrote from Rome to Boisrobert, speaking of scented waters: "I escape to my room, swimming in the midst of perfumes." But with all these faults, he could nevertheless delight the ear. Rhetoric has such power over men that Balzac was admired in his own day for having discovered that small, neglected but necessary branch of art which consists in the harmonious choice of words; he was even admired for having used it in the wrong contexts.

Voiture gave us some idea of the easy grace of which this epistolary style is capable, though it is not the best style, since it consists of witticisms. Two volumes of letters, in which there is not a single one which is instructive, which speaks from the heart or which depicts the customs of the time or the characters of men, are really nothing more than a lengthy frivolity, an abuse rather than an exercise of wit.

The language began to attain greater purity and to take on a more permanent form, a development which we

---

[3] Guez de Balzac (1594-1654).

owe to the French Academy, and above all to Vaugelas. His *Translation of Quintus Curtius,* which appeared in 1646, was the first really good book to be written in a pure style, and very few of its expressions and turns of phrase have since become obsolete.

Olivier Patru, who came soon after, did a great deal to regulate and purify the spoken language, and although he was not considered to be a learned advocate, he was nevertheless responsible for the introduction of order, clarity, decorum and elegance into legal discourse; these qualities had hitherto been entirely unknown at the bar.

One of the works which contributed most to form the nation's taste and to give it a feeling for accuracy and precision was the short collection of *Maximes* by François, Duke of La Rochefoucauld. Although there is hardly more than one truth in this book, namely that self-love is the motive force behind all our actions, yet the truth is presented in so many different lights that it almost always retains its freshness. The work is not so much a book as material for embellishing a book. This little collection was eagerly read; it accustomed people to think and to express their thoughts in lively, precise and delicate phrases. This was something no European writer had achieved since the Renaissance.

But the first real work of genius written in prose was the collection of *Lettres Provinciales* of 1656. It contains every variety of rhetoric. There is not a single word in it which, in the last hundred years, has been adversely affected by the changes to which all living languages are liable. This work marks the date of the fixing of the language. The Bishop of Luçon, son of the famous Bussi, has told me that when he asked the Bishop of Meaux what work he would best have liked to have written if he had not written his own, Bossuet replied, "The *Lettres Provinciales.*" They have lost much of their piquancy since the Jesuits were abolished,[4] and since then the objects of their disputes have come to be despised.[5]

---

[4] The Jesuits were banned in France in 1764, much to the delight of Voltaire, who had been their pupil but had become their opponent.

[5] Though he profoundly disagreed with much of Pascal's the-

The good taste which dominates this book from beginning to end, and the vigor of the last letters, did not immediately correct the loose, diffuse, incorrect and disconnected style which had long been that of the majority of writers, preachers and advocates.

One of the first preachers to combine reason and eloquence was Father Bourdaloue, about 1668. He transformed pulpit oratory, and others subsequently followed in his footsteps, such as Father Massillon, Bishop of Clermont, filling their sermons with greater elegance and with finer and more penetrating pictures of the manners of the age. However, none of these have eclipsed him; with his sinewy rather than florid style, devoid of imaginative imagery, he seemed more concerned with convincing his audience than with appealing to their emotions, and he never thought of merely pleasing them.

It might have been a good thing if in banishing from the pulpit the bad taste which debased it, he had also banished the custom of preaching on a text. Indeed the practice of giving a long speech on a quotation of a couple of lines, and of straining oneself to make everything relevant to this quotation, seems almost like a game, and hardly worthy of the gravity of the ministry. The text becomes a sort of motto, or rather riddle, which it is the job of the sermon to unravel. The Greeks and Romans never knew this practice; it began when letters had decayed, and time has consecrated it.

The habit of always dividing into two or three points things which, like questions of morality, need no dividing, or like matters of controversy need dividing even further, is another of these irritating customs which Father Bourdaloue found already established and to which he conformed.

He had been preceded by Bossuet, later Bishop of Meaux. When he was still very young, Bossuet, who was to become such a great man, had been engaged to Mlle

---

ology and philosophy (he had devoted one of his own *Philosophical Letters*, as well as other works, to refuting him), Voltaire greatly admired Pascal as a writer. Here he concentrates on this aspect of Pascal's work and gives no hint of the many criticisms he makes elsewhere.

Desvieux, a girl of remarkable personality. His aptitude for theology and for the type of rhetoric which was characteristic of him revealed themselves so early in his life that his parents and friends persuaded him to enter the Church. Mlle Desvieux herself urged him to do so, preferring the glory he was to acquire to the happiness of living with him. While he was still young, in 1662, he preached before the King and the Queen Mother, long before Father Bourdaloue had been heard of. His sermons, helped by a noble and touching delivery, were the first ever heard at court which approached the sublime, and his success was so great that the King sent a message to his father, the intendant of Soissons, congratulating him on having such a son.

Yet when Bourdaloue appeared, Bossuet was no longer regarded as the most distinguished preacher. He had already turned his attention to funeral orations, a type of eloquence which demands imagination and a majestic grandeur which has something poetic about it; for when one aims at sublimity, one must always borrow something, albeit discreetly, from poetry. The funeral oration for the Queen Mother, which he delivered in 1667, won him the bishopric of Condom; but this oration was not yet worthy of him, and like his sermons was never printed. The funeral oration for the Queen of England, widow of Charles I, which he gave in 1669, seemed to have almost all the qualities of a masterpiece. For this type of eloquence, the most promising subjects are the men and women who have experienced the most misfortune in their lives. The case is rather like that of tragedy, where the great misfortunes of the main characters are what interest people most. The funeral oration for Madame,[6] who was carried off in the prime of life and who died in his arms, had the greatest and rarest of successes, that of causing the court to shed tears. He was obliged to stop after these words: "Oh, disastrous night, terrible night, in which there suddenly resounded like a thunderclap the shattering news: Madame is dying, Madame is dead, etc." The whole audience burst out sobbing,

[6] The Duchess of Orleans was commonly known by this title.

and the orator's voice was interrupted by his own sighs and weeping.

The French were the only people to be successful in this type of rhetoric. And some time after this Bossuet invented yet another type; one in which scarcely anyone save himself could succeed. He applied the art of oratory to history itself, a field where at first sight it seems inappropriate. His *Discours sur l'Histoire Universelle,* written for the education of the Dauphin, has neither a model nor any imitators. If the system which he adopted to reconcile the chronology of the Jews with that of other nations has had its critics among the scholars, his style has only had admirers. People were amazed by the majestic power with which he describes the customs, the governments and the rise and fall of great empires as well as by the liveliness and veracity with which he paints and judges the nations.[7]

Almost all the most distinguished works of this age were in genres unknown to antiquity. *Télémaque* is a case in point. Fénelon, the disciple and friend of Bossuet, who later unwillingly became his rival and enemy, wrote this curious book which is half novel and half poem and uses rhythmic prose instead of versification. He seems to have wanted to treat the novel as Bossuet treated history, by giving it a new dignity and charm and above all by extracting from these fictions a moral useful to the human race, the sort of moral which had been totally neglected in almost all such fabulous inventions. It has been thought that he composed the book for the instruction of the Duke of Burgundy, whose tutor he was, just as Bossuet had written his *Universal History* for the education of the Dauphin. But his nephew, the Marquis of Fénelon, who inherited the virtues of this famous man, and who was killed at the battle of Rocourt, has assured me that this was not the case. Indeed it would hardly

[7] Bossuet's *Discours,* which traced the course of history from the Creation to the time of Charlemagne, was published in 1681 and was generally regarded in Voltaire's time as the best account of universal history. In Voltaire's assessment of it here, there is only a hint of criticism, but elsewhere he attacks the work much more strongly.

have been fitting if Télémaque's love affairs with Calypso and Eucharis had formed the basis of the first lessons given by a priest to the royal children of France.

He only wrote this work when he had been relegated to his archbishopric of Cambrai. Steeped in the classics, and gifted with a lively and tender imagination, he had created a style all his own and one which flowed easily and abundantly. I have seen his original manuscript; there are not ten corrections in it. He composed it in three months, in the midst of his unhappy disputes about quietism,[8] never realizing how much this relaxation was superior to his main occupations. It is said that a servant stole a copy from him and had it printed. If that is true, the Archbishop of Cambrai owed his European reputation to this act of infidelity; but he also owed to it the fact that he was disgraced forever at court. *Télémaque* was interpreted as being an indirect criticism of the government of Louis XIV. Sesostris, who triumphed with too much pomp, and Idoménée, who established luxuries in Salente and forgot about necessities, were taken to be portraits of the King, although one cannot, after all, have a superfluity in one's home except by having a superabundance of necessities. The discontented also saw the Marquis of Louvois in the character of Protésilas, who was vain, harsh and haughty, and an enemy of the great generals who served the state and not the minister.

The allies who united against Louis XIV in the war of 1688 and who later made his throne shake in the war of 1701 took great pleasure in recognizing him in this selfsame Idoménée, whose haughtiness revolts all his neighbors. These allusions made a profound impression by virtue of Fénelon's harmonious style, which so subtly and gently instills moderation and concord. Foreigners, and even the French themselves, tired of so many wars, found a certain malicious consolation in discovering a satire in a work written to teach virtue. There were in-

[8] Fénelon's acceptance of the religious heresy known as quietism brought him into conflict with many leading churchmen of his day, particularly Bossuet, and led to his partial disgrace. Voltaire describes these quarrels in Chapter XXXVIII of *The Age of Louis XIV*.

numerable editions; I myself have seen fourteen in English. It is true that since the death of the King—who was so feared, so envied, so respected by all and so hated by some—when human malice could no longer take pleasure in spotting allusions which allegedly criticized his conduct, some judges with strict standards have treated *Télémaque* rather harshly. They have criticized its longwindedness, its details, the lack of coordination between its episodes, the too frequently repeated and too monotonous descriptions of country life; yet this book has always been looked on as one of the finest monuments of a flourishing age.

Among the works which are unique of their kind may be counted La Bruyère's *Caractères*. Like *Télémaque*, it has no parallels among the works of the ancients. A rapid, concise and sinewy style, picturesque expressions, a new but in no way irregular use of language—all these features impressed the public. The allusions which were found in the work set the seal on its success. When La Bruyère showed the manuscript of his work to M. de Malézieu, the latter said to him, "This work will bring you many readers and many enemies." The book became less appreciated when the whole generation attacked in it had passed away. Yet as it contains things which belong to every age and every place, it will probably never be forgotten. *Télémaque* produced a number of imitators; La Bruyère's *Caractères* produced even more. It is easier to make brief sketches of things which strike one than to write a long work of imagination which both instructs and pleases.

The delicate art of introducing a certain charm even into works of philosophy was likewise something new, and the *Pluralité des Mondes*[9] was the first example of it. It was a dangerous example, for the real ornaments of philosophy are order, clarity and, above all, truth. What might deter posterity from ranking this work among our

[9] The *Entretiens sur la Pluralité des Mondes* (1686) was by Fontenelle. The work is a popularization, in conversational form, of astronomical theories of the time, based mainly on the principles of Descartes. Despite Voltaire's criticism of the work here, it has considerable affinities with his own popularizations of scientific questions.

classics is the fact that it is partly based on Descartes's fantastic theory of vortices.

To these novelties one must add that produced by Bayle, who gave us a sort of dictionary of reasoning.[10] It was the first work of this kind from which one could learn how to think. There are certain articles in this collection which contain only insignificant facts unworthy of Bayle, of the serious reader and of posterity; these must be left to the fate which befalls ordinary books. I may add that, in placing Bayle among the authors who have done honor to the age of Louis XIV, despite the fact that he was a refugee in Holland, I am only conforming to the decree of the parlement of Toulouse, which declared his will valid in France despite the rigors of the law, asserting expressly that "such a man cannot be considered as a foreigner."

We shall not burden the reader by discussing the multitude of good books written in this century; we are only considering those new and striking works of genius which characterize it and distinguish it from other ages. The rhetoric of Bossuet and Bourdaloue, for example, was not and could not be that of Cicero; it was of a new kind and had new merits. If anything approaches the work of the Roman orator, it is the three memoirs which Pellisson composed for Fouquet. They are like a number of Cicero's orations in being a mixture of legal matters and affairs of state, treated in a thorough way with an art that is unobtrusive, and adorned by a moving eloquence.

We have had historians, but no Livy. The style of the *Conjuration de Venise*[11] can be compared with that of Sallust. The Abbé de Saint-Réal had clearly taken him for his model, and may have surpassed him. All the other writings of which we have just spoken seem to be original creations. It is this above all that distinguishes this illustrious age. The sixteenth and seventeenth cen-

[10] Bayle's *Dictionnaire Historique et Critique*, a vast work of historical criticism filled with the skeptical spirit which characterized its author, first appeared in 1697. It had considerable influence on Voltaire and on most of the philosophers of his day.

[11] Saint-Réal's account of the plot to overthrow the Venetian republic was published in 1674. It is an exciting if not altogether accurate historical narrative, which Voltaire greatly admired.

turies had had plenty of scholars and commentators; but they had not manifested real genius in any form.

Who would believe that all these fine prose works would probably never have existed if they had not been preceded by poetry? Yet such is the way the human mind works in all countries: verse was everywhere the first child of genius and the first master of rhetoric.

Peoples are like individuals. Plato and Cicero began by writing verses. Men knew by heart the finest stanzas of Malherbe before they could cite a single noble and sublime passage of French prose. It seems highly probable that without Pierre Corneille the genius of prose writers would never have developed.

Corneille is all the more admirable in that he was surrounded by very bad models when he first began to write his tragedies. What might have further diverted him from the right road is the fact that these models were greatly esteemed, and even more discouraging, they were favored by Cardinal Richelieu, who was the protector of men of letters, though not of good taste. He rewarded wretched writers of the sort that are usually obsequious. His proud spirit, so valuable in other spheres, led him to try to humble those in whom he somewhat resentfully sensed real genius; but real genius rarely submits to dictation. It is very rare for a powerful man, when he is an artist himself, to protect other good artists sincerely.

Corneille had to struggle against his age, his rivals and Cardinal Richelieu. I shall not repeat here what has been written about *Le Cid*.[12] I shall merely note that the Academy, in judging between Corneille and Scudéry, showed too much of a desire to please Richelieu when it condemned Chimène's love. To love one's father's murderer and at the same time to demand vengeance for the murder—this was an admirable thing. To have overcome that love would have been a capital fault in tragedy, which consists principally in such struggles in the mind

[12] Corneille's first great tragedy, *Le Cid* (1636), was widely criticized. The French Academy was asked to mediate in the dispute, and published its conclusions, which were themselves often critical of Corneille.

and heart; but no one understood this art of tragedy save Corneille himself.

Le Cid was not the only work of Corneille's to arouse Richelieu's hostility. The Abbé d'Aubignac informs us that the minister disapproved of *Polyeucte*.

Le Cid, after all, was a greatly improved imitation of Guillén de Castro, and in some places a mere translation. *Cinna,* which followed it, was unique. I knew a former servant in the Condé household who told me that the great Condé,[13] at the age of twenty, being present at the first performance of *Cinna,* wept when Augustus pronounced these words:

> Myself I govern, as the world I rule,
> In act and will. O Time! O Memory!
> Hear and record this my new victory!
> Behold me triumph over my just ire,
> And let posterity the deed admire!
> Cinna, let us be friends: 'tis Caesar asks it.

These were hero's tears. The great Corneille making the great Condé weep with admiration—this was a notable date in the history of the human spirit.

The fact that several years later he wrote a number of plays which were unworthy of him did not prevent the nation from regarding him as a great man, just as the considerable faults one finds in Homer do not prevent him from being sublime. It is the privilege of real genius, and especially of the genius who strikes out on a new path, to make great mistakes with impunity.

Corneille formed himself; but Louis XIV, Colbert, Sophocles and Euripides all contributed to form Racine. An ode which he wrote at the age of eighteen for the King's marriage brought him a gratification which he did not expect and determined his poetic vocation. His reputation has constantly increased, while that of Corneille's works has somewhat diminished. The reason is that Racine, in all his works, beginning with *Alexandre,* is

[13] The great Condé (1621-86) was one of the most distinguished French generals under Louis XIII and Louis XIV.

always elegant, correct and true and that he speaks to the heart, whereas Corneille often fails to achieve these ends. Racine greatly surpassed both the Greeks and Corneille in the understanding of human passions, and he carried the sweet harmony of poetry and all the graces of discourse to the greatest heights they can ever hope to attain. Both these men taught the nation how to think, how to feel and how to express itself. Their audiences, whom they alone had taught, finally became severe judges, even of those who had enlightened them.

In Richelieu's time, there were very few people in France capable of discerning the faults of *Le Cid*. In 1702, when *Athalie*, the greatest of all dramatic masterpieces, was performed before the Duchess of Burgundy, the courtiers thought they knew enough to condemn it. Time has avenged the author; but this great man died without enjoying the success of his finest work. There was always a numerous party who took pride in refusing to recognize Racine's greatness. Mme de Sévigné, outstanding in her age as a letter writer, and still more for the charming way in which she related trivial anecdotes, always believed of Racine that "he will not go far." She judged him as she did coffee, of which she said, "People will soon tire of it." Time is needed for reputations to mature.

The strange destiny of this age made Molière a contemporary of Corneille and Racine. It is not true that Molière, when he first appeared, found the theater denuded of good comedies. Corneille himself had written *Le Menteur*, a play of character and intrigue, borrowed, like *Le Cid*, from the Spanish theater; and Molière had only produced two of his masterpieces when Quinault's *La Mère Coquette* appeared, a play of character and intrigue, and even a model of intrigue. It was first performed in 1664, and is the first comedy to portray those who have since been called *les marquis*. The majority of the great lords of Louis XIV's court tried to imitate the air of grandeur, splendor and dignity which characterized their master. This haughty air was copied by those of a lower order; and in the end there were a large number of the lesser nobility who made themselves highly ridiculous by the extent to which they gave themselves airs and tried to show off.

This fault lasted a long time. Molière often attacked it, and he did much to rid the public of these lesser fry among the self-important, as he did to free them from the affectation of the *précieuses*, from the pedantry of the *femmes savantes,*[14] and from the robes and the Latin of the doctors. Molière was, if one may say so, a legislator of social proprieties. I am speaking here only of the services he rendered his age; his other merits are well known.

Future generations will look back with envy on the age in which the heroes of Corneille and Racine, the characters of Molière, the orchestral works of Lully were entirely new to the nation, and (as we are considering here only the arts) the voices of Bossuet and Bourdaloue were heard by Louis XIV, by Madame, so renowned for her good taste, by Condé, Turenne and Colbert and by a host of men who had distinguished themselves in every field. Never again shall we see an age in which a Duke of La Rochefoucauld, author of the *Maximes,* can leave a conversation with Pascal and Arnauld to go to see a Corneille play.

Despréaux[15] rose to the same heights as these great men, not indeed in his early satires, for posterity will hardly concern itself with the *Embarras de Paris* or names like Cassaigne and Cotin; but he instructed this same posterity with his fine epistles, and above all with his *Art Poétique,* from which Corneille could have learned a great deal.

La Fontaine was a good deal less refined in style and less correct in his use of language; yet his unique simplicity and individual charm place his totally unaffected work almost on the same level as that of these other men of genius.

---

[14] *Les Précieuses Ridicules* and *Les Femmes Savantes* were two of Molière's plays which satirized the affectation of the women of the time, just as the pretentions of the minor nobility were satirized in the characters of the marquis in plays like *Le Misanthrope.*

[15] Better known as Boileau, the author of satires and epistles, and above all of the *Art Poétique* (1764), the celebrated attempt to summarize the theory and practice of French classical poetry.

Quinault, who excelled in a new genre[16] which was all the more difficult because it looked easy, earned a place among his illustrious contemporaries. Boileau's unjust denigration of him is well known, but Boileau had never made a sacrifice to the Graces, and he spent his life trying to humiliate a man who owed his inspiration to them. The greatest praise one can bestow on a poet is to learn his verses by heart, and there are whole scenes of Quinault which are known in this way—an advantage no Italian opera can claim to share. French music has retained a simplicity which is to the taste of no other nation; but the simplicity and beauty of nature, which are often so charmingly portrayed by Quinault, still find admirers among all Europeans who understand our language and have a cultivated taste. If a poem like *Armide* or *Atys* were discovered in antiquity, it would be received with rapturous enthusiasm. But Quinault was a modern.

All these men were recognized and protected by Louis XIV, except La Fontaine. His extreme simplicity, which he carried to the extent of self-neglect, kept him apart from a court which he had no wish to enter. But the Duke of Burgundy welcomed him, and he received in his old age a number of benefits from that prince. Despite his genius, he was almost as naïve as the heroes of his fables. A priest of the Oratory called Pouget could boast of having treated this utterly harmless man in the same way as if he had been speaking to la Brinvilliers or la Voisin.[17] His tales are borrowed from Poggio, Ariosto and Margaret of Navarre. Voluptuousness may be dangerous, but joking about it cannot be said to inspire it. One could apply to La Fontaine himself his admirable fable of the *animaux malades de la peste,* who accuse themselves of their faults: the lions, wolves and bears are forgiven

16 Quinault wrote many tragedies and comedies in traditional form, but the new genre to which Voltaire is referring is that of the operatic libretto. In his later years (after 1670), Quinault wrote many such librettos, particularly for the composer Lully.

17 These were two celebrated seventeenth-century poisoners. La Fontaine's *Contes* contained a number of improprieties which shocked many people, particularly churchmen.

everything; and an innocent animal is condemned for having eaten a little grass.

In the school of these men of genius, who will delight and instruct future generations, a multitude of attractive writers were formed from whom we have an infinity of charming lesser works which gave pleasure to cultured people, just as we have many charming painters who cannot be classed with Poussin, Le Sueur, Le Brun, Lemoyne or Vanloo.

Yet toward the end of Louis XIV's reign, two men stood out from the crowd of relatively mediocre minds and gained a great reputation. One was La Motte-Houdar, a man of judgment and wide interests rather than of genius, a delicate and methodical writer of prose, but often lacking spirit and elegance in his poetry, and even lacking that exactitude which one can only risk neglecting if one is sure of achieving something sublime. At first he produced fine stanzas rather than fine odes. His talents declined soon afterward; but we have many fine passages of his in more than one genre and these will prevent him from ever being classed as worthless. He showed that even a second-class author could have his value.

The other was Rousseau,[18] who had less wit, less subtlety and less facility than La Motte-Houdar, but had a far greater talent for the art of versification. He only started writing odes after La Motte-Houdar, but his were more beautiful, more varied and richer in images. In his psalms he equaled the grace and harmony to be found in the sacred songs of Racine. His epigrams are more polished than those of Marot. He was less successful in opera, which demands sensibility; in comedy, which needs gaiety; and in moral epistles, which must contain truth. He lacked these qualities, and so failed in those genres which were foreign to him.

He could have corrupted the French language if the style of Marot,[19] which he used in serious works, had

[18] This is Jean Baptiste Rousseau (1671-1741). He quarreled violently with Voltaire, and something of Voltaire's hostility to him is visible in the account which follows.

[19] Marot was an early sixteenth-century poet, whose style was often characterized by its conceits.

been imitated by others. Fortunately this mixture of the purity of our language with the deformity of that which was spoken two hundred years ago had only a passing popularity. Some of his epistles are rather forced imitations of Despréaux, and are not based on ideas as clear as his, nor on recognized truths. *Le vrai seul est aimable.*[20]

He degenerated a great deal when he went abroad; possibly because age and misfortune had weakened his talents, possibly because he was no longer in a position to receive the help he needed. His principal merit consisted in his choice of words and in happy turns of phrase—a merit which is both more necessary and rarer than is generally thought. Far from his native land, he could count among his misfortunes that of no longer having any severe critics.

His continual misfortunes resulted from an *amour-propre* which was both incorrigible and mixed with jealousy and animosity. His example must be a striking lesson for all men of talent; but here we are considering him only as a writer who contributed not a little to the honor of literature.

Since the time when these illustrious writers flourished, scarcely any great geniuses have arisen; and by the time of Louis XIV's death, nature seemed to be taking a rest.

The road was a hard one at the beginning of the century because no one had trodden it; it is hard today because it has been trodden flat. The great men of the past century taught people to think and to speak; they said things which were previously unknown. Those who follow them can scarcely do more than repeat what is known. And the multitude of masterpieces has resulted in a feeling of surfeit.

So the age of Louis XIV has had precisely the same fate as those of Leo X, Augustus and Alexander. The ground which in these illustrious times brought forth so many fruits of genius had been well prepared for a long time beforehand. People have searched in vain for the moral and physical causes of this late fecundity, followed

[20] "Truth alone is pleasing." The quotation is from Boileau.

by a long sterility. The real reason is that peoples that cultivate the arts need many years to purify their language and their taste. When the first steps have been taken, then genius can develop, and emulation and the public favor lavished on these new efforts will inspire all the talents. Every artist seizes on the natural beauties proper to his own form of art. Anyone who goes deeply into the theory of the arts which really require genius must, if he has a spark of that genius himself, know that these primary beauties, these central natural characteristics which belong to these arts and which suit the nation for which they are intended, are very few in number. Subjects, and the embellishments proper to these subjects, have far narrower limits than is usually imagined. The Abbé Dubos, an extremely shrewd man who wrote his treatise on poetry and painting about 1714, found that in the whole of French history, the only subject really worthy of an epic poem was the destruction of the League by Henry the Great.[21] He should have added that the epic embellishments which suited the Greeks, the Romans and the Italians of the fifteenth and sixteenth centuries are proscribed in France. The gods of mythology, oracles, invulnerable heroes, monsters, magic spells, metamorphoses and romantic adventures are no longer in season, and the beauties proper to an epic poem are confined within a very narrow circle. So if ever an artist does succeed in making use of those few ornaments which are really appropriate to his time, his subject and his public, and executes what hitherto has only been attempted, those who come after him will find that this task has been accomplished once and for all.

The same is true of tragedy. It would be wrong to imagine that one can go on indefinitely creating new and striking forms of great tragic passions and sentiments. There are limits to everything.

Serious comedy has its limits too. In human nature there are at most a dozen characters that are truly comic and sufficiently striking. The Abbé Dubos, lacking genius

[21] There is perhaps an element of self-advertisement in this paragraph, as Voltaire himself had written his epic poem *The Henriad* on precisely this subject.

himself, believes that men of genius can go on finding a host of new characters; but nature would have to create them first. He imagines that the little differences which exist between the characters of men can be handled as successfully as can major subjects. It is true that variations in shade are innumerable, but striking colors are few in number, and it is these primary colors that the great artist must use.

The rhetoric of the pulpit, particularly that of funeral orations, is in the same situation. Once moral truths have been eloquently enunciated, once the pictures of human weakness and misery, of the vanity of power and of the ravages of death, have been sketched by able hands, then they become commonplace. One is reduced either to imitating them or to going astray. When a sufficient number of fables have been written by a La Fontaine, anything anyone else may add expresses the same morality and relates almost the same adventures. So genius can only belong to a single age, and after that it is bound to degenerate.

Genres whose subjects are constantly being renewed, like history or the physical sciences, and which only demand hard work, judgment and common sense, can maintain themselves much more easily; and manual arts, like painting and sculpture, can avoid degeneration if patrons follow Louis XIV's example and employ only the best artists. For in painting and sculpture one can treat the same subjects a hundred times. The Holy Family is still being painted despite the fact that Raphael depicted it with all the superiority of his art; but one would not be allowed to treat *Cinna, Andromaque, l'Art Poétique* and *Tartuffe* in the same way.

It should further be noted that, now that our age has absorbed the lessons of the previous one, it has become so easy to write mediocre works that we have been flooded with frivolous books and, what is even worse, with useless serious books. But among this multitude of mediocre writings, an inevitable evil in a large, rich and idle city where one half of the citizens is constantly occupied in amusing the other, there are now and then some excellent works, be they history, reflections or those lighter writings which bring relaxation to all kinds of minds.

The French nation has produced more of these works than any other. Its language has become the language of Europe. To this end everything has contributed: the great authors of the age of Louis XIV and those who followed them; the Calvinist pastors in exile who carried rhetoric and method into foreign countries; Bayle above all, who, writing in Holland, was read everywhere; Rapin de Thoyras, who wrote in French the only good history of England;[22] Saint-Evremond, whose company was sought by the whole court of London;[23] the Duchess of Mazarin, whom men were ambitious to please; Mme d'Olbreuse, who became Duchess of Zell and took with her to Germany all the grace of her native land. Sociability is the natural inheritance of Frenchmen; it is a merit and a pleasure which other peoples have felt the need of. The French language is of all languages the one which expresses most easily, clearly and delicately all the objects of conversation of cultivated people; in this way it contributes, throughout Europe, to one of the greatest pleasures of life.

CHAPTER XXXIII

The Arts (Continued)

The arts which do not depend solely on the mind, like music, painting, sculpture and architecture, had made little progress in France before the time we call the age of Louis XIV. Music was still in its infancy; a few languishing songs and a few airs for violin, guitar or lute, most of them composed in Spain, were all that were known. Lully astonished people by his taste and knowledge. He was the first composer in France to introduce

[22] Rapin de Thoyras's *History of England* was published in the 1720's. Written from the Whig viewpoint, it was regarded as the standard history of England until the appearance of Hume's work.

[23] The poet and philosopher Saint-Evremond had lived for many years in exile in London during the late seventeenth century.

bass and middle parts and fugues. At first people found difficulty in playing his compositions, which today seem so simple and straightforward. A thousand people know music today for every one who knew it in Louis XIII's time, and the art has been developed correspondingly. There is no large town without public concerts now, whereas in those days there were none even in Paris, and twenty-four royal violins were the only orchestra France possessed.

Knowledge of musical matters, and of the arts which depend on music, has made such progress that toward the end of Louis XIV's reign a notation was invented for dancing, so that today it is true to say that one can dance at sight.

We had some great architects at the time of the regency of Marie de Médicis. She had the Luxembourg palace built in the Tuscan style, to honor her own country and to embellish ours. The same de Brosse to whom we owe the gateway of Saint-Gervais built this palace for a queen who was never to enjoy it. Richelieu had her greatness of mind, but he was very far from having her taste. The Cardinal's palace, now called the Palais-Royal, is proof of this. We conceived the greatest hopes when we saw the construction of that fine façade of the Louvre, which makes one wish so strongly to see this palace completed. Many citizens have built magnificent houses, but more effort has gone into making their interiors attractive than into making them externally impressive, and they have satisfied the taste for luxury of private individuals much more than they have embellished the city.

Colbert, the Maecenas of all the arts, created an academy of architecture in 1671. It is not enough that there should be men like Vitruvius;[1] there must also be men like Augustus to employ them.

It is equally necessary that municipal magistrates should be zealous and enlightened in taste. If there had been two or three provosts like President Turgot,[2] Paris would not be reproached for the bad construction and

---

[1] A famous writer on architecture who lived in the time of Augustus.

[2] The father of the celebrated finance minister of Louis XVI.

bad situation of her city hall, for her tiny and irregular square, famous only for its gibbets and its little firework displays, for the narrow streets of its most populous quarters; in short, for allowing traces of barbarity to remain in the midst of splendor and artistic greatness.

Painting began under Louis XIII with Poussin. The mediocre painters who preceded him are not worth considering. Since his day we have had a number of great painters, though not in that profusion which constitutes one of the riches of Italy. But without stopping to consider Le Sueur, who had no master but himself, or Le Brun, who equaled the Italians in design and composition, we have had over thirty painters who have left works worthy of study. Foreigners are beginning to deprive us of them. I have seen, in the palace of a great king,[3] galleries and apartments decorated entirely with our pictures, whose merit we are perhaps unwilling to recognize. In France I have seen a picture by Santerre failing to fetch twelve thousand francs. There is scarcely anywhere in Europe a larger work of painting than Lemoyne's ceiling at Versailles, and I doubt if there are any finer ones. Later, when Vanloo appeared, even foreigners regarded him as the greatest painter of his time.

Not only did Colbert give the Academy of Painting its present form, but in 1667 he persuaded Louis XIV to establish an academy in Rome. A palace was bought in the city to house the director, and every year pupils who have won prizes at the Paris Academy are sent there. Their travel and maintenance expenses are paid by the King. In Rome they copy the works of antiquity and study Raphael and Michelangelo. This desire to imitate ancient and modern Rome is a noble act of homage to her, and this homage still continues despite the huge collections of Italian paintings which have since been made by the King and the Duke of Orleans and the masterpieces of sculpture which France has produced. These have made it unnecessary for us to look elsewhere for masters.

---

[3] Voltaire is referring to Frederick the Great, whose Palace of Potsdam was largely decorated with the work of French artists.

It is principally in sculpture that we have excelled, and in the art of casting colossal equestrian statues in a single mold.

Future generations, digging among the ruins of our time, may someday discover works like the Baths of Apollo, now exposed to the weather in the woods of Versailles; the tomb of Cardinal Richelieu in the Sorbonne chapel, which is all too rarely shown to the public; the equestrian statue of Louis XIV, made in Paris to decorate Bordeaux; the Mercury which Louis XV gave to the King of Prussia; and many other works, the equal of those I have cited. If this were to happen, one may well believe that these productions of our own time would be placed side by side with the finest works of Greek antiquity.

We have equaled the ancients in our medals. Warin, at the end of Louis XIII's reign, was the first to raise this art above mediocrity. All these stamps and dies ranged in historical order in that part of the gallery of the Louvre assigned to artists make an admirable sight. They are worth two millions and most of them are masterpieces.

We have been equally successful in the art of engraving precious stones. That of reproducing and perpetuating pictures by the use of copper plates, thus making it easier to hand on the representations of nature and of art to posterity, was still undeveloped in France before this time. It is one of the most pleasant and useful of the arts. We owe it to the Florentines, who first invented it in the middle of the fifteenth century; it has been developed further in France than in its place of origin because we have produced a greater number of works of this kind. The King's collections of prints have often been considered one of the most magnificent presents he can give to ambassadors. Chasing in gold and silver, which is dependent on both design and taste, has been brought to the highest degree of perfection of which the human hand is capable.

After having surveyed all these arts which contribute to the delight of individuals and to the glory of the state, we should not fail to mention the most useful of all the arts, in which the French have surpassed all other nations: I mean surgery, where progress in this period was so rapid and noteworthy that people came to Paris from every corner of Europe for all those cures and operations which demand exceptional dexterity. Not only were there hardly any first-rate surgeons outside France, but it was the only country in which the necessary instruments were properly made; it supplied them to all its neighbors, and I have been told by the famous Cheselden, the greatest surgeon of London, that when in 1715 he began manufacturing the instruments of his art in London, he was the first to do so. Medicine, which helped to perfect surgery, was not developed further in France than it was in England, or under the celebrated Boerhaave in Holland. But as is the case with philosophy, it has attained the degree of perfection of which it is capable by profiting from the discoveries of our neighbors.

This, in general terms, is a faithful picture of France's contribution to the progress of the human spirit in the century which began in Cardinal Richelieu's times and ends with our own. It will be difficult to surpass it; and if it is surpassed in some fields, it will nevertheless remain a model for the more fortunate ages to which it will have given rise.

CHAPTER XXXIV

The Arts in the Rest of Europe in Louis XIV's Time

Throughout the course of this history, we have constantly insinuated that the public disasters of which it is composed, and which follow each other almost without interruption, are in the long run erased from the registers of time.[1] The details and intrigues of politics are forgotten; the good laws, the institutions, the monuments produced by the arts and sciences exist forever.

The multitude of foreigners who now visit Rome, not

[1] Voltaire is thinking here not just of *The Age of Louis XIV*, but of the whole of history since the time of Charlemagne, which he has described in the *Essay on Customs*.

as pilgrims but as men of taste, take little interest in Gregory VII or Boniface VIII. They admire the temples built by the Bramantes or Michelangelos, the paintings of the Raphaels and the sculptures of the Berninis. If they are cultured, they read Ariosto and Tasso and pay their respects to the ashes of Galileo. In England people mention Cromwell only occasionally and never discuss the Wars of the Roses, but they spend years studying Newton. No one is surprised to read in his epitaph that he was "the glory of the human race," but they would be surprised to find the ashes of any statesman in that country honored with a similar title.

In this chapter I should like to render justice to all the great men who, like him, were the ornaments of their country in the last century. I have called this century the age of Louis XIV, not only because this monarch protected the arts more than all the other kings of his day put together, but also because he reigned for as long as three generations of the other princes of Europe. The period I have chosen begins a few years before Louis XIV and ends a few years after his death, and this in fact is the period in which the human spirit has made the greatest progress.

Between 1660 and our own time, the English have made greater strides toward perfection in every field than they did in all previous ages. I shall not repeat here what I have said elsewhere about Milton.[2] It is

---

[2] Voltaire first discussed Milton in his *Essay on Epic Poetry*, which he wrote in English during his period of exile in England. At this time he was favorably disposed toward Milton, but by the time he returned to France and produced a French version of the *Essay*, his views had changed, and his attitude was to remain a predominantly hostile one. This is very visible here, for despite the praise contained in his final sentence, Voltaire spends most of his time giving his reasons for disliking Milton.

One cannot give the exact originals of Voltaire's quotations (the most important of which come from Book X of *Paradise Lost*), for even when he uses quotation marks, he is in fact summarizing rather than quoting. In what he has to say about "cold and dry and warm and damp," he in fact juxtaposes two completely unrelated passages, one from Book II and the other from Book X. It is clear that Milton's allegory found no favor with his own classical taste, that he set out to criticize Milton, and then, in his final sentence, tried not very successfully to redress the balance.

true that several critics have reproached him for the oddity of his descriptions; for his paradise of fools; for his alabaster wall surrounding the Garden of Eden; his devils, transformed from giants into pygmies in order to take up less room in the council chamber of Hell, a great hall built of pure gold; for cannons which are fired in Heaven and mountains which people throw at each other's head; and for his angels on horseback and his angels which, when cut in two, immediately reunite themselves. People complain of his prolixity and his repetitions and say that he is not the equal of Ovid or Hesiod in his long description of the way in which the earth, the animals and man were formed. His digressions on astronomy have been criticized for their aridity and his inventions have been condemned as extravagant rather than marvelous and disgusting rather than powerful; as examples one may quote his long bridge across chaos; Sin and Death making love and having children from their incest; Death, who "turns up his nose to sniff across the immensity of chaos the changes which have taken place on earth, like a raven scenting corpses"; Death, again, smelling the odor of Sin and striking with his petrifying club on cold and dry; this cold and dry, together with warm and damp, then become four brave generals who lead lightly armed embryon atoms into battle. But if criticism of this work has been exhaustive, one cannot exhaust praise of it. Milton remains the glory and admiration of England; he is compared to Homer, who had equally great faults, and he is preferred to Dante, whose imagination is even more extravagant.

Among the many pleasing poets who adorned the reign of Charles II, like Waller, the Earls of Dorset and Rochester, the Duke of Buckingham, etc., special mention should be made of the famous Dryden, who distinguished himself in every branch of poetry. His works are full of details which are at one and the same time natural, brilliant, lively, vigorous, bold and impassioned, and his merits are unequaled in his own country and unsurpassed among the ancients. If Pope, who came later, had not, toward the end of his life, written his *Essay on Man,* he would not be comparable to Dryden.

No nation has discussed moral questions in verse with more energy and depth than the English; here, it seems to me, lies the greatest merit of her poets.

There is another type of literature, more varied in its forms, which demands a mind that is still more cultivated and universal; this is the type of which Addison was a master. Not only did he immortalize himself with his *Cato*,[3] the only English tragedy written with continuous elegance and nobility, but his other moral and critical works are full of taste; common sense abounds there, adorned with the flowers of imagination, and his way of writing is an excellent model for any country. Dean Swift has produced a number of works for which there are no parallels in antiquity: he is Rabelais brought to perfection.

Funeral orations are hardly known in England; it is not their custom to praise kings and queens in churches; but pulpit oratory, which was very crude in London before Charles II's time, developed suddenly. Bishop Burnet, in his memoirs, confesses that this was a result of imitating the French. Perhaps they have surpassed their masters, for their sermons are less formal, less affected and less declamatory than the French.

It is also surprising that these islanders, separated from the rest of the world and instructed so belatedly, have acquired at least as much knowledge of antiquity as has been gathered in Rome, for so long the center of all nations. Marsham pierced the darkness of ancient Egypt. No Persian knew the religion of Zoroaster as well as did the learned Hyde. The history of Mohammed and of the times which preceded him was unknown to the Turks, and has been discovered by the Englishman Sale, whose travels in Arabia proved so fruitful.

There is no country in the world in which the Christian religion has been so strongly criticized and so learnedly defended as England. From Henry VIII's time to that of Cromwell, people had disputed and fought

[3] Addison's *Cato* is now almost forgotten, but this rather dull tragedy, which followed strict classical precepts, was regarded by Voltaire as the greatest work of the English stage, preferable by far to the barbarities of Shakespeare.

like those ancient gladiators who descended into the arena with a scimitar in their hands and a bandage over their eyes. A few small differences in forms of worship and in dogma had produced horrible wars. But in the period since the Restoration and up to our own times, when Christianity has been attacked almost every day, these disputes have not produced the slightest disturbance The attacks have been refuted with learning; formerly it would have been with fire and sword.

It is above all in philosophy that the English have been the masters of other nations. With them it ceased to be a matter of ingenious systems. The philosophical fables of the Greeks should have been forgotten long ago, and those of the moderns should never have appeared. Bacon had taken the first step by saying that one should interrogate nature in a new way, by performing experiments; Boyle spent his life doing just this. This is not the place for a dissertation on physics; it is enough to say that after three thousand years of vain researches, Newton was the first to discover and prove the great law of nature by which all the elements of matter attract each other reciprocally. It is by this law that all the stars are kept in their courses. He was the first who really understood light; before him its nature was unknown.

His principles of mathematics, which contain a view of the physical world both original and true, are founded on the discovery of the calculus, which is improperly called "of infinities." This discovery is the latest achievement of geometry, and one which he made at the age of twenty-four. It led a great philosopher, the learned Halley, to exclaim that "no mortal will ever be permitted to approach nearer to the divinity."

A host of able geometers and physicists were enlightened by his discoveries and spurred to further efforts by him. Bradley finally discovered the aberration of light from the fixed stars, placed at least twelve million million leagues away from our tiny globe.

The same Halley, whom I have just quoted, although he was simply an astronomer, had command of one of the King's ships in 1698. On it, he determined the position of the stars of the South Pole, and marked all the variations of the compass in every part of the known world. The voyage of the Argonauts, in comparison, was that of a boat crossing from one bank of a river to the other. Halley's voyage has hardly been spoken of in Europe.

This indifference which we can show toward great things which have become too familiar contrasts with the admiration the ancient Greeks had for little things, and is a further proof of the prodigious superiority of our own age over that of the ancients. Boileau, in France, and Sir William Temple, in England, obstinately refused to recognize this superiority; they wanted to decry their own age in order to place themselves above it. This dispute between the ancients and the moderns has finally been decided, at least as far as philosophy is concerned. There is not a single ancient philosopher who is now used for the education of the young in enlightened nations.

The example of Locke would itself suffice to illustrate the superiority of our century over the finest ages of Greece. Between Plato and him there is nothing; no one in the intervening years explained the operations of the human mind, and a man who knew the whole of Plato, but knew nothing but Plato, would have very little knowledge and even that would be wrong.

It is true that the Greek philosopher was eloquent; his apology for Socrates is a service rendered to the wise men of all nations; it is right to respect him, since he made oppressed virtue so respectable and its persecutors so odious. For a long time people thought it impossible that his excellent moral doctrine could be accompanied by a bad metaphysical one; because of his *Ternary*,[4] which nobody has ever understood, he was almost a Church Father. But what would we think today of a philosopher who told us that matter was *other*, that the world is a figure of twelve pentagons, and that fire, which is a pyramid, is linked to the earth by numbers? Would he be well received if he proved the immortality

---

[4] By this word Voltaire is no doubt referring to the theory of three substances contained in Plato's *Timaeus;* some Neoplatonic Christians had seen affinities between this doctrine and that of the Trinity.

of the soul and metempsychosis by saying that sleep is born of waking, waking of sleep, life of death and death of life? These are the reasonings which so many centuries have admired; and even more extravagant ideas have since been employed in the education of men.

Locke alone has explained *Human Understanding,* in a book in which there are nothing but truths; and what makes this work perfect is that these truths are clear.[5]

To complete the picture of the ways in which this century surpasses all others, we must glance at Germany and the North. Helvetius, at Danzig, was the first astronomer really to study the moon; no one before him had examined the heavens more thoroughly. Moreover, none of the great men produced by this age illustrates more clearly why it should be called the age of Louis XIV. Helvetius lost an immense library in a fire: the King of France recompensed the astronomer of Danzig with a present which far outweighed his loss.

Mercator, in Holstein, was Newton's precursor in the field of geometry; the Bernoullis of Switzerland were the great man's disciples. Leibnitz was for some time considered as his rival.

The celebrated Leibnitz was born at Leipzig; he died at Hanover like a true philosopher, adoring God as Newton did, without consulting men's opinions. He was perhaps the most universal scholar in Europe: a historian tireless in his researches; a profound jurist, who used philosophy to illuminate the law, although it might seem inappropriate to this study; a metaphysician who was sufficiently unprejudiced to try to reconcile theology with metaphysics; a Latin poet even; and finally, a sufficiently good mathematician to dispute with Newton the invention of the calculus *of infinities* and to cause people to hesitate for some time between Newton and himself.[6]

---

[5] In his early *Philosophical Letters,* Voltaire devoted a lengthy chapter to expounding the ideas of Locke's *Essay on Human Understanding,* and throughout his life he continued to regard Locke as the greatest of all philosophers. He has, however, curiously little to say about Locke here, and in fact spends more time telling us what is wrong with Plato than what is right with Locke.

[6] It is interesting to note the variations in Voltaire's attitude to earlier writers in *The Age of Louis XIV,* especially when these

This was the great age of geometry; mathematicians often sent challenges to each other; that is, they sent problems to be solved, in the same way as the ancient kings of Egypt and Asia sent each other riddles. The problems proposed by the geometers were more difficult than the riddles, but there was not one of them which was not solved somewhere in Germany, England, Italy or France. Never had correspondence between philosophers been so universal; Leibnitz did much to promote it. Gradually a republic of letters became established in Europe, despite the wars and despite the differences of religion. In this way all the arts and sciences helped each other. The academies helped to form this republic. Italy corresponded with Russia. Englishmen, Germans and Frenchmen went to study at Leiden. The famous physician Boerhaave was consulted by both the Pope and the Czar. His greatest pupils similarly attracted foreigners, and became, in some degree, the doctors of all nations. In every field the truly learned have strengthened the bonds of this great society of minds which has its branches everywhere and is everywhere independent. This correspondence still continues, and helps to console us for the evils which ambition and politics spread throughout the world.

Italy, in this century, has kept its ancient glory although it has had no new Tassos or new Raphaels; to produce them once was sufficient. Chiabrera, and later Zappi and Filicaia, have proved that the Italians have not lost their delicacy. Maffei's *Mérope* and the dramatic works of Metastasio are fine monuments of the age.

The study of physics, established by Galileo, has been continually maintained despite the contradictions between it and an ancient philosophy which has become

---

earlier writers are men to whom he feels a certain hostility. We have noted how, in the case of Descartes, criticism outweighs praise. But Leibnitz was also a philosopher to whom Voltaire was predominantly hostile, for not only was he the creator of a *Monadology* which Voltaire regarded as nonsense, but his *Theodicy* contained the theory that this was the best of all possible worlds, the theory which Voltaire satirized so mercilessly in the best-known of all his works, *Candide*. Yet here there is not a hint of this hostility. Voltaire is far from consistent in his critical viewpoints.

all too sacrosanct. Cassini, Viviani, Manfredi, Bianchini, Zanotti and many others have made Italy as enlightened as other countries, and although the most powerful rays of this light came from England, the schools of Italy did not turn their eyes away from it.

Every branch of literature has been cultivated in this ancient home of the arts to the same extent as in other countries, except for those matters in which freedom of thought has given other nations an advantage. Above all, this age has had a better knowledge of antiquity than preceding ones. Italy contains more monuments than the rest of Europe put together, and knowledge has increased as more of these have been discovered.

All this progress has been the work of a few wise men, of a few men of genius scattered in different parts of Europe, usually living for many years in obscurity and often persecuted. It is they who have enlightened and consoled the world while wars ravaged it. Elsewhere the reader can find lists of names of those who have been the ornaments of Germany, England and Italy. A foreigner is perhaps not the appropriate person to give an appreciation of the merit of all these illustrious men. It is enough if we have shown here how, in the past century, men from one end of Europe to the other have acquired more knowledge than in all previous ages put together.

CHAPTER XXXV

Ecclesiastical Affairs/Memorable Disputes

Numerically the Church is the smallest of the three orders of the state, and France is the only kingdom in which the clergy have become such an order. This, as we have already said, is as surprising as it is true, and nothing more clearly demonstrates the power of custom. But ever since it has held this position, the clergy has always been the order of state which the King has needed to handle with the greatest delicacy and tact. To conserve the union with the see of Rome and at the same time preserve the liberties of the Gallican Church, which are the rights of the early Church; to see that the bishops obey as subjects without infringing the rights of the episcopacy; to subject them, in many things, to secular jurisdiction, and yet allow them to remain judges in others; to make them contribute to the needs of the state without attacking their privileges—all this requires a mixture of dexterity and firmness which Louis XIV almost always possessed.

The clergy in France was gradually restored to the order and respectability from which it had departed as a result of the civil wars and the licentiousness of the times. The King no longer allowed laymen to hold benefices under the name *confidentiaires;*[1] nor did he permit those who were not priests to hold bishoprics, like Cardinal Mazarin, who had held that of Metz without even being a subdeacon, or like the Duke of Verneuil, who had enjoyed a similar privilege as a layman.

The clergy of France and of the conquered cities paid, in an average year, about two million five hundred thousand francs, and since the devaluation of the currency, they have aided the state with about four millions a year through grants known as tenths, extraordinary subventions and free gifts. This term "free gift" and the privilege which it implies have been conserved as a remnant of the old usage according to which all feudal lords accorded free gifts to the King when the state was in need. In the days of feudal anarchy, bishops and abbots, who by an ancient abuse were lords of fiefs, were obliged only to furnish soldiers. In those days the kings had only their own domains, like other lords. Later, when everything else changed, the clergy remained unchanged and conserved the right of helping the state by free gifts.

To this ancient custom, which a body that meets frequently can preserve but which would inevitably be lost by one which did not, may be joined the immunity on which the Church has always insisted, and its maxim that *its property is the property of the poor;* not that it claims to owe nothing to the state from which it holds everything, for when the state is in need, it is the first

[1] These were men who held benefices for a certain time on the condition that they later handed them over to others.

of the poor; but it claims the right to give only voluntary help. Louis XIV always asked for such help in such a way that he could not be refused.

People are amazed in Europe and in France that the clergy pays so little; they calculate that it enjoys a third of the income of the kingdom. If this really were the case, then no doubt it ought to pay a third of the charges, which, in an average year, would amount to over fifty millions not counting the duties on articles consumed, which it pays like all other subjects. But people have vague ideas and prejudices about everything.

It is undeniable that, of all the Catholic Churches, the French Church is the one that has accumulated the least wealth. Not only has no bishop acquired major sovereignty, as has the Bishop of Rome, but no abbot enjoys regal rights, as do the Abbot of Monte Cassino and those of Germany. In general the income of French bishoprics is not unduly large. Strasbourg and Cambrai are the wealthiest, but this is because they originally belonged to Germany, and the German Church was far richer than the empire.

Giannone, in his *History of Naples,* assures us that ecclesiastics have two thirds of the revenue of that country. France is not afflicted with such an enormous abuse. People say that the Church owns a third of the kingdom in the same casual way as they say that Paris has a million inhabitants. But if they would take the trouble to calculate the revenue of bishoprics, they would see, from the value of the leases made about fifty years ago, that all the bishoprics put together were valued on the basis of an annual revenue of four million, and the commendatory abbeys at four million five hundred thousand francs. It is true that these leases were undervalued by a third, and that if we add the increase in land revenues, then the total revenue of all consistorial benefices will amount to about sixteen millions. One must not forget that a considerable part of this money is sent every year to Rome, that it never returns and is thus a complete loss to the state. In allowing this to happen the King shows great liberality toward the Holy See. In the space of a century the state loses more than four hundred thousand silver marks; this would be enough to impoverish the kingdom in the long run, if commerce did not abundantly repair the loss.

To these benefices which pay their first year's income to Rome, we must add vicarships, convents, collegiate churches and religious communities, as well as all other benefices; but if we calculate them to be worth fifty millions a year throughout the whole extent of the present kingdom, we shall not be far wrong.

Those who have examined this matter with strict attention have been unable to put the total of all the revenues of the Gallican Church, secular and regular, at over ninety millions. This is not an exorbitant sum to maintain ninety thousand members of religious orders and about a hundred and sixty thousand priests, which was the figure calculated in 1700. And of these ninety thousand monks, more than a third live on charity or by saying masses. Many conventual monks do not cost their monastery two hundred francs a year; but there are abbots of monasteries who enjoy incomes of two hundred thousand francs. It is this enormous disproportion which is so striking and which causes dissatisfaction. People pity a country vicar whose arduous labors earn him only a bare living of three hundred francs, which is all he is entitled to plus four or five hundred as a supplementary grant, while an idle monk who has become an abbot without becoming any less idle possesses an immense sum and is addressed by pompous titles by those who are subject to him. These abuses are even more pronounced in Flanders, in Spain, and above all in the Catholic states of Germany, where one finds monks who are princes.

Abuses end by being observed like laws in almost every country; and if the wisest men gathered together to make laws, where is the state whose present form would remain unchanged?

The French clergy pay the King a free gift of several millions for a number of years, and make this payment more burdensome to themselves by a custom which they still observe in doing so. They borrow the money, and after having paid the interest, repay the capital to their creditors, thereby paying twice. It would be much more advantageous for the state and for the clergy in general, as well as being more reasonable, if the ecclesiastical body contributed to the needs of the nation by contributions proportional to the value of each benefice. But men are always attached to their ancient customs. The same spirit is visible in the fact that the clergy, although they assemble every five years, have never possessed an assembly hall or even a piece of furniture they could call their own. It is clear that they could have helped the King more while spending less and that they could have built themselves a palace in Paris which would have been a new ornament for the capital.

The principles of the French clergy, during the minority of Louis XIV, had not yet been completely cleansed of the disorders which had been introduced by the League.[2] The last meeting of the States-General, held in 1614 when Louis XIII was still young, had witnessed the vain attempt by the Third Estate, the most numerous part of the nation and the backbone of the country, to get the Parlement to assert that it was a fundamental law that "no spiritual power can deprive kings of their sacred rights, which they hold from God alone, and it is a crime of high treason to teach that kings can be deposed or killed." This was the substance, in so many words, of the nation's demand. It was made at a time when the blood of Henry the Great was still warm. However, a bishop of France and one who was born in France, Cardinal Duperron, violently opposed this proposal, on the pretext that it was not the province of the Third Estate to propose laws on matters which could concern the Church. Why then did not he and the clergy themselves do what the Third Estate wanted to do? He was, in fact, so far from having any such intention that he even said "that the power of the Pope was complete, utterly complete indeed, that it was direct in spiritual matters and indirect in temporal ones, and that he was charged by the clergy to state that they would excom-

[2] The Catholic League, which led the resistance against the Protestant Henry IV during the civil wars of the sixteenth century.

municate anyone who suggested that the Pope could not depose kings." The nobility were won around to this point of view, and the Third Estate was silenced. The Parlement renewed its old decrees declaring the crown independent and the person of the King sacred. The ecclesiastical chamber, while admitting that the King's person was sacred, insisted that the crown was dependent. This was the same spirit which in former times had deposed Louis the Pious.[3] This spirit prevailed to such an extent that the court was obliged to acquiesce and to imprison the printer who had published the Parlement's decree under the title "Fundamental Law." This, they said, was done for the sake of peace; but it was really to punish those who had furnished the crown with a weapon of defense. There were no such scenes in Vienna, for at that time France feared Rome, whereas Rome was afraid of the House of Austria.

The cause thus defeated was so much that of kings everywhere that James I of England wrote against Cardinal Duperron a book which is his finest work. It was also the peoples' cause, for their tranquillity demands that sovereigns should not be dependent on a foreign power. Gradually reason prevailed; and Louis XIV had no difficulty in making people listen to this reason, supported as it was by the weight of his power.

Antonio Perez had recommended three things to Henry IV: *Roma, Consejo, Pielago.*[4] Louis XIV possessed the last two in such abundance that he had no need of the first. He was careful to preserve the right of appeal to the Parlement from ecclesiastical ordinances, in all the cases where these ordinances affected royal jurisdiction. The clergy often complained of this and occasionally congratulated themselves on it, for if, on the one hand, these appeals maintained the rights of the state against episcopal authority, they also, on the other, affirmed this same authority by maintaining the privileges of the Gallican Church against the claims of the court of Rome; in this way the bishops looked on the Parlements both as adversaries and as defenders, and the government was care-

[3] The son of Charlemagne who was deposed by his three sons.
[4] "Rome, prudence, control of the seas."

ful to see that, despite the religious quarrels, the bounds which could so easily have been overstepped were in fact infringed by neither side. The same can be said of the power of bodies and companies as of the interests of commercial towns: it is up to the legislator to keep a balance between them.

The Liberties of the Gallican Church

This word "liberties" presupposes subjection. Liberties and privileges are exemptions from the general servitude. One should say the rights, and not the liberties, of the Gallican Church. These rights are those of all the ancient churches. The bishops of Rome have never had the slightest jurisdiction over the Christian societies of the Eastern empire. But when the Western empire fell in ruins, they extended their power everywhere. The Church of France was for long the only one which disputed with the See of Rome the ancient rights which each bishop had given himself when, after the first Council of Nicaea, ecclesiastical and purely spiritual administration modeled itself on civil government, and each bishop had his own diocese just as each imperial district had its own area. Certainly none of the Gospels said that a bishop of the city of Rome could send legates *a latere* into France to judge, reform, issue dispensations and collect money from the peoples;

To order French prelates to go to Rome to plead;

To impose taxes on the benefices of the kingdom under such names as vacancies, assets, successions, first fruits, incompatibilities, commands, ninths, tenths and annates;

To excommunicate the King's officers in order to prevent them from fulfilling their proper functions;

To make bastards capable of inheriting;

To invalidate the wills of those who died without giving part of their property to the Church;

To allow French ecclesiastics to alienate their landed property;

To delegate judges to inquire into the legitimacy of marriages.

In fact, one can count up to seventy such usurpations, against which the parlements of the kingdom have always maintained the natural liberty of the nation and the dignity of the crown.

However much credit the Jesuits may have had under Louis XIV, and however much the King, once he assumed power, put a curb on the remonstrances of the parlements, yet none of these distinguished bodies ever lost an opportunity of opposing the claims of the Roman court; and the King always approved this vigilance, because in this matter the essential rights of the nation were those of the crown.

The most important and most delicate affair of this sort was that of the *régale*. This is the right which the kings of France possess of appointing their nominees to any ordinary benefice in a diocese while the see is vacant and of disposing as they think fit of the revenues of the bishopric. This prerogative is now peculiar to the kings of France; but every state has its own. The kings of Portugal enjoy a third of the revenues of all the bishoprics in their kingdom. The Emperor has a prerogative of presentation; he has always been able to nominate to the first livings which fell vacant. The kings of Naples and Sicily have even greater rights. The rights of Rome itself are, for the most part, founded on custom rather than on any original titles.

The Merovingian kings appointed all bishops and other churchmen on their own authority. In 724, for example, Carloman created Archbishop of Mainz the very same Boniface who later, as an act of gratitude, anointed Pepin. There are still many relics of the power which kings used to possess of disposing of these important posts; the more important they are, indeed, the more they should be dependent on the head of state. The participation of a foreign bishop seemed dangerous; and giving a foreign bishop full power to nominate has often seemed an even more dangerous usurpation. More than once it has sparked a civil war. As the kings used to confer the bishoprics, it seemed reasonable that they should keep the minor privilege of disposing of the revenue and nominating to a number of ordinary livings during the short space of time between the death of a bishop and the registration of the oath of loyalty of his successor. Several bishops of towns annexed to the crown under the third dynasty refused to recognize this right, which private overlords had been too weak to uphold. The popes declared themselves for the bishops, and these claims remained shrouded in uncertainty. In 1608, under Henry IV, the Parlement declared that the right of *régale* applied throughout the kingdom; the clergy complained, and the King, who did not want to antagonize either the bishops or Rome, reserved the affair for his Council and took good care to come to no decision.

Richelieu and Mazarin had several decrees of Council issued, demanding that the bishops who said they were exempt should produce their titles. Until 1673 the whole question remained undecided, and at that time the King did not dare bestow a single benefice in almost all the dioceses south of the Loire, during the period in which the see was vacant.

Finally, in 1673 the chancellor Etienne d'Aligre signed an edict by which all the bishoprics of the kingdom were subjected to the right of *régale*. Two bishops, who unfortunately were the two most virtuous men in the kingdom, stubbornly refused to submit; they were Pavillon, Bishop of Aleth, and Caulet, Bishop of Pamiers. They began by defending themselves with plausible reasons; others, equally strong, were advanced against them. When enlightened men go on arguing for a long time, there is a distinct probability that the question is not clear. It was, indeed, most obscure; but it was clear that neither religion nor public order were concerned with stopping a king from doing in two of his dioceses what he was doing in all the others. Yet the two bishops were inflexible. Neither of them had registered his oath of loyalty, and the King considered he had the right to fill the canonries of their churches.

The two bishops excommunicated those whom the King appointed in this way. They were both suspected of Jansenism. Innocent X had been opposed to them; but when they declared themselves against the royal claims they were supported by Innocent XI, Odescalchi; this Pope, who was as virtuous and stubborn as they were, took their part wholeheartedly.

The King contented himself, in the first place, with exiling the principal officers of these bishops. He showed more moderation than two men who prided themselves on their holiness. The great age of the Bishop of Aleth was respected, and he was allowed to die in peace. The Bishop of Pamiers remained alone, but he was undismayed. He repeated his excommunications and persisted in refusing to register his oath of loyalty, in the persuasion that this oath made the Church too dependent on the monarchy. The King seized his temporal property. The Pope and the Jansenists indemnified him. He gained by being deprived of his revenues, and died in 1680, convinced that he had defended the cause of God against the King. His death did not extinguish the quarrel; canons nominated by the King came to take possession of the see, but monks who claimed to be canons and grand vicars drove them out of the church and excommunicated them. The metropolitan, Montpezat, Archbishop of Toulouse, within whose jurisdiction the matter lay, vainly condemned these so-called grand vicars. They appealed to Rome, following the custom of referring to the court of Rome ecclesiastical cases judged by French archbishops. This custom contradicted Gallican liberties; but all human governments are full of contradictions. The Parlement issued decrees. A monk called Cerle, who was one of the grand vicars we have been talking about, pronounced both the decisions of the metropolitan and the decrees of the Parlement to be invalid. The Parlement condemned him in his absence to be beheaded and dragged through the streets. He was executed in effigy, but from the depths of his hiding place he continued to insult the Archbishop and the King, and had the Pope's support in doing so. The Pope went further; convinced, like the Bishop of Pamiers, that the right of *régale* was a scandal to the Church, and that the King had no right in Pamiers, he quashed the decisions of the Archbishop of Toulouse and excommunicated the new grand vicars nominated by the Archbishop as well as those who had accepted benefices from the King and their abettors.

The King convoked an assembly of the clergy, consisting of thirty-five bishops and as many deputies of the lower clergy. The Jansenists, for the first time, took the side of the Pope and the Pope himself, because of his enmity toward the King, favored them without liking them. He considered it an honor to resist Louis XIV whenever he could; and even later, in 1689, he joined the allies against King James because Louis XIV was protecting this monarch. The situation was such that people said that the only way to end the troubles of Europe and the Church was for King James to become a Huguenot, and the Pope a Catholic.

However, the assembly of the clergy, in 1681 and 1682, pronounced unanimously for the King. Once again a small issue had become important; the election to a priory in a Paris suburb brought the King and the Pope into conflict. The Roman pontiff had quashed an ordinance by the Archbishop of Paris and annulled his nomination to the priory. The Parlement had declared this procedure illegal. The Pope had issued a bull ordering the Inquisition to burn the Parlement's decree and the Parlement had ordered the suppression of the bull. For a long time now, such struggles have been the usual and inevitable result of the traditional combination of the country's natural freedom to govern itself, with submission to a foreign power.

The assembly of the clergy adopted a policy which shows that wise men can submit to their sovereign with dignity, without any other power intervening. It agreed to the extension of the right of *régale* to the whole country; but this was a concession on the part of the clergy, who relinquished some of their claims out of gratitude to their protector, rather than as a formal admission of the absolute right of the crown.

The assembly justified its action to the Pope by a letter in which there is a passage which ought in itself to suffice as an eternal rule in such disputes. It says "that it is better to sacrifice something of one's rights than to disturb the peace." The King, the Gallican Church and the Parlements were all satisfied. The Jansenists wrote a few pamphlets. But the Pope was inflexible: he sent a pastoral letter annulling the resolutions of the assembly and ordered the bishops to retract. The situation had become so serious that it might easily have resulted in the final separation of the Church of France from that of Rome. In the time of Richelieu and Mazarin, people had talked of creating a patriarch. The magistrates were unanimous in demanding that the tribute of annates should no longer be paid to Rome; that Rome should no longer have the right of appointing to livings in Brittany during six months of the year; and that French bishops should no longer be called bishops *by permission of the Holy See*. Had the King so desired, he had only to utter a word; he was master of the assembly of the clergy, and he had the nation on his side. Rome would have lost everything as a result of the obduracy of a virtuous pontiff who, alone of all the popes in this century, could not move with the times. However, there are ancient barriers which cannot be shifted without violent upheavals. A greater clash of interests, a greater degree of passion and a more explosive frame of mind would have been needed to effect a sudden break with Rome; and it would have been very difficult to split off in this way, while at the same time trying to destroy Calvinism. The government even thought they were being exceptionally daring when, in 1682, they published the four famous decisions of this same assembly of the clergy, the substance of which was as follows:

1. God has given Peter and his successors no power, direct or indirect, over temporal matters.
2. The Gallican Church approves the decision of the Council of Constance, which declares that general councils are superior to the Pope in spiritual matters.
3. The rules, usages and practices established in France and in the Gallican Church must remain inviolable.
4. The decisions of the Pope in matters of faith are only certain after the Church has accepted them.

All the tribunals and all the faculties of theology registered these four propositions in their entirety; and an edict prohibited the teaching of anything contrary to them. This firmness was regarded in Rome as an act of rebellion, and by all European Protestants as a feeble effort by a Church which had once been free, and which was only breaking four links of its chain.

At first the nation accepted these four maxims with enthusiasm. But later support for them tended to cool off, and by the end of Louis XIV's reign they were beginning to be regarded as doubtful. In the end Cardinal Fleury had them partially disavowed by an assembly of the clergy, and this disavowal did not cause the slightest disturbance, both because tempers were no longer heated, and because, during Fleury's ministry, nothing appeared startling. However, they have since been taken up again with great vigor.

Innocent XI, however, became more bitter than ever. He refused to issue bulls to any of the bishops and commendatory abbots appointed by the King, so that when he died, in 1689, there were twenty-nine dioceses in France with no bishop. The priests the King had appointed received their revenues; but they did not dare to have themselves consecrated, or to exercise their episcopal functions. The idea of creating a patriarch was revived. The quarrel about the privileges of ambassadors in Rome[5] poisoned the wound even further, and led people to think that the time had at last arrived to establish in France a *Catholic and Apostolic* Church which would no longer be *Roman*. The attorney general, Harlay, and the advocate general, Talon, made this quite clear when they appealed in 1687 against the bull restricting ambassadorial privileges. They fulminated against the stubbornness of the Pope, who was leaving so many churches without pastors. But the King would never agree to this step, which, despite its apparent boldness, would really have been an easy one.

However, the cause of Innocent XI became that of the Holy See. The four propositions of the French clergy attacked the phantom of papal infallibility (which Rome

[5] This affair (1661) started as a quarrel over matters of precedence between the French and Spanish ambassadors in Rome and developed into a series of brawls. Voltaire describes it in Chapter VII.

maintains without really believing in it), as well as the real power associated with this phantom. Alexander VIII and Innocent XII followed in the footsteps of the proud Odescalchi, although in a less rigid way: they confirmed the decision condemning the assembly of the clergy; they refused bulls to the bishops; in short, they did too much because Louis XIV had not done enough. The bishops, tired of being merely nominated by the King and then finding themselves unable to exercise their functions, asked the court of France for permission to appease that of Rome.

The King, tiring of his firmness, gave his permission. Each bishop wrote separately to the Pope to say that he was "grievously afflicted by the proceedings of the assembly," and to declare that he did not accept as decided what had in fact been decided, or as established what had in fact been established. Pignatelli (Innocent XII), who was more conciliatory than Odescalchi, was satisfied with this proceeding. The four propositions were nonetheless taught in France from time to time, but these arms tended to rust when they were no longer used, and the dispute was quietly buried without being decided, as almost always happens in a state which has no invariable and recognized principles on such matters. So Rome is alternately resisted and appeased, all depending on the characters of those who govern and on the private interests of those who wield influence over those who govern.[6]

Apart from this, Louis XIV had no other ecclesiastical quarrels with Rome; nor was he ever opposed by the clergy in temporal matters.

Under his rule the clergy became respected for a decorum which had been unknown in the barbarous years of the first two dynasties and in the even more barbarous days of feudal government, and absolutely unknown during the civil wars, the agitations of Louis XIII's reign and

---

[6] In this long discussion of the quarrels between Louis XIV and Rome, Voltaire, especially in a number of his general comments, reveals his sympathy for the Gallican viewpoint. At the same time he makes a very real effort to present a balanced picture and to show the Popes and men like Pavillon and Caulet in a not unfavorable light.

above all during the *Fronde*. There are a few exceptions to this, as there always are to both dominant vices and dominant virtues.

It was only then that the people's eyes began to be opened to the superstitions which it always mingles with its religion. Despite the Parlement of Aix, and despite the Carmelites, people were permitted to know that Lazarus and Mary Magdalene had never visited Provence. The Benedictines failed to convince them that Denys the Areopagite[7] had governed the Church of Paris. Imaginary saints, false miracles and supposed relics began to be discredited. Sound reason, which enlightened philosophers, began to penetrate everywhere, although slowly and with difficulty.

The Bishop of Châlons-sur-Marne, Gaston-Louis de Noailles, brother of the Cardinal, was in 1702 sufficiently enlightened in his piety to remove and throw away a relic which had been carefully preserved for many centuries in the church of Notre-Dame and which had been worshiped under the name of the navel of Jesus Christ. All Châlons murmured against the Bishop. Presidents, councilors, royal officers, treasurers of France, merchants, leading citizens, canons and vicars, all protested unanimously, in legal form, against the Bishop's initiative, demanding the return of the holy navel and quoting the examples of Christ's garment preserved at Argenteuil, his kerchief at Turin and at Laon, one of the nails of the Cross at Saint-Denis, and a host of other relics which are preserved and yet despised and which do so much harm to a religion we revere. But the Bishop's wise resolution finally triumphed over the credulity of the people.

A number of other superstitions attached to respectable customs have remained. The Protestants point to them in triumph, but they are obliged to admit that there is no Catholic Church in which such abuses are less common and more despised than that of France.

The truly philosophical spirit, which took root only about the middle of this century, did not put an end to

---

[7] Denys the Areopagite, of the first century, had been confused with the Parisian St. Denis of the third.

theological quarrels old and new, for they were not within its province. We shall now speak of these dissentions, which are a disgrace to human reason.

CHAPTER XXXVI

Calvinism in Louis XIV's Time

It is no doubt an appalling thought that the Christian Church has been constantly torn by quarrels, and that blood has been shed through so many centuries by those who preached the God of peace. This fury was unknown to paganism. It covered the world in darkness, but rarely shed any blood other than that of animals; and if, occasionally, among the Jews and among the pagans, human victims were sacrificed, these sacrifices, horrible though they were, did not result in civil wars. Pagan religion merely consisted in a moral doctrine and a number of festivals. Morality is what is common to all men in all times and places, and the festivals, which were only celebrations, could never disturb mankind.

The spirit of dogmatism inspired men with the fury of the religious wars. I have long sought to discover how and why this dogmatic spirit, which divided the schools of pagan antiquity without causing the least disturbance, should have produced such horrible disorders among us. Fanaticism cannot be the only cause, for the gymnosophists and the Brahmans were the most fanatical of men, and yet never harmed anyone but themselves.[1] Might one not find the origin of this new plague which has ravaged the earth in the natural struggle between the republican spirit which animated the early churches, and authority, which hates resistance in any form? The secret assemblies which began by braving the laws of Roman emperors in caves and cellars gradually became a state within a state, a hidden republic in the midst of

[1] It is, of course, untrue that Christianity was the only religion to produce fanatical civil wars. But Voltaire probably sincerely believed that this was the case, and his attempt to show why Christianity should have led to these disturbances is an interesting and at times shrewd historical hypothesis.

the empire. Constantine rescued it from this underground existence and installed it beside the throne. Soon the authority attached to great sees found itself in opposition to the popular spirit which had hitherto inspired all Christian assemblies. Often, as soon as a metropolitan bishop uttered one opinion, a suffragan bishop, a priest or a deacon found they held the opposite one. All men are secretly jealous of authority, especially as all authority always tries to expand. When, in order to resist it, we find a pretext which we believe sacred, we soon make a duty of revolt. In this way some men become persecutors while others become rebels, both sides claiming that God is their witness.

We have seen how the urge to dominate men's souls has brought trouble to the world ever since the disputes between the priest Arius and a bishop.[2] To proclaim one's own opinions as the will of God and to command people to believe them under pain of bodily death and the eternal torment of the soul has been the final stage of spiritual despotism in a number of men, and to resist these two threats has been, in others, the last effort of natural liberty. If you have read the *Essay on Customs*, you will have seen, ever since the time of Theodosius, a perpetual struggle between the secular jurisdiction and the ecclesiastical, and ever since Charlemagne, the repeated rebellions of the holders of large fiefs against their sovereigns, bishops in revolt against kings, and the popes locked in combat with both priests and bishops.[3]

In the first centuries of the Latin Church, there were few disputes. The continual invasions of the barbarians hardly left time for thought, and doctrines had not been sufficiently elaborated to fix the universal faith. Almost the whole of the West rejected the cult of images in Charlemagne's time. A bishop of Turin, called Claudius, attacked them heatedly and maintained a number of doctrines which even today are the foundation of the

---

[2] Arius, who lived in the fourth century, was the founder of the heretical doctrine of Arianism. His great opponent was St. Athanasius.

[3] These subjects form one of the main themes of the chapters dealing with the Middle Ages in the *Essay on Customs*. Voltaire also deals with them at some length in his *Annals of the Empire*.

Protestant religion. These opinions persisted in the valleys of Piedmont, Dauphiné, Provence and Languedoc; they burst forth again in the twelfth century, and soon after produced the Albigensian crusade. Later they spread to the University of Prague, and stirred up the Hussite wars. Barely a hundred years elapsed between the end of the disturbance which arose from the ashes of John Huss and Jerome of Prague, and those which were started by the sale of indulgences. The ancient doctrines embraced by the Vaudois, the Albigensians and the Hussites, revived and differently interpreted by Luther and Zwingli, were eagerly received in Germany as a pretext for seizing many lands possessed by bishops and abbots, and for resisting the emperors, who were then making great strides toward despotic power. These doctrines triumphed in Sweden and Denmark, countries in which the people lived in freedom under their kings.

The English, endowed by nature with the spirit of independence, adopted them, modified them and made them into a religion suitable only for themselves. In Scotland, in these times of misfortune, Presbyterianism succeeded in establishing a type of republic whose pedantry and harshness were a good deal more intolerable than the rigors of the climate, and even than the tyranny of the bishops, which had excited so many complaints. It ceased to be dangerous in Scotland only when reason, law and force had repressed it. The Reformation spread to Poland and made rapid progress there in those towns where the people were not slaves. The largest and richest part of the Swiss republic had no hesitation in welcoming it. It was on the point of establishing itself in Venice for the same reasons, and would have succeeded in doing so if Venice had not been the neighbor of Rome and perhaps if the government had not been afraid of democracy, the condition to which the people naturally aspire in every republic and which was then the great aim of the majority of the preachers. The Dutch adopted this religion only when they threw off the Spanish yoke. Geneva became a completely republican state when it became Calvinist.

The house of Austria kept these doctrines out of the

states under its control as far as was possible. They barely managed to reach Spain. They were wiped out with fire and sword in the states of the Duke of Savoy, which had been their cradle. In 1655 the inhabitants of the valleys of Piedmont experienced what the peoples of Merindol and Cabrieres suffered in France under Francis I. The Duke of Savoy, an absolute monarch, exterminated the sect in his territories as soon as it seemed to him dangerous; today only a few feeble remnants are left, forgotten amid the rocks which hide them. Under the strong governments of Francis I and Henry II, Lutherans and Calvinists did not cause great disturbances in France; but once the government became weak and divided, religious quarrels became violent. The Condés and Colignys, who had become Calvinists because the Guises were Catholics, shook the state to its foundations. The inconsistency and impetuosity of the nation, its mania for novelty and its religious enthusiasm, turned the most polite of peoples into a race of barbarians for a period of forty years.

Henry IV was born into the Protestant sect, which he loved, though without any immoderate zeal. Despite his victories and his virtues, he found it impossible to reign without abandoning Calvinism. Having become a Catholic, he was not so ungrateful as to wish to destroy a party which had for so long been the enemy of kings, but to which he partly owed his crown. Even if he had wanted to destroy this faction, he would have been unable to do so. He cherished it, protected it, but kept it firmly under control.

The Huguenots in France at this time made up about a tenth part of the nation. Among them there were powerful lords, and whole towns were Protestant. They had made war on the kings, and forced them to allow them fortified strongholds; Henry II had granted them fourteen of these in Dauphiné alone. They also held Montauban and Nîmes in Languedoc, Saumur and above all La Rochelle, which was like a separate republic, and which could become powerful, thanks to the trade and favor of England. Finally Henry IV seemed to satisfy his taste, his political ideals and even his duty when, in

1598, he granted the Protestants the celebrated Edict of Nantes. This edict was basically only the confirmation of the privileges which the French Protestants had obtained from previous kings by armed force, and which Henry the Great, once he was secure on his throne, allowed them to keep from sheer good will.

By this Edict of Nantes, which the name of Henry IV rendered more famous than all others, every lord of a fief vested with plenary judicial powers was allowed, in his own castle, the full exercise of the so-called reformed religion; any lord without these powers might admit thirty people to his religious services. Complete freedom to practice this religion was authorized in all places which were under the immediate jurisdiction of a parlement.

The Calvinists could, without having to consult higher authority, have all their books printed in the towns where their religion was permitted.

They were declared capable of holding all the offices and dignities of the state; and the King showed he meant this by making the lords of La Trimouille and Rosny dukes and peers.

A special chamber was created in the parlement of Paris composed of a president and sixteen councilors which judged all cases concerning Protestants, not only in the immense district under the jurisdiction of Paris, but also in those of Normandy and Brittany. It was called the Chamber of the Edict. It is true that only one Calvinist was ever admitted to sit by right among the councilors of this court. However, as it had been created in order to put a stop to the vexations of which the party complained, and as men always pride themselves on fulfilling a duty which honors them, this chamber, composed as it was of Catholics, always rendered to the Huguenots, as they themselves admitted, the most impartial justice.

They had a sort of small parlement of their own at Castres, independent of that of Toulouse. At Grenoble and Bordeaux there were chambers which were half Calvinist and half Catholic. Their churches met in synods as did the Gallican Church. These privileges, and many others, incorporated the Calvinists into the body of the nation. It is true that this meant linking enemies together; but the authority, kindness and tact of the great King kept them from quarreling during his lifetime.

After the unforgettable horror and tragedy of Henry IV's death, during the weakness of a minority, and under a divided court, it was very difficult for the republican spirit of the Calvinists to avoid abusing its privileges, and for the court, weak though it was, to avoid trying to restrict them. The Huguenots had already established *circles* in France, in imitation of those of Germany. The deputies of these small assemblies were often seditious, for the party contained a number of highly ambitious nobles. The Duke of Bouillon, and above all the Duke of Rohan, the generally accepted leader of the Huguenots, soon led the restless spirit of the preachers and the blind zeal of the people into revolt. In 1615 the general assembly of the party took the daring step of presenting the court with a memorandum in which, among other insolent claims, they demanded the reform of the King's Council. By 1616 they had taken up arms in a number of places, and this audacious act, coupled with the divisions of the court, the hatred of royal favorites and the general uneasiness of the nation, led to a long series of disturbances. There were seditions, intrigues, threats, calls to arms and treaties of peace hastily made and equally hastily broken; all this led the celebrated Cardinal Bentivoglio, the papal nuncio in France, to say that he had witnessed nothing but storms.

In 1621 the reformed Churches of France offered Lesdiguières, who later became constable, the general command of their armies and a hundred thousand crowns a month. But Lesdiguières, who was more clear-sighted in his ambition than they were in their factions, and who knew them because he had commanded them, preferred to fight against them rather than to lead them; and by way of reply to their offers, he became a Catholic. The Huguenots then approached the Marshal Duke of Bouillon, who said that he was too old; finally they gave this unhappy post to the Duke of Rohan, who, together with his brother Soubise, dared to make war on the King of France.

This same year, the constable, de Luynes, conducted

Louis XII on an armed tour of the provinces. More than fifty towns surrendered to him almost without resistance; but he failed before Montauban, and the King had the mortification of being forced to decamp. La Rochelle was besieged in vain; it resisted thanks to its own strength and to the help it obtained from England. The Duke of Rohan, guilty of high treason, negotiated a peace with his King, almost like one crowned head with another.

After this peace, and after the death of the constable, de Luynes, the war had to be begun all over again. La Rochelle, still leagued with England and the Calvinists in the rest of the kingdom against its rightful sovereign, was besieged a second time. A woman (the Duke of Rohan's mother) defended this town for a whole year against the royal army, against the activities of Cardinal Richelieu and against the valor of Louis XIII, who risked death more than once at this siege. The town suffered all the rigors of hunger, and its final surrender was brought about only by the five-hundred-foot-long mole which Richelieu had built in imitation of the one which Alexander had constructed before Tyre. It tamed both the sea and the inhabitants of La Rochelle. The mayor, Guiton, who had wanted to be buried beneath the ruins of the town, had the audacity, after having surrendered unconditionally, to appear with his guards in the presence of Richelieu. The mayors of the principal Huguenot towns had such guards. Guiton was deprived of his, and the town deprived of its privileges. The Duke of Rohan, leader of the rebellious heretics, continued the war on behalf of his party. Abandoned by the English, although they were Protestants, he allied himself with the Spaniards, although they were Catholics. But the firm behavior of Cardinal Richelieu forced the Huguenots, who were defeated on all sides, to submit.

All the edicts which had been granted them up to this time had in fact been negotiated with the kings. Richelieu insisted that the one he issued should be called the Edict of Grace. In it the King spoke as a sovereign who offers pardon. La Rochelle, Ile de Ré, Ile d'Oléron, Privas and Pamiers were forbidden to practice the new religion; in other respects the Edict of Nantes, which the Calvinists continued to regard as their fundamental law, remained unchanged.

It seems curious that Richelieu, absolute and strong-minded as he was, did not abolish this famous edict; but at that time he had another aim in view, one which was perhaps more difficult to achieve, but one which was no less in accordance with his ambition and with the greatness of his designs. He sought the glory of subjugating men's minds; and he thought he was capable of doing this through his understanding, his power and his political skill. His aim was to win over some of the preachers whom the reformed Church then called ministers and who are now known as pastors. He would begin by getting them to agree that the Catholic religion was not a crime in the eyes of God, and then gradually lead them on from here by granting them a number of unimportant points and yet giving the court of Rome the impression that he had granted nothing. He calculated that he could dazzle one section of the Protestants in this way, win over the others with presents and favors, and end by giving every impression of having reunited them with the Church, leaving time to complete the task, and envisaging only the glory of having achieved or prepared this great work, or at least of having it attributed to him. The famous Capuchin Father Joseph, on the one side, and two ministers who had been won over, on the other, began these negotiations. But it soon appeared that Cardinal Richelieu had presumed too much, and that it was far more difficult to get theologians to agree than to build dikes across the ocean.

After this rebuff Richelieu decided to crush the Calvinists. But other preoccupations prevented him from doing so. He had to struggle at one and the same time with the great lords of the kingdom, the royal household, the whole house of Austria and often with Louis XIII himself. Finally, in the midst of these storms, he died a premature death. All his designs remained unfulfilled, and he left behind a name which was more dazzling than loved or revered.

However, after the capture of La Rochelle and the Edict of Grace, the civil wars ceased and only the disputes remained. Both sides produced those large volumes which nobody ever reads today. The clergy and above all the Jesuits strove to convert the Huguenots. The ministers tried to attract a number of Catholics to their opinions. The King's Council spent its time issuing decrees over a village cemetery claimed by both religions, over a Protestant house of worship built on land formerly belonging to the Church, over schools, over the rights of owners of castles, over burials and over bells; and rarely did the Protestants win their case. After so much devastation and pillage, all that remained was these trifling disputes. The Huguenots no longer had a leader after the Duke of Rohan had ceased to hold the post, and after the house of Bouillon had lost Sedan. They even made a virtue of remaining at peace in the midst of the factions of the *Fronde* and the civil wars which the princes, parlements and bishops stirred up, claiming thereby to serve the King against Cardinal Mazarin.

During the life of this minister the religious question was hardly ever raised. He saw no objection to giving the post of controller general of finances to a foreign Calvinist called Hervart. The Protestants then became tax-farmers and held posts in all branches of tax collection.

Colbert, who revived the nation's industry and who can be regarded as the founder of its commerce, employed many Huguenots in the arts, in industry and in the navy. The fact that they were usefully occupied in this way gradually diminished their outbursts of controversial zeal; and the glory which for fifty years surrounded Louis XIV, together with his power and the firm and vigorous nature of his government, deprived the reformed party, as it did all other orders of the state, of any idea of resistance. The magnificent entertainments of a pleasure-loving court even made the pedantry of the Huguenots look ridiculous. With the development of good taste, the psalms of Marot and Besa gradually came to evoke nothing but distaste. These psalms, which had charmed the court of Francis II, appealed only to the populace under Louis XIV. Sound philosophy, which began to make its way in the world toward the middle of the century, was bound to contribute even further in the long run to making decent people disgusted with controversial disputes.

But even before reason gradually forced men to listen to her, the very spirit of dispute itself served to maintain the Jansenists first began to gain a reputation, and they had their share of support among the people, who nourished themselves on these subtleties. They wrote against both the Jesuits and the Huguenots; the latter answered both Jesuits and Jansenists; the Lutherans of Alsace attacked all three. A paper war among so many parties, while the state was achieving great things and the government was all-powerful, inevitably soon became an occupation for idle people, of the sort which sooner or later ends by being greeted with complete indifference.

Louis XIV was roused to anger against the reformers by the continual remonstrances of his clergy, by the insinuations of the Jesuits, by the court of Rome and lastly by the chancellor Le Tellier and his son Louvois, who were both enemies of Colbert and who wanted to root out the Calvinists as rebels because Colbert was protecting them as useful subjects. Louis XIV, who knew nothing of the fundamentals of their doctrine, looked on them, not without some reason, as former rebels who had been subdued with difficulty. He began by applying himself to the task of undermining from every side the edifice of their religion. Their churches were closed on the slightest pretext; they were forbidden to marry Catholic girls, a prohibition which perhaps showed a lack of shrewdness in that it failed to take advantage of the power of a sex with which the court, nevertheless, was well acquainted. The intendants and bishops tried, on the most plausible grounds, to take Huguenot children away from their parents. In 1681 Colbert was ordered not to employ any man of this religion in the administration of taxation. They were excluded, as far as possible, from the guilds of arts and crafts. The King, however, while keeping them under the yoke, did not always make them feel the full weight of it. Decrees prohibited all acts of violence against them. Persuasion was mixed with severity, and it was only in the formalities of justice that full rigor was employed.

One method of conversion which often proved effective was used more than all others: this was money; yet even this was not used enough. Pellisson was charged with this secret undertaking—the same Pellisson who had long been a Calvinist, and who was so well known for his writings, for his abundant eloquence and for his attachment to the superintendent Fouquet, of whom he had been both the secretary and favorite, and the victim. He had the good fortune to be enlightened and to change his religion at a time when this change could lead him to dignities and fortune. He entered orders and obtained benefices and a post of master of requests. About 1677 the King gave him the revenues of the abbeys of Saint-Germain-des-Prés and Cluny, together with the revenues of a third of the vacant benefices so that he might distribute them to those who were willing to be converted. Cardinal Lecamus, Bishop of Grenoble, had already used this method. Pellisson, when he was put in charge of this department, sent money to the provinces, trying to secure a large number of conversions for very little money. Small sums distributed to the poor swelled the list that Pellisson presented every three months to the King, making him believe that nothing could resist his power and his generosity.

The Council, encouraged by these small successes, which time would have rendered more considerable, took a bold step in 1681 by issuing a declaration which required all children to renounce the Protestant religion at the age of seven; under the sanction of this declaration, large numbers of children were seized in the provinces in order to force them to abjure, and troops were billeted on their parents.

In 1681 this precipitate step, taken by the chancellor Le Tellier and his son Louvois, resulted in the desertion of many families from Poitou, Saintonge and the neighboring provinces. Foreign countries hastened to take advantage of this.

The Kings of England and Denmark, and above all the city of Amsterdam, invited the French Calvinists to take refuge in their states and assured them of a livelihood. Amsterdam even promised to build a thousand houses for the refugees.

The Council, seeing the dangerous consequences of this hasty assertion of their authority, thought it could remedy them by other measures equally authoritarian. They realized the importance of artisans in a commercially prosperous country, and of sailors at a time when a powerful navy was being built up. They therefore ordered that any member of these professions who tried to escape should be condemned to the galleys.

A number of Calvinist families were found to be selling their landed property. Immediately a declaration was issued confiscating all this property in the event the seller left the country within a year. There followed an intensification of the stern measures against the Protestant ministers. At the slightest infringement of the law, their churches were closed. All the income bequeathed to their consistories was used instead for the upkeep of hospitals throughout the kingdom.

Calvinist schoolmasters were forbidden to receive pensioners. Ministers were made subject to the taille; Protestant mayors were deprived of their nobility. Those officers of the royal household and King's secretaries who were Protestants were ordered to resign their offices. Adherents of this religion were no longer allowed to become notaries, advocates or even attorneys.

The clergy were enjoined to make converts, and the reformed pastors were forbidden to do so on pain of banishment for life. All these decrees had been pressed for openly by the French clergy. They were, after all, the children of the family, and they did not want to have to share with strangers introduced by force.

Pellisson continued to buy converts; but Mme Hervart, widow of the controller general of finances, animated by the sort of religious zeal to which women throughout the ages have always been prone, offered as much money to prevent conversions as Pellisson did to achieve them.

Finally, in 1682 the Huguenots in a number of places dared to disobey. They assembled together in Vivarais and in Dauphiné near the places where their churches had been demolished. They were attacked, and they defended themselves. This was but a dying spark of the old fire of civil war. Two or three hundred wretches, without leaders, without strongholds and even without plans, were dispersed in a quarter of an hour. Their defeat was followed by their torture and execution. The intendant of Dauphiné had the grandson of Pastor Chamier, who had drawn up the Edict of Nantes, broken on the wheel. He is among the most famous martyrs of the sect and his name has long been venerated by the Protestants.

In 1683 the intendant of Languedoc had the preacher Chomet broken on the wheel. Three others were condemned to the same torture, and ten more to hanging; they saved themselves by flight and were only executed in effigy.

All this inspired terror, but at the same time increased the stubbornness of resistance. It is well known that men become more attached to their religion the more they have to suffer for it.

It was then that the King was persuaded that after having sent missionaries into all the provinces, the next step was to send dragoons. These acts of violence seemed untimely; they resulted from the view, prevalent in the court at that time, that the very name of Louis XIV should suffice to silence all opposition. People did not reflect that the Huguenots were no longer what they had been at Jarnac, Moncontour and Coutras;[4] that the rage of civil war was spent; that this disease, which had lasted so long, was no longer virulent; that nothing human is unchanging and that if the fathers had been rebels under Louis XIII, the children were loyal subjects of Louis XIV. In England, Holland and Germany, one could witness the spectacle of several sects who had been busy cutting each other's throats in the previous century now living peacefully together in the same towns. Everything showed that an absolute monarch could be served equally well by Catholic and Protestant alike. The Lutherans of Alsace offered convincing proof of this. In short, it seems that

[4] These were famous battles of the civil wars of the sixteenth century.

Queen Christine[5] was quite right when she wrote in one of her letters, referring to these acts of violence and to the emigrations: "I consider France to be like a sick man who is having his arms and legs cut off to cure a disease which could have been completely cured by kindness and patience."

Louis XIV, who protected Lutheranism when he occupied Strasbourg in 1681, could have tolerated Calvinism in the rest of the country, for time might well have abolished it just as it is gradually diminishing the number of Lutherans in Alsace. Did the government really never stop to think that by using force against a large number of the King's subjects, they might end by losing an even greater number, who, despite edicts and guards, would succeed in escaping from a violence which seemed to them horrible persecution? Finally, why should they have wished to make more than a million men hate a dear and precious name and one to which Protestants and Catholics, Frenchmen and foreigners alike had attached the epithet "great"? Even political considerations might have persuaded them to keep the Calvinists, for their presence would have helped them to resist the constant claims of the court of Rome. It was precisely at this time that the King was in open conflict with Innocent XI, the enemy of France. But Louis XIV, trying to conciliate the interests of his religion with those of his grandeur, wanted simultaneously to humiliate the Pope with one hand and crush Calvinism with the other.

In both these enterprises, he sought only the glory which he admired in all things. The bishops, several of the intendants and the whole Council persuaded him that his soldiers had only to show themselves in order to complete the work which his generosity and the missions had begun. He thought he was merely using his authority; but those to whom this authority was entrusted exercised it with extreme rigor.

Toward the end of 1684 and at the beginning of 1685, when Louis XIV, still powerfully armed, had nothing to fear from his neighbors, troops were sent into all the

[5] Christine of Sweden, whose abdication and subsequent sojourn in France are described in Chapter VI of *The Age of Louis XIV*.

towns and castles where the Protestants were strongest; and as the dragoons, who were rather badly disciplined in those days, committed most excesses, this action was known as the *dragonnade*.

The frontiers were as carefully guarded as possible, to prevent the flight of those whom it was intended to convert. It was like a hunt carried out in a vast enclosure.

A bishop, an intendant, a subdelegate, a priest or some other authorized person marched at the head of the soldiers. The principal Calvinist families were gathered together, especially those who were thought most open to persuasion. They renounced their religion in the name of the others, and those who refused were handed over to the soldiers, who could do anything with them except kill them. A number of people, however, were so cruelly maltreated that they died. The children of the refugees in foreign countries still cry out in horror at the sufferings of their fathers, comparing them to the most violent persecutions of the early Church.

It was a strange contrast to see such harsh and pitiless orders emanating from a pleasure-loving court famous for its gentle manners, its graces and its social charm. Behind the actions taken, one could clearly detect the stern hand of the Marquis of Louvois, the man who had wanted to drown Holland beneath the sea and had reduced the Palatinate to ashes.[6] There still exists a letter he wrote in this year 1685, which reads as follows: "His majesty wishes those who are unwilling to accept his religion to be treated with the utmost rigor; and those who are stupid enough to seek the glory of being the last should be reduced to the last extremity."

Paris was not exposed to these vexations; the sounds of distress would have been heard all too near the throne. It is all very well to make men suffer, but it is painful to have to listen to their cries.

While the Protestant churches were being destroyed everywhere, and armed force was being used in the provinces to make their adherents abjure, the Edict of Nantes itself was finally revoked in October, 1685, there-

[6] Voltaire describes these actions of the war minister, Louvois, in earlier chapters of *The Age of Louis XIV*.

by completing the ruin of an edifice which was already undermined on every side.

The Chamber of the Edict had already been suppressed. The Calvinist councilors of the parlement were ordered to resign. In quick succession the King's Council issued a large number of decrees, all designed to stamp out the remains of the proscribed religion. The one which seemed cruelest was the order to seize the children of Protestants and hand them over to the nearest Catholic parents; this order was so blatantly unnatural that it was never executed.

However, this celebrated edict revoking that of Nantes in fact produced a result which was the complete opposite of the one aimed at. The intention was to reunite the Calvinists with the Church within the kingdom. We know that when Gourville, who was a most judicious man, was consulted by Louvois, he proposed that all the ministers should be locked up and that none should be released except those who, having been won over by secret bribes, would abjure their religion in public, thereby serving the cause of reunion much more effectively than the missionaries and the soldiers. Instead of following this shrewd advice, the government ordered that all ministers who refused to be converted should leave the country within a fortnight. It was blind folly to think that if they drove away the shepherds, a large part of the flock would not follow. It showed a rash overestimation of their power and little understanding of human nature to think that all these wounded hearts and all these imaginations inflamed by the idea of martyrdom, especially in the south of France, would not take every risk to escape abroad, there to make known their constancy and the glory of their exile among the many nations who envied Louis XIV and were holding out their arms to these swarms of refugees.

When he signed the Edict, the old chancellor, Le Tellier, cried out in his joy: *"Nunc dimittis servum tuum, Domine . . . quia viderunt oculi mei salutare tuum."*[7] He

---

[7] "Now lettest thou thy servant depart, O Lord . . . for mine eyes have seen thy Salvation" (Luke 2:25).

did not know that he was signing one of France's greatest misfortunes.

Louvois, his son, was equally deceived when he thought that an order signed by him would be sufficient to guard all the frontiers and all the coasts against those who decided it was their duty to escape. When people apply all their skill to breaking the law, they are always stronger than authority. It was enough to bribe a few guards to ensure the escape of a whole host of refugees. Nearly fifty thousand families left the country in three years, and they were later followed by others. They took with them, for the benefit of foreign countries, their skill, their industry and their wealth. Almost the whole of northern Germany, a land still rural and devoid of industries, was transformed by the arrival of these multitudes. They peopled whole towns. The cloths, the braids, the hats and the stockings which formerly had been bought from France were now made by them. A whole suburb of London was populated by French silk workers; others took there the art of making cut glass, which was then lost to France. It is still common to find in Germany the gold circulated there by the refugees. And so France lost about five hundred thousand inhabitants, a vast amount of money and above all the skills which went to enrich her enemies. Holland acquired some excellent officers and soldiers. The Prince of Orange and the Duke of Savoy had complete regiments made up of refugees. The same sovereigns of Savoy and Piedmont who had treated their own reformers so cruelly took those of France into their pay; and it was certainly not because of religious zeal that the Prince of Orange enrolled them. Some of them even settled as far away as the Cape of Good Hope. The nephew of the famous Duquesne, lieutenant general of the navy, founded a little colony in this far-off land. It did not prosper, and the majority of those who set sail perished. Yet some remnants of this colony still remain as neighbors of the Hottentots. The French were dispersed even farther than the Jews had been.

The prisons and galleys were filled with those who were caught in flight; but in vain. What could be done with so many wretched people whose belief had been strengthened by their sufferings; how could one send lawyers and infirm old men to the galleys? Several hundred were shipped off to America. Finally the Council conceived the idea that once people were no longer forbidden to leave the country, and their minds were no longer influenced by the secret pleasure of disobedience, there would be fewer desertions. They were wrong again; and after having opened the frontiers, they closed them a second time, but to no avail.

In 1685 Calvinists were forbidden to have Catholic servants for fear that these might be converted by their masters; and in the following year another edict ordered them to get rid of Huguenot servants, who could then be arrested as vagabonds. There was no uniformity in the way they were persecuted, except in the general plan to use oppression as a means of conversion.

When all the Protestant churches were destroyed, and all their ministers banished, the question arose as to how those who had recanted, whether from persuasion or through fear, were to be kept within the Roman communion. Over four hundred thousand of them remained in France. Some, who refused the sacrament after having first received it, were condemned to be burned alive. The bodies of those who refused the last rites were dragged on a hurdle through the streets and buried in the refuse dump.

When used against those filled with a burning enthusiasm, persecution often merely reinforces their convictions. Everywhere, the Calvinists gathered to sing their psalms despite the fact that such meetings were punishable by death. Death was also the punishment for any minister who returned to France and five thousand five hundred francs reward was offered to anybody who denounced one of them. Several did return, and were either hanged or broken on the wheel.

Though it seemed crushed, the Calvinist sect lived on. In the war of 1689, it entertained the hope that King William, after he had dethroned his Catholic father-in-law, would come to the aid of the Protestants of France. The hope proved vain, but in the war of 1701 there was a real outbreak of rebellion and fanaticism in Languedoc and the neighboring areas.

This rebellion was stirred up by prophecies. Such predictions have always been used to delude the simple and inflame the fanatical. If a charlatan makes a hundred predictions and chance brings about the fulfillment of one of these, the others are forgotten and the one remains as a token of God's favor and as proof of a miracle. If none of them comes true, then explanations are offered, and a new interpretation put on the words; this is adopted by enthusiasts and believed by fools.

The minister Jurieu was one of the most ardent prophets. He proclaimed himself superior to predecessors such as Cotterus, Cristine Somebody-or-other, Justus Velsius and Drabitius,[8] all of whom he regarded as being inspired by God. Later he placed himself almost on a level with the author of the *Apocalypse* and with St. Paul; his followers, or rather his enemies, had a medallion struck in Holland with the inscription "*Jurius propheta.*" For eight years he promised the deliverance of God's people. His school of prophecy established itself in the mountains of Dauphiné, Vivarais and the Cévennes, a country ready to receive such predictions since it was peopled by ignorant and hotheaded men who were excited by the heat of the climate and still more by their preachers.

The first school of prophecy was set up in a glassworks on a mountain in Dauphiné called Peira; there an old Huguenot called De Serre announced the destruction of Babylon and the re-establishment of Jerusalem. He showed the children the words of the Gospel, which said: "When three or four are gathered together in my name, my spirit is in the midst of them and with a grain of faith you shall move mountains." Then he received the Spirit; it was conferred on him by being breathed into his mouth, for it is said in St. Matthew that Jesus breathed on his disciples before his death. Next he went into a trance; he had convulsions; his voice was transformed; he remained motionless, distracted, his hair

[8] These were all "prophets" in various parts of Europe in the first half of the seventeenth century.

standing on end, according to the ancient custom of all nations and the rules of inspired madness handed down from age to age. In this way children received the gift of prophecy; and if they did not move mountains, it was because they had sufficient faith to receive the Spirit but not to work miracles; so they redoubled their fervor in the hope of receiving this ultimate gift.

While the Cévennes were thus becoming a school of religious enthusiasm, ministers, who were called "apostles," were secretly returning to preach to the people.

Claude Brousson, who came of a reputable Nîmes family, an eloquent and zealous man much respected abroad, returned to his native land in 1698 and was convicted not only of having continued his ministry despite the edicts, but also of having been in correspondence, ten years before, with the enemies of the state. He had, in fact, conceived the plan of introducing English and Savoyard troops into Languedoc. This plan, written in his own hand, and addressed to the Duke of Schomberg, had been intercepted long ago, and was in the hands of the intendant of the province. Brousson, wandering from town to town, was captured at Oléron and transferred to the citadel of Montpellier. The intendant and his judges interrogated him; he replied that he was the apostle of Jesus Christ, that he had received the Holy Spirit, that he could not betray the faith entrusted to him and that his duty was to distribute the bread of the Word to his brothers. He was asked if the apostles had any written plans to stir up the provinces; he was shown his own incriminating letter, and his judges unanimously condemned him to be broken on the wheel (1698). He died as the early martyrs did. The whole sect, far from regarding him as a state criminal, saw in him nothing but a saint who had sealed his faith with his blood; and they published *The Martyrdom of M. de Brousson.*

After this the prophets became more numerous and their fury intensified. In 1703 there was an unfortunate incident. An abbé of the house of Du Chaila, an inspector of missions, obtained from the court an order to have two daughters of a recently converted nobleman shut up in a convent. Instead of taking them straight to the convent, he took them first to his own castle. A crowd of Calvinists gathered, broke down the gates and freed the two girls and a number of other prisoners. The rebels seized the Abbé Du Chaila; they offered him his life if he would accept their religion. He refused. One of the prophets then shouted at him, "Die then. The Spirit condemns thee. Thy sin is against thee," and he was at once shot. Immediately afterward the rebels seized the collectors of the poll tax and hanged them with their account rolls tied around their necks. Then they proceeded to attack and kill any priests they met. They were pursued, but they retreated among the woods and rocks. There, their numbers increased; their prophets and prophetesses announced to them, in God's name, the re-establishment of Jerusalem and the fall of Babylon. Suddenly an abbé called La Bourlie appeared among them in their desolate hiding place, bringing them money and arms.

He was the son of the Marquis of Guiscard, deputy governor to the King and one of the wisest men in the kingdom. The son was most unworthy of such a father. He had fled to Holland after committing a crime and now came to the Cévennes to stir up a revolt. Some time later, he arrived in London, where he was arrested in 1711 for betraying the English government after having betrayed his own country. Brought before the Council, he seized from the table one of those long penknives which can quite easily kill someone, and struck the chancellor, Robert Harley, later Earl of Oxford. He was taken to prison, loaded with chains. He avoided the punishment which awaited him by taking his own life. Such was the man who, in the name of the English, the Dutch and the Duke of Savoy, came to encourage the fanatics and to promise them powerful assistance.

In 1703 a large part of the country secretly supported them. Their war cry was "No taxes and freedom of conscience," a cry which always appeals to the populace. The fury showed by the rebels justified, in the eyes of the people, Louis XIV's aim of rooting out Calvinism; but if it had not been for the revocation of the Edict of

Nantes, it would never have been necessary to fight against such fury.[9]

The King began by sending Marshal Montrevel with a number of troops. He waged war on these wretches with a barbarity that surpassed their own. Prisoners were broken on the wheel and burned, though the soldiers who fell into the hands of the rebels also died cruel deaths. The King, now at war with Europe, could send only a few troops against them. It was difficult to surprise them amid their rocks, which were then almost inaccessible, in their caves, and in the woods, which they reached by unfrequented paths and from which they sallied forth suddenly like wild beasts. They even defeated a body of naval troops in a fixed battle. Three marshals of France were successively used against them.

In 1704 Marshal Montrevel was succeeded by Marshal Villars. Discovering that it was even more difficult to find them than to beat them, Marshal Villars, after making himself feared, proposed an amnesty. Some of them agreed, disillusioned with the promises of help received from the Duke of Savoy, who like so many sovereigns persecuted them at home but had aided them in the countries of his enemies.

Their most accredited leader, and the only one worth naming, was Jean Cavalier. I met him later in Holland and England.[10] He was a slight, fair-haired man with a kind and pleasant face. His party gave him the name of David. Starting off as a butcher's boy, he had, at the age of twenty-three, become the leader of a considerable multitude, thanks partly to his own courage and partly to the help of a prophetess who had him recognized as leader

---

[9] This paragraph, in which Voltaire almost seems to contradict himself by suggesting first that popular support was on one side and then that it was on the other, is typical of his own dual attitude toward the Calvinists and their opponents. As a believer in national unity and a strong monarchy, he tends to side with the King until he is revolted by the latter's religious intolerance. His love of liberty and tolerance lead him to sympathy with the Calvinists, but this sympathy tends to be dissipated both by the fact that the Calvinists are allied with the country's enemies and still more by the fanaticism of their religious beliefs.

[10] Voltaire had known Cavalier in Holland. He later met him again when he went into exile in England in 1726.

on an express order from the Holy Ghost. When the amnesty was proposed, he was at the head of eight hundred men, whom he was forming into regiments. He asked for hostages and was given them. Followed by another of the leaders, he came to Nîmes to treat with Marshal Villars.

In 1704 he promised to form four regiments of rebels who would serve the King under four colonels, of whom he was to be the first, with the right to choose the other three. These regiments were to be free to practice their own religion, as were other foreign troops in French pay; but this freedom should not be allowed anywhere else. These conditions were on the point of being accepted when Dutch emissaries arrived, armed with money and promises to prevent their being put into effect. They succeeded in detaching the leading fanatics from Cavalier; but having given his word to Marshal Villars, he intended to keep it. He accepted a colonel's commission and began to form his regiment with a hundred and thirty men who remained faithful to him.

I have often heard Marshal Villars say that he asked this young man how, at his age, he managed to have so much authority over men so fierce and undisciplined. He replied that when people disobeyed him, his prophetess, who was known as Great Mary, immediately became inspired and condemned to death the offenders, who were then killed without further argument. Later, when I asked Cavalier the same question myself, I received the same reply.

These curious negotiations took place after the battle of Blenheim. Louis XIV, who had proscribed Calvinism with such haughty self-assurance, now made peace (albeit under the name of an amnesty) with a butcher's boy; and Marshal Villars presented him with his colonel's commission and an annuity of twelve hundred francs.

The new colonel went to Versailles to receive the orders of the minister of war. The King saw him and shrugged his shoulders. Cavalier, kept under observation by the Ministry, took fright and sought refuge in Piedmont. From there he went to Holland and England. He fought in Spain, and commanded a regiment of French refugees at the battle of Almansa. The fate of this regiment serves to illustrate the fury of civil wars and the extent to which religion increases this fury. Cavalier's troops found themselves opposing a French regiment. As soon as they recognized each other, both sides, without waiting to fire a shot, rushed into the attack with the bayonet. We have already remarked that the bayonet is rarely actually used in fighting. After a volley has been fired, it is usually the resolute behavior of the first line, composed of three ranks, that decides the result of the engagement. But these men were filled with a fury which surpassed all ordinary courage. Of the two regiments, less than three hundred men survived. Marshal Berwick often told this astonishing story.

Cavalier died as a general officer and governor of the island of Jersey, with a great reputation for courage. This was the one quality he had kept from the days of his wild youth, as he had gradually developed prudence in the place of a fanaticism which had become outmoded.

Marshal Villars was recalled from Languedoc and replaced by Marshal Berwick. The defeats which the King's armies were suffering encouraged the fanatics of Languedoc, who hoped for help from heaven and received it from the allies. They were sent money by way of Geneva. They were waiting for officers who were to be sent from Holland and England. They had their agents in every town in the province.

Their plot to seize the Duke of Berwick and the intendant Bâville in Nîmes, to raise a revolt in Languedoc and Dauphiné, and to bring in enemy troops, may be classed among the great conspiracies. The secret was kept by over a thousand conspirators, until the indiscretion of a single individual revealed the whole plot. More than two hundred people died cruel deaths at the hands of the executioner. With fire and sword, Marshal Berwick exterminated all he could find of these wretches. Some died fighting, others on the wheel or at the stake. Some, who were better prophets than they were soldiers, managed to escape to Holland. There they were received by the French refugees like messengers from heaven.

They walked before them, singing psalms and strewing their path with branches. Several of these prophets went to England; but finding that the Episcopal Church was too like the Roman one, they tried to make their own dominant. They were so utterly convinced that great faith could work miracles, they offered to resuscitate a dead man, in fact any dead man who was chosen for them. The people are the same everywhere, and the Presbyterians might have allied themselves with these fanatics against the Anglican clergy. It seems hardly believable that one of the greatest geometers in Europe, Fatio Duiller, and an extremely learned man of letters called Daudé were at the head of these enthusiasts. But fanaticism makes even science its accomplice and silences reason.

The English government took the line that should always be taken with these miracle workers. They were allowed to dig up a corpse in the cemetery of the cathedral church. The area was surrounded by guards. Everything was done in a proper legal fashion, and the scene ended with the prophets being put in the stocks.

These excesses of fanaticism had little chance of success in England, where philosophy was becoming dominant. They had caused no trouble in Germany ever since the Treaty of Westphalia had given equal rights to the three religions, Catholic, Evangelical and Reformed. The United Provinces, by a wise policy of tolerance, allowed all religions in their midst. In short, by the end of the century France alone, despite the progress made by reason, still suffered from major ecclesiastical quarrels. This reason, which spread so slowly among the learned, had hardly begun to make any progress among the doctors of theology, and still less among ordinary citizens. It must first gain a hold among men of outstanding capacity; then it will gradually spread to others, and end by ruling the people themselves, who, though they cannot understand it, can see the moderation of their superiors and learn to be moderate themselves. This, however, is one of the great works of time, and the hour of its accomplishment had not yet arrived.

Essay on the Customs and the Spirit of Nations

INTRODUCTION

I. Physical Changes in Our Globe

You[1] wish that philosophers had written ancient history because you would like to read it in a philosophical spirit. All you are interested in is useful truths, and all you have found, you say, is useless errors. Let us try to sort things out together; let us see if we can unearth a few precious monuments from beneath the ruins of centuries.

Let us begin by considering whether the earth we inhabit was the same in the past as it is now.

It is quite possible that our earth has undergone as many changes as states have experienced revolutions. It seems certain that the sea used to cover immense areas where nowadays there are large cities or fertile crops. The sea has encroached on or retreated from every coastline.

Take the moving sands of North Africa and of the lands between Syria and Egypt; can they be anything other than sea sand left behind in heaps as the sea gradually retreated? Herodotus, who does not always tell lies,[2] is no doubt telling us an important truth when he

---

[1] The *you* Voltaire is addressing is in all probability his mistress, the Marquise du Châtelet. Her intellectual interests were almost exclusively scientific and she had no time for history. It was partly to try to convert her that Voltaire wrote the *Essay on Customs*. Though this Introduction, in its final form, was written long after her death, parts of it, such as this first section, probably date from much earlier.

[2] Voltaire's attitude to most ancient historians tends to be a "debunking" one, and both in this work and in others he spends considerable time pointing out the errors of Herodotus.

says that, according to the account of the Egyptian priests, the Nile delta has not always been dry land. Cannot the same be said about the sandy areas around the Baltic? And do not the shallows which surround the Cyclades and the vegetation which is easily discovered under the surrounding water offer visible proof that these islands were once part of the mainland?

The Straits of Messina, the ancient gulf of Charybdis and Scylla, which is still dangerous today for small boats, surely teaches us that Sicily used to be joined to Apulia, as the ancients always believed. Mount Vesuvius and Mount Etna have the same foundations under the sea which separates them. Vesuvius began to be a dangerous volcano only when Etna ceased being one; one of the two vents is still active when the other is extinct: a violent shock destroyed the part of the mountain which used to join Naples to Sicily.

The whole of Europe knows that the sea has swallowed up half Frisia. Forty years ago I saw the steeples of eighteen villages near Mordick, which were still sticking out above the floods and have since been washed away by the waves. There are plenty of examples to show that the sea does not take long to withdraw from its former shores. Take the cases of Aigues-Mortes, Fréjus and Ravenna, which used to be ports and are so no longer; look at Damietta, where we landed at the time of the Crusades and which is now ten miles inland: the sea is withdrawing daily from Rosetta. Everywhere nature offers evidence of these changes, and if stars have been lost in the immensity of space, if the seventh of the Pleiades disappeared long ago and several others have vanished from the Milky Way, should we be surprised to find that our own little globe undergoes continual changes?

I am not attempting to assert that the sea has formed, or even been near, all the mountains of the earth. The shells which have been found near these mountains may have been the homes of little shellfish which lived in lakes; these lakes, destroyed by earthquakes, may have emptied themselves into lower lakes. Ammonites, star-shaped stones, lentil-shaped stones, Judean stones and the glossopetrae seem to me to be land fossils.[3] I have never had the temerity to believe that these glossopetrae could be the tongues of dogfish, and I agree with the man who said that one could just as well believe that thousands of women had come to leave their *conchas Veneris* on the shore as that thousands of dogfish had brought their tongues there. Some people have dared to suggest that seas without tides, or those with tides seven or eight feet high, have formed mountains four or five hundred fathoms high; they have suggested that the whole earth has been burned, or that it has become a ball of glass. Such fantasies dishonor physics, and such quackery is unworthy of history.[4]

Let us avoid mixing the doubtful with the certain, and fantasy with truth; we have sufficient proofs of the great changes which have taken place on our globe, without going looking for new ones.

The greatest of all these changes would have been the loss of Atlantis, if it were true that this part of the world had ever existed. But it seems probable that this land was merely the island of Madeira, discovered, perhaps, by the Phoenicians, the most daring navigators of antiquity, forgotten again, and finally rediscovered at the beginning of our own fifteenth century.

[3] By the middle of the eighteenth century, it had been established that the "figured stones" which puzzled earlier scientists were fossils, and most people were agreed that they were marine fossils. But controversy continued to rage on the question of how they had reached the tops of mountains. Some saw their presence there as proof of the Biblical story of the Flood. Others, like Buffon, were beginning to grope their way toward a more modern geological explanation.

Voltaire's views on this question may fairly be described as reactionary. Though he insists on the great age of the human race and on the fact that some changes have taken place in the physical form of the world, he has little sense of either geological or biological evolution and tends to assume that things have been basically the same since the Creation. His refusal to accept the presence of marine fossils in mountains is largely attributable to this, though probably partly due, also, to his hostility to anything which seemed to corroborate the Old Testament story.

[4] Eighteenth-century theories of the early history of the earth put forward by men like de Maillet and Buffon had combined truly scientific hypotheses with more than a little fantasy. Here again Voltaire's view is limited, and he is only able to see the fantasy.

Finally, it seems clear, from the indentations in all the lands washed by the oceans, from the gulfs formed by the breaking-in of the sea, and from the archipelagoes strewn in the midst of the waters, that the two hemispheres have lost more than two thousand leagues of land on the one hand and regained it on the other. But the sea cannot have covered the Alps and the Pyrenees for centuries: such an idea is contrary to all the laws of gravity and hydrostatics.

II. The Different Races of Men

More interesting to us are the obvious differences between the kinds of men who people the four parts of the known world.

Only a blind man could doubt that the whites, Negroes, albinos, Hottentots, Laplanders, Chinese and Americans are entirely different races.[1]

Every scientifically minded traveler who has passed through Leiden has been to have a look at the part of the *reticulum mucosum* of a Negro, dissected by the famous Ruysch. The rest of this membrane was taken by Peter the Great to St. Petersburg and placed in the collection of curiosities there. It is this membrane, which is black, that gives the Negroes their inherent blackness, which they only lose in certain illnesses. These damage this tissue and allow the fat which has escaped from the cells to form white patches under the skin.

Their round eyes, their flattened noses, their lips, which are always thick, their ears, which have a different shape from ours, the woolly hair of their heads, and the very degree of their intelligence make them vastly different from all other kinds of men. That they do not owe this difference to their climate is proved by the fact that Negroes and Negresses, when transported to the coldest climates, always continue to produce animals of the same

[1] Some eighteenth-century theorists, such as the authors of the *Encyclopedia*, were beginning to develop a theory of evolution and were suggesting that the human race had a common ancestor. Once more, Voltaire's blindness to evolutionary ideas leads him to oppose this view.

kind. Half-castes are a mongrel race and can only be born from the union of a white parent and a black one.

Albinos are both small in stature and few in numbers. They inhabit central Africa and are so weak that they hardly ever leave the caves in which they live. However, sometimes the Negroes catch them, and we buy them from them out of curiosity. I have seen two myself, and thousands of Europeans have seen them. To suggest that they are dwarf Negroes whose skin has been whitened by a sort of leprosy is like saying that Negroes themselves are only white men who have been blackened by leprosy. An albino no more resembles a Guinea Negro than he does an Englishman or a Spaniard. Their whiteness is not like ours; there is nothing flesh-colored about it; nothing of a mixture of white and brown. It is the color of linen or rather of white wax; their hair and eyebrows are of the finest, softest silk; their eyes are unlike those of any other men but very similar to those of a partridge. In stature they are like Laplanders, but their heads are like nobody else's, for they have different hair, different eyes and different ears; the only thing human about them is the general form of their bodies and the fact that they have faculties of speech and thought, though to a far lesser degree than ourselves. At least, the ones I have seen and examined were like this.

The apron which nature has given the Kaffirs, and which consists of loose, soft skin falling from their navel over their thighs; the black nipples of the Samoyed women; the beards of the men of our continent and the beardless chins of the American Indians constitute such clear differences that it is hardly possible to imagine that these are not all different races.

Moreover, if one asks where these American Indians came from, one must also ask where the inhabitants of Australasia came from. The answer has already been given: Providence, which has placed men in Norway, has also placed them in America and within the Antarctic Circle, just as It has planted trees and grass there.

Several scholars have suspected that some races of men, or of animals akin to man, have perished; the albinos are so few in numbers, so weak and so ill-treated by the Negroes that it is to be feared that this race will not last for very long.

Almost all ancient authors speak of satyrs. I do not see why their existence should be impossible; even today, in Calabria, they occasionally have to suffocate monsters to which women have given birth. It is not improbable that in warm climates apes have ravished girls. Herodotus, in Book II, says that during his travels in Egypt a woman mated publicly with a goat in the province of Mendes; and he says the whole of Egypt will bear witness to this. In Leviticus 17, such intercourse with goats is forbidden. It must, therefore, have been common, and pending further clarification we must presume that races of monsters may have been born of such abominable unions. But if they did exist, they could not have influenced the human race; like mules, which cannot reproduce, they could not have caused other species to degenerate.

As to the length of human life (if you exclude the long line of Adam's descendants consecrated by the books of the Jews and unknown for so long to anyone else), it seems probable that all races of men have enjoyed roughly the same short span of life as ourselves. As animals, trees and all the other products of nature have always lasted for the same length of time, it is ridiculous to imagine that we are an exception.

But one must remember that, since trade did not always bring the human race the products and diseases of other climates, and since men were more robust and hardworking in the simplicity of the rural state for which they were born, they probably enjoyed both better health and a somewhat longer life than they do living in indolence, or amid the unhealthy occupations of big cities; so if in Constantinople, Paris and London one man in a hundred thousand reaches the age of a hundred, it is probable that in ancient times twenty men in a hundred thousand attained that age. This is what has been observed in a number of places in America, where the human race has remained in the state of nature.

The plague and smallpox, which Arab caravans gradually carried to the peoples of Asia and Europe, had been unknown before. So the human race multiplied more easily than elsewhere in Asia and the fertile climates of Europe. It is true that accidental illnesses and a number of wounds could not then be cured as they can today; but the advantage of never being attacked by the plague or smallpox was enough to compensate for all the dangers attached to our nature so that all things considered it is probable that the human race, in favorable climates, used to enjoy a healthier and happier life than it has done since the establishment of great empires. This is not to say that men have never lived for three or four hundred years; this is a highly respectable miracle you find in the Bible; but anywhere else it would be an absurd fairy tale.

III. The Antiquity of Nations

Almost all peoples, but above all those of Asia, claim to have existed for a startlingly long period of time. The fact that they agree to this extent should at least lead us to examine whether their ideas about this antiquity are devoid of all probability.

For a nation to exist as a social unit, and for it to be powerful, warlike and learned, a prodigious period of time is certainly necessary. Take the case of America: when it was discovered only two kingdoms were found there, and in these the art of writing had not yet been invented. The rest of this vast continent was, and still is, divided among little societies which know nothing of the arts. All these tribes live in huts, clothing themselves in the skins of beasts in cold climates and going almost naked in temperate ones. Some live by hunting, others live on roots; they have never sought after a different way of life, for men do not desire what they do not know. Their industry could never have gone beyond supplying their most pressing needs. The Samoyeds, the Laplanders, the inhabitants of northern Siberia and those of Kamchatka are still less advanced than the peoples of America. The majority of Negroes and all the Kaffirs are sunk in the same morass of stupidity, and will remain there for a long time.

A conjunction of favorable circumstances over many centuries is necessary for the formation of a large society of men, gathered under the same laws; it is needed even for the formation of a language. Men would not articulate if they were not taught to pronounce words; they would only utter confused cries and make themselves understood by signs. A child speaks only by imitation, and then only after some time; and if he did not learn to talk in his early years, he would never be able to express himself other than with extreme difficulty.

It may well have taken even longer for men gifted with exceptional talents to devise and teach others the first rudiments of an imperfect and barbarous language than it took to progress from there to the establishment of some sort of society. There are even whole nations which have never succeeded in forming a proper language and pronouncing it distinctly; according to Pliny, this was the case with the Troglodytes, and it is still the case with the natives of the Cape of Good Hope. The distance between such a barbarous jargon and the art of describing one's thoughts is an immense one.

This brutish state in which man existed for so long must have made the human species very rare in every part of the world. Men could scarcely provide for their own needs, and as they could not understand one another, they could not help one another. Carnivorous animals, who are instinctively better adapted to life than men, must have roamed the earth and preyed on the human species.

Men could defend themselves against wild beasts only by throwing stones and by arming themselves with stout branches of trees; this is perhaps the origin of antiquity's confused notion that the early heroes fought against lions and wild boars with clubs.

The most populous countries were no doubt those with a warm climate, for there man could easily find abundant food in coconuts, dates, pineapples and in rice, which grows by itself. It is very probable that India, China and the banks of the Euphrates were thickly populated when all other regions were still almost uninhabited. In our northern latitudes, on the other hand, one was much more likely to meet a pack of wolves than a society of men.

IV. *Knowledge of the Soul*

What notion could all these early peoples have had about the soul? No doubt one very similar to that of our country folk before they have heard the catechism, or even after they have heard it. They acquire only a confused idea and they never trouble to reflect about it. Nature, which is everywhere and always the same, has been too kind to them to make metaphysicians of them. She made the first human societies feel that there was some being superior to man when she visited them with extraordinary plagues. Equally, she made them feel that there is something within man which acts and thinks. They did not distinguish this faculty from that of life itself; and the word *âme* (soul) always meant "life" to the ancients, whether they were Syrians, Chaldeans, Egyptians or Greeks, or belonged to the tribe that finally established itself in part of Phoenicia.[1]

By what steps could people have reached the idea of the existence, within our physical being, of another, metaphysical being? Certainly when men were solely occupied in providing for their own needs they did not know enough to start making philosophical mistakes.

As time passed, partially civilized societies began to be formed in which a small number of men began to acquire the leisure to reflect. It must have been the case that a man, deeply moved by the death of his father, his brother or his wife, saw in a dream the person he was mourning. Two or three dreams of this sort would have worried a whole little community. Here is a dead man appearing to the living; and yet this dead man, eaten by worms, is still in the same place. Therefore it must be something that was in him and is walking in the air; it

[1] **The Jews. Disrespectful and contemptuous remarks about the Jewish people and history are frequent in this work, reminding one that it is a piece of anti-Church propaganda as well as a study of history.**

is his soul, his shade, his spirit; it is some slight semblance of his former self. Such is the natural reasoning of ignorance which is just beginning to reason. This opinion is that of all the early times we know, and consequently must have been that of the early times we don't know. The idea of a purely immaterial being could not have presented itself to minds that knew only matter. There must have been blacksmiths, carpenters, masons and farm workers before there existed a man who had leisure enough to meditate. All the manual arts must, without doubt, have preceded metaphysics by many centuries.

Let us note, in passing, that in the Homeric age of Greece, the soul was nothing but an aerial image of the body. Ulysses sees shades and ghosts in the underworld: could he have seen pure spirits?

Later we shall examine how the Greeks borrowed from the Egyptians the ideas of Hades and the apotheosis of the dead; how, like other peoples, they believed in an afterlife without suspecting the spirituality of the soul. On the contrary, they could not imagine how a being without a body could experience good or evil. And Plato may well be the first to speak of a purely spiritual being. Here we have what is perhaps one of the greatest achievements of the human intelligence. Even then, the spirituality of Plato is often contested, and the majority of the Church Fathers accepted the idea of a corporeal soul, although they were Platonists. But we have not yet arrived at such recent times and we are considering the world as still unformed and scarcely out of its primitive state.

V. *The Religion of the First Men*

When, after a large number of centuries, a few societies had become established, it is probable that there existed some sort of crude religious cult. Men, who were then uniquely occupied in staying alive, could not achieve knowledge of the author of life; they could not understand the relations between all the different parts of the universe, these innumerable ends and means which announce to wise men the existence of an eternal architect.

The knowledge of a God who created the universe, rewarded virtue and punished vice is the fruit of cultivated reason.[1]

All peoples, then, were for many centuries what the inhabitants of many of the southern coasts of Africa and half of America are today. These peoples have no idea of a unique god who has created everything, who is omnipresent and who exists, of himself, in eternity. Yet they should not be called atheists in the normal sense of the word, for they do not deny the Supreme Being; they are ignorant of him; they have no idea of him. The Kaffirs take an insect as their protector, the Negroes a serpent. Among the Americans, some worship the moon, others a tree; many have absolutely no cult at all.

The Peruvians, when they became civilized, adored the sun; either Manco Capac had made them believe that he was the son of this star or their budding reason had told them that they owed some debt of gratitude to the heavenly body which gives life to nature.

To find out how these cults, or these superstitions, became established, it seems to me that we must try to trace the way in which the human mind develops when left to its own devices. Suppose that a small community of primitive men see the fruits on which they feed wither; or perhaps some of their huts are destroyed by floods, or others burned by lightning. Who, they ask, has caused this evil? It cannot be one of their fellows, for they have all suffered equally. Therefore it must be some secret power. It has ill-treated them; therefore it must be propitiated. How can this be done? By treating it in the same way as one treats anyone one wants to please; that is, by giving it little presents. There is a serpent in the neighborhood; it might very well be this serpent; so some

---

[1] This formula *(Un dieu formateur, rémunerateur et vengeur)* is one Voltaire is constantly using in his own deistic writings. While it seems highly probable that his belief in a creator God was sincere, it is much more doubtful whether he really believed in rewards and punishments in an after life. He was convinced, however, that such a belief was necessary to keep the lower orders of society in their place; hence his God has sometimes been referred to unkindly as *"un dieu gendarme."*

milk is left as an offering for it, near the cave in which it takes refuge. From then onward it becomes sacred; it is invoked when there is war with the neighboring village, and this village, for its part, has chosen a different protector of its own.

Other small communities were in the same situation. But they did not have any object in the immediate neighborhood on which to focus their fears and their adoration, so they gave some general title to the being whom they suspected of having done them harm, such as the Master, the Lord, the Chief, the Ruler.

This idea fitted in far better than did the others we have mentioned with the spirit of reason which the passage of time was gradually developing and strengthening; it therefore tended to dominate men's minds by the time the nation had become numerous. And so we find a large number of nations with no other god but the master, the lord. To the Phoenicians he was Adonai; to the peoples of Syria, Baal, Melcom, Adad, Sadai. All these names mean "The Lord," "The Powerful One."

So, as time passed, each state had its tutelary god, without even knowing what a god was, and without being able to avoid thinking that every neighboring state had a similar protector of its own. For how could one imagine, when one had a lord of one's own, that other peoples did not have one too? The only remaining question was which of these masters, lords or gods would triumph when nations fought against each other.

This was no doubt the origin of the lasting and widespread belief that every people was really protected by the divinity it had chosen. This idea was so deeply rooted in men that in much later times you find Homer making the gods of Troy fight those of Greece without giving the slightest suggestion that this was something new and extraordinary. Among the Jews, you find Jephtah saying to the Ammonites: "Do you not possess by right what your Lord, Chamos, has given you? Allow us, then, to possess the land which our Lord, Adonai, has promised us."

There is another passage no less conclusive; it is that from Jeremiah 49:1, which reads: "What reason did the Lord Melcom have for taking possession of the land of

Gad?" It is clear from these expressions that the Jews, although they served Adonai, also recognized the Lord Melcom and the Lord Chamos.

In the first chapter of Judges, you will find that "the god of Judah made himself master of the mountains, but could not conquer in the valleys." And in the third book of Kings you find the opinion established among the Syrians that the god of the Jews was only the god of the mountains.

Even more striking is the fact that nothing was more common than the habit of adopting foreign gods. The Greeks recognized those of the Egyptians; by this I do not mean the bull Apis and the dog Anubis, but Ammon and the twelve great gods. The Romans worshiped all the gods of the Greeks. Jeremiah, Amos and St. Stephen tell us that during their forty years in the desert the Jews recognized only Moloch, Remphan or Kium, and that they made no sacrifice and presented no offering to the god Adonai, whom they worshiped later. It is true that the Pentateuch only speaks of the golden calf, which is not mentioned by any prophet; but this is not the place to clear up this great difficulty; it is enough that we should revere equally Moses, Jeremiah, Amos and St. Stephen, who seem to contradict each other and whom the theologians manage to reconcile.

The only point I am making is that, if one excepts those periods of war and bloody fanaticism which extinguish all feelings of humanity and which make the customs, laws and religion of one people an object of horror to another, then every nation found it perfectly acceptable for their neighbors to have their own gods and often imitated the cults and ceremonies of foreigners.

Even the Jews, despite the horror they felt for the rest of humanity (a horror which time only served to augment), imitated circumcision from the Arabs and the Egyptians. Like the latter, they made distinctions between clean and unclean meats, and they also took from them ritual ablutions, processions, sacred dances, the goat Hazazel and the sacred heifer. They often worshiped the gods Baal and Belphegor, who belonged to their other neighbors; such is the extent to which nature and custom almost always prevail over the law, especially when this law is not generally known by the people. In the same way Jacob, the grandson of Abraham, had no scruples about marrying two sisters who were what we call idolaters and daughters of an idolatrous father. Moses himself married the daughter of an idolatrous Madianite priest. Abraham was the son of an idolater. The grandson of Moses, Eleazar, was an idolatrous priest of the idolatrous tribe of Dan.

These same Jews, who in much later times protested so loudly against foreign cults, described the idolatrous Nebuchadnezzar and the idolatrous Cyrus as the Lord's anointed in their sacred books. One of their prophets was sent to idolatrous Nineveh, while Elisha allowed the idolatrous Naaman to enter the temple of Rimmon. But we must not anticipate; we know perfectly well that men always contradict themselves in their customs and in their laws. Let us avoid digressing from the subject with which we are dealing and let us continue to see how different religions became established.

The most civilized peoples of Asia this side of the Euphrates worshiped the stars. The Chaldeans, before the first Zoroaster, paid homage to the sun as the Peruvians did later in another hemisphere. This error must have been natural to man since it has so many devotees in Asia and America. A small and primitive people has only one protector. When it becomes more numerous, it increases the number of its gods. The Egyptians began by worshiping Isheth or Isis and ended up by adoring cats. The first acts of homage of the rustic Romans were addressed to Mars; when they had become masters of Europe they paid tribute to the goddess of the act of marriage or the god of latrines.[2] And yet Cicero, together with all philosophers and initiates,[3] recognized a supreme and all-powerful god. Reason had led them all back to the point of view which primitive men had held by instinct.

Apotheoses can only have been thought of long after

---

[2] *Dea Pertunda, Deus Stercutius* [Voltaire's note].

[3] The initiates of the Greek and other mysteries, which Voltaire describes in a later chapter of this Introduction.

the first cults. It is not natural, at first sight, to make a god out of a man who, as we have seen for ourselves, was born like us, suffered the illnesses, sorrows and misfortunes of humanity like us, was subject to the same humiliating needs and ended by dying and being eaten by worms. But here now is what happened in almost every nation, after the revolutions of several centuries.

A man who had done great things and rendered services to the human race could not indeed be regarded as a god by those who had seen him trembling with fever or going to the closet; but his enthusiastic admirers persuaded themselves that as he had eminent qualities he must have them from a god; he must, therefore, be a son of god. And so the gods started having children all over the world; for, without counting the fables of the many peoples who preceded the Greeks, Bacchus, Perseus, Hercules, Castor and Pollux were sons of gods; Romulus was the son of a god; Alexander was declared the son of a god in Egypt; a certain Odin, among our own northern nations, was the son of a god; Manco Capac, in Peru, was the son of the sun. The historian of the Mongols, Abulcazi, relates that one of the female ancestors of Genghis, called Alanku, while still a virgin, was made pregnant by a ray of light from heaven. Genghis himself was taken to be the son of a god; and when Pope Innocent IV sent Friar Ascelin to Batu Khan, the grandson of Genghis, this monk, who only managed to get himself presented to one of the viziers, told the latter that he came on behalf of the vicar of God. The minister answered, "Is this vicar not aware that he owes homage and tributes to the son of God, the great Batoukan, my master?"

Among men enamored of the marvelous, the distance between being a son of god and being a god is a small one. Only two or three generations are needed to make the son share the domain of his father; so, as time passed, temples were built to all those who were supposed to have been born from the supernatural union of a god with a human girl or woman.

Volumes could be written on this question; but all they would really tell us can be said in a few words: the bulk of the human race has always been, and will long remain, senseless and stupid; and perhaps the most senseless of all have been those people who have tried to find some sense behind these absurd fables and to introduce reason into folly.

VI. The Usages and Sentiments Common to Almost All Ancient Peoples

Nature being the same everywhere, men necessarily had to adopt the same truths and the same errors about all those things which are most obvious to the senses and at the same time most stimulating to the imagination. They must all have attributed the noise and the effects of thunder to the power of a superior being living in the sky. Peoples living near the ocean, seeing great tides flooding their shores at the full moon, must have believed that the moon was the cause of everything that happened in the world at the time of its different phases.

In their religious ceremonies, they almost all turned toward the east, not realizing that there is really neither an east nor a west, but paying a sort of homage to the sun which rose before their eyes.

Among the animals, the snake must have seemed to them to be gifted with a superior intelligence because when they saw it sloughing its skin they must have thought it was rejuvenating itself. Therefore, by changing its skin, it could remain eternally young; hence it was immortal. As a result it became, in Egypt and in Greece, the symbol of immortality. Large serpents which were to be found near springs prevented timid men from approaching; soon it was thought that they were guarding treasures. In this way, a serpent guarded the golden apples of the Hesperides; another kept watch over the Golden Fleece; and in the mysteries of Bacchus there was carried the image of a serpent which seemed to be guarding a bunch of golden grapes.

So the serpent was considered to be the cleverest of the animals; this is why we get the old Indian fable which tells how God, having created man, gave him a nostrum which would ensure him a long and healthy life.

The man loaded this divine present on his donkey; but when the donkey became thirsty on the way home, the serpent showed him a spring and took the nostrum while the donkey was drinking; and so man lost immortality by his negligence and the serpent acquired it by his cunning. A host of stories of donkeys and serpents come from the same source.

These serpents were harmful; but as there was something divine about them only a god could have taught men how to destroy them. So the serpent Python was killed by Apollo, and the great serpent Ophion fought the gods long before the Greeks had thought of their Apollo. A fragment of Pherecydes proves that this fable of the great serpent who was an enemy of the gods was one of the oldest in Phoenicia. And a thousand years before Pherecydes, the first Brahmans had imagined that one day God sent a great snake on earth which gave birth to ten thousand other snakes; and these were so many sins in the hearts of men.

We have already seen that dreams must have introduced the same superstition throughout the world. I am uneasy, during waking hours, about the health of my wife or my son; in my sleep I see them dying; and in fact they do die a few days later; there can be no doubt that the gods sent me this dream which turned out to be true. And if my dream was not fulfilled, then it was a deceptive dream which the gods had sent me. So, in Homer, Jupiter sends a deceptive dream to Agamemnon, leader of the Greeks. So, in I Kings 22, the god who is leading the Jews sends an evil spirit to lie in the mouth of the prophets and to deceive the King, Ahab.

All dreams, true or false, come from heaven; and in the same way, oracles become established throughout the world.

A woman comes to ask some wise men if her husband will die within the year. One says yes and the other no: it is quite certain that one or the other will be right. If the husband lives, the woman keeps silent; if he dies, she tells the whole town that the man who has predicted this death is a divine prophet. So very soon you find, in every country, men who predict the future and who discover the most hidden things. These men are called seers in Egypt, as Manetho tells us, and as Josephus himself says in his discourse against Apion.

There were seers in Chaldea and in Syria. Every temple had its oracles. Those of Apollo obtained such high repute that Rollin, in his *Ancient History,* repeats the oracles rendered by Apollo to Croesus.[1] The god guesses that the king is having a turtle cooked in a copper dish, and tells him that his reign will end when a mule is on the throne of Persia. Rollin never looks to see whether these predictions, worthy of Nostradamus, were made after the event; he does not doubt the science of the priests of Apollo and believes that God permitted Apollo to tell the truth; apparently this was in order to strengthen the pagans in their religious beliefs.

A more philosophical question, and one on which all the great civilized nations from India to Greece have agreed, is that of the origin of good and evil.

In India, people were taught that Adimo, the son of Brahma, produced just men through his navel on the right side and unjust ones on the left side; and it was from this left side that all moral and physical evil came. The Egyptians had their Typhon, who was the enemy of Osiris. The Persians imagined that Ahriman pierced the egg which Ormazd had laid, and introduced sin into it. The story of the Greek Pandora is well known; it is the finest of all the allegories which antiquity has transmitted to us.

The allegory of Job was certainly written in Arabic, for the Hebrew and Greek translations have conserved a number of Arabic terms. This book, which is of great antiquity, depicts Satan, who is the Ahriman of the Persians and the Typhon of the Egyptians, walking over the earth and asking God's permission to afflict Job. Satan appears to be subordinate to the Lord, but it is clear that he is a very powerful being, capable of sending diseases on earth and of killing animals.

Basically, although they did not realize it, all these

[1] The *Ancient History* by the Jansenist Rollin was published in the 1730's. It was a popular but not very critical work, and is a frequent target of Voltaire's mockery.

peoples were at one in believing in two principles; so that all the known world was in some sense Manichaean.[2]

Every people must have accepted the idea of expiation; for where was the man who had not committed great faults against society? And where was the man whose instinctive reason did not lead him to feel remorse? Water washed away stains from the body and from clothes, and fire purified metals; so water and fire must be able to purify souls. As a result, no temple was without its salutary waters and fires.

Men bathed in the Ganges, the Indus and the Euphrates at the time of the new moon and during eclipses. This immersion expiated sins. If the Nile was not used for similar acts of purification, this was because the crocodiles would have devoured the penitents. But the priests, who purified themselves for the people, bathed in large vats which they also used for immersing criminals who came to ask pardon of the gods.

In all their temples, the Greeks had sacred baths and sacred fires, for these were universal symbols of purity of the soul. Indeed superstition appeared to be established among all nations, except among the mandarins of China.

VII. Savages

By "savages," does one mean rustics who live in huts with their wives and a few animals, ceaselessly exposed to all the inclemency of the weather; knowing only the land which feeds them and the market which they visit occasionally to sell their goods and to buy a few clothes; speaking a jargon which is not understood in the towns; having few ideas and consequently few expressions; subject, without knowing why, to a man who wields a pen and to whom they take every year half of what they have earned by the sweat of their brows; assembling, on certain days, in a sort of barn to celebrate ceremonies they do not understand and to listen to a man dressed dif-

---

2 The Manichaeans believed in two opposing and roughly equal principles of good and evil. One of the best-known Manichaeans in literature is the character of Martin in Voltaire's *Candide*.

ferently from them making speeches whose meaning they cannot grasp; sometimes, when the drums beat, leaving their cottages and going off to be killed in foreign lands and to kill their fellow men for a quarter of what they would earn by staying at home and working? If this is what is meant by "savages," then Europe is full of them. Moreover, one cannot deny that the peoples of Canada and the Kaffirs, whom it pleases us to call savages, are infinitely superior to ours. The Hurons, the Algonquins, the Illinois, the Kaffirs and the Hottentots know how to make everything they need, which is not the case with our rustics. The tribes of America and Africa are free, whereas our savages have not even an idea of liberty.

The so-called savages of America are sovereigns who receive ambassadors from our colonies which have been transplanted into territories adjoining theirs by avarice and thoughtlessness. They understand honor, a word our European savages have never even heard. They have a motherland which they love and defend; they make treaties; they fight with courage and often speak with heroic energy. Is there in the whole of Plutarch's *Great Men* a finer reply than that which a Canadian chief made to a European nation which suggested that he should cede his patrimony to them: "We were born in this land and our fathers are buried here; should we say to the bones of our fathers: Arise and come with us to a foreign land?"

These Canadians were Spartans in comparison with the rustics who vegetate in our villages and the voluptuaries who degenerate in our towns.

However, by "savages" one may mean animals with two feet, walking on their hands when the need arises, solitary, wandering in the forests, *Salvatici, Selvaggi,* mating as the fancy takes them and then forgetting the women they have taken; knowing neither their sons nor their fathers; living like brutes without the instincts or the resources of brutes. At least one writer has said this is the true state of man and that we have done nothing but degenerate into wretchedness since we left it.[1] I do

---

[1] The writer referred to is Jean-Jacques Rousseau, who, in his *Discourse on Inequality* (1755), had presented a picture of

not believe that this solitary life attributed to our fathers is really in accordance with human nature.

Unless I am much mistaken, we are in the first rank (if one may be allowed to say so) of animals who live gregariously, like bees, ants, beavers, geese, hens, sheep and so on. If you meet a wandering bee, should you conclude that this bee is in a state of pure nature and that those who work together in the society of the hive have degenerated?

Has not every animal an irresistible instinct which it must necessarily obey? What is this instinct? The natural arrangement of its organs whose functions develop with time. This instinct cannot develop immediately because the organs are not yet sufficiently mature.

Can we not in fact observe that every animal and every other being invariably conforms to the law which nature has given to the species? The bird makes its nest just as the stars keep to their courses: by an unchanging principle. How could man be the only one to change? If he had been destined to lead a solitary life like other carnivorous animals, would he have been able to contradict the law of nature to the extent of living in society? And if he were destined to live in troops, like farmyard animals and many others, could he have perverted his destiny to the extent of living for centuries in solitude? He is capable of improvement; and from this it has been concluded that he has become perverted. But why not conclude that he has improved up to the limit which nature has set to such improvements?

All men live in society: can one infer from this that they did not do so in the past? Would not this be like concluding that the reason bulls have horns today is because they have not always had them?

Man in general has always been what he is now; this does not mean that he has always had fine cities, twenty-four-pounder cannons, comic operas and convents full of

---

primitive man very similar to the one Voltaire goes on to attack. By the 1760's, Voltaire and Rousseau had become markedly hostile to one another, both because of their philosophical and political differences, and as a result of Rousseau's open hostility to Voltaire's attempt to get a theater established in Calvinist Geneva.

nuns. But he has always had the same instinct which leads him to find satisfaction in himself, in the companion of his pleasures, in his children, in his grandchildren and in the work of his hands.

Here is something that never changes from one end of the world to the other. As the basis of society has always existed, society itself must have always existed in some form; we were not made to live like bears.

Sometimes children are found lost in the woods and living like brutes; but the same is true of sheep or geese; this does not alter the fact that sheep and geese are destined to live in flocks.

There are fakirs in India who live alone, loaded with chains. This is true, but they only live like this so that passers-by who admire them will come and give them alms. They are only doing, from a mixture of fanaticism and vanity, the same as our roadside beggars do when they lame themselves to excite compassion. These excrements of human society are merely proof of the abuse which can be made of this society.

It is very probable that men remained in the rural state for thousands of years, as an infinity of peasants still do today. But men could never have lived like badgers or hares.

What law, what secret bonds, what instinct can have led man to live a family life without the help of any arts and crafts, and without even having formed a language? The answer is his own very nature; the inclination which leads him to union with a woman; the attachment which a Molak, an Icelander, a Laplander or a Hottentot feels for his companion when her swelling womb gives him the hope of seeing a being like himself born of his blood; the need which this man and this woman have of each other and the love which nature inspires in them for the child once it is born; the authority which nature gives them over this child and the habit of loving it; the way in which the child necessarily comes to obey its parents and the help they get from it when it is five or six years old; the further children which this man and woman have; and finally, when they are old, the pleasure with which they see their sons and daughters having children of their own, who have the same instincts as their fathers and mothers.

Admittedly these are all very primitive people; but do the charcoal burners of the German forests, the inhabitants of the far North or a hundred peoples of Africa live very differently today?

What language will these savage and barbarous families speak? No doubt a long time will elapse before they speak any at all; they will communicate perfectly well by cries and gestures. All nations have been savages if one takes the word in this sense; that is, there must have been a long period in which families wandered through the forests, fighting for their food with other animals, arming themselves against them with stones and stout branches, living on wild vegetables, fruits of every kind and finally on other animals.

There is in man an instinct for mechanical invention which, as we can see, daily produces remarkable results in very primitive men. We find machines invented by the inhabitants of the mountains of the Tyrol or the Vosges which astonish scientists. The most ignorant peasant knows how to move the heaviest burden with the help of a lever without having the slightest idea that the ratio of the balancing force to the weight is the same as that between the distance between the fulcrum and the weight and the distance between the fulcrum and the force. If this had had to be known before levers could be used, how many centuries would have passed before men ever succeeded in moving a large stone!

Suggest to children that they jump a ditch; they will all automatically set about this by drawing back a few paces and then running toward the obstacle. But they certainly do not know that in this case their force is the product of their mass multiplied by their speed.

It is certain, then, that nature on its own is capable of inspiring in us useful ideas which precede all our reflections. The same is true in the field of morals. We all have two feelings which are the foundation of society: commiseration and justice. If a child sees one of his fellows being savagely attacked, he will feel sudden anguish which he will express by his cries and tears; if he can, he will help the sufferer.

Ask an uneducated child, who is just beginning to reason and to speak, if the grain which a man has sown in his field belongs to him and if the thief who has killed the proprietor has a legitimate right to this grain; you may be sure that the child will reply as would all the legislators on earth.[2]

God has given us a principle of universal reason just as he has given feathers to birds and fur to bears; and this principle is so constant that it continues to exist despite all the passions which fight against it, despite the tyrants who would like to drown it in blood, and despite the impostors who want to annihilate it in superstition. It is for this reason that the most primitive people is always, in the long run, a sound judge of the laws which govern it, because it can sense whether these laws conform to or are opposed to the principles of commiseration and justice which it carries in its heart.

But before a numerous society, a people or a nation can be formed, there must be a language; and this step is the most difficult one. Without the gift of imitation, it would never have been achieved. No doubt men began with cries which expressed their most obvious needs; then the more ingenious men, born with more flexible organs, must have formed a few articulate sounds, which their children must have repeated; their mothers must have been primarily responsible for getting them to talk. Every language must have originally been composed of monosyllables, for these are the easiest to form and to remember.

In fact, we find that the oldest nations, who have kept something of their early language, still use monosyllables to express the most familiar things and those which are

[2] Voltaire does not appear to realize the extent to which he is prejudicing the issue by the terms he uses here. His statement may be contrasted with that of Rousseau at the beginning of the second part of the *Discourse on Inequality,* where a similarly tendentious argument is used to prove that the real criminal was the man who first instituted private property.

most obvious to the senses; even today, Chinese is almost entirely founded on monosyllables.

Look at Old Germanic and at all the languages of the North and you will hardly find a single necessary and common object expressed by more than a single articulation. These are monosyllables everywhere: *zon,* the sun; *moun,* the moon; *ze,* the sea; *flus,* the river; *man,* the man; *kof,* the head; *boum,* a tree; *drink,* to drink; *march,* to walk; *shlaf,* to sleep, etc.

It was with this brevity that men expressed themselves in the forests of Gaul and Germany and throughout the North. The Greeks and Romans had more composite words only long after they had formed an organized society.

But how did we become wise enough to invent different tenses? How did we find out the way to express shades of meaning like *I should like to, I would have liked to,* and to indicate the difference between affirmative and conditional statements?

It can only have been among nations which had already become highly civilized that men succeeded, as time passed, in creating composite words to express the secret operations of the human mind. And in fact we find that barbarous peoples have only two or three tenses. Hebrew had only a present and a future. The lingua franca which is so common in the ports of the Levant is still in a similar state of poverty. Finally, despite all men's efforts, there is still no language which approaches perfection.

VIII. America

Can people still go on asking where the men came from who peopled America? If so, one must certainly ask the same question about the peoples of Australasia. These lands are a good deal farther from Christopher Columbus' point of departure than are the Antilles. Men and animals have been found everywhere where the earth is habitable. Who has put them there? We have already answered this question: it was He who makes the grass to grow in the fields. One should be no more surprised at finding men in America than at finding flies there.

It is amusing to find the Jesuit Lafitau claiming, in the Preface to his *History of the American Savages*,[1] that only atheists can say that God created the Americans.

Even today, maps of the ancient world are still drawn in which America appears under the name of the Island of Atlantis. The Cape Verde Islands appear under the name of Gorgades, and the Caribbean islands under that of Hesperides. Yet the only basis of all this is the ancient discovery of the Canary Islands and probably of Madeira, which were reached by the Phoenicians and Carthaginians. These islands are very close to Africa, and in ancient times they may have been even closer than they are today.

Let us leave Father Lafitau to derive the Caribbeans from the peoples of Caria because of the similarity of names and especially because the women of the Caribbean cook for their husbands as did the women of Caria; let us leave him to imagine that the women of the Caribbean were only born red and Negresses only born black because of the habit their fathers had of painting themselves black or red.

What happened, or so he tells us, is that Negresses, seeing their husbands painted black, were so impressed by this that their whole race was affected forever. The same thing happened to the Caribbean women, who, through the same power of the imagination, gave birth to red children. He quotes the example of Jacob's sheep, which were born mottled because the patriarch had had the ingenious idea of showing them branches from which he had removed half the bark. As these branches seemed to have two colors, they gave two colors to the patriarch's lambs. But the Jesuit should have known that not all the things which happened in Jacob's time happen today.

If the son-in-law of Laban had been asked why his sheep, which spent their time looking at grass, did not

[1] **Lafitau's comparative study of the American natives and the peoples of classical antiquity appeared in 1724. Though it contained absurdities such as those described by Voltaire, it was in some ways a pioneer work of comparative anthropology.**

produce green lambs, he would have had a hard task finding an answer.

Finally, Lafitau derives the Americans from the ancient Greeks; and here are his reasons. The Greeks had fables and so have some of the Americans. The early Greeks went hunting and so do the Americans. The early Greeks had oracles and the Americans have sorcerers. People danced at Greek festivals and people dance in America. One must admit that these reasons are convincing.

There is one reflection one can make about the peoples of the New World that Father Lafitau did not make: that is that the people farthest removed from the tropics have always been invincible and the peoples nearest the tropics have almost always been ruled by kings. The same was true for a long time of our own continent. But we do not find that the peoples of Canada have ever conquered Mexico in the way the Tartars spread throughout Asia and Europe. It seems that the Canadians were never numerous enough to send colonies elsewhere.

Generally speaking, America could never have been as populous as Europe and Asia; it is covered with immense marshes which make the air extremely unhealthy; the land produces a tremendous number of poisons; arrows, dipped in the juices of these venomous herbs, invariably produce mortal wounds. Finally, nature had given the Americans a far less industrious spirit than it had the men of the Old World. The combined effect of all this must have been very harmful to the growth of population.

Among all the physical observations which can be made about this fourth part of our universe, which remained unknown for so long, the most curious, perhaps, is that there is only one people there that have beards: these are the Eskimos. They live in the North, around the fifty-second parallel, where it is colder than the sixty-sixth in our continent. Their neighbors are beardless. So here we have two races of men completely different, living side by side with each other; supposing, that is, that the Eskimos actually do have beards. But recent travelers say that the Eskimos are beardless and that we have taken their dirty hair for beards. Whom is one to believe?[2]

Near the Isthmus of Panama you find the race of Dariens, who are very similar to the albinos, and shun the light and live in caves. They are a feeble race and consequently far from numerous.

The lions of America are weak and cowardly; the wool-bearing animals are large and so vigorous that they are used as beasts of burden. All the rivers are at least ten times as broad as ours. In short, the natural products of this land are not the same as those of our hemisphere. So there is variety everywhere, and the same Providence which has produced the elephant, the rhinoceros and the Negroes has produced, in another world, elks, condors, animals who have long been thought to have their navels in their backs, and men with a character very different from our own.

IX. Theocracy

It would appear that the majority of ancient nations were governed by a sort of theocracy. Take India first; you notice that the Brahmans ruled there for a long time. In Persia, the Magi had great authority. The history of the ears of Smerdis may be a fable, but it does prove that a Magus was on the throne of Cyrus. Many Egyptian priests prescribed to their kings exactly how much they should eat and drink; they brought them up in childhood and judged them after their death; often they became kings themselves.

Turning to the Greeks, their history, fabulous though it is, surely shows us that the prophet Calchas had sufficient power in the army to sacrifice the daughter of the king of kings.

And if we pass on even further, to savage nations who

---

[2] The sudden change of viewpoint here is explained by the fact that the final two and a half sentences were added after the first edition of the work, when Voltaire had obtained evidence contradicting his first opinion. He takes the trouble to introduce this evidence, but not to rewrite the paragraph as a whole, an indication of the hurried way in which some of his later works were written and revised.

came long after the Greeks, we find the Druids governing the Gallic nation.

It does not seem possible that the first peoples to become reasonably strong could have had any government other than a theocratic one; for as soon as a nation has chosen its tutelary god, this god has his priests. These priests dominate the mind of the nation; they can only dominate in the name of their god; so they make him speak constantly and repeat his oracles; everything is carried out on the express orders of god.

From this source have arisen the human blood sacrifices which have stained almost the whole world. What father or what mother would ever forswear nature to the extent of presenting their child to a priest to be sacrificed on an altar, if they were not convinced that the god of the country ordered this sacrifice?

Not only did theocracy reign for a long time, but its tyranny was responsible for the most horrible excesses ever perpetrated by human folly; and the more this government claimed to be divine, the more abominable it was.

Almost all peoples have sacrificed children to their gods; so they must have believed they received this unnatural order from the mouths of the gods they worshiped.

Among the peoples who are so incorrectly called civilized, the only one I can find which never practiced these absurd horrors is the Chinese. China is the only one of the ancient states we know which was never governed by the priesthood; for the Japanese lived under priestly laws six hundred years before our era. Almost everywhere else theocracy was so well established, so deeply rooted, that the first histories are those of the gods themselves who have become incarnate in order to govern men. The gods, so the peoples of Thebes and Memphis said, reigned for twelve thousand years in Egypt. Brahma became incarnate to reign in India; Sammonocodom in Siam; the god Adad governed Syria; the goddess Cybele had been sovereign of Phrygia; Jupiter, of Crete; Saturn, of Greece and Italy. The same spirit is present in all these fables; everywhere men have the confused idea that in ancient times the gods descended on the earth.

X. The Chaldeans

The Chaldeans, the Indians and the Chinese seem to me to have been the first nations to become civilized. We can even fix a definite date to Chaldean science. It is to be found in the nineteen hundred and three years of astronomical observations sent from Babylon by Callisthenes to Alexander's tutor. These astronomical tables go back precisely as far as the year 2234 B.C. It is true that this date is very close to the time at which the Vulgate places the Flood. But this is not the place to discuss the profundities of the different chronologies of the Vulgate, the Samaritan and the Septuagint versions of the Bible, all of which we revere.[1] The Universal Flood is a great miracle which has nothing in common with our researches. Here we are reasoning only according to natural notions, while always being prepared to submit the feeble gropings of our limited intelligence to illumination of a higher order.

A number of ancient authors, quoted by George Syncellus, tell us that in the time of a Chaldean king called Xixoutrou, there was a terrible flood. Apparently the Tigris and the Euphrates overflowed their banks more than usual. But only revelation could have told the Chaldeans that this same scourge had submerged all the habitable world. Again I must emphasize that I am here examining only the ordinary course of nature.

---

[1] A chronology derived from the computation of the ages of the patriarchs in the Old Testament, which indicated that the world had been created about 4000 B.C., was accepted by the Church and by the historians generally, in the seventeenth and early eighteenth centuries. It became increasingly difficult to reconcile this figure with new discoveries about antiquity, and as a result, the Samaritan and Septuagint versions of the Bible were pressed into service, as they provided a considerably longer period than did the Vulgate. Voltaire would doubtless have liked to deny the historical validity of these figures absolutely, but he dared not do so, and so contented himself with pointing to the absurdity of regarding the three different figures as all equally divinely inspired and true.

It is clear that if the Chaldeans had existed for only nineteen hundred years before our own era, this short space of time would not have been enough for them to discover the true system of our universe; yet in fact they had achieved this amazing discovery. Aristarchus of Samos tells us that the sages of Chaldea had realized the impossibility of the earth occupying the center of the planetary system; that they had assigned this place to the sun, its rightful occupant; and that they made the earth and the other planets travel around the sun, each in a different orbit.

The progress of human understanding is so slow, the apparent evidence of the eyes is so powerful, and man's subjection to accepted ideas is so tyrannical that it is impossible that a people which had existed for only nineteen hundred years would have made such an advanced scientific discovery which contradicts the evidence of the eyes and demands the most profound theoretical knowledge. One is not surprised to find that the Chaldeans themselves claimed they were four hundred and seventy thousand years old. Even then, the knowledge of the true system of the universe was only shared, in Chaldea itself, by a small number of philosophers. Such is the fate of all great truths; and the Greeks, who came later, adopted only the common system, which is the system of children.

Four hundred and seventy thousand years is a long time for us who were only born yesterday, but it is very little for the universe as a whole. I know perfectly well that we cannot accept this calculation; that Cicero ridiculed it, that it is exorbitant, and above all that we must believe the Pentateuch rather than Sanchoniatho or Berossus; yet I must repeat that (humanly speaking) it is impossible that men succeeded in discovering such astonishing truths in nineteen hundred years. The first art is to provide for one's own subsistence, a task which used to be harder for men than for beasts; the second, to form a language, and this certainly demands a very considerable space of time; the third is to build oneself a few huts and the fourth to clothe oneself. After that, in order to forge iron or to find something to take its place, so many fortunate chances, so much industry and so many centuries must have been needed that it is hard to imagine how men ever succeeded. And what a leap from this state to astronomy!

For a long time the Chaldeans engraved their observations and their laws on brick, using hieroglyphs, which were speaking characters; several centuries later, this usage was adopted by the Egyptians. The art of transmitting one's thoughts by using alphabetical characters must have been invented only very late in this part of Asia.

It is probable that it was about the time the Chaldeans built their cities that they began to use the alphabet. How had they managed before, you may ask. As they still do in my village and in hundreds of villages throughout the world where nobody can read or write and where nevertheless they understand each other very well, and where the necessary arts are cultivated, sometimes even with genius.

Babylon was probably a very old township before it was turned into an immense and superb city. But who built this city? I have no idea. Was it Semiramis, was it Belus, was it Nabonassar? Very possibly there never was, in the whole of Asia, a woman called Semiramis or a man called Belus. It is rather as if we gave Greek towns the names of Armagnac and Abbeville. The Greeks, who changed all the endings of the barbarians into Greek words, deformed all Asiatic names. Moreover, the history of Semiramis reads just like an Oriental fairy tale.

Nabonassar, or rather Nabon-assor, was probably the man who embellished and fortified Babylon and made it into such a superb city. He is a real king, known in Asia by the era which bears his name. This era, about which there can be no doubt, begins only 747 years before our own; so it is very modern in relation to the number of centuries needed to arrive at the establishment of great dominions. The very name of Babylon suggests that it existed long before Nabonassar. It is the city of *Father Bel. Bab* means "father" in Chaldean, as d'Herbelot tells us. Bel is the name of the Lord. In the East, it was known only under the name of Babel, the city of the

Lord, the city of God, or, according to others, the gate of God.

Probably a Ninus, founder of Nineveh, never existed any more than did a Belus, founder of Babylon. No Asiatic prince ever had a name ending in *us*.

The circumference of Babylon may have measured twenty-four leagues; but it seems unbelievable that a Ninus should have built, on the Tigris so close to Babylon, a city called Nineveh of equal size. We are told of three powerful empires existing at the same time: that of Babylon, that of Assyria or Nineveh, and that of Syria or Damascus. This seems highly improbable; it is rather as if one said there existed simultaneously, in one part of Gaul, three powerful empires, whose capitals were Paris, Soissons and Orleans, and that each had a circumference of twenty-four leagues.

I must admit I am at a loss to understand the two empires of Babylon and Assyria. Several scholars who have tried to throw some light on this darkness have affirmed that Assyria and Chaldea were really the same empire, sometimes governed by two princes, one of whom lived in Babylon and the other in Nineveh; and this reasonable idea may well be adopted until we find a more reasonable one.

What serves to make the antiquity of this nation seem highly probable is the famous tower built to observe the stars. Almost every commentator, unable to deny the existence of this monument, has felt obliged to imagine that it was a remnant of the tower of Babel, which men had wanted to raise up to the sky. It is far from clear what these commentators meant by the sky. Was it the moon? Was it the planet Venus? They are rather far away. Did they merely want to build a very high tower? There is nothing wrong in that, and no difficulty about it, assuming that there were plenty of men and plenty of instruments and provisions.

The tower of Babel, the dispersal of the peoples and the confusion of tongues are, as is well known, highly respectable things which we are not discussing. We are only speaking here of the observatory, which has nothing in common with the stories of the Jews.

If Nabonassar built this edifice, then at least one must admit that the Chaldeans had an observatory more than two thousand four hundred years before our time. Imagine, then, how many centuries the slowness of the human mind must have required to achieve the construction of such a monument to the sciences.

It was in Chaldea and not in Egypt that the zodiac was invented. There are, it seems to me, three fairly conclusive proofs of this: the first is that the Chaldeans were an enlightened nation before Egypt, which was constantly being flooded by the Nile, could have been habitable; the second is that the signs of the zodiac fit the climate of Mesopotamia and not that of Egypt. The Egyptians could not have the sign of the bull for the month of April, for that is not their season for plowing; they could not represent the month which we call August by a girl laden with ears of corn, since that is not their harvest time. They could not represent January by a water jug, as it rains very rarely in Egypt and never in January. The third reason is that the ancient signs of the Chaldean zodiac were one of the articles of their religion. They were under the government of twelve secondary or mediatory gods, each one of whom presided over one of these constellations, as Diodorus Siculus tells us in Book II. This religion of the ancient Chaldeans was Sabianism, that is to say the adoration of a supreme God and the veneration of the stars and the celestial intelligences which presided over the stars. Their cult was so linked with astronomy that when they prayed they turned toward the North Star.

Vitruvius, in his ninth Book, in which he talks of sundials, of the height of the sun and the length of shadows, and of light reflected from the moon, always quotes the ancient Chaldeans and not the Egyptians. This seems to me a fairly strong proof that it was Chaldea and not Egypt that was regarded as the cradle of this science, so that nothing is truer than the old Latin proverb: *Tradidit Aegyptis Babylon, Aegyptus Achivis.*[2]

---

2 "The Egyptians learned from the Babylonians, and the Greeks from the Egyptians."

CHAPTER I

China: Its Antiquity, Its Forces, Its Laws, Its Customs and Its Sciences [1]

At this time the empire of China was already more extensive than that of Charlemagne, especially if one includes Korea and Tonkin, which were vassals of China. It covered about thirty degrees of longitude and twenty-four of latitude. We have noted that this state has existed in all its splendor for four thousand years without the laws, customs, language and even the manner of dress having undergone significant changes.

Its history, which in general matters cannot be doubted and which is the only one based on astronomical observations, goes back, according to a most reliable system of chronology, as far as an eclipse observed two thousand one hundred and fifty-five years before our own era. This eclipse has been verified by missionaries who were mathematicians and who, sent out in recent centuries to this unknown people, both admired it and instructed it. Father Gaubil examined a series of thirty-six eclipses of the sun reported in the books of Confucius; he found only two which were false and two which were doubtful. The doubtful ones did in fact take place, but they could not have been seen from the place where the observer was supposed to be; and this in itself proves that Chinese astronomers were then in a position to calculate eclipses, for they made errors in two calculations.

It is true that Alexander had sent to Greece from Babylon the observations of the Chaldeans, which went a little further back than those of the Chinese and which are undoubtedly the finest monument of antiquity. But these Babylonian astronomical tables were not linked to the history of events, whereas the Chinese joined the

---

[1] On the significance of Voltaire's decision to devote the first chapter of his *Essay* proper to China, see page xvii.

history of the heavens to that of the earth and thus justified one by the other.

In an uninterrupted succession supported by authentic testimonies, their chronology goes back two hundred and thirty years before the eclipse we have mentioned, to the time of the Emperor Hiao, who himself worked to reform astronomy and who, in a reign of about eighty years, strove, it is said, to make men both wise and happy. His name is still venerated in China, as those of Titus, Trajan and Antoninus are in Europe. If he was a capable mathematician for his age, this shows that he was born in an already civilized nation. One does not find the ancient chiefs of German or Gaulish townships reforming astronomy: Clovis did not have an observatory.

Before Hiao there were six earlier kings, but the length of their reigns is uncertain. When chronology is silent, one cannot, I think, do better than refer to the rule worked out by Newton, who calculated the number of years reigned by the kings of many different countries and found that the average reign was one of about twenty-two years. According to this calculation, which is all the more reasonable for being moderate, these six kings would have reigned for about a hundred and twenty years; this is much more in conformity with the order of nature than, for example, the two hundred and forty years given to the seven kings of Rome, and many other calculations to which the experience of all ages gives the lie.

The first of these kings, called Fo-hi, reigned, therefore, more than twenty-five centuries before our era, at the time when the Babylonians already had a series of astronomical observations; and already, at that time, China obeyed a sovereign. Its fifteen kingdoms, united under a single man, prove that long before this time this state had been well-populated, civilized and split up into a large number of sovereignties; for no great state is ever formed except from a number of little ones; it can only be the result of political skill, courage and above all, of time; there is no greater proof of antiquity.

The five *Kings*, the most ancient and the most authentic book in China, informs us that, under the Emperor

Yo, the fourth successor of Fo-hi, a conjunction of Saturn, Jupiter, Mars, Mercury and Venus was observed. Our modern astronomers are in dispute about the time of this conjunction, and should stop arguing. But even if the Chinese had made a mistake in this celestial observation, it was a fine thing to be able to make such a mistake. The Chinese books say explicitly that from time immemorial it was known in China that Venus and Mercury revolved around the sun. One would have to renounce the light of reason to deny that such knowledge supposes a multitude of previous centuries, even if this knowledge was only a series of doubts.

What makes these first books particularly admirable and gives them a recognized superiority over all those which relate the origins of other nations is the fact that no miracles or predictions are found there; we do not even find those politic frauds which we attribute to other founders of states. The one exception, perhaps, is that Fo-hi is said to have tried to convince people that he saw his laws written on the back of a dragon. But this imputation itself shows that writing was known before Fo-hi. In any case, it is hardly up to us, far away in the West, to doubt the authenticity of the archives of a nation which was completely civilized when we were still savages.

It is true that a tyrant called Chi-hoangti ordered all the books to be burned; but this senseless and barbarous order warned people to look after them carefully, and they reappeared after his death. And after all, what does it matter whether these books contain a completely reliable chronology or not? I am not interested in knowing precisely when Charlemagne lived; once it is certain that he made vast conquests with large armies, it is clear that he belonged to a nation of considerable size, which had been formed into a society by a long succession of centuries. So since the Emperor Hiao, who indubitably lived more than two thousand four hundred years before our era, conquered the whole of Korea, it is certain that his people must have existed since the most remote antiquity. Moreover, the Chinese invented a time cycle or calendar which begins two thousand six hundred and two years before our own. Should we throw doubt on a chronology unanimously accepted by them, we who have sixty different systems of calculating ancient times, which is as good as having none at all?

Let me repeat that men do not multiply as easily as is thought. A third of all children born are dead within ten years. Those who have calculated the rate of propagation of the human species have remarked that rare and favorable circumstances are needed for a nation to grow by a twentieth in a hundred years; and it often happens that the population diminishes instead of increasing. Learned chronologists have calculated that, after the Flood, when a single family was constantly occupied in peopling the world and its children were similarly occupied, there were more people at the end of two hundred and fifty years than there are in the whole world today. Even the *Talmud* and the *Arabian Nights* do not contain anything quite so silly. We have already said that children cannot be created by strokes of the pen. Look at our colonies; look at the immense archipelagoes of Asia from which people never emigrate: the Maldives, the Philippines and the Moluccas have not enough inhabitants. All this gives further proof of the prodigious antiquity of the population of China.

In Charlemagne's time, as indeed for a long time before, its population was even more remarkable than its size. The last census we know of, carried out only in the fifteen provinces of China proper, produced a total of almost sixty million men capable of military service. This figure did not include veteran soldiers, old men over sixty, young people under twenty, mandarins, the multitude of literate people, or priests; still less did it include women, who are everywhere within a fifteenth or a sixteenth of being equal in numbers to men, as has been observed by the most accurate compilers of human statistics. On this basis, it seems unlikely that there are less than a hundred and fifty million inhabitants in China; Europe has not many more than a hundred millions, counting twenty millions in France, twenty-two in Germany, four in Hungary, ten in the whole of Italy as far as Dalmatia, eight in Great Britain and Ireland, eight in Spain and Portugal, ten or twelve in European Russia, five in Poland, the same number in European Turkey, Greece and the Islands, four in Sweden, three in Norway and Denmark and about four in Holland and the neighboring Low Countries.

So one should not be surprised if Chinese cities are immense; if Peking, the new capital of the empire, has a circumference of almost six leagues and contains three million inhabitants; if Nanking, the old capital, used to have even more; and if an ordinary town called Kientzeng, where porcelain is made, contains about a million inhabitants.

The journal of the Chinese empire is the most authentic and useful journal in the world, since it contains the details of all public needs and of the resources and interests of all the orders of society. This journal tells us that in the year 1725 A.D., the woman whom the Emperor Yontchin declared Empress commemorated this occasion by following the ancient custom of distributing gifts to all the poor women of China who were over seventy years old. The journal calculates that, in the province of Canton alone, 98,222 over seventy received these presents. 40,893 who were over eighty, and 3,453 who were approaching a hundred. Think how many women there must have been who did not receive a present! Among those who are no longer counted as useful to society, here are more than a hundred and forty-two thousand who received presents in a single province. How vast the population of the whole state must be! And if everyone in the empire who received a present got ten francs, what a tremendous sum these acts of generosity must have added up to!

According to the accounts of the most intelligent men who have ever traveled, the armed forces of the state consist of a militia of about eight hundred thousand well-equipped soldiers. Five hundred and seventy thousand horses are maintained, either in stables or in the Emperor's grazing grounds, to serve as mounts for soldiers, for the journeys of the court or for public messengers. Several missionaries, whom the Emperor, moved by his love of science, recently allowed to approach his person, relate how they followed him in his magnificent hunts in the direction of Great Tartary when he was accompanied by a hundred thousand horsemen and sixty thousand foot soldiers marching in battle order; this is an age-old custom in every part of the world.

Chinese towns have never had any fortifications other than those which common sense inspired all nations to build in the days before artillery: a ditch, a rampart, a strong wall and towers; even since the Chinese have started using cannon they have not adopted our type of fortifications. However, while other peoples fortify their towns, the Chinese fortified their whole empire. The Great Wall, which separated and defended China from the Tartars, was built a hundred and thirty-seven years before our era and still stretches for five hundred leagues, climbing mountains, descending precipices, having a uniform breadth of twenty feet and a height of thirty. As a monument it is superior to the pyramids of Egypt, both for its utility and for its immensity.

This wall did not prevent the Tartars from profiting, as time passed, from the divisions within China, nor from finally conquering it; but the constitution of the state was neither weakened nor changed as a result. The homeland of the victors became a part of the vanquished state; and the Manchu Tartars, when they became masters of China, merely submitted, sword in hand, to the laws of the country they had invaded.

In his third book Confucius mentions a detail which illustrates the antiquity of the use of chariots. In his day the viceroys or governors of provinces were obliged to furnish the head of state or emperor with a thousand war chariots each drawn by four horses, a thousand *quadrigae*. Homer, who lived long before the Chinese philosopher, only speaks of chariots with two or three horses. The Chinese had no doubt been the first to introduce and develop the use of quadrigae; but as far as can be seen, neither they nor the Greeks of the time of the Trojan war made use of ordinary cavalry. And yet it seems certain that people fought on horseback before they used chariots. There is evidence that the pharaohs of Egypt had cavalry, but they also used chariots; however, it seems probable that in a country like Egypt which was muddy and intersected by so many canals, the number of horses was always very restricted.

As to financial matters, the ordinary revenue of the Emperor, according to the most probable calculations, reaches the figure of two hundred million taels of pure silver. One must note that the tael is not precisely equivalent to our ounce and that the silver ounce is not intrinsically worth five francs as is stated in the *History of China* compiled by the Jesuit Du Halde. The coinage does not have an intrinsic value, but two hundred million taels make 246 million ounces of silver, and this, at the rate of fifty-four francs, nineteen sous to the mark, is the equivalent of 1,690 millions of our money in 1768. I give the precise date because the arbitrary value of our money has changed all too frequently and may well change again; this is something which is often forgotten by writers who know more about books than they do about business and who consequently often make big mistakes in calculating the value of foreign money.

The Chinese had stamped gold and silver coinage long before the coins of Darius were manufactured in Persia. The Emperor Kang-hi had made a collection of three thousand of these coins, and among them there were many which came from India; this is a further proof of the antiquity of the arts in Asia. But gold has long since ceased to be a means of exchange in China; it is an article of merchandise as in Holland; silver is no longer used for coinage and is valued only according to weight and degree of purity; the only coinage now made is of copper, and it alone is given an arbitrary value. In difficult times the government has made payment in paper money, as has happened since in more than one European state; but China has never had public banks, which increase the wealth of a nation by multiplying its credit.

This country, favored as it is by nature, possesses almost all the fruits which have been transplanted from Europe as well as many others which we lack. Corn, rice, grapes, vegetables and trees of all kinds grow in profusion; but people have made wine there only in recent times, having long been contented with the fairly strong liquor which they extract from rice.

The precious insect which produces silk originated in China; much later it passed from there to Persia, together with the art of making fabrics from the down which covers it; these fabrics were so rare, even in Justinian's time, that silk was worth its weight in gold in Europe.

Paper of fine texture and brilliant whiteness has been made in China since time immemorial: it was made with strips of boiled bamboo wood. It is not known when porcelain was first made, nor the fine lacquer which Europe is beginning to imitate and equal.

For two thousand years they have known how to make glass, though it is less beautiful and less transparent than our own.

They invented printing about the same time. As is well known, this printing consists of engraving on wooden plates, similar to those first made by Gutenberg at Mainz in the fifteenth century. The art of engraving characters on wood has been brought to a greater degree of perfection in China; our method of employing movable cast type, which is greatly superior to theirs, has not yet been adopted by them, because it would have necessitated their accepting the alphabet, and they are so attached to their ancient methods that they have never been willing to give up their symbolic writing.

The use of bells is of the greatest antiquity among them. We have had them in France only since the sixth century. They have developed chemistry; and though they have never become good physicists, they invented gunpowder. However, they used it only to make fireworks for festivals, though they are far better at this than all other nations. It was the Portuguese who, in recent centuries, taught them the use of artillery and it is the Jesuits who have taught them how to cast cannon. If the Chinese did not apply themselves to inventing these instruments of destruction, this is no reason for praising them for their virtue, for they made war nonetheless.

They made considerable progress in astronomy, in so

far as this science is a matter of observation and patience. They studied the heavens assiduously, noticing all the phenomena and recording them for posterity. As we do, they divided the sun's course into three hundred and sixty-five and a quarter parts. They had an idea, if a somewhat confused one, of the precession of equinoxes and solstices. What is perhaps most worthy of attention is that, from time immemorial, they divided the month into weeks of seven days. The Indians did the same; the Chaldeans adopted this method which later passed into the little land of Judea; but it was not adopted in Greece.

The instruments used by one of their famous astronomers, who worked in quite a small town a thousand years before our own era, are still shown today. In Nanking, the former capital, there is a bronze globe so large that three men could not put their arms around it. It is mounted on a brass cube which opens to allow a man to get in and turn the globe on which the meridians and parallels are drawn.

Peking has an observatory full of astrolabes and armillary spheres; it is true that these instruments are less exact than ours, but they do bear striking witness to the superiority of the Chinese over the other peoples of Asia.

They had invented the compass, but did not use it for its real purpose of guiding ships at sea. They sailed only near the coast. As they owned a country which provided everything they wanted, they had no need to go to the ends of the earth as we do. The compass, like gunpowder, was merely a curiosity to them, but they are hardly to be pitied for this.

It is surprising that this inventive people never got beyond the elements of geometry. They certainly knew these elements many centuries before Euclid formulated them among the Greeks of Alexandria. In our own times, the Emperor Kang-hi assured Father Parennin, one of the wisest and most learned of the missionaries who had access to this monarch, that the Emperor Yu had made use of the properties of the right-angle triangle to draw a geographical map of a province over 3,960 years ago. Father Parennin himself quotes a book, written eleven hundred years before our own era, which shows that the famous demonstration attributed in the West to Pythagoras had long been among the best-known theorems.

One may well ask why the Chinese, having progressed so far in these distant times, have never progressed any farther; why their astronomy is so old and so limited; why they are still ignorant of half-tones in music. It would seem that these men, who are so different from ourselves, have been endowed by nature with organs capable of discovering immediately all they needed to discover, but incapable of going beyond this. We, on the other hand, acquired knowledge very late, but we have developed it very rapidly. What is less surprising is the credulity which these peoples have always shown in combining astrology with real astronomical knowledge. This superstition was once shared by all men and it is not long since we were cured of it ourselves; so much does error seem to be the natural lot of mankind.

However, if one asks why so many arts and sciences have been cultivated uninterruptedly for so long in China and yet made so little progress, there are two possible answers: the first is the prodigious respect which these people feel for everything which has been handed down by their fathers, and which makes everything ancient seem perfect in their eyes; the other is the nature of their language, the foundation of all knowledge.

The art of expressing one's ideas in writing, which ought to be something very simple, is something extremely difficult for them. Each word is expressed by a different character. A scholar, in China, is a man who knows most characters; some of them have reached old age before knowing how to write well.

The subjects which they have understood, cultivated and perfected most are morals and law. The respect shown by children to their parents is the basis of the government of China. Paternal authority is never weakened there. A son can plead against his father only with the consent of all his relations, his friends and the magistrates. The educated mandarins are looked on as fathers of towns and provinces, and the king as the father of the empire. This idea, which is rooted in every heart, makes the whole state into a single family.

Because it is a fundamental law that the empire is a family, the pursuit of public good has always been regarded there, more than anywhere else, as man's first duty. This is the reason for the constant care taken by the Emperor and the tribunals to repair roads, link rivers, dig canals and encourage agriculture and industry.

We shall discuss the government of China in another chapter; but it is worth mentioning here that travelers, and above all missionaries, have thought they saw despotism everywhere. They judge everything from the outside; they see men prostrating themselves and immediately take them to be slaves. A man before whom people prostrate themselves must be the absolute master of the lives and fortunes of a hundred and fifty million men; his will alone must be law. Yet this is not really the case, as we shall try to show. Here it is enough to say that in the most ancient times of the monarchy, men were allowed to write down, on a long table placed in the palace, everything they considered reprehensible in the government. This usage was introduced in the reign of Venti, two centuries before our own era; in time of peace, moreover, the representations of the tribunals have always had the force of law. This important observation destroys the vague charges made in the *Esprit des Lois* against the oldest government in the world.

All the vices exist in China as they do elsewhere, but they are certainly more effectively repressed by the laws because the laws are always uniform. The learned author of the *Memoirs* of Admiral Anson expresses contempt and anger against the Chinese because the populace of Canton cheated the English whenever it could; but should one judge the government of a great nation on the behavior of the populace on its frontiers? And what would the Chinese have said of us if they had been shipwrecked on our coasts in the days when the laws of European nations ordered the confiscation of all shipwrecked property, and custom allowed the proprietors to be murdered?

The constant ceremonial which restricts social life in China and which is only laid aside by friends in the interior of their homes has established throughout the nation a modesty and decency which give their manners both gravity and kindness. These qualities are found even among the ordinary people. Missionaries have told us that often, in public market places and in the midst of all the upheaval and confusion which in our part of the world so often leads to noisy scenes and unpleasant outbursts of anger, they have seen peasants going down on their knees before one another, as is the custom in the country, asking pardon for the troubles which each accused himself of causing, helping each other and quietly clearing everything up.

In other countries the laws punish crime; in China they do more than this, they reward virtue. If news of a rare and generous action spreads through a province, the mandarin is obliged to inform the Emperor; and the Emperor sends a mark of his esteem to the man who has deserved it. Recently, a poor peasant called Chicou found a purse full of gold which a traveler had lost; he carried it as far as the traveler's province and there handed it over to the magistrate of the district without asking any reward for his trouble. The magistrate was obliged, under pain of dismissal, to inform the supreme tribunal of Peking; this tribunal was obliged to inform the Emperor; and the poor peasant was created a mandarin of the fifth class, for there are ranks of mandarin available to peasants who distinguish themselves by their moral actions as there are for those who are conspicuously successful farmers. It must be confessed that the only distinction the peasant would have received among us would have been an increase in his taxes, on the grounds that he must have been well off. This morality, this obedience to the laws, combined with the worship of a supreme being, make up the religion of China, that of the Emperor and of the educated classes. The Emperor is, since time immemorial, the high priest; it is he who sacrifices to the Tien, to the sovereign of heaven and earth. He has to be both the first philosopher and the first preacher of the empire; his edicts are almost always both informative and morally wise.

CHAPTER LXXX

France in the Time of Charles VII, the Maid of Orleans and Jacques Coeur

This English invasion of France[1] was rather like the French invasion of England in Louis VIII's time, except that it was longer and more destructive. Charles VII had to win back his country inch by inch. He had to fight the regent Bedford, who was as absolute as Henry V had been, as well as the Duke of Burgundy, who had become one of the most powerful princes of Europe following the inclusion of Hainaut, Brabant and Holland in his domains. Charles VII's friends were as dangerous to him as were his enemies; the majority of them took advantage of his misfortunes to such an extent that his constable, the Count of Richemont, brother of the Duke of Brittany, had two of his favorites strangled.

The deplorable state to which Charles was reduced may be judged from the extent to which he found it necessary to devalue the currency in all those parts of the country which remained faithful to him; the franc, which at the end of the reign of Charles V was worth more than eight of our francs, was reduced to fifteen per cent of its present value; in this way it became worth only a fiftieth part of its value a few years earlier.

It was soon necessary to have recourse to an even stranger expedient: to a miracle. A nobleman from the frontier area of Lorraine, called Baudricourt, found a young servant girl in a Vaucouleurs tavern and thought her admirably fitted for the role of warrior-prophetess. This was Joan of Arc, who most people think was a shepherdess, but who was in fact an inn servant. Monstrelet describes her as "robust, capable of riding bareback, and with many other skills which young girls do

[1] These were the invasions of the Hundred Years' War, which Voltaire has described in previous chapters.

not usually possess." She was passed off as an eighteen-year-old girl, though she herself admitted, in her confession, that she was then twenty-seven. She had enough courage and wit to undertake this enterprise, which was great from the beginning and which ended up by being heroic. She was taken to the King at Bourges. She was examined by women, who did not fail to pronounce her a virgin, and by a number of councilors of the parlement, who had no hesitation in declaring her inspired, whether because she deceived them or because they themselves were sufficiently astute to take part in the deception. The mass of the people believed what they said, and this was enough.

In 1429 the English were besieging the city of Orleans, Charles's last remaining stronghold, and were on the point of capturing it. This warrior girl, dressed as a man and advised by experienced captains, undertook to relieve the city. She spoke to the soldiers on God's behalf and inspired them with the enthusiastic courage which all men have when they believe God is fighting for them. She marched at their head, saved Orleans, defeated the English, predicted to Charles that she would have him crowned in Rheims and, sword in hand, fulfilled her promise. She took part in the coronation, holding the standard with which she had fought.

These rapid victories achieved by a girl, the signs of miraculous intervention, the coronation which made the King's person more venerable—all this was soon to lead to the re-establishment of the legitimate king and the expulsion of the foreigners. But Joan herself, the instrument of these miracles, was wounded and captured while defending Compiègne. A man like the Black Prince would have honored and respected her courage; but the regent Bedford thought it necessary to destroy her reputation in order to revive the fortunes of the English. She had feigned a miracle; Bedford pretended to believe she was a sorceress. My aim throughout this work is to observe the spirit of the age, for it is this spirit which directs the great events of the world. The University of Paris presented a petition against Joan of Arc, accusing her of heresy and magic. Either the University believed what the regent wanted it to believe, or if not, it was committing a detestable act of cowardice. This heroine, who was worthy of the miracle she had feigned, was tried at Rouen by Cauchon, Bishop of Beauvais, five other French bishops and a single English bishop, who were assisted by a Dominican monk, a representative of the Inquisition, and by doctors of the University. She was described as "superstitious, a sorceress of the devil and a blasphemer of God and his saints, who had strayed far from the faith of Christ." As such she was condemned to life imprisonment on a diet of bread and water. She answered her judges in terms worthy of being remembered forever. Asked why she had dared take part, with her standard, in Charles's coronation, she replied: "It is only right that someone who has had a share of the work should have a share of the honor."

Finally she was accused of having dressed in her man's clothes again after these had been deliberately left with her in order to tempt her. Her judges, who certainly had no right to judge her, as she was a prisoner of war, then declared her a relapsed heretic. They burned at the stake a woman who had saved her King and would have had altars raised to her in the heroic times when men raised them to their liberators. Charles VII later re-established her memory, which was already sufficiently honored by the manner of her death.[2]

Cruelty in itself is not enough to make men carry out such deeds; there must also be present that fanaticism, composed of superstition and ignorance, which has been the disease of almost every age. Some time later, the English condemned the Princess of Gloucester to do penance in the Church of St. Paul and condemned one of her friends to be burned alive on the pretext of some sort of witchcraft employed against the King's life. Baron

[2] Joan of Arc had been the heroine of Voltaire's mock epic poem *La Pucelle,* a work which is comical throughout, and often obscene. Here he is trying to be more objective, but it is interesting to see how he fluctuates between admiration for Joan's bravery and pity for her cruel fate on the one hand, and on the other, the "rationalistic" conviction that she and her advisers must have been engaged in deliberate deceit.

Cobham had been burned as a heretic and, in Brittany, Marshal Retz had suffered the same penalty after being accused of magic and of having cut the throats of children in order to use their blood in his so-called magical rites.

Let the inhabitants of a great city, where arts, entertainments and peace now reign, and where reason itself is gradually making progress, compare these times with their own, and let them complain if they dare. This is a reflection one should make at every page of this history.

In these sad times communications were so interrupted in the provinces, and neighboring peoples were so foreign to one another, that in Lorraine, a few years after the death of the Maid, an adventuress dared to take her name and assert boldly that she had escaped execution and that an effigy had been burned in her place. What is even more strange is that people believed her; she was loaded with honors and presents; in 1436 a member of the House of Armoise married her, believing that he was marrying the real heroine, who, although of obscure birth, would have been at least his equal through her great deeds.

During this war, which was longer than it was decisive and which caused so many misfortunes, another event proved to be the salvation of France. The Duke of Burgundy, Philip the Good, earned this name by finally pardoning the King for the death of his father,[3] and uniting with him against the foreigner. It is true that he made the King pay dearly for this murder, for the treaty gave him all the towns on the River Somme, together with Roye, Montdidier and the county of Boulogne; he freed himself from any act of homage during his lifetime and became a great sovereign; but he had the generosity to liberate the Duke of Orleans, son of the one who had been killed in Paris, from his long imprisonment in London. He paid his ransom, which was said to amount to three hundred thousand golden crowns. This figure is an exaggeration typical of the writers of the time, but at

[3] He had been murdered in 1419 in the struggle between the rival Bourguignon and Armagnac factions, which Voltaire describes in an earlier chapter.

least Philip's conduct showed his great virtues. There are always noble souls even in the most corrupt times. His virtues did not prevent him from being a voluptuary as far as women were concerned, but this can only be a vice when it leads to evil actions. It was this same Philip who, in 1300, had instituted the Order of the Golden Fleece in honor of one of his mistresses. His court was the most brilliant in Europe; Antwerp and Bruges were flourishing centers of trade and spread prosperity throughout his domains. France owed him both her peace and her greatness, which continued to increase after that time despite misfortunes and despite foreign and civil wars.

Charles VII won back his kingdom in more or less the same way as Henry IV was to conquer it a hundred and fifty years later. It is true that Charles did not have the outstanding courage, the prompt and active mind or the heroic character of Henry IV. But like him, he was often obliged to handle friends and enemies carefully, to fight little battles and to surprise and even buy towns. He entered Paris as Henry IV was later to do, by a mixture of intrigue and force. Both of them were declared incapable of possessing the crown, and both pardoned their enemies. They had also a weakness in common, that of allowing love to play too great a part in their lives; for love almost always has an influence on the affairs of state of Christian kings, though this never happens in the rest of the world.

Charles only made his entry into Paris in 1437. The citizens, who had distinguished themselves by so many massacres, greeted him with all the demonstrations of joy and affection which were customary among these uncultured people. Seven girls representing the so-called mortal sins and seven others impersonating the theological and cardinal virtues, all bearing placards, received him near the gate of Saint Denis. He stopped for a few minutes at a crossroads to watch the religious mysteries which players were performing on stages. The inhabitants of the capital were as poor as they were rustic in these days; those of the provinces were even more so; twenty years were needed for the state to recover. It was not until about 1450 that the English were completely driven out of France; they kept only Calais and Guînes, and lost forever all the vast domains which the three victories of Crécy, Poitiers and Agincourt had been unable to secure for them. The divisions of the English contributed to the reunification of France almost as much as did Charles VII. Henry VI, who had been king of both countries and had even come to Paris to be crowned, was dethroned by his relatives in London, re-established and dethroned once again.

Charles VII, master of a peaceful France at last, established the kind of order which had ceased to exist since the decadence of Charlemagne's family. He maintained a standing army of fifteen hundred gendarmes; each of these gendarmes provided six horses, so that the whole force consisted of nine thousand horsemen. The captain of a hundred men received seven hundred francs a year, the equivalent of about ten thousand francs today; every gendarme was paid three hundred and sixty francs a year and each of the five men who accompanied him had four francs a month, which would be about twenty-four of ours. So in peacetime the upkeep of the army cost about six millions of our money. Things have changed greatly in Europe. The establishment of companies of archers shows that muskets were not then in common use; this instrument of destruction became widespread only in the time of Louis XI.

Apart from these troops, which were continually under arms, each village maintained an archer, who was exempt from the taille. It was through this exemption, normally a privilege of the nobility, that so many people soon came to claim for themselves the titles and qualities of noblemen. Those who held fiefs directly were dispensed from the *ban,* which was no longer convoked; there only remained the *arrière-ban,*[4] composed of under vassals who were still liable for service when occasion demanded.

It seems surprising that, after so many disasters, France still had so many resources and so much money;

---

[4] Roughly speaking, the *ban* consisted of the feudal levies who were first called on for service, and the *arrière-ban* of the reserves.

but a country which is rich in its produce never ceases to be rich unless cultivation is neglected. The civil wars shook the body of the state, but did not destroy it. The killings and plunderings, which impoverished some families, enriched others; merchants became all the more skillful because greater ingenuity was needed to survive amid all these storms. Jacques Coeur is a great example of this; he had established the largest trading concern that any private individual in Europe had ever controlled; and after his time only Cosimo de' Medici equaled him. Jacques Coeur had three hundred factors in Italy and the Levant; he lent the King two hundred thousand gold crowns, without which he would never have managed to reconquer Normandy; his industry was far more useful during the peace than Dunois and the Maid had been during the war. It is perhaps a great blot on the memory of Charles VII that such an important man was persecuted; the reason is unknown, for who knows the secret motives for the faults and injustices of men?

The King had him imprisoned and the Parlement of Paris tried him. Nothing could be proved against him except that he had sent back to his Turkish master a Christian slave who had deserted and betrayed him, and that he had sold arms to the Sultan of Egypt. For these two deeds, one of which was permissible and the other virtuous, he was condemned to lose all his property. His clerks acted in a more upright way than did the courtiers who condemned him; they almost all contributed to help him in his misfortune. It is said that Jacques Coeur left to carry on his business in Cyprus and that he was too strong-minded to return to his ungrateful country although he was recalled. But this anecdote is not well attested.

Otherwise, the end of Charles VII's reign was a fairly happy period for France, although most unhappy for the King himself, for his days ended in bitterness as a result of the rebellion of his unnatural son, who later became Louis XI.

CHAPTER LXXXI

Customs, Usages, Commerce and Wealth in the Thirteenth and Fourteenth Centuries

I should like to discover what society was like in those days, how people lived in their family circles and what arts were cultivated, rather than describe all those misfortunes and battles which form the tragic subject matter of history and are but the commonplaces of human wickedness.

Toward the end of the thirteenth century and at the beginning of the fourteenth, it seems to me that in Italy, despite all the dissentions, people were beginning to emerge from the barbarism which had covered Europe ever since the fall of the Roman empire. The necessary arts had not perished, for artisans and merchants, whose very obscurity saves them from the ambitious fury of the great, are like so many ants who go on quietly building their homes while the eagles and vultures are tearing each other to pieces.

Even in these uncivilized times, certain useful inventions were made, the fruit of the mechanical inventiveness which nature has given to men and which is quite independent of their scientific or philosophical knowledge. For example, the secret of helping old men with weak eyesight to see, with the aid of glasses which are known as *spectacles*, was discovered in the thirteenth century; we owe this fine achievement to Alexander Spina. Windmills became known in Italy about the same time. La Flamma, who lived in the fourteenth century, speaks of them, and no one did so before his day, although they had been known much earlier among the Greeks and the Arabs and are mentioned by Arab poets of the seventh century. Faïence, which was made chiefly at Faenza, took the place of porcelain. Panes of glass had been used for a long time, but they were still rare and were considered a luxury. The art of making them was taken by Frenchmen to England about 1180 and their use was regarded as a sign of great magnificence.

In the thirteenth century the Venetians were the only ones who knew the secret of making glass mirrors. There were a few clocks using wheels in Italy; the one at Bologna was famous. The discovery of the compass was potentially of far greater importance; but it was due purely to chance, and men were not yet looking far enough afield to make full use of it. The invention of paper, which was made by crushing and boiling linen rags, belongs to the early fourteenth century. Cortusius, the historian of Padua, speaks of a certain Pax who established there the first factory for making it, almost a century before the invention of printing. In this way the useful arts were gradually created, usually by inventors whose names have not come down to us.

The rest of Europe was very far from possessing towns like Venice, Genoa, Bologna, Siena, Pisa and Florence. Almost all the houses in the towns of France, Germany and England were thatched with straw, and the same was true of the less wealthy towns of Italy, such as Alexandria *della paglia,* Nice *della paglia,* etc.[1]

Although forests had covered a great deal of land which had long remained uncultivated, yet people still did not know how to use chimneys to protect themselves from the cold, though today these are both an asset and an ornament to all our houses; a whole family would gather in the middle of a smoky common room around a large round hearth with a pipe going up to the ceiling.

In the fourteenth century, we find La Flamma, as is the habit with uncritical writers, complaining that frugal simplicity has given way to luxury: he regrets the days of Frederick Barbarossa and Frederick II, when the people of Milan, the capital of Lombardy, ate meat only three times a week. Wine was very rare then, wax candles were unknown and even tallow candles were a luxury. He tells us that even the best citizens burned pieces of dry wood to provide light; that they ate hot meat only three times a week; that their shirts were of

[1] *Della paglia* is the Italian for "of straw."

serge, not linen; that the dowry of even the most important middle-class girls did not exceed a hundred francs. Things have indeed changed, he adds; nowadays people wear linen; women dress in silks, which are sometimes even interwoven with gold and silver; they have dowries of anything up to two thousand francs, and they even adorn their ears with gold pendants. Yet these luxuries of which he complains are still in some respects far inferior to what today are regarded as the necessities of life among rich and industrious peoples.

Table linen was very rare in England; wine was sold there only by apothecaries as a cordial; all private houses were of coarse wood covered with a kind of mortar called cob; the doors were low and narrow; the tiny windows hardly let in any light; to be drawn in a carriage through the streets of Paris, unpaved and muddy as they were, was a luxury; and this luxury was forbidden to ordinary citizens by Philip the Fair. In Charles VI's time a ruling was made that: *Nemo audeat dare praeter duo fercula cum potagio*—"Let no one dare to provide more than two dishes with the soup."

A single fact should suffice to illustrate the lack of money in Scotland and even in England, as well as the rusticity of those times, which people called simplicity. In public papers we read that when the kings of Scotland came to London the English court assigned them thirty shillings a day, a dozen loaves, a dozen cakes and thirty bottles of wine.

Yet the lords of fiefs and the principal prelates still lived as magnificently as the times allowed, as was bound to be the case with great landowners. For a long time, bishops had traveled only with a retinue of a prodigious number of servants and horses. A Lateran Council held in 1179 under Alexander III reproached them with the fact that churches and monasteries often had to sell their gold and silver vases in order to receive them and pay the expenses of their visits. The retinues of archbishops were reduced by canons of these councils to fifty horses, those of bishops to thirty, and those of cardinals to twenty-five; for a cardinal, who did not hold a bishopric and who, in consequence, owned no land, was less wealthy than a bishop. This magnificence of the prelates was even more odious then than it is today, because there was no middle class between great and small and between rich and poor: it is only with time that commerce and industry have succeeded in forming this middle class, which creates the wealth of the nation. Silver dishes were almost unknown in the majority of towns. Mussius, a Lombard writer of the fourteenth century, looks on forks, spoons and silver cups as great luxuries.

He tells us too that the father of a family with ten mouths to feed and a pair of horses was obliged to spend up to three hundred florins a year; this is, at the very most, two thousand francs of our money.

In the twelfth, thirteenth and fourteenth centuries, then, money was very rare in certain parts of Italy and still rarer in France. The Florentines and Lombards, who, together with their brokers the Jews, controlled all the trade of France and England, were in a position to extract interest of twenty per cent per annum on ordinary loans to the English and the French. A high rate of interest is an infallible sign of a poor people.

Charles V amassed a certain amount of wealth by his economies, by the wise administration of his domains (which were then the principal source of royal revenue) and by the taxes invented under Philip of Valois, which, although they were not heavy, caused much grumbling among a poor people. His minister, Cardinal de la Grange, made his own fortune only too well: but all these treasures were dispersed to other countries. The Cardinal took his to Avignon; the Duke of Anjou, Charles V's brother, lost those of the King in his ill-fated Italian expedition. France remained sunk in poverty until the last days of Charles VII's reign.

Things were very different in the flourishing commercial cities of Italy. People lived comfortably and even opulently there, and they were the only places where one could enjoy the pleasures of life. Finally wealth and liberty gave birth to genius there, just as they also nourished courage.

CHAPTER LXXXII

Arts and Sciences in the Thirteenth and Fourteenth Centuries

In Frederick II's time the Italian language was still unformed; this can be seen from the Emperor's own verses, which are the last example of the romance language free from Germanic harshness:

> *Plas me el cavalier Frances,*
> *E la donna Catalana,*
> *El l'ovrar Genoes,*
> *E la danza Trevisana,*
> *E lou cantar Provensales,*
> *Las man e cara d'Angles,*
> *E lou donzel de Toscana.*[1]

This literary monument is worth more than people think and is far superior to all those ruins of medieval buildings which are eagerly sought after by those who possess an uneducated and tasteless curiosity.[2] It shows that nature has not changed in any of the nations of which Frederick speaks. The women of Catalonia are still, as in his day, the most beautiful in Spain; the French nobility still has the same martial graces as were admired then; a soft white skin and beautiful hands are still common in England. Young people are more attractive in Tuscany than anywhere else; the Genoese have kept their industriousness and the inhabitants of Pro-

---

[1] "I like the French knight
And the Catalan lady
And the workmanship of Genoa
And the dancing of Treviso
And the songs of Provence,
The hands and faces of the English
And the youths of Tuscany."

[2] Interest in medieval art, architecture and customs was beginning to revive in the second half of the eighteenth century, but this comment, and many others later in the chapter, show that Voltaire was far too classical in taste to have any sympathy with this revival.

vence their taste for poetry and song. It was in Provence and Languedoc that the romance language was first made harmonious, and the poets of Provence were the masters of the Italians. Nothing is better known to those interested in this type of research than the verses on the Vaudois of the year 1100:

Que non voglia maudir ne jura ne mentir,
N'occir, ne avoutrar, ne prenre de altrui,
Ne s'avengear deli suo ennemi,
Los dison qu'es Vaudes et los feson morir.[3]

This quotation also has its utility for it is a proof that all reformers have always had rigorous moral standards.

Unfortunately this jargon survived unchanged in Provence and Languedoc, whereas with the coming of Petrarch, Italian achieved strength and grace and, far from degenerating, has developed even further. Italian became a fully formed language at the end of the thirteenth century in the days of good King Robert, the grandfather of the unfortunate Joan.[4] Even before this, the Florentine Dante had shown what Tuscan was capable of when he wrote his *Commedia,* a bizarre poem but one resplendent with natural beauties. In this work there are many detailed descriptions in which the author rises above the bad taste of the age and of his subject, and it is full of passages which are as pure in style as if they belonged to the age of Ariosto and Tasso. One should not be surprised that the author, who was one of the leaders of the Ghibelline faction persecuted by Boniface VIII and Charles of Valois, expresses in his poem his grief at the quarrels between the empire and the papacy. I should like to quote here a passage of Dante concerning these dissentions; these monuments of the human mind form a welcome relaxation from the long story of the misfortunes which have vexed mankind:

---

[3] "If someone does not want to curse or swear or lie or kill or commit adultery or steal from others or avenge himself on his enemy, they say he is a Vaudois and they put him to death." Voltaire speaks of the religious views of the Vaudois in Chapter XXXVI of *The Age of Louis XIV*. See page 216.

[4] See page 300.

Soleva Roma, che il buon mondo feo,
Due soli aver, che l'una e l'altra strada
Facean vedere, e del mondo e di Deo.
L'un l'altro ha spento; ed è giunta la spada
Col pastorale, e l'un con l'altro insieme
Per viva forza mal convien che vada;
Però che, giunti, l'un l'altro non teme:
Se non mi credi, pon mente alla spiga;
Ch'ogni erba si conosce per lo seme.[5]

After Dante came Petrarch, who was born in 1304 in Arezzo, the native city of Aretino. He purified the language still further, and used it in the most harmonious way possible. In these two poets, above all in Petrarch, we find a large number of features similar to those of the masterpieces of the ancients, and which combine the strength of antiquity with the freshness of modernity. Here is the beginning of his fine ode to the Fountain of Vaucluse:

Chiare, fresche, e dolci acque,
Ove le belle membra
Pose colei, che sola a me par donna;
Gentil ramo, ove piacque
(Con sospir mi rimembra)
A lei, di fare al bel fianco colonna;
Erba, e fior, che la gonna
Leggiadra ricoverse
Con l'angelico seno;
Aer sacro sereno,
Ov' amor co' begli occhi il cor m'aperse;
Date udienza insieme
Alle dolenti mie parole estreme.[6]

---

[5] Voltaire himself gives a fairly free French verse translation of this passage and of the one from Petrarch.

"Rome, which made the good world, used to have two suns which showed the way to two different roads: one of the world, the other of God. One of these has quenched the other and the sword has been joined to the shepherd's crook and it is a bad thing that one should be forced to go along with the other, for when they are joined, one does not fear the other; if you do not believe me then look at the fruits of this union, for every plant is known by its seeds."

[6] "Clear, fresh and sweet waters where she who seems to me

These poems, known as *canzoni,* are considered to be his masterpiece; his other works did him less honor, but he immortalized the Fountain of Vaucluse, Laura and himself. If he had never loved, he would be much less famous. However imperfect a translation may be, it gives some idea of the immense distance which separated the Italians from all other nations at that time. I have preferred to give you some idea of Petrarch's genius, of the sweetness and elegant gentleness of his character, rather than repeat what many others have said about the honors he was offered in Paris and those he received in Rome. His triumphant procession to the Capitol in 1341 was a celebrated act of homage which his amazed contemporaries paid to a genius who was then unique, but who has since been surpassed by Ariosto and Tasso. But I must mention that his family had been banished from Tuscany and stripped of all their wealth during the struggles of the Guelphs and Ghibellines, and that the Florentines sent Boccaccio to beg him to return and honor his native city with his presence and enjoy the inheritance which had been restored to him. Never did Greece, even in her most glorious days, show greater taste or greater esteem for talent.

This same Boccaccio gave permanent form to the Tuscan language; he is still the best model of prose style, both for his exactitude and purity and for the naturalness of his narrative. Perfected by these two writers, the language underwent no further changes, whereas all other European nations, even the Greeks, have altered theirs.

There followed an uninterrupted succession of Italian poets whose work has come down to posterity. Pulci followed Petrarch, Boiardo, Count of Scandiano, followed Pulci, and Ariosto surpassed them all in the fecundity of his imagination. We should not forget that Petrarch and

---

to be the only woman rested her fair limbs; gentle branch of which she liked (as I remember with a sigh) to make a column to rest her fair side; grass and flowers which her pretty dress covered as it did her angelic bosom; holy and calm air where love opened my heart with its fair eyes; listen all together to my dying and lamenting words."

Boccaccio had sung the praises of the unfortunate Joan of Naples, whose cultivated mind fully recognized their merit, and who was even one of their disciples. She was at that time entirely devoted to the arts, the charms of which helped her to forget the criminal days of her first marriage. The transformation which culture wrought in her way of living should have saved her from the cruel tragedy which ended her life.[7]

The arts, which seem to go hand in hand and which usually perish and revive together, were all emerging now in Italy from the ruins of a barbarous past. Cimabue, who worked in the thirteenth century with no predecessors to guide him, almost seemed to invent painting afresh. Giotto painted pictures which can still be seen with pleasure. His most famous remaining work has been set in mosaic and represents the first apostle walking on the waters; it is to be seen above the great gate of St. Peter's in Rome. Brunelleschi began the reform of Gothic architecture. Guido d'Arezzo, as early as the end of the eleventh century, had invented a new system of musical notation and made this art much easier and much more widespread.

All these fine achievements were the work of Tuscans. Their native genius recreated everything even before the little knowledge which had remained in Constantinople spread to Italy, together with the Greek language, as a result of the Ottoman conquests. Florence, at this time, was like a new Athens, and among the orators who came from every part of Italy to congratulate Boniface VIII on his election as Pope, eighteen were Florentines. This clearly shows that the renaissance of the arts was not due to the fugitives from Constantinople. All that these Greeks could teach the Italians was the Greek language; they had hardly any knowledge of real sciences, and the little physics and mathematics that were known in those days came from the Arabs.

It may seem surprising that so many men of genius appeared in Italy at this time when they had no pro-

[7] Voltaire has described her tragic life and cruel death in Chapter LXIX.

tectors and no models and lived in the midst of dissentions and wars. But if one looks at the Romans, one finds that Lucretius had written his poem on nature, Virgil his bucolics and Cicero his philosophical works in the midst of the horrors of civil war. When once a language begins to reach maturity, it is an instrument which great artists find ready to hand and which they use without bothering who is governing and disturbing the world.

If this renaissance was confined to Tuscany alone, this was not because there were no talents anywhere else. St. Bernard and Abelard, in twelfth-century France, might have been looked on as men of genius, but their language was still a barbaric jargon, and they paid tribute in Latin to the bad taste of their time. Rhyme, to which these Latin hymns of the twelfth and thirteenth centuries were subjected, was the very stamp of barbarity; this was not the way in which Horace sang of the secular games. Scholastic philosophy, the bastard daughter of a badly translated and misunderstood Aristotelian philosophy, did more harm to reason and useful studies than the Huns and the Vandals had done.

The art of Sophocles was nonexistent; in early times in Italy there were only a few naïve representations of stories from the Old and New Testaments; and this was the origin of the French mystery plays. These spectacles had originated in Constantinople. The poet St. Gregory of Nazianzus had introduced them in opposition to the dramatic works of the ancient Greeks and Romans; and as the choruses of Greek tragedies were religious hymns and their theater was a sacred institution, Gregory of Nazianzus and his successors wrote sacred tragedies; but unfortunately the new theater did not have the same superiority over that of Athens that the Christian religion had over that of the Gentiles. A remnant of these pious farces is to be found in the traveling theaters which still exist among the shepherds of Calabria. On solemn occasions they act the birth and death of Christ. The populace of more northerly nations soon adopted these customs. In more recent times the same subjects have been treated in a more dignified way, and in our own time we find examples of them in the little operas known as oratorios; finally, Frenchmen have created dramatic masterpieces based on the Old Testament.

In the sixteenth century in France, the brotherhood of the passion portrayed Christ on the stage. If the French language had been majestic then, instead of being naïve and crude, and if there had been a man of genius among all these ignorant dullards, then one may well believe that the death of a just man persecuted by Jewish priests and condemned by a Roman praetor might have given rise to a work of sublime genius; but a more enlightened age would have been needed, and in a more enlightened age such representations would not have been permitted.

The arts had not disappeared in the East, and as the poems of the Persian Saadi are often heard today in Persia, Turkey and Arabia, they must have been of some merit. He was a contemporary of Petrarch, and is equally famous. It is true that, generally speaking, Orientals lack good taste; their works are like the titles they give to their sovereigns, which are full of references to the sun and the moon. The spirit of servitude always produces an inflated style, just as that of liberty is sinewy and that of true greatness is always simple. The Orientals lack delicacy because women are not admitted into society; they lack order and method because each individual abandons himself to his imagination in the solitude in which they all spend part of their lives, and imagination on its own tends to get out of control. They have never known true eloquence like that of Demosthenes or Cicero. After all, who would there be to persuade in the East? The slaves? And yet their works contain some brilliant shafts of light; they paint in words, and although their figures of speech are often exaggerated and incoherent, they can be sublime. Perhaps you would like, here, to look at a passage from Saadi which I have translated into blank verse and which is rather like some passages from the Hebrew prophets. It depicts the greatness of God; admittedly this is a commonplace theme, but it will give you some idea of the spirit of Persia:

He knew distinctly that which ne'er existed:
His ear is filled with sounds that ne'er were heard:

Though prince, he wants no cringe nor bended knee;
Though judge, he needs no written rule nor law.
The pencil of his sure eternal prescience
Portrayed our features in our mother's womb.
From east to west he drives the rapid sun,
And scatters rubies 'mid the rugged mountains.
He takes two drops of water: this forms man,
That the translucent pearl in the deep.
At his command existence rose from nothing.
He speaks: and lo, the universe recoils
Into the immensity of space and void.
He speaks: and lo, the universe returns
From nothing's dark abyss to bright existence.[8]

If literature like this was cultivated on the banks of the Tigris and the Euphrates, this proves that the other arts which contribute to the pleasures of life were well known. The superfluous can come only after the necessary; but even this necessary was still lacking in almost the whole of Europe. What did people know in Germany, France, England, Spain and northern Lombardy? A few barbarous feudal customs, as uncertain as they were riotous, duels, tourneys, scholastic theology and witchcraft.

In many churches they still celebrated the festival of the ass, as well as that of innocents and fools. They used to lead an ass to the altar and chant out an anthem: *"Amen, Amen, Asine, eh, eh, eh, Mr. Ass, eh, eh, eh, Mr. Ass."*

Du Cange and his successors, the most accurate of compilers, quote a five-hundred-year-old manuscript which contains the hymn to the ass:

Orientis partibus
Adventavit asinus
Pulcher et fortissimus.

Eh! sire ane, ça chantez,

[8] This is a contemporary English translation from Voltaire's French.

Belle bouche, rechignez,
Vous aurez du foin assez.[9]

A girl played the part of the Mother of God traveling to Egypt mounted on this ass and holding a child in her arms. She led a long procession, and at the end of the Mass, instead of saying *"Ite, missa est,"* the priest brayed three times as loud as he could and the people replied with similar noises.

This barbaric superstition came, nevertheless, from Italy. But although in the thirteenth and fourteenth centuries some Italians were beginning to emerge from darkness, the populace was still sunk in it. In Verona people had imagined that the ass which bore Christ had walked across the sea and come as far as the banks of the Adige by way of the Gulf of Venice. They imagined too that Christ had assigned it a meadow for its pasture and that it had lived there for many years and died there. Its bones were enclosed in an artificial donkey which was deposited in the Church of Santa Maria in Organo under the protection of four canons; these relics were carried in procession three times a year with the greatest solemnity.

It was this ass of Verona which made the fortune of Our Lady of Loreto. Pope Boniface VIII, seeing that the procession of the ass attracted many strangers, thought that the house of the Virgin Mary would attract even more, and he was not mistaken. He lent this fable the full weight of his apostolic authority. If the people believed that an ass had walked on the sea from Jerusalem to Verona, there was no reason why they should not believe that Mary's house had been transported from Nazareth to Loreto. The little house was soon enclosed in a superb church; the crowds of pilgrims and the presents of princes made this temple as rich as that of Ephesus.

---

[9] "From the East
Came the ass,
Beautiful and exceedingly strong.

Eh! Mr. Ass, now sing
With your fair mouth, jib,
You will have fodder enough."

The Italians at least grew rich on the blindness of other peoples; but elsewhere people embraced superstitions for their own sake, merely by abandoning themselves to their crude instincts and to the spirit of the age. You have observed more than once that this fanaticism, to which men have such a strong inclination, has always served not only to make them stupider but also to make them wickeder. Pure religion refines manners by enlightening the mind, and superstition, by blinding it, inspires every form of fury.

In Normandy, the so-called land of wisdom, there was a figure entitled the Abbé of Fools who was drawn through the streets of several towns on a cart with four horses. He had a miter on his head and a crozier in his hand and distributed blessings and instructions as he passed.

A king of jesters was established at court by letters patent. He was originally the chief or judge of a little palace guard and later became a court jester who had rights over all thieves and prostitutes. Every town had its guilds and brotherhoods of artisans, citizens and women, who made sacred mysteries out of the most extravagant ceremonies; this is the origin of the society of Freemasons, which alone has survived while time has destroyed all the others.

The most contemptible of all these brotherhoods was that of the flagellants, and it was also the most widespread. It had its beginnings in the insolence of a few priests who abused the weakness of those who did penance in public to the extent of beating them. A trace of this custom can still be seen in the sticks with which the Roman penitentiaries are armed. Then monks began to beat themselves, imagining that nothing pleased God more than the scarred back of a monk. In the eleventh century Pierre Damien excited laymen into whipping themselves naked. In 1260 several brotherhoods of pilgrims traveled through Italy armed with whips, and they later visited other countries in Europe. This association even became a sect, which finally had to be dispersed.

While bands of beggars were scouring the world beating themselves, fools walked at the heads of processions in almost all the towns, dressed in crumpled clothes, wearing bells and carrying baubles, and this custom still exists in the towns of Holland and Germany. The only literature in the native tongue of these northern nations consisted of the farces called "moralities," followed by others called "The Foolish Mother" and "The Prince of Fools."

Revelations, possessions and witchcraft were constantly in the news. The wife of Philip III was accused of adultery and the King consulted a devout nun to find out whether she was guilty or not. The children of Philip the Fair entered into an association in writing whereby they promised to help each other against anyone who tried to kill them by magic. A sorceress who with the help of the devil had forged a deed in favor of Robert of Artois was burned by order of the parlement. The illness of Charles VI was attributed to witchcraft, and a magician was summoned to cure him. In England the Princess of Gloucester was condemned to do penance before the Church of St. Paul, as we have already remarked, and a baroness of the realm, who was said to be her accomplice, was burned alive as a witch.

If credulity could expose the leading figures of the kingdoms of Europe to horrors like these, one can well imagine what ordinary citizens were exposed to. And this was the least of their misfortunes.

Germany, France, Spain and the whole of Italy except for the great trading cities were absolutely without police. The walled towns of Germany and France were plundered during the civil wars. The Greek empire was overrun by the Turks. Spain was still divided between the Christians and the Arab Moslems and both parts were often torn by civil wars. Finally, in the time of Philip of Valois, Edward III, Louis of Bavaria and Clement VI, a general plague destroyed those who had escaped the sword and famine.

This happened in the fourteenth century, just after the crusades had depopulated and impoverished Europe. If we look back beyond these crusades to the centuries which followed the death of Charlemagne, we find that they are no less miserable and are even more barbarous.

A comparison of these centuries with our own (whatever perversities and misfortunes we may suffer) must make us aware of our good fortune despite the almost invincible proneness of human nature to praise the past at the expense of the present.

It would be wrong to think that barbarism was universal: there were great virtues in all ranks of society, on the throne and in the cloisters among the knights and among the churchmen; but neither a St. Louis nor a St. Ferdinand could cure the wounds from which the human race was suffering. The long quarrel between the emperors and the popes, the stubborn struggle for liberty which the Romans waged against both the German emperors and the Roman pontiffs, the frequent schisms and finally the great schism of the West never allowed popes who were elected in times of trouble to exercise the virtues which more peaceful times would have inspired in them. Could they avoid being affected by the general corruption of manners? Every man is molded by his age and very few manage to rise above the manners of the times. The crime in which many of the popes became involved and their scandalous behavior, which seemed authorized by the general example, cannot be buried in oblivion. Of what use, then, is the description of their vices and their disasters? To show how fortunate Rome is, now that decency and tranquillity have become established there. What greater lesson can we learn from all the vicissitudes described in this *Essay on Customs* than the realization that every nation has been wretched until law and legislative power have become properly established?

Just as a few monarchs and a few pontiffs who were worthy of better times could not put a stop to all these disorders, so a few intelligent men, born amid the darkness of these northern nations, could not introduce arts and science there.

The King of France, Charles V, who collected about nine hundred volumes a hundred years before the Vatican library was founded by Nicholas V, tried in vain to encourage talents; the soil was not prepared for these exotic fruits. Some of the wretched compositions of these days have been collected, but this is like hoarding a heap of stones from some ancient hovel when one lives in a palace. Charles was obliged to send to Pisa for an astrologer, and Catherine, the daughter of this astrologer, who wrote in French, claims that the King said: "So long as learning shall be honored here, this kingdom will continue to flourish." But learning was unknown, and good taste still more so. France was a wretched country, without stable laws, torn by civil wars, lacking commerce, police or written customs and governed by a thousand different usages; half the country was called the *langue d'oui* or *d'oil,* and the other half the *langue d'oc;*[10] how could it be anything other than barbarous? Its only advantage was that the French nobility was outwardly more brilliant than that of other nations.

When Charles of Valois, brother of Philip the Fair, had invaded Italy, even the Lombards and Tuscans adopted French fashions. These fashions were extravagant: bodices which laced at the back like those of girls today, large hanging sleeves and cowls with points which hung down to the ground. Yet the French nobles gave a certain grace to this masquerade and justified Frederick II's opinion: *"Plas me el cavalier Frances."*[11] They would have done better to learn military discipline, for then France would not have been the prey of foreigners as it was under Philip of Valois, John and Charles VI. But why was this discipline more familiar to the English? Perhaps they felt a greater need of it because they were fighting far from home; perhaps nature has endowed them with a calmer and more reflective type of courage.

---

[10] The word for "yes" in northern French was *oil* (later *oui*); that in Provençal and other southern dialects was *oc*. Because of this, the language of the north became known as the *langue d'oil* and that of the south as the *langue d'oc* (language of *oc*) and these same terms were later applied to the areas in which the different languages were spoken. Languedoc is still today the name of a province of southern France.

[11] The complete text of the poem is on page 297.

CONCLUSION AND EXAMINATION OF THIS HISTORICAL TABLEAU

[*Voltaire begins with a page of summary of recent historical events, particularly those associated with the Seven Years War. He then continues:*]

. . . It is the task of the historians of the individual states which have been at war to give posterity an account of all the misfortunes which man suffered, to describe all the pillage, the crimes, the losses, the ineffective measures and the inadequate resources.

As I am concerned here only with the customs and the spirit of nations in these upheavals which have shaken the world, I want to stress that, even in the midst of all the cruelty inseparable from armed conflict, there has been more than one occasion when the spirit of humanity and civilization has mitigated the horrors of war. The French who were prisoners of war in Prussia received the kindest possible treatment from the King of Prussia and from his brother, Prince Henry. The two Princes of Brunswick were as notable for their generosity as they were for their victories. The princes, generals and officers of France exhibited all the generosity of their character.

The English made a collection to help the sailors they had captured; and this generous act had no other motive than the humanistic philosophical spirit which is beginning to penetrate many states and which will probably at least put an end to religious wars even if it cannot stop those which result from political mistakes.

It is this spirit which has led to the growth of academies in every kingdom and republic and which has given greater scope to the human mind by spreading knowledge; its gradually expanding light has led men to apply themselves more than ever to agriculture, and taught the wise to think of methods of making the land more fertile while ambitious men were drowning it in blood.

Finally, one cannot but believe that reason and human industry will continue to make further progress; that the useful arts will be developed; that prejudices, which are not the least of the many scourges which afflict mankind, will gradually disappear among all the leaders of nations, and that philosophy, widespread throughout the world, will go some way toward consoling human nature for the calamities which it will suffer in every age.

It was with this intention and this hope that the *Essay on Customs* was published. It was dictated by a feeling of humanity and written in the spirit of truth. Some people, who can only be looked on as enemies of society, have accused the creator of this vast tableau of having painted crimes, above all those of religion, in too somber colors, and of having made fanaticism execrable and superstition ridiculous.

The only thing the author can really be reproached with is that he has perhaps not said enough; the complaints of the fanatics themselves prove how necessary this history was. It is clear that there are still unfortunates who are the victims of this spiritual disease and who are afraid to be cured.

"History," from the Philosophical Dictionary

SECTION I

DEFINITION

History is the narrative of events which are supposed to have actually happened, as opposed to fable, which is the narrative of events which are admittedly false.

One kind of history is the history of opinions; but this is little more than a compilation of human errors.

The history of the arts can be the most useful of all when it combines an account of the invention and the progress of the arts with a description of the way they work.

Natural history, which is improperly called "history," is essentially a branch of the physical sciences. The history of events has been divided into sacred and secular; sacred history is the succession of divine and miraculous operations by which it formerly pleased God to lead the Jewish nation and which now serve to exercise our faith.

> *Si j'apprenais l'hébreu, les sciences, l'histoire,*
> *Tout cela, c'est la mer à boire.*
> (La Fontaine, Book VIII, Fable 25)[1]

THE FIRST FOUNDATIONS OF HISTORY

The first foundations of all history are the tales fathers tell to their children and which are then handed down

[1] "If I learned Hebrew, science and history, it would be like trying to drink up the sea."

from one generation to another; even in their original form they are never more than probably true, and then only when they do not outrage common sense, and they lose a degree of probability with every generation. As time passes, the fabulous element increases and the truth is lost: that is why all the stories of the origin of peoples are absurd. So, for example, the Egyptians were governed by gods for many centuries; subsequently they were governed by demigods and finally they had kings for 11,340 years; during this period the sun had changed four times from east to west.

The Phoenicians of Alexander's time claimed to have been established in their country for thirty thousand years; and these thirty thousand years were filled with as many miracles as was Egyptian chronology. I admit that it is physically very possible that Phoenicia has existed not only for thirty thousand years but for thirty thousand billion centuries and that it has, like the rest of the world, experienced thirty million revolutions. But we have no knowledge of these.

The extent to which ridiculous myths predominate in the ancient history of Greece is well known.

The Romans, despite their seriousness, nevertheless shrouded in fables the history of their first centuries. This people, so recently compared with the nations of Asia, existed for five hundred years without historians. So it is not surprising that Romulus is said to be the son of Mars, that a she-wolf is supposed to have suckled him, that he is supposed to have marched with a thousand men from his village of Rome against twenty-five thousand warriors from the village of the Sabines and eventually to have become a god. Nor are we surprised to hear that Tarquinius the Elder is said to have cut a stone with a razor and a vestal to have drawn a ship to land with her girdle, etc.

The first annals of all modern nations are no less fabulous. These prodigious and improbable stories must sometimes be told, but mainly as proofs of human credulity. They find their place in the history of opinions and stupidities; but the field is a vast one.

MONUMENTS

There is only one way of knowing anything about ancient history with some degree of certainty, and that is by seeing if any incontestable monuments remain. We have only three written ones:

The first is the collection of astronomical observations made during nineteen hundred successive years at Babylon and sent to Greece by Alexander. This series of observations which goes back 2,234 years before our era proves unquestionably that the Babylonians existed as an organized people several centuries earlier; for the arts are only the work of time and the laziness natural to men leaves them for thousands of years with no other knowledge or talents save those of feeding themselves, protecting themselves against the climate and cutting each other's throats. This fact may be illustrated by the examples of the Germanic tribes, the English in Caesar's time or the Tartars of today, two thirds of Africa, and all the peoples we have found in America with the partial exception of the kingdoms of Peru and Mexico and the republic of Tlaxcala. Remember that in the whole of this new world nobody knew how to read or write.

The second monument is the central eclipse of the sun calculated in China 2,155 years before our era and recognized as authentic by all our astronomers. The same must be said of the Chinese as of the peoples of Babylon: they must already have formed a vast civilized empire. But what places the Chinese above all the other peoples of the earth is that their laws, their customs and the language spoken by literate people there have not changed in nearly four thousand years. This nation and India are the oldest of all those which still exist today; they possess the vastest and the finest countries and had invented almost all the arts before we had learned even a few of them. Yet these same people have always been omitted, up to the present day, from our so-called universal histories.[2] Whenever a Spaniard or a Frenchman

[2] This is one of Voltaire's main grievances against Bossuet. But most universal histories written in the eighteenth century before

listed the different nations, he never failed to call his own country the first monarchy in the world, and his king the greatest king in the world, flattering himself that his king would give him a pension as soon as he had read his book.

The third monument, much inferior to the other two, is that of the Arundel marbles. The chronicle of Athens was carved there 263 years before our era; but it goes back only as far as Cecrops, 1,319 years before the time in which it was carved. In the whole of ancient history these are the only incontestable dates we have.

Let us look closely at these marbles brought back from Greece by Lord Arundel. Their chronicle begins 1,582 years before our era. That makes them now 3,353 years old and yet you do not find there a single miraculous or prodigious fact. The same is true of the Olympiads: it is not about them that one can say *Graecia mendax*—lying Greece. The Greeks knew perfectly well how to distinguish history from fable and real facts from the stories of Herodotus. In the same way, in serious matters, their orators never borrowed from the speeches of the Sophists or the images of the poets.

The date of the capture of Troy is given in these marbles but there is no mention of the arrows of Apollo, the sacrifice of Iphigenia or the ridiculous combats of the gods. The dates of the inventions of Triptolemus and Ceres are found there; but Ceres is not called "goddess." There is a mention of a poem on the abduction of Proserpine; but it does not say she was a daughter of Jupiter and a goddess and that she was the wife of the god of Hades.

Hercules is initiated into the Eleusinian mysteries; but there is not a word about his twelve labors, nor his crossing to Africa in his cup, nor his divinity, nor about the big fish by which he was swallowed and which, according to Lycophron, kept him three days and three nights in its belly.

With us, on the other hand, a standard is brought from heaven by an angel to the monks of Saint-Denis; a

---

Voltaire's time follow Bossuet's example and confine themselves (as far as antiquity is concerned) to the Middle East and Europe.

pigeon brings a bottle of oil into a church in Rheims; two armies of serpents fight a pitched battle in Germany; an archbishop of Mainz is beseiged and eaten by rats; and, to crown everything, great care is taken to give the dates of these adventures. The Abbé Lenglet[3] keeps on compiling these impertinences, the almanacs repeat them a hundred times. And that is how the young are taught; all these pieces of nonsense have found their way into the education of princes.

All history is recent. It is not surprising that there is no profane ancient history more than about four thousand years old. The changes in the world and the long and universal ignorance of the art of transmitting facts by writing are the reasons for this. A number of peoples are still ignorant of this art; in earlier times only a very few civilized nations possessed it and even among them it was known only by a small minority. Among the French and the Germans literacy was very rare; up to the fourteenth century almost all acts were only attested by witnesses. In France it was only under Charles VII, in 1454, that some of the customs of the nation began to be written down. The art of writing was still rarer among the Spaniards and that is why their history is so dry and uncertain up to the time of Ferdinand and Isabella. Thus one can see how the very small number of people who knew how to write could deceive the others, and how easy it was to get us to believe the most enormous absurdities.

There are nations which have conquered whole areas of the world without being able to write. We know that Genghis Khan conquered part of Asia at the beginning of the thirteenth century; but it is not through him nor through the Tartars that we know it. Their history, written by the Chinese and translated by Father Gaubil, tells us that these Tartars were then unable to write.

This art must have been equally unknown to the Scythian Oguskan, called Madies by the Persians and the Greeks, who conquered part of Europe and Asia long be-

[3] Lenglet Dufresnoy was a prolific though not very original writer on historical and geographical subjects in the early eighteenth century.

fore the reign of Cyrus. It is almost certain that out of a hundred nations, only two or three could then use written characters. Perhaps in some former world which has been destroyed, men knew writing and the other arts; but in ours they are all extremely recent.

There remain monuments of another kind which serve only as evidence of the remote antiquity of certain peoples and which precede all known epochs and all books; these are the marvels of architecture like the pyramids and palaces of Egypt, which have resisted time. Herodotus, who lived 2,200 years ago and who had seen them, was unable to find out from the Egyptian priests when they had been built.

The earliest pyramids can hardly be less than four thousand years old; but one must consider that these ostentatious works of the kings could only have been begun long after the establishment of towns. And we should note that to build towns in a country which was flooded every year, it must first have been necessary to raise their foundations on pilings so as to keep them above the mud and render them inaccessible to floods; before taking this necessary step and before being in a position to undertake such major works, the people must have made themselves refuges, while the Nile was in spate, among the rocks which formed two chains to right and left of the river. These assembled peoples must have had implements of agriculture and of architecture and must have had a knowledge of surveying as well as laws and police. All this inevitably demands a prodigious amount of time. We see, from the tedious details of our own affairs—even the most necessary and insignificant ones—how difficult it is to achieve great things; not only is stubborn persistence needed, but several generations imbued with this same persistence.

However, whether it was Menes, Thaut or Cheops, or Ramses who raised one or two of these stupendous masses, we shall not be much wiser about the history of ancient Egypt. The language of this people is lost, and so all we know is that even before the most ancient historians, there was material from which ancient history could have been written.

SECTION II

As we already have twenty thousand works, most of them in several volumes, on the history of France alone, and as a studious man who lived to be a hundred would not have time to read them, it is useful, I think, to limit our interests. We are obliged to study the history of our own country and that of our neighbors. It is even more important that we should know something of the great deeds of the Greeks and Romans and of their laws, which are still largely ours. But if we tried to add to this the study of more remote antiquity, we should be like a man who left Tacitus and Livy in order to give serious study to the *Arabian Nights.* All the accounts of the origins of peoples are clearly fables; the reason is that men must have lived a long time in societies and have learned to make bread and clothes (which was difficult) before learning how to transmit their thoughts to posterity (which was even more difficult). The art of writing is certainly not more than six thousand years old among the Chinese and, whatever the Chaldeans and Egyptians say, it is most unlikely that they could read and write fluently any earlier.

The history of earlier times, then, could only have been transmitted by memory and we know how the memory of past events is corrupted in passing from one generation to another. Imagination alone wrote the first histories. Not only did each people invent its own origin, but it invented also the origin of the whole world.

If we are to believe Sanchoniatho, things began, first of all, with a thick air which the wind rarefied; from it were born desire and love, and from the union of desire and love the animals were formed. The stars only came later and simply to ornament the heavens and to delight the sight of the animals who were on the earth.

The Knef of the Egyptians, their Oshireth and their Isheth, which we call Osiris and Isis, are scarcely less ingenious and ridiculous. The Greeks embellished all these fictions; Ovid collected them and ornamented them with the charms of the finest poetry. What he has to say about a god who reduces chaos to order and about the formation of man is sublime:

Sanctius his animal mentisque capacius altae
Deerat adhunc, et quod dominari in cetera posset,
Natus homo est. . . .

(Metamorphoses, I, 76-8)

Pronaque cum spectent animalia cetera terram,
Os homini sublime dedit, coelumque tueri
Jussit, et erectos ad sidera tollere vultus.

(Metamorphoses, I, 84-6)[4]

Hesiod and others who wrote much earlier were far from expressing themselves with the same sublime elegance. But from this wonderful moment when man was created, up to the time of the Olympiads, everything is plunged in profound darkness.

Herodotus arrives at the Olympic games and tells stories to the assembled Greeks like an old woman talking to children. He begins by saying that the Phoenicians sailed from the Red Sea into the Mediterranean, which could be true only if one supposes that they had gone around the Cape of Good Hope and circumnavigated Africa.

Then comes the abduction of Io, then the fable of Gyges and Candaules, then some fine stories of thieves and that of the daughter of the King of Egypt, Cheops, who, having demanded an ashlar stone from each of her admirers, had enough of them to build one of the finest pyramids.

Add to this oracles, prodigies and the tricks of priests and you have the whole history of the human race.

The early history of Rome seems to have been written by men like Herodotus; our conquerors and our legislators could count their years only by having nails stuck in a wall by their high priest.

---

[4] "An animal more sacred than these and more capable of higher understanding and that might rule over the rest was wanting. Man was born. . . ."

"And while other animals look downward upon the earth, He gave man a lofty face and ordered him to look at heaven and lift his countenance upright toward the stars."

The great Romulus, king of a village, is the son of the god Mars and of a nun who went to fetch water in her pitcher. He has a god for a father, a whore for a mother and a she-wolf for a wet nurse. A shield falls specially from heaven for Numa. The splendid books of the Sybils are found. An augur cuts a large stone with a razor by permission of the gods. A vestal floats a large stranded ship by pulling it with her girdle. Castor and Pollux come to fight for the Romans, and the trace of their horses' hoofs remains printed in the stone. The Gauls from across the Alps come and sack Rome; some say they were chased away by geese, others that they carried back a great deal of gold and silver with them; but it is probable that in those days, in Italy, geese were more plentiful than silver. We have imitated the early Roman historians at any rate in their taste for fables. We have our oriflamme brought by an angel, our holy phial brought by a pigeon, and when we add to that St. Martin's cloak, we are doing pretty well!

What would useful history be? Surely it would be the history which taught us our duties and our rights yet without seeming to claim to be actually instructing us.

People often ask whether the fable of the sacrifice of Iphigenia is taken from the history of Jephtha, if Deucalion's flood was invented in imitation of that of Noah, if the adventure of Philemon and Baucis is based on that of Lot and his wife. The Jews admit that they had no communication with foreigners and that their books were unknown to the Greeks before the translation made on the orders of one of the Ptolemys; but long before this, the Jews had been courtiers and usurers among the Greeks of Alexandria. The Greeks never went to sell their old clothes in Jerusalem. It seems probable that no other people imitated the Jews, but that they themselves took a great deal from the Babylonians, the Egyptians and the Greeks.

The whole of Jewish antiquity is sacred for us, despite our hatred and contempt for this people. Reason, indeed, cannot make us believe the Jews; but we submit to them by faith. There are about eighty different systems of calculating their chronology and even more ways of explaining the events of their history. We do not know which is the true one, but we are keeping our faith in reserve for it, hoping that some day it will be discovered.

There are so many things which we have to believe about this learned and magnanimous people that all our belief is used up and we have none left for the prodigies of which the history of other nations is full. It is no use Rollin telling us about the oracles of Apollo and the marvels of Semiramis; it is no use his transcribing everything that has been said about the justice of the ancient Scythians who pillaged Asia so often and who ate men on occasions; he finds us rather incredulous.

What I admire most in our modern compilers is the wisdom and good faith with which they prove to us that everything that happened in former days in the greatest empires in the world happened only in order to instruct the inhabitants of Palestine.[5] If the kings of Babylon, in the course of their conquests, fall in passing on the Hebrew people, it is solely in order to punish this people for its sins. If the king known as Cyrus becomes master of Babylon, it is in order to allow some Jews to return home. If Alexander conquers Darius, it is to establish Jewish old-clothes dealers in Alexandria. When the Romans annex Syria to their vast domains and enclose the little country of Judea in their empire, it is once again in order to instruct the Jews. The Arabs and the Turks appear on the scene only in order to chastise this attractive people. It must be admitted that it has had an excellent education; no other nation has had so many teachers; and all this shows how useful history is!

But what is even more instructive is the exact justice which our clerics have rendered to all the princes whom they disliked. Look at the impartial candor with which St. Gregory of Nazianzus judges the Emperor Julian the philosopher.[6] He declares that this prince, who did not be-

[5] This is Voltaire's other great grievance against Bossuet and his successors, who saw the hand of God behind all historical events. Though a deist himself, Voltaire rejects the idea of any divine intervention in history.

[6] Better known as Julian the Apostate. His apostasy endeared him to Voltaire, who often portrays him as one of the wisest and best of the Roman emperors.

lieve in the devil, had secret dealings with the devil, and that one day, when the demons appeared to him in flames and in hideous form, he drove them away by inadvertently making signs of the cross.

He calls him madman and wretch; he assures us that Julian sacrificed young boys and girls every night in his cellars. This is how he speakes of the most merciful of men who never revenged himself for the insults which this same Gregory uttered against him during his reign.

An excellent way of justifying the calumnies which you heap on an innocent man is to write an apology for a guilty one. In this way you make up for everything. This method was used by the same saint of Nazianzus. The emperor Constantius, uncle and predecessor of Julian, had, on coming to the throne, massacred his mother's brother Julius and his two sons, all three of whom had been declared august; this was a method he had learned from his father, Constantine the Great. Later he assassinated Gallus, Julian's brother. He treated the empire as a whole with the same cruelty as he treated his family. But he was devout; in a decisive battle which he fought against Magnentius, he prayed to God in a church during the whole of the time the armies were fighting. Such was the man whose panegyric Gregory writes. If this is how saints tell us the truth, what may we not expect of laymen, above all when they are ignorant, superstitious and partisan?

Nowadays, a somewhat curious use is occasionally made of the study of history. Charters of the time of Dagobert are dug up, most of them suspect and misunderstood, and it is inferred from them that the customs, rights and prerogatives which existed in those days ought to be revived today. I advise those who study and argue in this way to say to the sea: In the past you were at Aigues-Mortes, at Fréjus, at Ravenna, at Ferrara; go back there immediately![7]

---

[7] This is an important statement from the point of view of Voltaire's own method. Though he makes propaganda out of history, he hardly ever does so in the traditionalist sense; i.e., he never argues that because an institution or constitution has existed for centuries it is therefore "right." Such arguments, however, were very common in the eighteenth century, particularly

SECTION III

THE USE OF HISTORY

The use of history consists above all in the comparison which a statesman or an ordinary citizen can make between the laws and customs of other countries and those of his own; this is what leads modern nations to emulate each other in the arts, in agriculture and in commerce.

The great faults of the past are also very useful in many ways; the crimes and misfortunes of history cannot be too frequently pondered on, for whatever people say, it is possible to prevent both. The history of the tyrant Christian of Denmark may stop a nation from giving absolute power to a tyrant; and the disaster of Charles XII at Poltava should warn a general not to invade the Ukraine without supplies.

It was because he had read the details of the battles of Crécy, Poitiers, Agincourt, Saint-Quentin, Gravelines, etc. that Marshal Saxe determined, as far as possible, to turn his battles into struggles for positional advantage.

Examples can have a great effect on the mind of a prince who reads attentively. He will see that Henry IV undertook his great war, which was to change the system of Europe, only after having assured himself of enough money to be able to survive several years' fighting without needing further financial aid.

He will see that Queen Elizabeth, aided only by the resources of trade and a wise economy, resisted the powerful Philip II, and that out of the hundred vessels which she sent to sea against the invincible armada, three quarters were provided by the commercial towns of England.

The fact that France was not invaded under Louis

---

over the question of the origin of the French monarchy. Aristocratic theorists such as Boulainvilliers, monarchists such as Dubos, and democrats such as Mably all interpreted the history of the Frankish conquests of Gaul in different ways, each striving to prove thereby that the system he supported was both right and natural for France. Voltaire will have nothing to do with this type of argument.

XIV after nine years of the most disastrous war clearly shows the value of the frontier fortifications which he built. It is no good the author of the *Causes of the Fall of the Roman Empire*[8] blaming Justinian for having pursued the same policy; he should blame only the emperors who neglected these frontier fortifications and who opened the gates of the empire to the barbarians.

One advantage which modern history has over ancient is that it teaches all rulers that ever since the fifteenth century the remaining European powers have always united against any power which threatened to become too preponderant. This system of balance of powers was unknown to the ancients, and this accounts for the success of the Roman people, who, having formed a militia superior to that of other peoples, were able to conquer them one by one from the Tiber to the Euphrates.

One ought to spend a great deal of time reading about the usurpations of the Popes, the scandalous discords of their schisms, the madness of controversial disputes, the persecutions and the wars caused by this madness and the horrors which they have produced. If this knowledge were not made familiar to young people, if only a small number of scholars knew these facts, the public would be as stupid as it was in the days of Gregory VII. The calamities of these times of ignorance would inevitably reappear because no precautions would be taken to prevent them. Everybody in Marseilles knows how the plague was once inadvertently brought from the East, and the result is that they are able to protect themselves against it.

Destroy the study of history and you would very possibly see St. Bartholomew's[9] Days in France and Cromwells in England.

---

[8] Montesquieu. Voltaire expressed admiration for his illustrious predecessor, but had little real sympathy for him and often, as here, went out of his way to criticize him.

[9] The massacre of St. Bartholomew's Day in 1572 was one of the most horrible events of the civil wars. Voltaire frequently refers to it, and even claimed to suffer from fever every year on its anniversary.

THE CERTAINTY OF HISTORY

Any certainty which is not mathematical demonstration is only extreme probability: this is all that historical certainty can ever be.

Marco Polo was the first and at that time the only person to speak of the greatness and of the population of China; he was not believed and he could not expect to be believed. The Portuguese, who entered this vast empire several centuries later, made its existence probable. It is now certain, with that certainty which arises from the unanimous testimony of a thousand eyewitnesses of different nations when this testimony is challenged by no one.

If only two or three historians had described how Charles XII insisted on remaining in the dominions of the Sultan, his benefactor, despite the latter's opposition, and fought with his servants against an army of Janizaries and Tartars, I should have suspended judgment; but having spoken to several eyewitnesses and never having heard this action doubted, I was forced to believe in it; for after all, if it was neither a wise nor an everyday action, it was in no way contrary to the laws of nature nor to the character of the King.

What is contrary to the ordinary course of nature should not be believed unless it is attested by men visibly inspired by the divine spirit and whose inspiration it is impossible to doubt. That is why the article "Certainty" in the *Encyclopedia* puts forward a great paradox when it asserts that one should be just as willing to believe everyone in Paris if they affirmed they had seen a dead man brought to life again, as to believe everyone in Paris when they said that we had won the battle of Fontenoy. It seems obvious that the testimony of the whole of Paris about something which is improbable cannot have the same value as the testimony of the whole of Paris about something probable. These are surely elementary notions of sound logic. A work like the *Encyclopedia* should be dedicated only to truth.

VOLTAIRE

THE UNCERTAINTY OF HISTORY

We distinguish historical times from fabulous ones; but in these historical times themselves we ought to distinguish between truths and fables. I am not speaking of the fables which are nowadays recognized as such; I am not, for example, discussing the prodigies with which Livy has embellished or spoiled his history; but even in the case of the most generally accepted facts, how many reasons for doubt still remain!

When one considers that the Roman republic existed for five hundred years without historians; that Livy himself deplores the loss of other monuments, which almost all perished in the great fire of Rome, *pleraque interiere;* when one remembers that during the first three hundred years, the art of writing was very rare, *rarae per eadem tempora litterae;* one may then feel quite free to doubt all the events which are not in the ordinary order of human affairs.

Is it very likely that Romulus, grandson of the king of the Sabines, would have been forced to carry off the Sabine women when his men needed wives? Is the history of Lucretia very likely? Should one believe without difficulty, on the word of Livy, that King Porsena fled full of admiration for the Romans, because a fanatic had wanted to kill him? Should not one rather prefer to believe Polybius, who came two hundred years before Livy? Polybius says that Porsena conquered the Romans; that is a good deal more probable than the adventure of Scaevola, who plunged his hand into the fire because it had made a mistake. I would have defied Poltrot to do the same.

Does the adventure of Regulus, shut up by the Carthaginians in a cask lined with iron spikes, really deserve to be believed? Would not Polybius, who was a contemporary, have mentioned it if it had been true? He has not a word to say about it; is there not a great presumption that this story was only invented much later to make the Carthaginians odious?

Open Moreri's *Dictionary* at the article "Regulus"; he

assures you that the torture of this Roman is related in Livy; yet the decade in which Livy might have spoken of it is lost; we have only the supplement by Freinshemius; so what has happened is that this *Dictionary* has quoted a seventeenth-century German while believing that it was quoting a Roman of Augustus' time. Immense volumes could be written about all the celebrated and accepted facts which one ought to doubt. But the limits of this article do not permit me to expatiate.

ARE TEMPLES, FESTIVALS, ANNUAL CEREMONIES AND EVEN MEDALS HISTORICAL PROOFS?

One naturally tends to believe that a monument erected by a nation to celebrate an event is proof that it happened; yet if these monuments were not erected by contemporaries and if they commemorate some improbable deed, do they prove anything except that people have wanted to consecrate a popular opinion?

The rostral column erected in Rome by the contemporaries of Duilius is no doubt a proof of Duilius' naval victory; but does the statue of the augur Naevius, cutting a stone with a razor, prove that Naevius had actually worked this miracle? And were the statues of Triptolemus and Ceres in Athens incontestable witnesses that Ceres had descended from some planet or other to teach agriculture to the Athenians? Does the famous Laocoön statue, which still exists today in such a complete form, prove the truth of the story of the Trojan horse?

Ceremonies and the annual festivals established by entire nations are no better evidence for the origins which are attributed to them. The festival commemorating Arion's being carried on a dolphin's back was celebrated by the Romans as by the Greeks. That of Faunus recalled his adventure with Hercules and Omphale when the god, in love with Omphale, took the bed of Hercules for that of his mistress.

The famous festival of Lupercalia was established in honor of the she-wolf who suckled Romulus and Remus.

What was the foundation of the feast of Orion, celebrated on the fifth of the Ides of May?[10] Here is the story. Hyrieus received at his house Jupiter, Neptune and Mercury, and when his guests took their leave, this fellow who had no wife and wanted to have children expressed his grief to the three gods. We dare not describe what they did on the hide of the ox which Hyrieus had given them to eat; later they covered this hide with some earth and nine months after, Orion was born.

Almost all Roman, Syrian, Greek and Egyptian festivals were founded on similar tales, as were the temples and statues of the ancient heroes; they were monuments consecrated by credulity to error.

One of our oldest monuments is the statue of St. Denis carrying his head in his arms.

A medal, even a contemporary one, is not always a proof. How many medals have been struck for reasons of flattery after very indecisive battles, qualified as victories, or after unsuccessful enterprises which have come to fruition only in legend? Was there not a medal struck quite recently during the war of 1740 between England and Spain which attested the capture of Cartagena by Admiral Vernon at the very time when this admiral was raising the siege?

Medals are irreproachable evidence only when the event is attested by contemporary authors; then these different proofs support each other and together demonstrate the truth.[11]

SHOULD ONE INCLUDE HARANGUES AND PORTRAITS IN HISTORY?

If, on an important occasion, the general of an army or a statesman has spoken in a striking and powerful manner which characterizes his genius and that of his age, then no doubt his speech should be reported word for word; such harangues are perhaps the most useful

[10] May 10.

[11] Some early eighteenth-century writers, such as Hardouin, had become so suspicious of written documents that they were prepared only to trust the evidence of coins, medals and inscriptions. Voltaire is here attempting to redress the balance.

part of history. But why put into a man's mouth words that he has never uttered? One might just as well attribute to him actions he has never committed. This is a fiction imitated from Homer; but what is fiction in a poem becomes, strictly speaking, lying in a historian. Several of the ancients used this method; but this proves nothing except that several of the ancients wanted to make a parade of their eloquence at the expense of truth.[12]

PORTRAITS

Portraits, too, often show far more desire to impress than to instruct. Contemporaries have the right to sketch the portraits of statesmen with whom they have negotiated or generals under whom they have made war. But there is a great danger that their brush may be guided by passion. It would appear that the portraits one finds in Clarendon are drawn with much more impartiality, gravity and wisdom than those which one enjoys reading in Cardinal Retz.

But to want to paint the ancients, to try to penetrate their souls, to look on events as if they were signs by which one could read people's innermost hearts—such an enterprise is a very delicate one and, in some cases, a puerility.

CICERO'S MAXIM CONCERNING HISTORY: THAT THE HISTORIAN SHOULD NOT DARE TELL A LIE OR HIDE A TRUTH

The first part of this precept is incontestable; the second must be examined. If a truth can be of some use to the state you would be wrong to keep silent. But suppose you are writing the history of a prince who has confided a secret to you: ought you to reveal it? Ought you to tell

[12] The inclusion of harangues and portraits in historical writing (many of them purely imaginary) was characteristic of many sixteenth- and seventeenth-century historians who revived the humanist tradition. The question whether such a practice was legitimate was frequently debated in the late seventeenth and early eighteenth centuries. Voltaire's firm stand is characteristic of his "philosophical" outlook.

posterity something which you could not tell secretly to a single individual without being guilty? Should the duty of a historian overrule a greater duty?[13]

Let me suppose further that you have witnessed an act of weakness which has had no influence on public affairs; should you reveal this weakness? In that case history would become satire.

It must be admitted that most writers of anecdotes are more indiscreet than useful. But what should one say about those insolent compilers who, making a virtue of slander, print and sell scandals as La Voisin sold poisons?

SATIRICAL HISTORY

If Plutarch criticized Herodotus for not having sufficiently extolled the glory of certain Greek towns and for having omitted several well-known facts worthy of being remembered, how much more reprehensible are those who today, without having any of the merits of Herodotus, impute odious actions to princes and nations without the slightest sign of any proof? The history of the war of 1741 has been written in England. And in this history we find that at the battle of Fontenoy "the French fired on the English with poisoned balls and pieces of poisoned glass and that the Duke of Cumberland sent the King of France a box full of these so-called poisons found in the bodies of wounded Englishmen." The same author adds that, the French having lost forty thousand men in this battle, the parlement of Paris made an order forbidding people to speak of it on pain of physical punishment.

The fraudulent memoirs recently printed under the name of Madame de Maintenon are full of similar absurdities. One of them is that at the siege of Lille, the allies threw notes into the town which read like this: "French-

---

[13] This was another favorite subject of debate, and a problem Voltaire himself had faced, particularly in his *History of Russia Under Peter the Great.* His main aim was to praise Peter's social reforms, but he was in some perplexity as to the extent to which he ought to give an account of some of the more barbarous of the Czar's actions.

men, be consoled; la Maintenon will never be your queen."

Almost every page is stained with impostures and with offensive expressions against the royal family and against the principal families of the kingdom without any evidence to give the slightest color of probability to these lies. This is not writing history; it is writing down, haphazardly, calumnies which deserve the stocks.[14]

There has been printed in Holland, under the name of "history," a host of libels in which the style is as coarse as the insults and the facts as false as they are badly written. People say this is an evil fruit of the excellent tree of liberty. But if the wretched authors of these stupidities were free to deceive their readers, we must use our freedom to undeceive them here.

SECTION IV

THE METHOD AND MANNER OF WRITING HISTORY, AND STYLE

So much has been said on this question that we must say very little more. It is well known that the method and style of Livy, his gravity and his wise eloquence, are appropriate to the majesty of the Roman republic; that Tacitus is better at portraying tyrants; Polybius at giving instruction in the art of war; Dionysus of Halicarnassus at explaining antiquities.

But while modeling oneself in general on these ancient masters, one has, today, a heavier burden to bear. Modern historians are expected to provide more details, more attested facts, precise dates and authorities, and to give more attention to customs, laws, manners, commerce, finance, agriculture and population; history is in the same situation as mathematics and physics: its scope has increased tremendously. Just as it is easier today to

[14] Voltaire's abusive language here is explained by the fact that the author of these memoirs, La Beaumelle, was a personal enemy who had been responsible for publishing a pirated edition of *The Age of Louis XIV*. In the final version of this section, further paragraphs containing abuse of La Beaumelle were inserted. We have omitted them here.

make collections of gossipy articles, so it is more difficult to write history.

Daniel[15] thought he was a historian because he transcribed dates and accounts of battles which nobody understands. He should have been instructing me in the rights of the nation, the rights of the principal bodies within the nation, its laws, its customs and its manners and the ways in which they have changed. The nation has the right to say to him: I insist that you write *my* history rather than that of Louis the Fat or Louis Hutin. You tell me, on the authority of an old chronicle written without plan, that when Louis VIII was attacked by a mortal illness, and was worn out, languishing and at the end of his tether, the doctors ordered this cadaverous body to sleep with a pretty girl to help him recover, and that the King indignantly refused to commit such an immoral act. Ah! Daniel, so you don't know the Italian proverb: *Donna ignuda manda l'uomo sotto la terra.*[16] You should have a little more knowledge of both political history and natural history.

People now insist that the history of a foreign country should not be written in the same way as that of one's own.

If you write a history of France, you are not obliged to describe the course of the Seine and the Loire; but if you publish an account of Portuguese conquests in Asia, then you must describe the topography of the countries you are dealing with. You are expected to take your reader by the hand along the coast of Africa and those of Persia and India; you are expected to provide instruction on the customs, laws and usages of those nations which are new to European readers.

We have twenty histories of Portuguese establishments in India; but not one of them tells us about the different governments of this country, its religions, its antiquities, the Brahmans, the disciples of St. John, the Ghebers, and the banians. It is true that the letters of

[15] The Jesuit author of a well-known history of France (1713) often criticized by Voltaire.

[16] "A naked woman sends man to his grave."

Xavier and his successors have been preserved. We have been presented with histories of India written in Paris from the accounts of these missionaries who did not know the language of the Brahmans. We are told a hundred and one times that the Indians worship the devil. Almoners of a company of merchants set off convinced that this is the case, and as soon as they see symbolical figures on the coasts of Coromandel, they invariably write saying that these are portraits of the devil, that they are in his empire, and that they are going to fight him. They do not consider that it is we who worship the devil Mammon, and are traveling six thousand leagues from our native land to pray to him for money.

As for those who are employed by Parisian booksellers of the Rue Saint-Jacques and who are ordered to write a history of Japan, Canada or the Canary Islands based on the memoirs of a few Capuchin monks, I have nothing to say to them.

It is enough that one should realize that the method appropriate to the history of one's own country is not fitted for describing the discoveries of the New World; that one should not write about a small town in the same way as about a great empire; that one should not write the personal history of a prince as if it were that of France or England.

If you have nothing to say other than to tell us that one barbarian succeeded another barbarian on the shores of the Oxus and the Ixarte, what use are you to the public?

These rules are fairly well known; but the art of writing good history will always be very rare. People realize that a grave, pure, varied and pleasant style is needed.

There are laws for writing history as there are for all the creative arts; there are plenty of precepts, but very few great artists.

SECTION V

THE HISTORY OF THE JEWISH KINGS AND THE BOOKS OF CHRONICLES[17]

All peoples have written their history as soon as they were able to write. The Jews too have written theirs. Before they had kings, they lived under a theocracy; they were held to be governed by God himself.

When the Jews wanted a king like other neighboring peoples, the prophet Samuel, who was very interested in not having a king, told them, on God's behalf, that God himself rejected the idea; and so theocracy ended among the Jews at the moment that monarchy began.

So without blaspheming, one can say that the history of the Jewish kings was written in the same way as that of other peoples, and that God did not take the trouble to dictate himself the history of a people he no longer governed.

We only advance this opinion with the greatest hesitation. What might confirm it is the fact that the Chronicles very often contradict the Book of Kings both in chronology and in facts, in the same way as our secular historians sometimes contradict each other. Moreover, if God has always written the history of the Jews, then presumably he is still writing it; for the Jews are still his favored people. Someday they will be converted, and it seems that then they will be every bit as justified in regarding the history of their dispersal as sacred as they are in asserting that God wrote the history of their kings.

One may make a further reflection; it is that, as God was for a long time their only king and then became their historian, we should have the most profound respect for all Jews. There is no Jewish old-clothes dealer who

---

[17] In this section Voltaire has a double aim. On the one hand he wants to attack orthodox Christianity by pointing out that the Old Testament is far from being a moral work. On the other he wants, for tactical reasons, to separate the moral from the historical aspects of the Old Testament and to assert the historian's right to investigate the latter from a purely historical viewpoint without laying himself open to theological censure.

is not infinitely superior to Caesar and Alexander. How can one avoid prostrating oneself before an old-clothes dealer who proves to you that his history has been written by God himself while Greek and Roman histories have only been transmitted by secular hands?

If the style of the History of the Kings and the Chronicles is divine, it is still possible that the actions related in these histories are not divine. David slays Uriah. Ish-Bosheth and Mephibosheth are slain. Absolom slays Ammon; Joab slays Absolom; Solomon slays Adonijah, his brother; Baasha slays Nadab; Zimri slays Elah; Omri slays Zimri; Ahab slays Naboth; Jehu slays Ahab and Joram; the inhabitants of Jerusalem slay Amaziah, son of Joash; Shallum, son of Jabesh, slays Zachariah, son of Jeroboam; Menahem slays Shallum, son of Jabesh; Pekah, son of Remaliah, slays Pekahiah, son of Menahem; Hoshea, son of Elah, slays Pekah, son of Remaliah. We will not bother to mention a number of minor slayings. It must be confessed that, if the Holy Spirit did write this history, he did not choose a particularly edifying subject.

SECTION VI

WICKED ACTIONS CONSECRATED OR EXCUSED IN HISTORY

It is only too common among historians to praise very wicked men who have rendered service to the dominant sect or to the nation. Such praise may be that of a zealous citizen, but this zeal is an outrage to the human race. Constantine cut his son's throat, suffocated his wife and murdered almost the whole of his family; he has been praised in Church Councils, but history should express detestation of his barbarities. It is doubtless fortunate for us that Clovis was a Catholic; it is fortunate for the Anglican Church that Henry VIII abolished the monks; but it must be admitted that Clovis and Henry VIII were monsters of cruelty.

When the Jesuit Berruyer, who was no less a fool for being a Jesuit, decided to paraphrase the Old and New Testaments in a more gallant style, with no intention other than that of making people read them, he used all the flowers of rhetoric in describing the two-edged knife which the Jew Aod drove up to the hilt into King Eglon's belly and the sword with which Judith cut off Holofernes' head after having prostituted herself to him, and several other actions of the same sort. The parlement, while respecting the Bible which recounts these actions, condemned the Jesuit who praised them, and had the Old and New Testaments burned; I mean, of course, the Jesuit's versions of them.

But as human judgments are always different in such cases, the same thing happened to Bayle in the precisely opposite situation; he was condemned for not having praised all the actions of David, King of the province of Judea.[18] A certain Jurieu, a refugee preacher in Holland, together with other refugee preachers, wanted to force him to retract. But how can one retract on facts which are stated in the Bible? Had not Bayle some reason for thinking that not all the facts reported in the Jewish books are saintly actions: that David, like other men, committed extremely criminal acts, and that if he is called the man after God's own heart, it is because of his penitence and not because of his misdeeds?

Let us put aside the names and think only of the actions. Let us suppose that during the reign of Henry IV, a priest of the League had secretly poured a bottle of oil over the head of a shepherd from Brie. The shepherd comes to court; the priest introduces him to the King as a good violin player who will drive away the King's melancholy; the King makes him his squire and gives him one of his daughters in marriage; then the King quarrels with the shepherd and the latter takes refuge with a German prince who is the enemy of his father-in-law; he arms five hundred brigands, sunk in debt and debauchery, scours the country with this scum, killing friends and enemies and even exterminating the women and babes in arms so that there shall be no one left to bear the news of this butchery; I suppose, further, that

[18] The cause of this controversy was Bayle's article on David in his *Dictionnaire Historique et Critique*. Bayle did more than merely refrain from praising David; he pointed out the moral impossibility of doing so.

this same shepherd from Brie becomes King of France after the death of Henry IV, and that he kills his grandson after having made him eat at his table and has seven other grandchildren of his King put to death; where is the man who would not admit that this shepherd from Brie was a little harsh?

The commentators are agreed that David's adultery and the murder of Uriah are faults which God has pardoned. In which case, one may agree that the massacres mentioned above are also faults which God has pardoned.

Yet Bayle was allowed no quarter. However, recently, when some preachers in London compared George II to David, one of the servants of the King published a little book complaining of the comparison.[19] He examined the whole of David's conduct and went much farther than Bayle, treating David more severely than Tacitus treats Domitian. This book did not excite the least protest in England; all its readers recognized that bad actions are always bad, that God may pardon them when the penitence is proportional to the crime, but that no man should approve them.

So there is more reason in England than there was in Holland in Bayle's time. People realize today that they should not pretend that actions deserving the supreme punishment are a model of saintliness; and they recognize that if one should not consecrate crime, one should not believe absurdities.

---

[19] This work, *David: The Man After God's Own Heart*, was by the English deist Peter Annet.

J. H. Brumfitt, D.Phil., is currently Senior Lecturer in French Language and Literature at the University of St. Andrews. He is a leading scholar in the field and has published several notable works on French literature, among which are a book on *Voltaire, Historian* and an edition of Anatole France's *Les Dieux ont Soif*. He has been honored with two fellowships from Oxford University, where he also lectured prior to his joining the faculty of St. Andrews.

Hugh R. Trevor-Roper, general editor of *The Great Histories Series*, is the distinguished Regius Professor of Modern History at Oxford University. He is probably most well known to American readers for his book *The Last Days of Hitler*, which is a classic in the field of modern German history and was the result of official investigations carried out by Professor Trevor-Roper at the behest of British Intelligence in an attempt to unshroud the mystery surrounding the dictator's fate. The book has already been translated into nineteen foreign languages. Professor Trevor-Roper is a specialist in sixteenth- and seventeenth-century history and has published several other notable works, including *Archbishop Laud* and *Man and Events*. He has contributed numerous articles on political and historical subjects to the journals and is familiar to American readers of *The New York Times Magazine* and *Horizon*.

Index

INDEX

INDEX